SEX AND SEXUALITY

SEX AND SEXUALITY

Volume 2
SEXUAL FUNCTION
AND DYSFUNCTION

Edited by Richard D. McAnulty and M. Michele Burnette

PRAEGER PERSPECTIVES

Westport, Connecticut
London

Library of Congress Cataloging-in-Publication Data

Sex and sexuality / edited by Richard D. McAnulty and M. Michele Burnette.
    v. cm.
   Includes bibliographical references and index.
    Contents: v. 1. Sexuality today : trends and controversies—v. 2. Sexual function
and dysfunction—v. 3. Sexual deviation and sexual offenses.
    ISBN 0–275–98581–4 (set : alk. paper)—ISBN 0–275–98582–2 (v. 1 : alk.
paper)—ISBN 0–275–98583–0 (v. 2 : alk. paper)—ISBN 0–275–98584–9
(v. 3 : alk. paper)
    1. Sex.   2. Sex customs.   3. Sexual disorders.   4. Sexual deviation.
I. McAnulty, Richard D.   II. Burnette, M. Michele.
HQ21.S4716   2006
306.77—dc22   2006001233

British Library Cataloguing in Publication Data is available.

Library of Congress Catalog Card Number: 2006001233
ISBN: 0–275–98581–4 (set)
      0–275–98582–2 (vol. 1)
      0–275–98583–0 (vol. 2)
      0–275–98584–9 (vol. 3)

First published in 2006

Praeger Publishers, 88 Post Road West, Westport, CT 06881
An imprint of Greenwood Publishing Group, Inc.
www.praeger.com

Printed in the United States of America

The paper used in this book complies with the
Permanent Paper Standard issued by the National
Information Standards Organization (Z39.48–1984).

10 9 8 7 6 5 4 3 2 1

Contents

Preface

We have had many opportunities to teach and interact with both college students and professional audiences about some very important topics and issues in human sexuality in our roles as authors and college professors. When we were approached to write this three-volume set on sex and sexuality, we were intrigued with the idea of having a forum in which to reach a broader audience. That is our goal for this work. With that in mind, we encouraged our contributors to "talk to" a general audience when writing about the topics that were most important to them. The authors we selected to write these chapters represent both established authorities and budding scholars on the various topics in human sexuality. We are confident that they have all helped us accomplish our goal.

To us, few, if any, other topics in the realm of human behavior are more interesting, exciting, or controversial than sex. And we hope that you will agree after reading the chapters from this set. Each chapter stands alone, and you can choose to read as many or as few as you would like—pick the ones that interest you. We hope that you will find this work to be of significant value to you, whether you are in pursuit of a better general understanding of sexuality or are looking for answers to specific questions.

One theme you will find throughout these texts is that human sexual function is affected by a whole host of factors. These factors are biological, sociocultural, and psychological in nature. The scientific study of sexuality is for all practical purposes a "young" field, and we have only touched the surface in an attempt to fully understand how these factors interact and impact sexuality.

Another theme or concern you will find throughout this work is the question whether "scientific" views of sex are biased by social judgments about normal versus abnormal and/or functional versus dysfunctional sexual behavior. U.S. culture, in particular, holds many strong values and prohibitions about sex. In this context, studying and interpreting research on sexuality in an unbiased manner can be a challenge. Many of our authors caution the reader about this concern.

We wish to thank all the researchers and clinicians, past and present, who have contributed to the science of sex. Many of them have contributed chapters to this set, and for that we are grateful. We also thank our colleagues, families, and friends who supported us during the writing and editing process. Finally, we thank "the team" at Praeger Publishers.

Introduction

Sexual arousal and response is a natural and essential condition of life. Without it, animals would not reproduce and would cease to exist. It seems that a function so essential to our survival would be straightforward so as to ensure that this process would not fail. But observe human sexual behavior, and you will see that it is far from uncomplicated. Human sexual arousal and response is multiply influenced by the integration of emotional, cognitive, interpersonal, physiological, biological, sociocultural, environmental, and perhaps even evolutionary factors. So complex and dynamic are these interrelationships that we will likely always lack a full and complete understanding of them.

Volume 2 of *Sex and Sexuality* opens with an overview of our remarkable reproductive anatomy. Chapter 1, by Burnette, covers the structure and function of all the major reproductive organs of the male and female. This chapter, combined with Chapter 2 by Demakis on the role of the brain and the endocrine system, enhances our understanding of how multiple body systems interact to produce sexual arousal and response. This complex picture becomes even clearer with the addition of Rowland's chapter, Chapter 3, on the psychobiology of sex, in which he discusses models of sexual arousal and response as well as physiological mechanisms (e.g., the senses) and psychological processes (e.g., thoughts, feelings) that play a part in human sexual behavior.

Next, this volume addresses perspectives on sex and intimate relationships. In Chapter 4, Geary offers an interesting discussion of how male and female differences in sexual preferences and behavior may have evolved through time to improve the chances of species survival. The research on evolution and sexual behavior has largely involved nonhuman species and has been extrapolated to humans. A discussion of sex and interpersonal relationships would be incomplete without a discourse on love. Regan points out in Chapter 5 that a majority of adolescents and adults in the United States believe that sexual interactions should generally occur within the context of a love relationship. Regan discusses types and theories of love with an emphasis on the two types most linked to sexual expression, passionate and companionate love.

Most research aimed at understanding sexual response and function has focused on understanding what has caused inhibition or disruption in the process of sexual arousal and response. The next several chapters address this topic. As we learn from the models of sexual arousal and response, this process is arbitrarily divided into phases, including sexual desire, excitement, orgasm, and resolution. Dysfunction can occur in any of the first three phases. In Chapter 6, Bogaert and Fawcett talk about factors that increase, maintain, and/or decrease a person's desire to engage in sex. In Chapter 7, Febbraro addresses sexual problems that occur during the excitement phase of the sexual response related to difficulties either with feelings of sexual pleasure or with the physiological changes associated with sexual excitement (e.g., failure of a female to adequately lubricate, or premature ejaculation in a male). In Chapter 8, Millner discusses orgasmic problems and disorders, in which she raises and addresses the issue of what constitutes a true orgasmic disorder—for example, if a woman can successfully achieve an orgasm while masturbating but not while having intercourse, does she have an orgasmic disorder? This situational inorgasmia might be considered a problem if, for example, it caused discord between the couple, but it is not necessarily a dysfunction or disorder.

In light of the various sexual dysfunctions that individuals sometimes experience, research and clinical work over the years have focused on finding effective ways to resolve these problems for individuals and couples. Chapter 9 by Kleinplatz provides an overview of interventions for sexual problems and again touches on some of the controversies inherent in determining what constitutes an actual disorder, given the subjective nature of the human sexual experience.

Past research has focused mostly on sexual inhibition when addressing disorders of the desire and arousal phases of sexual response. More recently, hypersexuality, also called sexual compulsivity, has become a focus of research. Sexual compulsivity has become especially popularized by reports of individuals who access pornographic Internet sites uncontrollably. Reece, Dodge, and McBride provide a stimulating discussion of this popular topic and urge caution in making value judgments about what is and is not an appropriate level of sexual interest or activity in Chapter 10. Finally, this volume would be incomplete if we did not include a chapter addressing a long-ignored issue—sexuality in people affected in various degrees by chronic disease, physical disabilities, and the treatments of these conditions. Too often we discount individuals with significant disease process or physical limitations as asexual, not capable of or interested in sexual activity. This view is damaging to those who long to be complete human beings within the context of some real physical limitations. Fisher, Graham, and Duffecy, in Chapter 11, discuss the importance of this topic and review the impact of "major conditions" on sexual function as well as interventions aimed at reducing their impact on sexual function. Perhaps most importantly, they emphasize that quality of life and psychological well-being are improved when individuals can maintain satisfying sexual interactions.

Reproductive and Sexual Anatomy

M. Michele Burnette ◆

The reproductive or sex organs are a remarkable set of anatomical structures. These organs are referred to as both reproductive and sexual because they perform two interrelated functions. They produce and support the developing fetus, and they can provide intense sexual pleasure and intimacy between people. In this chapter, you will learn about all the major reproductive structures in the male and female, as well as the breasts, since they are so closely linked to sexual pleasure in the U.S. culture.

Female and male anatomy are presented in separate sections in this chapter; however, keep in mind that for each structure in the female sexual anatomy there is a corresponding structure in the male anatomy. These are called *homologous* structures because they develop from the same cells in the developing fetus. As you may know, the chromosomes of males and females are different, with males having an XY sex chromosome configuration, and females having an XX configuration. In addition, although we tend to refer to testosterone as a "male" hormone and estrogens as "female" hormones, males and females have varying amounts of both of these hormones in their bodies. However, if a fetus has a Y chromosome, male hormones are produced in greater amounts. And in the presence of adequate amounts of testosterone, the cells that are intended to become reproductive organs differentiate into male organs (e.g., penis, testes). In the absence of a Y chromosome, all fetuses develop female organs (e.g., uterus, ovaries). Thus, this chapter will begin the study of sexual anatomy with that of the female.

EXTERNAL GENITAL STRUCTURES OF THE FEMALE

The external genitals of the female serve two purposes. They both protect the internal structures and play a primary role in producing physical pleasure during sexual interactions (as they are highly sensitive to touch). Collectively, these external structures are referred to as the *vulva,* but this area is often wrongly referred to as the *vagina,* which is an internal structure, and only the opening of the vagina is visible from the outside. Please refer to the drawing of the external genitals (Figure 1.1) as you read this section.

The Mons Veneris

The *mons veneris,* also called the *mons pubis,* is a fatty mound found covering the pelvic bone. Like all the external sexual structures, it is sensitive to touch. During puberty, hair grows on this mound of tissue.

The Labia Majora

The *labia majora,* or *major lips,* are two flaps of fleshy tissue running from the mons veneris to the perineum, just above the anal opening. Sensitive to touch, these structures also become covered with pubic hair during puberty. In a nonsexually aroused state, the labia majora fold together to protect the vaginal and urethral openings. However, when the female is sexually aroused, these structures engorge with blood, which results in the labia opening and flattening out, ultimately exposing the vaginal opening.

The Labia Minora

The *labia minora,* or *minor lips,* are two smaller, hairless folds of skin found in the area within the labia majora. They serve a similar protective function as the labia majora and respond similarly during sexual arousal by opening up and exposing the vaginal opening. The area contained within the labia minora is often referred to as the *vestibule.* Both the labia majora and minora differ vastly in appearance across different females. The labia minora come together at the top to form the clitoral hood.

The Clitoris and Clitoral Hood

Above the urethral opening is the clitoris. The clitoris is the most highly innervated external sex structure—it is most sensitive to touch and temperature and is, therefore, the focal point of sexual stimulation. The clitoris is a cylindrical structure formed by a shaft and a glans. The glans is the most visible part, and, in fact, much of the shaft lies beneath the surface. During sexual arousal,

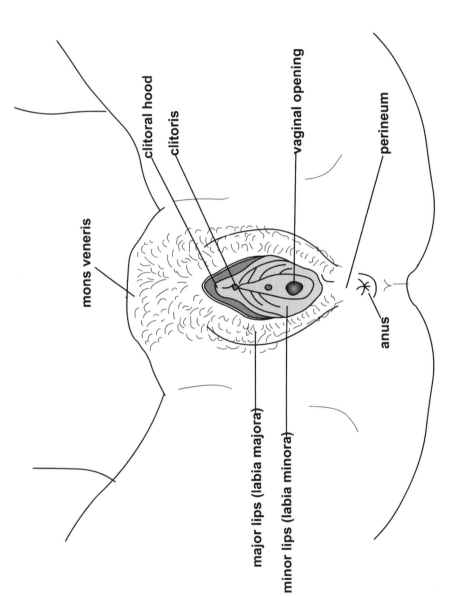

Figure 1.1. Female reproductive system external structures.

two spongy bodies, called *corpora cavernosa*, which are located inside the shaft, will become engorged with blood and cause the clitoris to expand in size and become more accessible to stimulation. The clitoral hood, which results from the labia minora joining together, generally covers the clitoris but will retract somewhat during arousal. Because the glans is so sensitive, it can become over stimulated in some women, causing an unpleasant sensation. At later points of sexual arousal, the glans actually retracts under the hood somewhat, protecting it from excessive stimulation. The amount of stimulation of the glans that is perceived as pleasurable varies considerably among women. Verbal and non-verbal communication from a woman about what does and does not feel good should always be a partner's guide during sexual interactions.

The Vaginal Opening

The vaginal opening, also referred to as the *introitus*, is located below the urethra (through which one urinates). It is the opening to the vaginal canal. It is through the vaginal canal that a woman menstruates and gives birth. Thus, this opening, while appearing very small, has the ability to expand tremendously. At the beginning of a girl's life, the vaginal opening usually has a partial-to-complete thin layer of tissue covering it. This tissue is referred to as the *hymen*. Usually, the hymen is merely a ring around the outer edges of the vaginal opening or a covering with multiple openings in it. Only rarely, the hymen is fully intact and must be opened to allow for menstrual flow once a girl reaches puberty and begins to menstruate. The function of the hymen is unclear beyond the possibility that it offers some protection to the vaginal opening. However, in ancient times and even in some cultures today in which the virginity of a woman before marriage is highly valued and expected, the hymen carries much significance. Upon having intercourse for the first time on her wedding night, a virginal bride is expected to show evidence of bleeding with the rupture of the hymen. In Deuteronomy 22: 13–17 of the Hebrew Bible, this is referred to as the "tokens of virginity," or proof that the female has not previously had sexual intercourse and is therefore worthy of being married. Unfortunately for brides in such oppressive cultures, a woman may not bleed when she has intercourse for the first time if the hymen does not cover the vaginal opening. Even an intact hymen can be ruptured through strenuous physical activity, injury, or through use of a tampon. Thus, the absence of bleeding during first intercourse is not a sign that the female is not "virginal."

The Perineum

The perineum is more of an area than an actual structure, but it is important in that touching or stroking this area can be highly sexually stimulating. This area is found between the vaginal and anal openings. It is also the area of tissue that is sometimes torn or cut (called an episiotomy) during a vaginal delivery.

INTERNAL GENITAL STRUCTURES OF THE FEMALE

The external structures, which are highly sensitive to sexual stimulation, play a primary role in sexual pleasure and a secondary role in reproduction. By contrast, the internal structures play a greater role in reproduction as opposed to sexual pleasure because they, for the most part, are not highly innervated with touch receptors. Following from the external structures, the discussion of the internal structures will begin with the outermost structure, the vaginal canal and move to the innermost structures. Please refer to the sketch of the internal structures (Figure 1.2) as they are discussed.

The Vagina

The vagina, or vaginal canal, is a tubular structure, but the walls rest against each other when in a nonaroused state. The canal is about four inches long when not in an aroused state and runs between the vaginal opening and the cervix. The walls of the vagina contain folded layers of muscle, which can stretch considerably during childbirth. The walls also constantly secrete a fluid, which provides an optimal environment for "good bacteria" that maintain vaginal pH at a healthy level. These secretions increase considerably during sexual arousal to lubricate the walls for vaginal intercourse. All women experience a small amount of vaginal discharge because of these fluids. This is natural and expected, but if the discharge seems excessive, causes irritation, or has a foul or strong odor, it may indicate infection, such as a yeast infection or sexually transmitted infection. If any of these signs are present, the woman should consult a medical professional.

Only the outer one-third of the vaginal canal is sensitive to touch; thus, it is the only part that plays much of a role in sexual stimulation. Some experts on female sexual anatomy and lay women alike contend that there is an area in the outer third of the vagina which is especially rich with nerve endings and, when stimulated, is most likely to cause an orgasm. This is called the Grafenberg or *G-Spot*. It is reportedly located about two inches up from the entrance of the vagina on the front of the body. Women report that they can feel a raised spot or series of ridges in this area.

The Cervix

The vaginal canal ends at the cervix. The cervix is located between the vaginal canal and the uterus. Viewing the cervix up through the vagina, it appears somewhat like a donut with a very small opening in the center. The opening is to the uterus and is called the *cervical os*. Two important substances

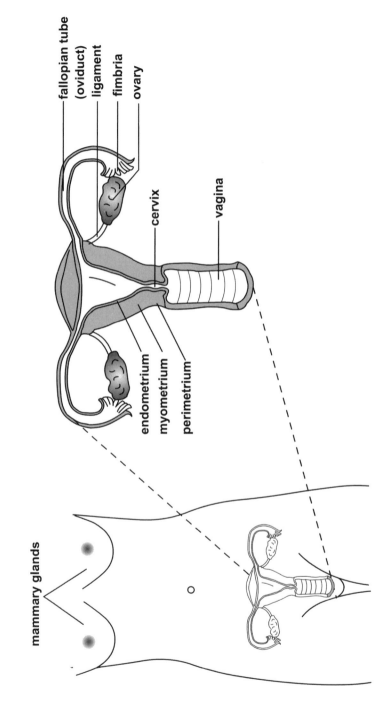

Figure 1.2. Female reproductive system internal structures.

pass through the cervical os—menstrual flow passes out of the uterus through this canal and into the vaginal canal, and during intercourse, ejaculate containing millions of sperm (the male contribution to ultimately producing a baby) must pass through the cervix to the uterus on the way to the fallopian tubes, where an egg, if present, might be fertilized. Mucus produced by glands in the cervix forms a plug in the cervical os, which protects the uterus from harmful bacteria. This plug dissolves during menstruation and ovulation (when an egg cell is available for fertilization by the sperm) to allow passage through the os.

The Uterus

The uterus is the structure that bears the resemblance of an upside-down pear. It has muscular walls and is hollow within. Measuring on average about three by two inches, it is obviously capable of expanding tremendously as this is the reproductive organ that is home to the developing fetus. The uterine walls are formed by three layers. The thin, outer layer is called the perimetrium. The middle layer, or myometrium, contracts during labor to help move the prenate into the vaginal canal. And the inner layer, or endometrium, thickens in response to hormonal changes in anticipation of pregnancy. Once an egg from the female is fertilized by a sperm from a male, the mass of cells that will become a human form attaches to the uterine wall and is nourished by the endometrium. If pregnancy does not occur, the inner lining sheds in the form of menstrual flow.

The Fallopian Tubes

The fallopian tubes, or *oviducts*, are the site of fertilization. These are tubes that connect to the upper portion of the uterus. At the opposite end are these fingerlike projections that partially surround, but are not actually attached to, the ovaries. When an egg is released from the ovary, these projections, called *fimbriae*, coax the egg into the fallopian tube, where millions of tiny, moving, hair-like structures on the fallopian tube walls, called cilia, further coax the egg cell along the tube. The sperm usually unites with the egg cell in the outer third of the tube, the area closest to the ovaries.

The Ovaries

The ovaries, located at the end of the fallopian tubes, are held in place by a ligament attached to the uterine wall. They are two egg-shaped structures measuring approximately $\frac{3}{4}$–$1\frac{1}{2}$ inches long. These critical organs produce egg cells as well as hormones that are essential to female reproduction.

SUMMARY OF MAJOR FEMALE REPRODUCTIVE ORGANS AND THEIR FUNCTIONS

External Organs	Function
Mons pubis	Sexual stimulation
Clitoris, primarily clitoral glans	Sexual stimulation and arousal
Clitoral hood	Sexual stimulation and protection of clitoral glans
Labia majora	Protection of vulva; sexual stimulation
Labia minora	Protection of vaginal opening; sexual stimulation
Perineum	Sexual stimulation

Internal Organs	Function
Corpora cavernosa	Erection of the clitoris
Vagina	Sexual intercourse, menstrual flow, vaginal delivery, possible sexual stimulation in outer one-third
Cervical os	Passage of menstrual flow, semen to and from uterus
Uterus	Fetal development
Fallopian tubes	Passage for egg cell from ovary to uterus; site where sperm joins egg (conception)
Ovaries	Production of egg cell; production of hormones

THE BREASTS

The breasts, also called *mammary glands*, are unique to mammals, which are capable of producing milk and nourishing their young. In the center of the surface of the breast is the *areola*, the circular, darkened area. The *nipple*, a rounded, protruding, and also darkly pigmented structure, is located in the center of the areola. Beneath the skin of the breasts lies a layer of fatty tissue (adipose). Found within this tissue are the *alveolar glands* and the *lactiferous ducts*. The alveolar glands produce breast milk after delivery of an infant. The alveolar glands empty into the lactiferous ducts. These ducts store milk produced by the alveolar glands, and they also open into the nipples, where they release milk when stimulated by a suckling infant.

The amount and distribution of adipose tissue determines the shape and size of the breasts; thus, the size of the breasts bears no relationship to how well the breasts function (e.g., milk production) or how sensitive they are to stimulation. Why, then, is our U.S. culture, and so many others, so concerned about the size of a woman's breasts? In fact, this obsession seems to be a growing trend—according to the American Society of Plastic Surgeons (n.d.), 264,041 women in North America underwent breast augmentation surgery in 2004 alone. The number of these surgeries has increased 676 percent since 1992 (American Society of Plastic Surgeons, 2005). Unlike most cultures around the world, the U.S. culture "hypersexualizes" breasts, rather than thinking of them as simply body parts intended for breastfeeding babies. The breasts are made taboo, and like the reproductive organs, are covered, and people are often embarrassed by public exposure of breasts (i.e., public breast-feeding). This view of breasts is unique to U.S. culture and those heavily influenced by the United States. In other cultures, however, it is not unusual to see uncovered breasts (e.g., sunbathing in Europe or simply never covering them, as in some African cultures), and they are not titillating. Author of the book *Breasts: The Women's Perspective on an American Obsession*, Carolyn Lat-teier, was interviewed in 2002 on a TV program called *All About Breasts* on the Discovery Health Channel. She said, "A lot of people think it's just the human nature to be fascinated with breasts, but in many cultures, breasts aren't sexual at all. I interviewed a young anthropologist working with women in Mali, in a country in Africa where women go around with bare breasts. They're always feeding their babies. And when she told them that in our culture men are fascinated with breasts there was an instant of shock. The women burst out laughing. They laughed so hard, they fell on the floor. They said, 'You mean, men act like babies?'" She further suggested that if more women breastfed, using breasts for what they were intended, people would not see breasts as taboo or sexual (Discovery Health Channel, 2002).

EXTERNAL GENITAL STRUCTURES OF THE MALE

The Penis

Please refer to the figure of the external male genitals (Figure 1.3). Perhaps the most prominent genital structure in the male is the penis. The penis is a cylindrical structure consisting of a *glans* and a *shaft*. The penis actually runs beyond the body wall into the pelvic region—this unexposed area is referred to as the *root*. The glans and shaft of the penis are homologous to the glans and shaft of the clitoris. The shaft runs the full length of the penis up to the glans, which is the acorn-shaped structure at the end of the penis. The opening to the urinary tract, called the *meatus,* is located at the tip of the glans. The raised edge where the shaft connects to the glans is called the *coronal ridge*. The glans and the area of the coronal ridge in particular are most heavily innervated and are, therefore, very sensitive to touch. As in women, direct stimulation to this area might become too intense at times for some men.

The skin covering the penis is hairless and very elastic, moving freely across the underlying structures and stretching when the penis becomes erect. The area of tissue on the underside of the penis is homologous to the labia minora in

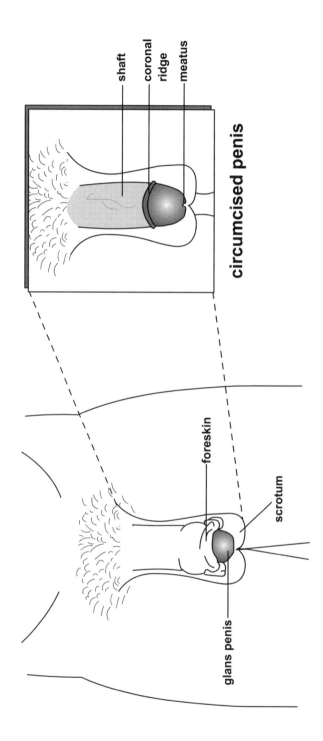

Figure 1.3. Male reproductive system external structures.

the female. A visible line that runs along the underside of the penis is where the tissues fused during prenatal development. Covering the glans is a fold of tissue called the *foreskin*. The foreskin usually retracts beyond the glans during an erection and only slightly when urinating. The foreskin is sometimes removed for cultural or religious reasons in a procedure called *circumcision*. This procedure is usually performed just after birth, although some adults choose to have it removed later in life. Contrary to popular opinion, circumcision is not a medical necessity. Circumcision has been shown to reduce the risk of infections such as urinary tract infections, and more seriously the human immunodeficiency virus; however, equal risk reduction occurs simply by practicing good hygiene (i.e., cleaning under the foreskin while bathing). Given the fact that circumcision is painful and has its own risks (e.g., infection, deformation), parents are urged to weigh all costs and benefits carefully (Kinkade & Meadows, 2005).

Penile Augmentation

Another current social concern regarding the penis is that of penile augmentation. Conduct a quick search of the Internet (or check your junk email box), and you will see that there are countless products being marketed to increase a man's penis size . . . because "size does matter." Manual stretching exercises, stretching by using penile weights, vacuum pumps, pills, and lotions are all scams designed to entice men who have fallen prey to the "male enhancement" industry's campaign to make men feel insecure about their penises and erections. In fact, some of these enhancement strategies can be harmful. For example, both manual stretching and using weights can damage penile tissue. Vacuum pumps can also damage the elastic penile tissue and eventually cause less-firm erections (Mayo Clinic Staff, 2005).

In recent years, penis augmentation surgery has become available, but medical societies do not endorse augmentation surgery for cosmetic reasons only. Surgery typically involves making an incision near the base of the penis and cutting the suspensory ligament that attaches the penis to the pubic bone allowing the root of the penis to hang outside the body. Skin is also grafted from the abdomen to the penile shaft. A potentially significant problem created by this procedure is that because the suspensory ligament stabilizes and supports the upward tilt of the erect penis, the penis may now wobble, or erections may occur at unusual angles. The girth of a penis can also be increased through several methods. A couple of common ones include injecting fat cells from another part of the body into the penile shaft or grafting skin and fat to the outside of the penis. These procedures are of questionable safety, and additional surgery is sometimes required to correct negative effects of the surgery. Some of these complications include low-hanging penises, loss of sensitivity, scarring, shorter penises, hair at the penis base, and fat concentrated in one or more areas causing lumps (Mayo Clinic Staff, 2005).

Interestingly, the typical male requesting this surgery has a penis length within the normal range (Mayo Clinic Staff, 2005; Mondaini et al., 2002). What is "normal?" A recent Italian study showed that the typical flaccid penis is 9 centimeters (3.54 inches) long while the stretched penis is 12.5 centimeters (4.92 inches). The typical circumference at the middle of the shaft is 10 centimeters (3.94 inches; Ponchietti et al., 2001). Other research has shown that 70 percent of men's erect penises range from 5 inches to 7 inches, and a penis is considered "abnormally" small only when it measures smaller than 3 inches when erect (Mayo Clinic Staff, 2005). Men seeking penile augmentation are typically in their late twenties, and they tend to think that the typical penis is larger than the above findings (i.e., they estimate that the normal flaccid penis is 12 centimeters or 4.72 inches). A large number of these males said their concerns started in childhood when they observed that a friend had a larger penis, and a smaller but significant number of them began to worry about their penis size in their teen years after viewing erotic images (Mondaini et al., 2002).

So, does size matter? In a recent Dutch study, 77 percent of the sexually active women surveyed responded that penis size was "unimportant" or "totally unimportant." Women who were concerned about length were also concerned about girth, with girth being more important to them than length (Francken, van de Wiel, van Driel, & Weijmar Schultz, 2002). Other research has shown that women tend to prefer average-sized penises. And some men with large penises express concerns about being too large because women respond in fear to the sight of a large penis or the man fears hurting his partner. In fact, some women do feel discomfort if an especially long penis is thrust against the cervix, and the man must be careful not to insert the penis too far. In addition, it is important to remember that the female has very little sensation in the upper two-thirds of her vagina, meaning that stimulation in this area is unlikely to enhance sexual arousal. In short, bigger is not necessarily better.

The Scrotum

The scrotum, a saclike structure behind the penis, is the homologous structure to the labia majora in the female. The scrotum houses organs called the testes. This sac is thin, hairless or slightly hair-covered skin, which hangs and moves loosely around the testes. The function of the scrotum is critical to reproduction—its job is to maintain the testes at a temperature that is neither too cold nor too hot and therefore damaging or lethal to sperm, which are formed, matured, and stored in the testes. Sperm must be maintained at a temperature of about 93° Fahrenheit, more than five degrees lower than normal body temperature. To maintain this safe temperature, the *dartos muscle*, in the middle layer of the scrotal sac, contracts and draws the testes up closer to the body when they become too cold and loosens so that the testes will fall farther away from the body when they become too hot. The scrotum sometimes contracts when a

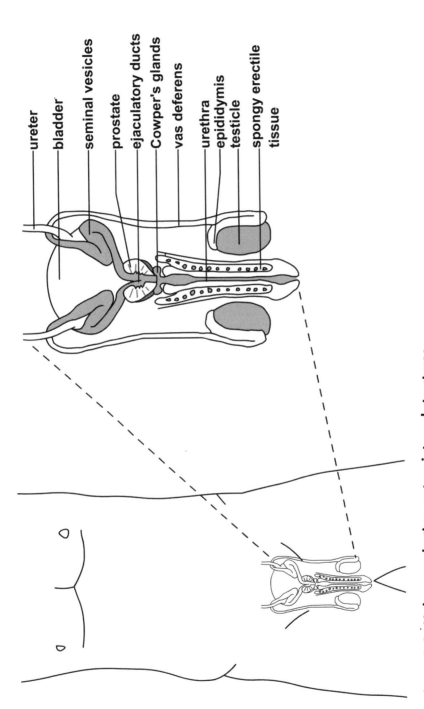

ureter

bladder

seminal vesicles

prostate

ejaculatory ducts

Cowper's glands

vas deferens

urethra

epididymis

testicle

spongy erectile
tissue

Figure 1.4. Male reproductive system internal structures.

man senses fear, an involuntary response intended to protect the testes from harm (Baldwin, 1993).

The Perineum

The perineum on the male body is the area located between the scrotum and the anal opening. Similar to the female, the perineum of the male is richly innervated and, therefore, sensitive to touch.

INTERNAL GENITAL STRUCTURES OF THE MALE

The internal structures of the male are essential for reproduction and they play a significant role in sexual arousal and response. For example, the first structures described, those found inside the penis, are necessary for a male to achieve an erection. Please refer to the drawing of the internal structures (Figure 1.4) as they are reviewed.

Internal Structures of the Penis

The penis contains three cylindrical bodies, two *corpora cavernosa* and one *corpus spongiosum*. The corpora cavernosa contain spongy, erectile tissue inside thick membranous sheaths. These structures are homologous to the corpora cavernosa in the female. The third cylindrical body, the corpus spongiosum, is also a spongy body containing erectile tissue bound in sheaths. All three of these structures engorge with blood to cause an erection during arousal. The *urethra*, a tube through which urine and ejaculate moves, runs the length through the middle of the corpus spongiosum.

Structures inside the Scrotal Sac

As mentioned earlier, the primary organ housed within the scrotum is the testes. There are two testicles or *testes* (sing.: testis), which are homologous to the two ovaries in the female. One testicle is usually slightly larger than the other. These oval structures are about 1 inch by 1.5 inches. The testicles are divided into lobes. A mass of coiled tubes called *seminiferous tubules* are located within these lobes and contained in a sheath called the *tunica albuginea*. The seminiferous tubules produce sperm. Special cells, called *Leydig's cells*, are also located among the tubules, and they are responsible for producing androgens, hormones that are important for male sexual functioning. These hormones are released into the bloodstream. After being produced in the seminiferous tubules, the sperm travel through the *rete testes*, another set of tubes, to the *epididymes* (sing.: *epididymis*) where they are stored and continue to mature. The epididymes are found resting against the back of the testicles and are best described as crescent-shaped structures. Each epididymis is actually made up of one coiled tube, which, if stretched and measured from end-to-end, is about 20 feet long. You can actually feel the epididymis by gently rolling the testis between your fingers. Each testis is held in place by a *spermatic cord*, which contains nerves and blood vessels that support the testes. The *cremaster* muscle is also located in the spermatic cord. During sexual arousal, the cremaster muscle contracts, pulling the scrotal sac closer to the body. As with the dartos muscle, contraction and expansion of the cremaster muscle also functions to regulate scrotal temperature. Finally, the spermatic cords also contain the *vas deferens*, which are discussed next.

The Vas Deferens and Ejaculatory Ducts

During ejaculation, the *vas deferens* provide an exit from the testes and a passageway to the *prostate gland*. As noted in Figure 1.4, the vas deferens go up and over the bladder before reaching their destination, which is to join with the *ejaculatory ducts*, through which the seminal vesicles empty into the vas deferens.

The Seminal Vesicles and Prostate Gland

The seminal vesicles are small, elongated structures located outside the prostate gland. The prostate gland is a walnut-sized structure located just beneath the bladder. The seminal vesicles and the prostate gland provide the seminal fluid, 70 percent coming from the seminal vesicles and 30 percent from the prostate gland. Seminal fluid provides a mode of transportation for the sperm. It also contains sugars to nourish the sperm, and it maintains the pH level around the sperm at a safe level; the pH of the vagina is too acidic and would kill the sperm in the absence of seminal fluid. Once the sperm and seminal fluid combine, they are ejaculated through the urethra.

How can the urethra function for urination and ejaculation without the two being mixed? It is simple. A wide sphincter muscle at the opening of the bladder relaxes (and opens) when a male needs to urinate and tenses (and closes) during ejaculation.

The Bulbourethral Gland

Located just below the prostate gland is a tiny, pea-sized gland called the *bulbourethral gland* or the *Cowper's gland*. During sexual arousal, this gland also emits an alkaline substance. Its purpose is not entirely understood, although the prevailing notion is that it neutralizes the acidity in the urethra of the male before ejaculate is released as a protective measure. Some people consider it as a lubricant for sexual intercourse, but it does not occur in sufficient amounts to adequately lubricate. The important thing to remember about this fluid is that it may contain thousands of stray sperm, which made their way to the gland during a previous ejaculation. Thus, barrier-method contraception (e.g., a condom) should be applied before Cowper's gland emissions and any penis to vulva contact if one would like to be absolutely certain to avoid pregnancy.

SUMMARY OF MAJOR MALE REPRODUCTIVE ORGANS AND THEIR FUNCTIONS

External Organs	Function
Shaft of penis	Sexual stimulation; intercourse
Glans of penis	Sexual stimulation
Foreskin	Protection of glans; sexual stimulation
Scrotum	Houses testicles; protects and regulates temperature of testicles
Perineum	Sexual stimulation

Internal Organs	Function
Corpora cavernosa	Erection of penis
Corpus spongiosum	Erection of penis; houses urethra
Testicles	Sperm production and storage; hormone production
Vas deferens	Transportation of sperm to meet seminal fluid
Seminal vesicles and prostate gland	Production of seminal fluid
Ejaculatory ducts	Joining of sperm and seminal fluid just before ejaculation
Cowper's glands	Production of fluid to neutralize acidity of urethra to protect sperm
Urethra	Passage of ejaculate and urine

CONCLUSION

At first, the idea of studying sexual anatomy may sound boring, but hopefully you learned that the sexual anatomy is quite interesting. The benefits of understanding how these organs function are considerable from both a psychological and physical standpoint. Such knowledge can make you more comfortable with your sexuality in general and help you to know how you and your partner can derive the most enjoyment from your sexual interactions. In addition, understanding how these organs work might help you to recognize when you might have a physical concern that needs to be addressed.

REFERENCES

American Society of Plastic Surgeons. (n.d.). *Top 5 cosmetic procedures*. Retrieved September 8, 2005, from www.plasticsurgery.org/public_education/loader.cfm?url=/commonspot/security/getfile.cfm&PageID=16732

American Society of Plastic Surgeons. (2005). *2004 cosmetic surgery trends*. Retrieved September 8, 2005, from www.plasticsurgery.org/public_education/loader.cfm?url=/commonspot/security/getfile.cfm&PageID=16150

Baldwin, D. (1993). *Understanding male sexual health*. New York: Hippocrene Books.

Discovery Health Channel. (2002). All about breasts [TV series episode]. *Berman and Berman: For Women Only*. Retrieved September 8, 2005, from www.newshe.com/allaboutbreasts1.shtml

Francken, A. B., van de Wiel, H. B., van Driel, M. F., & Weijmar Schultz, W. C. (2002). What importance do women attribute to the size of the penis? *European Urology, 42*(5), 426–431.

Kinkade, S., & Meadows, S. (2005). Does neonatal circumcision decrease morbidity? *Journal of Family Practice, 54*(1), 81–82.

Mayo Clinic Staff. (2005, May 24). *Beware of penis-enlargement scams*. Retrieved September 11, 2005, from www.mayoclinic.com/invoke.cfm?id=MC00026

Mondaini, N., Ponchietti, R., Gontero, P., Muir, G. H., Natali, A., Caldarera, E., Biscioni, S., & Rizzo, M. (2003). Penile length is normal in most men seeking penile lengthening procedures. *International Journal of Impotence Research, 14*(4), 283–286.

Ponchietti, R., Mondaini, N., Bonafe, M., Di Loro, F., Biscioni, S., & Masieri, L. (2001). Penile length and circumference: A study on 3,300 young Italian males. *European Urology, 39*(2), 183–186.

2

Sex and the Brain

George J. Demakis ◆

The brain is the most complex organ in the human body and is involved in nearly all that we do, from dancing to reading to having sex. Though its role in sexual behavior is still not fully understood, the increasing research on this topic in recent years has documented the brain's importance—one writer (Rodgers, 2002) even titled her chapter on the topic "Where It Really Happens"—in various areas such as sexual interest, arousal, and orientation, as well as sex differences. Many researchers, in fact, would agree that one cannot understand sex without understanding the brain and, more broadly, how it interacts with other organs and systems in the body to produce, control, and regulate sexual behavior. This chapter explores these issues. I first review common methods of studying sexual behavior, then outline basic neuroanatomy with an emphasis on brain regions important for sex, and then summarize the findings about brain-sex relationships framed by common research methods. What is not covered here and beyond the scope of this chapter are (a) physiological changes that accompany sexual arousal in the genitalia, such as erection in males, (b) brain differences between men and women and how such differences are manifested in behavior and cognition, and (c) brain differences that may be associated with sexual orientation. Each of the literatures on the above topics is voluminous, at times controversial, especially the final point, and deviates from our goal of understanding the brain's role in sexual behavior.

RESEARCH METHODS USED TO STUDY
SEX AND THE BRAIN

Our understanding of the brain's role in sex comes from three kinds of research (see Meston & Frohlich, 2000): various types of animal studies; laboratory studies of humans in which aspects of sexual interest or response are elicited; and clinical studies of humans with sexual dysfunction after brain injury. Each of these approaches has its own advantages and disadvantages. First, animal studies allow, in some ways, the most direct study of how various brain regions are important for sexual behavior and have been time-tested. In one approach, a lesion is created by destroying a part of the brain to assess the effect this has on the resulting behavior. If, for instance, a lesion to a specific region of the hypothalamus (described below) reduces the ability of the male rat to copulate (engage in intercourse with a female rat), it is assumed that that region is involved in copulation. This argument is strengthened when similar-sized lesions are made in surrounding brain regions without a reduction in copulatory behavior. In a related approach, the specific brain region of interest can be stimulated with mild electrical current to evaluate whether this induces or increases copulation. Again, if it does so, but stimulation to nearby brain regions does not, the likelihood that the region is involved in copulation increases. The practical advantages of this research are obvious because ethical considerations prevent such research on humans. In fact, huge amounts of such research have been done with different species and on a variety of topics, from behavior to organ systems to disease processes. However, because rats (and other species) are not as complex as humans and their sexual behavior tends to be more stereotyped (i.e., more routine and less variable), it is not always clear if findings obtained from these studies generalize or apply to humans, whose sexual behavior is anything but stereotyped. Clearly, cognition or thinking is more relevant for human behavior and helps generate the diversity of our sexual experience. Animal research also cannot address some of the more interesting aspects of human sexual behavior, such as the experience of orgasm, or the many ways in which culture influences our thinking about all things sexual.

A related line of work with animals that shares some of the above advantages and disadvantages is the large body of research on the influence of hormones—chemical messengers released by the brain—on sexual behavior. There are various ways of conducting such research. For instance, certain hormones can be introduced via injection of medication, or they can be reduced or eliminated with certain medications or through removal of a specific brain region or body part. The most common example of the latter approach is castration of the male animal early in life, which has been shown in numerous animal species to reduce testosterone and many aspects of sexual behavior. Similarly, removal of the ovaries in the female animal has been demonstrated to reduce estrogen and progesterone, hormones important in the regulation of the estrus (animal) or menstrual (human) cycles and mating behavior.

More broadly, hormones can be considered to have *activating effects,* in which they affect the functioning of the adult brain, and *organizing effects,* in which they affect brain development. An example of the former is the effect of testosterone on the amygdala which elicits sexual motivation in the male, and an example of the latter effect is when testosterone influences the preoptic area of the hypothalamus in the developing male rat, an important area for sexual behavior. As can be seen in these latter effects, hormones influence neural growth and death in certain brain regions pre- and postnatally, making the male and female brain different. In general, the research on hormones requires an understanding of how the brain (particularly the hypothalamus) influences and regulates the endocrine system, the system that controls and mediates hormonal influences on our bodies and behavior—understanding the complex relationships among chemistry, biology, and behavior is critical here. Whatever the approach, understanding how hormonal changes influence sexual behavior, and even brain function, has provided a wealth of information about brain-sex relationships.

The second type of research—the use of healthy individuals exposed to sexually relevant information or stimuli—better helps us to understand the brain's role in sexual arousal. This research is typically done in a controlled laboratory setting in which participants are exposed to sexually explicit stimuli, typically photos or video clips, while brain function is assessed. Some research has even had participants masturbate to evaluate brain changes during orgasm. Active brain areas, when compared to base line, or when exposed to other stimuli, are considered to be regions important for sexual arousal or orgasm. Brain activation in such studies can be measured by the electrical activity of neurons (brain cells) with electroencephalogram (EEG) or by the metabolic activity of brain regions with positron emission tomography (PET scan). An advantage of such research is that it provides a noninvasive and ethical view of brain involvement in humans. Moreover, because conditions of the experiment can be manipulated or controlled by the experimenter, it is possible to evaluate brain differences in conditions that share at least some basic similarities with sex, such as the experience of humor or positive emotion. Unfortunately, such research remains relatively rare as it is tremendously difficult to evaluate some aspects of sexuality (e.g., orgasm) in a controlled laboratory setting. Even if sexual arousal can be initiated, perhaps culminating in orgasm, such experiences in a lab are likely to be different than those in real life and may limit the applicability of the findings. A final issue here is that, at least traditionally, the above neuroimaging has been limited in how well it can visualize subcortical brain structures, regions of particular interest for the study of sex (described below), though this has improved in recent years.

The third and final common type of research is the study of changes in sexual functioning or behavior in individuals with brain damage or disease or, less commonly, psychiatric conditions, such as depression or schizophrenia. Ideally, the researcher examines sexual behavior in individuals with damage to specific brain regions and compares them to those with damage to other specific brain regions. Much like the animal studies mentioned above, when damage to an area is related to a decrease in sexual interest or motivation, that area is assumed to be involved in this aspect of sexuality. A variety of patient groups have been studied, including those with traumatic brain injury, stroke, and even Alzheimer's disease. The true challenge of this approach is that naturally occurring brain damage, as opposed to the experimentally placed lesions in animal studies, typically does not occur in only one specific area of the brain, making determination of the role of specific brain areas difficult. Moreover, damage to one area with a tumor or a stroke may also affect other brain areas far from the area of damage as blood flow is altered throughout the brain. A second related approach has evaluated patients treated for psychiatric disorders with psychosurgery, which entails surgical destruction of certain disordered brain regions thought to be causing the psychiatric difficulties. In the past, this approach was used for severe psychiatric difficulties, notably schizophrenia, and is used rarely today. At various times, the destruction or inhibition of brain regions can also be done with medications, an approach sometimes used in the treatment of individuals with severe sexual disorders, such as pedophilic sex offenders. Interpretation of such findings is complicated because there are likely to be complex differences in psychiatric patients involving not only the brain, but also cognition and behavior, that potentially limit our understanding of brain–sex relationships.

In total, what we know about the brain and sexual behavior comes from a variety of research approaches using a wide range of animal and human participants. Rather than competing, it is probably best to see these approaches as complementary—each provides a unique perspective and set of findings for our understanding of the brain's role in sexual behavior, but together, they provide the fullest understanding of brain–sex relationships. Before addressing what we know about such relationships, I briefly outline the main subdivisions and structures of the brain, to guide that discussion, with focus on those areas involved in sexual behavior.

NEUROANATOMY 101 WITH A FOCUS ON SEXUAL BEHAVIOR

I will focus below on the central nervous system, though it is important to note that it is connected with other parts of the nervous system that are responsible for behavior (somatic nervous system) and those responsible for automatic life-sustaining activity, such as heart beat, breathing, food digestion, and salivation (autonomic nervous system). The autonomic nervous system has a sympathetic division, which is responsible for stimulation or "fight or flight," and the parasympathetic, which is responsible for inhibition or "rest and digest." These systems balance our internal environment and work in opposition to each other; the sympathetic stimulates the heart to beat faster and inhibits digestion, whereas the parasympathetic slows heartbeat and stimulates digestion.

The central nervous system is divided into the brain and the spinal cord. The *spinal cord* is surrounded by the bony spinal column and consists of nerves connecting the brain and the rest of the body, including the muscles, skin, joints, and organs. In this way the brain receives information from the external and internal worlds and then, after processing it, makes decisions, generates emotions, or executes movement. There are also spinal reflexes, such as the knee-jerk reflex, when the leg kicks out after the kneecap is struck, that do not connect with the brain. The *brain* itself has three main subdivisions: the brainstem, the cerebellum, and the cerebrum. The *brain stem* emerges from the top of the spinal cord and hosts numerous structures that, most basically, are important for life-sustaining activities such as the control of breathing, heart rate and blood pressure, and sleep and wake cycles. The *cerebellum* is at the lower back region of the brain and is important for balance and the coordination and regulation of skilled motor movements. Both the brain stem and the cerebellum are typically not under conscious control and tend to function automatically.

Within the *cerebrum*, things become more complex, and it is divided into the *diencephalon* and *cerebral hemispheres*, of which we have two—the right and left hemisphere. The main structures of the diencephalon include the *thalamus* and the *hypothalamus*. A thalamus sits at the top of the brain stem in each hemisphere and is the brain's principal relay station; information from the world is routed through our senses to the thalamus and then to the respective brain areas where more complex processing occurs. Similarly, information from the brain to other body parts is routed through the thalamus. Just in front, and below the thalamus, is the *hypothalamus*, a small structure critical for motivated behaviors such as feeding, drinking, emotion, temperature control, and sex. The desire for any of these needs can be considered to motivate or drive behavior to reach the relevant goal, whether it be a meal when hungry or a mate when sexually aroused. To influence and control these complex behaviors, the hypothalamus sits at the connection of multiple brain regions and integrates emotional (limbic), hormonal (endocrine), and cognitive (cortex) information. In fact, the pituitary gland, considered the body's master gland as it controls the release of hormones, is directly connected to and controlled by the hypothalamus. Examples of hormones, which travel in the bloodstream and influence organs throughout the body, include insulin, which is released by the pancreas to control glucose storage and use; thyroid hormone, released by the thyroid gland to control metabolic rate; and sex hormones, released by the testes or ovaries, that are involved in the development of genitalia and secondary sex characteristics during puberty, as well as later control and maintenance of sexual behavior. The complex interrelationships among the pituitary gland, various other glands throughout the body, and the level of circulating hormones are controlled by the hypothalamus. We will return to the hypothalamus and the relevant sex hormones a bit later in more detail, as they are particularly important in our understanding of the brain's involvement in sexual behavior.

The two cerebral hemispheres comprise the remainder of the cerebrum. At the highest and most complex level, each can be divided into the four lobes or regions of the *cortex* where complex perception, thinking, language, and control of behavior occur (see Figure 2.1). These lobes, named for the underlying bones, are as follows: *occipital*, responsible for visual processing; *temporal*, responsible for auditory (hearing) processing; *parietal*, responsible for somato-sensory processing, such as touch, body position, and pressure; and *frontal*, responsible for inhibition or control of behavior/emotion, planning and execution of movement, motivation, higher-order thinking, and working memory. Because the frontal lobes will be further detailed below, it is important to note that their anterior regions are typically divided into three: orbitofrontal regions are at the base, medial prefrontal are in the middle, and dorsolateral prefrontal are at the sides (see Figure 2.2).

Language, that supreme function of humans, is localized in the left hemisphere in the vast majority of individuals; regions in the left temporal lobe are responsible for the comprehension of language, and regions in left frontal lobe are responsible for the expression of language. Below these cortical areas

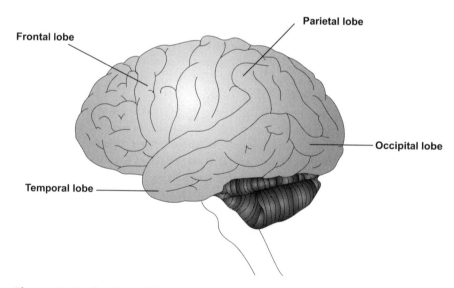

Figure 2.1. The four lobes of the brain, as viewed in the left hemisphere.

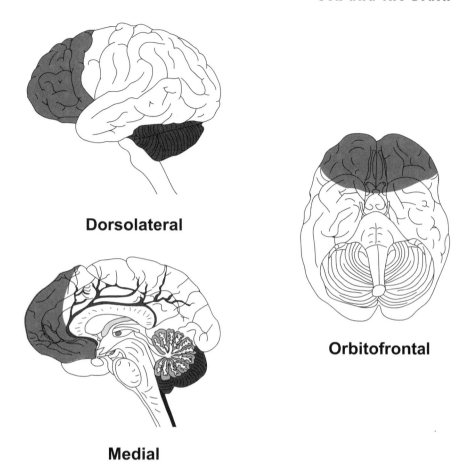

Figure 2.2. Dorsolateral (side), medial (middle), and orbital (bottom) regions of the human cerebral cortex illustrating the three major subdivisions of the prefrontal cortex.

(often termed subcortical), each cerebral hemisphere includes the *basal ganglia*, a set of structures important for the control of movement, and the *limbic system*, several connected brain structures important for, among other things, emotion, memory, and sex. Limbic means "border" in Latin; this system is a horseshoe-shaped rim at the junction of the diencephalon and each cerebral hemisphere. Key structures here include the *hippocampus*, curled into the base of the temporal lobe, responsible for the formation of new memories; and the *amygdala*, which sits just in front of the hippocampus and is involved in certain aspects of sexual and emotional behavior (see Figure 2.3). Other structures of the limbic system include the cingulate gyrus, the septal area, and, as described above, the hypothalamus. We will return to the limbic system, particularly the role of the hypothalamus, below.

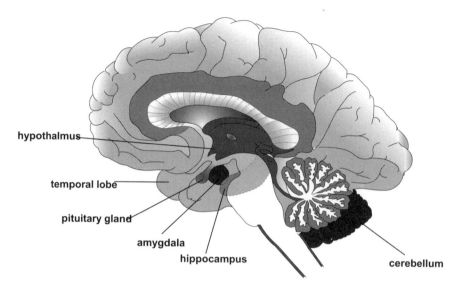

Figure 2.3. Medial view of the right hemisphere illustrating principal subcortical structures including the hippocampus, amygdala, hypothalamus, pituitary gland, and cerebellum.

WHAT DOES THE ANIMAL LITERATURE TELL US ABOUT SEX AND THE BRAIN?

A variety of animal studies have determined that structures within the hypothalamus are critical for sexual behavior (see Figure 2.4). For the male, the specific region appears to be the medial preoptic region (MPOA) of the hypothalamus and possibly surrounding structures as well. When this region is stimulated with a mild electric current, the male engages in copulatory behavior; when the region is damaged with a lesion, such behavior is either reduced or eliminated. While it is relatively clear that this region is important for the actual mechanics of mating, it may not be important for sexual interest or motivation. For instance, in one study, male rats with damage to this area still retained interest in females and sought access to them, despite their inability to mate (Everitt, 1990). Similarly, damaged brain areas in male monkeys have resulted in males that will not mate with females, but may masturbate in view of the females, again suggesting intact sexual interest and motivation. When the MPOA is electrically stimulated in male monkeys, penile erections and mounting occur. Given its clear role in male sexual behavior, it is not surprising that this region is a sexually dimorphic nucleus (i.e., different between the sexes): it is approximately five times larger in the male (Gorski, 1984). The MPOA is also sensitive to testosterone, a male sex hormone or androgen; a male rat castrated in adulthood will cease sexual behavior, but implantation of testosterone in this area reinstates sexual behavior. More

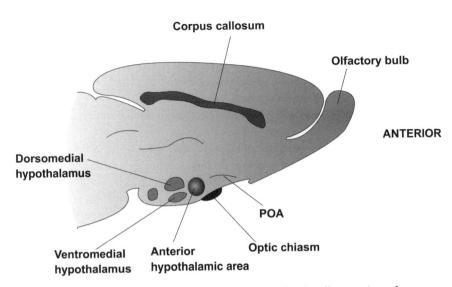

DORSAL

Corpus callosum

Olfactory bulb

ANTERIOR

Dorsomedial
hypothalamus

POA

Ventromedial   Anterior   Optic chiasm
hypothalamus   hypothalamic area

Figure 2.4. A medial view of the male rat brain illustrating the preoptic area (POA), which appears to be particularly important for successful copulation.

broadly, testosterone has been widely demonstrated to be necessary for male sexual behavior, including erections and ejaculations—and even sexual thoughts in humans—in a variety of species.

While the findings described above confirm the importance of the MPOA for male sexual behavior, it is important to be more precise about what this region actually accomplishes. At least as determined from studies on the rat, on which most of the research has been done, it seems important for the integration and organization of multiple sources of information, including that from environmental, physiological, and psychological sources, to copulate (see Nelson, 2000, pp. 199–271). Such information includes, for instance, data about the state of the male's own endocrine system and stimuli associated with the female rat, such as auditory, olfactory, and tactile information about her sexual availability. Without it, the male is unable to generate appropriate sexual behavior and responses in the presence of a receptive mate. Because it serves to integrate such diverse sources of bodily and environmental information, the MPOA is not only critical for sex, but also plays an important role in other motivated behaviors, such as thirst, temperature regulation, and maternal behavior in the female.

In females, the ventromedial hypothalamus (VMN), quite similar in location to the MPOA in males, appears to be critical for mating. In female rats, this region controls lordosis, the characteristic arching of the back and elevation of the rump while the animal remains still, necessary for copulation. In many animal species, this posture displays females' receptivity for sex and is stereotyped, showing little variability across individuals. Experimental damage to the VMN decreases or abolishes lordosis and other sex-related female behavior (e.g., ear wiggling), whereas electrical stimulation does the opposite. Similar to the males, when certain hormones, in this case estradiol or progesterone, are injected into this area, sexual behavior is activated, even in rats whose ovaries have been removed. The VMN also appears similar to the MPOA in the sense that it serves to integrate multiple sources of information such as that from the motor system, necessary for the characteristic posture of lordosis, and the endocrine system, necessary for the secretion of female sex hormones of estrogen and progesterone that accompany lordosis (see Nelson, 2000, pp. 273–335).

In addition to the findings on the hypothalamus, animal research has also demonstrated the importance of the amygdala—a limbic structure closely connected with the hypothalamus—and the temporal lobes for sexual activity. Another part of the Everitt (1990) study described above lesioned the amygdala rather than the hypothalamus in male rats. These rats did not seek access to females, suggesting decreased sexual motivation, but were capable of mating with females if they were provided. Later when amphetamines that induce the release of the neurotransmitter dopamine were injected into this area, sexual motivation increased. The amygdala, therefore, seems important for sexual motivation and initiation. In a quite different type of study, Kluver and Bucy (1939) removed bilateral (from both cerebral hemispheres) amygdalae and anterior temporal lobes of monkeys and observed a constellation of unique behaviors: tameness and loss of fear, hyperorality (i.e., a tendency to put anything into the mouth whether food or not), visual agnosia (i.e., inability to visually recognize objects), attentional difficulties (i.e., inability to focus on both relevant and irrelevant stimuli), and hypersexuality. In fact, such monkeys demonstrated indiscriminate sexual activity—whether heterosexual, homosexual, autoerotic (masturbation), and sexual activity with inanimate objects, such as chairs. While this research is usually used to highlight the role of the amygdala and related structures in emotion, it is clear that this region is involved in other activities, including sexual behavior. This issue and the potential causes of the increased sexuality will be described below in discussion of individuals who have suffered neurological damage.

WHAT DOES THE RESEARCH ON (MOSTLY) HEALTHY HUMANS TELL US ABOUT SEX AND THE BRAIN?

EEG research has, for the most part, concentrated on cortical involvement in sexual activity and has generally indicated the importance of the right hemisphere. For instance, Cohen, Rosen, and Goldstein (1976) found that right parietal regions became more activated than left parietal regions in both heterosexual men and women who self-stimulated to orgasm. This asymmetry (i.e., difference between sides of the brain) increased as sexual arousal increased. Another study by Waismann, Fenwick, Wilson, Hewett, and Lumsden (2003) using heterosexual men also found activation in right parietal regions when these men viewed sexually explicit slides. The authors suggested that these findings were obtained because regions of the parietal lobe are responsible for complex aspects of visual processing, such as visual association and pattern recognition. Given the visual nature of the stimuli, these findings would not be surprising. Using a somewhat different approach, Tucker (1983) had a small sample of experienced actors generate either intense feelings of sexual arousal or depression in a laboratory condition. Self-reported sexual arousal was associated with higher right-hemisphere activity. One exception to the above research was a study by Heath (1972), who found increased activity in the septum, a limbic system structure, but none in the right hemisphere, during orgasm in a man and woman undergoing psychiatric treatment. It is unclear how well these findings generalize to other populations because of the severe psychiatric difficulties of the sample. These various EEG studies have now been supplanted by more sophisticated neuroimaging technologies that provide a more detailed analysis of regional brain activation. Simply noting that right hemisphere activity increases during sexual arousal, as has been done in the past, does not provide much specificity nor does it advance our understanding of brain-sex relationships.

The newer generation of neuroimaging studies has provided better neuroanatomical detail of sexual arousal in humans. One well-done and technologically advanced study by Redoute et al. (2000) used PET scans to evaluate cerebral blood flow in heterosexual men presented with sexually explicit (but silent) video clips. This study used a whole-brain scanner that could evaluate specific cortical as well as subcortical brain areas. Specific areas of increased activation, as compared to when neutral video clips were observed, included the following brain regions: limbic system and related structures (anterior cingulate, right frontal orbitofrontal region), parietal lobes, basal ganglia, and the posterior hypothalamus. Areas of deactivation were primarily in the temporal lobes, bilaterally. Karama et al. (2002) used somewhat different technology, functional magnetic resonance imaging (fMRI) analysis of brain activation, during silent video clips of sexual interactions between a man and a woman. These authors found activation in the following brain regions for both sexes: bilateral medial prefrontal, orbitofrontal, insular, and occipitotemporal regions, as well as the amygdala, ventral striatum, and anterior cingulate cortex. Interestingly, hypothalamic activation was observed only in men and was positively correlated with self-reported sexual arousal during the video clips. Males also demonstrated higher levels of self-reported sexual arousal than females. Together, these studies have demonstrated that multiple cortical and subcortical brain regions are involved in sexual arousal; Redoute et al. (2000)

have argued that these areas highlight the cognitive, emotional, motivational, and physiological aspects of sexual arousal. As a caveat, it should be noted that these studies only evaluated arousal and not actual sexual behavior, which might be expected to involve other brain regions as well, particularly those responsible for motor behavior.

Moving from only sexual arousal, Tiihonen et al. (1994) conducted a unique and technically difficult study. They had heterosexual men masturbate to orgasm while being monitored by a PET scan and found increased activation in right prefrontal regions. Blood flow to other brain areas decreased. These authors concluded that this region was important for human male sexuality, particularly its emotional aspects, but not actual genital somatosensory stimulation. In fact, there was no activation in this brain area devoted to processing sensory information from the genitalia, suggesting that orgasm is more than simply the mechanical stimulation of these organs, but rather is a "higher" process mediated by the cortex, including sexually related thoughts, perceptions, memories, and fantasies. While this finding is confined to men and should be considered tentative until replicated, it does accord well with some clinical findings (see below).

Together with the older EEG research, the more recent PET and fMRI findings suggest the importance of the right hemisphere, particularly frontal regions, as well as a variety of limbic regions and structures connected to them for sexual arousal (and, in one study, orgasm). Unfortunately, because much of this research has been done with males, it is unclear how well these findings hold up in women, and one wonders if such patterns of brain activity associated with sexual arousal in a laboratory setting are the same as those experienced in real life. While these are reasonable caveats, research on individuals who have had brain surgery or have suffered neurological damage (described below) confirm these findings and provide an additional method of studying brain-sex relations.

WHAT DOES RESEARCH ON BRAIN-DAMAGED INDIVIDUALS TELL US ABOUT SEX AND THE BRAIN?

Though now relatively rare, previous research done on individuals who have had psychosurgery as a psychiatric treatment sheds light on brain-sex relationships. Probably the most well-known and, until recently, frequent psychosurgery was frontal lobotomy, in which regions of the frontal lobe are damaged, thus disrupting connections between frontal and subcortical regions thought to be disordered in psychiatric illness. These were done in wide numbers in the mid-1900s on individuals with severe psychiatric disorders such as schizophrenia. Walter Freeman (1973), who was the main proponent of this surgery in the United States, followed individuals after their surgeries for many years and concluded that frontal lobotomy tends to be followed by an increase in libido, at least in the short term. For instance, he described a single man with "religious obsessions" who had not had intercourse for twenty years prior to the surgery, but postsurgery commented on the "increased pleasure" he experienced with sex as he apparently sought out prostitutes. Freeman also described one woman who continued to live with her husband, but had many (fifty!) extramarital sexual relationships. In a classic case study, Ackerly (1964) described J. P., a patient born without a right frontal lobe and with only approximately 50 percent of his left frontal lobe. When he was in school his behavior was odd—at times he was seemingly polite and well-mannered, but at other times he would behave in a socially unacceptable fashion. For instance, he would excessively boast about accomplishments, steal things, wander about, expose himself, and masturbate in public. He was of normal intelligence and did not show remorse for such behavior. By the time he was an adult, he had been arrested for automobile theft, at which time the frontal lobe damage was identified. Similar hypersexuality can also occur in humans who have suffered Kluver-Bucy syndrome, which is relatively rare in complete form, as initially observed in monkeys after removal of the temporal lobes. In one case (Shraberg & Weisberg, 1978), a 23-year-old woman displayed the classic elements of this syndrome following a stroke after childbirth. For our purposes, most relevant was her hypersexuality—she would throw off her hospital gown and then writhe and gyrate her hips to simulate intercourse. This behavior often occurred when hospital staff was present; after approximately two months of hospitalization, it ceased. EEG analysis of this woman's brain revealed abnormalities in the right hemisphere, particularly in the parietal regions and the junction between the parietal and temporal lobes. In addition to the above disorders, poor control over sexual impulses and desires has been observed in many neurological conditions, including dementia and traumatic brain injury, which can obviously be a management and treatment challenge.

Briefly, in one of the few group studies on the topic, Sandel, Williams, Dellapietra, and Derogatis (1996) examined sexual functioning in a group of individuals several years after traumatic brain injury. Though as a group no major differences in sexual functioning were found compared to normative data, individuals with either a damaged right hemisphere or frontal lobe experienced increased sexual functioning on certain variables. Frontal lobe damaged individuals reported more sexual cognitions or thoughts and fantasies, whereas right hemisphere damaged individuals reported higher sexual arousal and more sexual experiences.

What do the above case studies and the research study on sexual impulsivity teach us about the brain-sex relationship? These abnormal increases in sexual interest and activity are likely due to the diminishment of the customary inhibiting effect of cortical structures, primarily frontal and anterior temporal lobes on subcortical brain structures. More precisely, the frontal lobes serve to inhibit or constrain these structures and, when they can no longer do so, the relative influence of these regions is magnified. Because these regions are involved in motivated behavior, such as sex and emotion, when they are damaged these behaviors emerge as poorly controlled, impulsive, and often socially unacceptable. These may be sexual, as described above, or emotional, as individuals with frontal damage also tend to control and regulate their emotional state poorly. Because of this and other cognitive and behavioral deficits in frontal lobe disorder (see above), it is not surprising that individuals with such damage tend to have difficulty in managing responsibilities, including those at work, home, and school.

Two other very different areas of research on individuals with damaged central nervous systems are relevant for our discussion of the brain and sex. Though considered unethical today, in the past, neurosurgery had been used as a method to reduce or control what was considered deviant sexual behavior. In Germany, Dieckmann, Schneider-Jonietz, and Schneider (1988) lesioned the hypothalamus in fourteen individuals with "aggressive sexual delinquency" that had "resulted in great disorder in their way of life." Though the type of individuals the surgery was performed on was not specifically mentioned here, similar research has been done on rapists and pedophiles. When they followed up eight of the fourteen patients one year postsurgery, all had reported decreased sexual compulsion, and seven of eight reported decreased sexual initiative. All or most reported improvement in their relationship with their partner, as well as in their behavior at home or school. In none of the patients was the fundamental character of sexual interest changed (e.g., a pedophile remained a pedophile), but self-reported sexual motivation and arousal diminished. Though well-done and large-scale studies have not been conducted on this topic, this study and related research supports the animal research that has indicated the important role of the hypothalamus in sexual interest and arousal. Moreover, this research suggests that because the cortex is not affected, individuals' thinking about and perception of the sexually alluring, whether considered legal and/or socially appropriate or not, does not appear to change.

A related area of research, again not widely used today, though advocated by some, is the administration of pharmacological agents, particularly anti-androgen medications, to reduce levels of testosterone in male sex-offenders (see Bradford, 1997, for review of this issue). These interventions have typically only been used with the most severe offenders such as rapists, pedophiles, and sexual sadists. Anti-androgens, particularly cyproterone acetate and medroxy-progesterone acetate (Depo Provera), which is the most frequently used in the United States, reduce the sensitivity of androgen receptors in key brain areas, such as the anterior hypothalamus, other limbic system structures, and the spinal cord and the penis. Such interventions have been known as "chemical castrations" and can be contrasted with surgical castrations (i.e., removal of the testes) that are no longer done today. Though research in this area has again typically not been well conducted, and long-term outcomes of such an approach are not well established, the medications have most commonly been shown to reduce self-reported sexual arousal, fantasy, behavior, as well as libido and erections in some male sex-offenders. Case studies or small-group studies have also been reported in which the sexual behavior ceased or was reduced or eliminated in male sex-offenders (see Grossman, Martis, & Fichtner, 1999). While chemical castration is legal in some states in the United States, there have been numerous legal challenges to this practice, including that it violates constitutional guarantees, including the right to privacy, equal protection, and the prohibition against cruel and unusual punishment (Miller, 1998). Partly as a result of this, and of the reluctance of some in the medical field to fully participate in such experiments, these approaches remain controversial and are not as widely used or advocated today as they have been in the past. Nevertheless, such findings highlight the important role of androgens in male sexual behavior.

The second and a quite different area of research, the sexual behavior and responsivity of spinal cord damaged patients, provides a somewhat different perspective on sex and behavior. While there is significant variability in location of injury on the spinal cord as well as the resulting sexual behavior, an interesting finding to emerge from this area is that individuals with complete severing of the spinal cord who are quadriplegic can still respond sexually. For instance, with genital stimulation of the penis, males are able to achieve erections and ejaculate, though they typically do not experience orgasm, as the sensory information necessary for this to occur from the penis and genitalia does not reach the brain because of the spinal injury. These men are also typically not able to achieve erection by simply thinking about or fantasizing about sex. Similar findings about the capacity of spinal cord damaged animals to achieve erections and to ejaculate have been observed. In a related case, a young man who was brain-damaged and in a coma was mechanically stimulated to ejaculate so that his wife could be artificially inseminated (Townsend, Richard, & Witt, 1996). Findings in women are a bit more complex, but it also appears that sexual arousal and stimulation are more common than orgasm in women with a variety of spinal cord injuries (Sipski, 2002). Together, these findings indicate that certain reflexive aspects of sexual behavior can be achieved without direct brain involvement and, traditionally, have been conceived of as spinal reflexes. Such reflexes are due to the connection of the external genitalia with the spinal cord and do not require higher-up cortical processing. Before moving on from this issue, it is important to note that while these reflexes may be retained after injury, sexual interest, arousal, and motivation typically decline post–spinal cord injury, which would be expected given the many physical, psychological, and medical challenges these individuals face. For instance, even assuming all aspects of sexuality were functioning normally, the motoric difficulties of an individual with quadriplegia would certainly make sexual activity challenging.

CONCLUSIONS AND CONTEXT

Like all motivated behavior, such as feeding and aggression, sexual behavior is enormously complex and involves multiple body systems, but particularly the central nervous, endocrine, and reproductive systems. This chapter has reviewed the role of the first two of these in sexual behavior. The various literatures detailed above point to the importance of multiple brain regions, particularly one subcortical structure, the hypothalamus, as well as cortical regions in the right hemisphere, particularly frontal regions. In fact, the hypothalamus has been long known to be critical in all types of motivated behavior, which reflects its unique location within the brain. The hypothalamus sits immediately above, and is directly connected with, the pituitary gland, the body's master gland that has considerable control over the production and distribution of hormones, including those responsible for sexual behavior. It also has close connections with the autonomic nervous system, which has excitatory and inhibitory functions over automatic activities, such as heart beat, breathing, and digestion, and the brain stem, all regions that are recruited in sexual behavior. Higher-up cortical regions of the brain provide the cognitive aspects of sexuality, including sexual thoughts, memories, fantasies, and imagination. Moreover, they provide some control or inhibition of sexual behavior—individuals with damaged frontal regions, particularly in the right hemisphere, demonstrate difficulties with socially appropriate displays of sexual behavior. So without these higher structures our sex lives would certainly be poorer and more poorly regulated, though some of the more physiological and reflexive aspects of sexual behavior may be retained, as they are in individuals with spinal cord injury. Taken together, sexual arousal and behavior is dependent on both the functioning and integration of cortical and subcortical brain regions. This final statement is true for other motivated behaviors too, like feeding, in which there is a strong physiological component, as reflected in decreased blood glucose that interacts with our thoughts, expectations, and even past experience about food to influence the initiation of eating. Similar processes affect the termination of eating.

In closing, one caveat should be kept in mind as the brain-based issues involved in sex are considered. Sole focus on the brain, despite its obvious importance in sexual behavior, is not sufficient. The influence of other factors needs consideration, particularly environmental issues including family, religious, and societal influences, as well as the individual's genetic endowment and previous sexual experience. Many of the other chapters in this volume address these issues. While the brain is key—it is the place where it "really happens"—the influence of these other factors needs to be incorporated for us to more fully understand the complexity of sexual interest, arousal, and behavior.

REFERENCES

Ackerly, S. S. (1964). A case of paranatal bilateral frontal lobe defect observed for thirty years. In J. M. Warren & K. Akert (Eds.), *The frontal granular cortex and behavior* (pp. 192–218). New York: McGraw-Hill.

Bradford, J. (1997). Medical interventions in sexual deviance. In D. R. Lewis & W. O'Donohue (Eds.), *Sexual deviance: Theory, assessment, and treatment* (pp. 449–464). New York: Guilford.

Cohen, H. D., Rosen, R. C., & Goldstein, L. (1976). Electroencephalographic laterality changes during human sexual orgasm. *Archives of Sexual Behavior, 5,* 189–199.

Dieckmann, G., Schneider-Jonietz, B., & Schneider, H. (1988). Psychiatric and neuropsychological findings after stereotactic hypothalamotomy in cases of extreme sexual aggressivity. *Acta Neurochirurgica, Supplement, 44,* 163–166.

Everitt, B. J. (1990). Sexual motivation: A neural and behavioral analysis of the mechanisms underlying appetitive and copulatory responses of male rats. *Neuroscience and Biobehavioral Reviews, 14,* 217–232.

Freeman, W. (1973). Sexual behavior and fertility after frontal lobotomy. *Biological Psychiatry, 6,* 97–104.

Gorski, R. A. (1984). Critical role for the medial preoptic area in the sexual differentiation of the human brain. *Progress in Brain Research, 61,* 129–143.

Grossman, L. S., Martis, B., & Fichtner, C. G. (1999). Are sex offenders treatable? A research overview. *Psychiatric Services, 50,* 349–361.

Heath, R. G. (1972). Pleasure and brain activity in man: Deep and surface electroencephalograms during orgasm. *Journal of Nervous and Mental Disease, 154,* 3–18.

Karama, S., Lecours, A. R., Lerous, J. M., Bourgouin, P., Beaudoin, G., Joubert, S., et al. (2002). Areas of brain activation in males and females during viewing of erotic film excerpts. *Human Brain Mapping, 16,* 1–13.

Kluver, H., & Bucy, P. C. (1939). Preliminary analysis of functions of the temporal lobes in monkeys. *Archives of Neurology and Psychiatry, 42,* 979–1000.

Meston, C. M., & Frohlich, P. F. (2000). The neurobiology of sexual function. *Archives of General Psychiatry, 57,* 1012–1030.

Miller, R. D. (1998). Forced administration of sex-drive reducing medications to sex offenders: Treatment or punishment? *Psychology, Public Policy, and Law, 4,* 175–199.

Nelson, R. J. (2000). *An introduction to behavioral endocrinology* (2nd ed.). Sunderland, MA: Sinauer.

Redoute, J., Stoleru, S., Gregoire, M. C., Costes, N., Cinotti, L., Lavenne, F., et al. (2000). Brain processing of visual sexual stimuli in human males. *Human Brain Mapping, 11,* 162–177.

Rodgers, J. E. (2002). *Sex: A natural history.* New York: W. H. Freeman.

Sandel, M. E., Williams, K. S., Dellapietra, L., & Derogatis, L. R. (1996). Sexual functioning following traumatic brain injury. *Brain Injury, 10,* 719–728.

Shraberg, D., & Weisberg, L. (1978). The Kluver-Bucy Syndrome in man. *Journal of Nervous and Mental Disease, 166,* 130–134.

Sipski, M. L. (2002). Central nervous system based neurogenic female sexual dysfunction: Current status and future trends. *Archives of Sexual Behavior, 31,* 421–424.

Tiihonen, J., Kuikka, J., Kupila, J., Partanen, K., Vainio, P., & Airaksinen, J. (1994). Increase in cerebral blood flow of right prefrontal cortex in man during orgasm. *Neuroscience Letters, 170,* 241–243.

Townsend, M. F., Richard, J. R., & Witt, M. A. (1996). Artificially stimulated ejaculation in the brain-dead patient: A case report. *Urology, 47,* 760–762.

Tucker, D. M. (1983). Asymmetries of coherence topography: Structural and dynamic aspects of brain lateralization. In P. Flor-Henry & J. Gruzelier (Eds.), *Laterality and psychopathology* (pp. 349–362). Amsterdam: Elsevier Science.

Waismann, R., Fenwick, P. B., Wilson, G. D., Hewett, T. D., & Lumsden, J. (2003). EEG responses to visual erotic stimuli in men with normal and paraphilic interests. *Archives of Sexual Behavior, 32,* 135–144.

3

The Psychobiology of Sexual Arousal and Response: Physical and Psychological Factors That Control Our Sexual Response

David L. Rowland ✦

INTRODUCTION AND OVERVIEW

The ease with which most people experience sexual arousal and response belies the complex integration of physiological, psychological, relationship, and cultural factors underlying it. Research over the past decade has revealed much of this complexity, yet, even now, our understanding of sexual arousal and response remains very incomplete. In fact, many of our insights about normal sexual arousal and performance have resulted from the study of disturbances in the system. Such situations provide strong motivation for us to analyze the system in order to understand and remediate the problem. In doing so, we discover that, despite its critical role in so basic a function as procreation, sexual arousal and response requires a great deal of integration at all levels of the organism.

In this chapter, we discuss the process of sexual arousal and response, including:

- *Models* of sexual arousal and response, reviewed briefly in order to provide a foundation for understanding sexual behavior.

- *Physiological mechanisms,* including (1) sensory systems that respond to both internal and external stimuli (e.g., sight of an attractive person; the smell of someone's cologne); (2) central neural mechanisms that underlie sexual arousal and guide the organism toward behavior (e.g., activity in areas of the spine and brain); and (3) peripheral response systems that prepare the person for sexual activity (e.g., vaginal lubrication, erection of the penis).

- *Psychological processes,* such as attention, thoughts, and feelings, which provide the link between erotic stimulation and sexual arousal.

CONCEPTUALIZATION OF SEXUAL AROUSAL AND RESPONSE

Various models of sexual arousal and response have been proposed over the past century. Some, for example, take a clinical or medical orientation toward sexual arousal and response, others, an experimental or research orientation that emphasizes the psychophysiological and cognitive-behavioral elements of sexual response.

General Models for Sexual Response

The seed for the modern conceptualization of sexual response was planted by Masters and Johnson (1966) whose "sexual response cycle" attempted to provide descriptive labels for the sequence of physiological (mainly genital) events occurring during sexual arousal and orgasm. The sequential phases of *sexual excitement, plateau, orgasm,* and *resolution* corresponded to specific genital changes beginning with increased blood flow to the genitalia, on to the muscular contractions of orgasm, and finally to the period of deactivation following climax. The model's strong focus on genital response (Rosen & Beck, 1988) and the semantic problem of using discrete verbal labels (Robinson, 1976) for a physiologically continuous process were its significant limitations.

Kaplan's (1974) model of sexual response incorporated three components: *desire, excitement,* and *orgasm,* essentially compressing Masters and Johnson's physiological phases into two components, excitement and orgasm. More importantly, desire, a psychological construct closely connected to motivation, was added to account for differences in the frequency and intensity of sexual activity among individuals. This triphasic model has strong clinical appeal since its components coincide with the types of problems often encountered by the clinician. Specifically, individuals with sexual problems may lack an interest or desire for sex, may not be able to become sexually excited (e.g., get an erection or show vaginal lubrication), or may indicate a problem with orgasm (e.g., too soon in men, or not at all in men and women). Indeed, Kaplan's approach to describing sexual response has been incorporated into diagnostic manuals for classifying sexual dysfunctions (*Diagnostic and Statistical Manual of Mental Disorders,* American Psychiatric Association, 2000). Like Masters and Johnson's model, Kaplan's was primarily descriptive, viewing sexual response as a set of interrelated components, with each component comprising a requisite step for the next. This triphasic model not only recognized separate physiological and psychological aspects for each component, but it also pointed out the inter-dependence among the response components. For example, problems with orgasm could result from insufficient arousal; or problems with arousal might actually be seated in the desire phase.

Since these initial conceptualizations, a number of alterations or alternative models have been proposed. For example, a distinction between spontaneous desire (libido) and stimulus-driven desire (arousability) has been suggested. Whereas the former seems more typical of men, the latter is more descriptive of women, a difference that may have evolutionary, physiological, and clinical significance (Basson, 2002; Levin, 2002, in press; Tiefer, 1991). Regarding the evolutionary perspective, males' success at producing offspring is largely tied to their willingness and ability to compete for females—hence a high level of biologically mediated sexual drive increases the likelihood of participating and succeeding in the competition. Because mammalian females expend greater effort than males toward the offspring (gestation, lactation, etc.), their success depends more heavily on choosing males with the "right" set of credentials or qualities. As a result, females will be more discriminating in their choice of males than vice versa, and this discrimination (and subsequent interest) will be driven largely by external (physical and behavioral) cues provided by the potential mate (Daly & Wilson, 1978). Such differences in reproductive strategies would be supported by physiological infrastructure (e.g., gonadal, endocrinal, sensory-perceptual, and emotional differences) between the sexes.

Most would agree that this sharpening of the conceptualization of desire is both warranted and overdue. Not only do the above distinctions fit well with many men's and women's reports of their own experiences of arousability, but they also recognize the importance of both internally and externally mediated stimuli essential for sexual interest and arousal. They also appear consistent with the kinds of problems that often surface in sexual dysfunction clinics. In addition, this reconceptualization provides greater linkage of desire with arousal, as for most women and many men, the stimuli that generate interest in becoming aroused (sexual interest) are the same as those that elicit arousal itself (e.g., behaviors and sight of the partner). Finally, this reconceptualization is important from a clinical perspective, as it formally incorporates an idea that has long been known to clinicians in the treatment of sexual problems, namely the importance of taking a systemic approach that includes physiological, psychological, and relationship factors toward understanding sexual response and its disorders.

Given the previous comment, it is not surprising that increasing emphasis has been placed on the role of the dyadic (i.e., a couple's) relationship in understanding (and treating) sexual response (Schnarch, 1988, 1991). According to the systemic or "biopsychosocial" model, sexual response is the culmination of three interacting domains. (1) The biological—the physiological mechanisms that prepare and enable genital response. (2) The psychological—the affective and cognitive predispositions and interpretations that lead to and sustain the response. And (3) the relational—the dyadic interactions that promote intimacy, meaning, and mutually satisfying outcomes in sex. Consideration of functioning within each domain is important to understanding overall sexual response. Not only can functioning within one domain affect that of another (i.e. negative feelings toward a sexual partner or situation may inhibit sexual interest and arousal) but factors within domains may interact with each other as well. For example, the experience of past sexual failures (e.g., inability to reach orgasm) may result in a negative predisposition toward future sexual interactions. Relevant to this approach, there is evidence that women are more likely than men to engage in sexual behaviors even when they do not find them to be sexually arousing (Geer & Broussard, 1990), suggesting a stronger role for sociocultural factors (e.g., pleasing one's partner) in determining their sexual behavior.

Focus on Sexual Arousal

While the above models are particularly useful for clinical analysis, they are primarily descriptive in nature and often provide little or no insight into the kinds of factors that might actually impact sexual arousal and response. As a result, some theorists have restricted their focus to the *arousal* or excitement component of sexual response, at the same time attempting to specify both direction and magnitude of effects of each of the domains (physiological, psychological, relational) on sexual response (subjective arousal as well as genital response). These models are often diagrammed with many boxes or circles (each representing a different domain of influence) and connecting arrows, suggesting bidirectional and interactive relationships that sometimes seem to bear little resemblance to the sexual problems brought to the clinician and much less to the personal experience of sexual arousal. Yet, while they lack the simplicity of descriptive models, they are important to researchers and clinicians in that they identify factors likely to influence each of the components of the sexual response cycle—desire, arousal, and orgasm—and suggest ways in which they themselves are likely to influence one another. In this respect, these detailed models are far more comprehensive, suggesting causal, correlated, and hierarchical relationships among factors. They also carry greater heuristic value (in that they suggest where to look for factors that cause variation in responses) than the rather simple models used for clinical categorization and diagnosis.

Because models of sexual arousal have typically emerged from the psychological and behavioral sciences (rather than the biomedical or clinical sciences), it is not surprising that one major element tying them together is their greater attention to the role played by informational, affective-emotional, and attitudinal factors. Byrne, for example (Byrne & Kelley, 1986; Fisher, Byrne, White, & Kelley, 1988), offers a model of sexual response based on the classic S-O-R (stimulus-organism-response) paradigm. Here, both innate and learned stimuli (the "S" in the model) operate on a number of brain-mediating processes (the "O" in the model) including those representing memories and images, beliefs and expectations, and emotions and subjective perceptions. These systems guide physiological responses and sexual activity (the "R" in the model). The end responses and activities are themselves evaluated and fed back to influence future sexual situations, leading people to exhibit differences on the "O" and "R" dimensions. Those people whose experiences, beliefs, and emotions are likely to lead them to seek out and respond to sexual interactions are categorized as *erotophilic*, while those who are likely to shun or avoid sexual interactions are categorized as *erotophobic*.

A model of male sexual arousal similar to Byrne's has been advanced by Barlow (1986; Cranston-Cuebas & Barlow, 1990), who has differentiated the response of sexually functional men from that of dysfunctional men mainly based on their cognitive (or thought) processing and attention. Thus, men who successfully become aroused to sexual stimuli do so because their thought processing is more "task-relevant." In contrast, men with erectile problems too often focus on "task-irrelevant" processing such as worrying about performance, trying to meet unrealistic expectations, or monitoring of their own response instead of attending to the erotic cues from the partner. This task-irrelevant processing interferes with arousal and sexual response.

The recently proposed "dual control" theory (Janssen & Bancroft, in press) represents an attempt to unify some of the above concepts into a single model. This model assumes that the weighing of excitatory and inhibitory processes determines whether or not sexual arousal or response occurs within an individual in a given situation. Although based primarily on data from men, the model empirically distinguishes between inhibitory factors due to the threat of performance failure (e.g., not getting an erection, ejaculating too early, and so on) and those due to the threat of performance consequences (e.g., the threat of a venereal disease, unwanted pregnancy, getting caught, etc.). These inhibitory factors are useful in predicting erection problems in men as well as their propensity toward sexual risk-taking behaviors (e.g., unprotected sex).

Synthesis of Models

Because various models differ in their focus or utility, some are frequently cited by clinicians, others by researchers. No single model can adequately serve all the needs within the field of sexology. Clearly, a good understanding of sexual arousal incorporates important aspects of a number of the models.

- First, a constellation of psychological (thoughts, attitudes, beliefs, emotions), relationship, and cultural factors influences and guides individuals to seek or shun sexual interactions.

- Second, certain preconditions are necessary for sexual response to occur, including the appropriate external stimuli (partner, sexual situation, etc.) and internal conditions (endocrine, neurophysiological pathways, etc.). These internal conditions are mediated through both psychological and physiological pathways and contribute to the ability to respond to psychosexual stimuli and thus experience sexual arousal.

- Third, sexual response itself consists of a progression of responses, beginning with sexual arousal, which has both a central (brain) component and a peripheral (autonomic/genital) component. The subsequent behavioral response (a sexual act) is maintained through ongoing psychological and peripheral physiological processes, which, through feedback mechanisms, may culminate in orgasm and resolution.

- Finally, the positive experiences associated with sexual arousal and response often reinforce and increase feelings of passion and intimacy between the couple, strengthening the partners' sexual bond. These, together with a sense of commitment, typically contribute to the satisfaction, longevity, and success of long-term relationships (Sternberg & Barnes, 1988).

PHYSIOLOGY OF SEXUAL AROUSAL AND RESPONSE: GENERAL FRAMEWORK

Physiological systems are involved in sexual response in three ways:

1. Physiological *input* systems ensure sexual readiness (arousability) or induce sexual arousal itself. These systems may show seasonal or circadian fluctuations, they may convey information about general environmental conditions or context (is it the right time, the right place, the right mate?), or they may transmit specific sensory stimulation from a potential mate. In humans, where there are few rigid biological constraints regarding sexuality, the roles of these systems are typically subtle and vary substantially across genders or from one individual to another. However, sensory neural pathways that transmit visual (e.g., sight of an attractive partner) and tactile (e.g., stroking of the genitals) information to the brain might fall into this category, as would endocrine factors that prime the organism for sexual action.

2. Spinal and brain systems mediate sexual arousal and feelings. Presumably, input systems produce alterations in neural activity in specific brain regions that, in turn, induce a state of central activation and arousal. While there is substantial evidence from the animal literature, in humans, the relevant mechanisms and brain systems are only now being clarified through PET and MRI studies.

3. Finally, physiological *response* systems are involved in the internal (autonomic) and external (somatic) responses necessary for preparing and maintaining the organism's body, including the sex organs, for sexual behavior. These changes have been documented quite extensively in humans, although the relevant

neuroanatomical structures and biochemical mechanisms that mediate these responses are not always well understood.

PHYSIOLOGICAL INPUT MECHANISMS THAT PREPARE THE INDIVIDUAL FOR SEX

Many physiological systems are responsible for maintaining the organism in a "motivated" (arousable) state and for mediating sensory information that induces sexual arousal. Many species, for example, require specific photoperiodic (day-night rhythms) stimulation related to seasonal cycles and/or ambient temperature conditions for seasonal development of the gonads. The gonads—ovaries in the female, testes in the male—must be active and producing hormones (e.g., estrogen in the female, testosterone in the male) for successful reproduction in all mammalian species. Furthermore, olfactory, visual, auditory, and tactile cues from a potential mate often serve as "releasers" of sexual response in many birds and mammals. In humans, the sexual meaning of most cues often results from subtle conditioning and socialization processes—processes about which most people (and scientists) are not fully aware. Furthermore, these processes are undoubtedly both complex and idiosyncratic (peculiar to each individual) and therefore defy easy investigation.

Nevertheless, some types of stimulation appear to be universally interpreted as sexual (e.g., tactile stimulation of the genitals), and therefore the physiological systems underlying them are likely to play an important role in sexual response. In both men and women, for example, stimulation of certain areas of the body (genitals, nipples) is interpreted as being erotic/sexual and therefore is reliably arousing (Barbach, 1974; Rowland & Slob, 1992). In addition, the sight and smell of the partner's (or another individual's) body may be arousing, although the nature and explicitness of effective stimulation appears to differentiate the sexes, a point discussed later. In most instances, however, the erotic nature of the stimulation is also defined by the context in which it occurs. For example, genital touching by one's sexual partner in the bedroom may be highly erotic whereas similar touching by a physician as part of a physical examination may be neither pleasant nor arousing.

Not only must the organism receive arousing stimulation, but it must also be in an *arousable* state. Variation in arousability in humans has typically been attributed more to psychosocial than biological factors. Nevertheless, in most mammals, arousability is largely under the control of the *gonadal hormones* (see Baum, 1992; Carter, 1992b; Pfaus, Kippin, & Coria-Avila, 2003, for reviews). These hormones, produced by the ovaries in the female and testes in the male, are secreted in response to stimulation from the brain via the pituitary gland and its gonadotropic hormones. In postpubescent females, the secretion of gonadal hormones is sequential, with estrogen dominating during the first half of the menstrual cycle and progesterone during the second half. In males, the picture is simpler. Secretion of pituitary gonadotropins is tonic rather than cyclic, and as a result, the production and secretion of androgens is fairly constant over long periods of time. Of the various androgens, testosterone exerts the greatest effect on the central nervous system and has been implicated most in sexual arousal and behavior.

In many nonhuman mammals, the relationship between gonadal hormones and sexual arousal is well understood. In males, circulating androgens cross the blood-brain barrier and act (probably after conversion to estrogen) upon hypothalamic, and other brain, structures to maintain the organism in a sexually prepared state. Without these hormones, sexually experienced males of some species show little or no interest in sexual behavior in the presence of a receptive female. In the nonhuman female, estrogen and progesterone serve essentially the same function as androgen in the male. This state of easy arousability controlled by the sex hormones in nonhumans is typically referred to as the "motivational" component of sexual response.

The human counterpart of motivation—libido or desire—is not controlled by gonadal hormones but may be influenced by them. Specifically, testicular hormones (particularly testosterone) contribute to a man's interest in sex: the removal of these hormones is associated with diminished interest in, and desire for, sex (see Bancroft, 1989; Carter, 1992a) whereas their reinstatement increases nocturnal erections, spontaneous sexual thoughts, and sexual desire. In this respect, testosterone appears to have much the same impact on both human and nonhuman males in that it underlies sexual interest. Yet, there is at least one important distinction between men and nonhuman males. Men with insufficient testosterone are quite capable of becoming sexually aroused in response to erotic visual stimulation (Davidson & Myers, 1988), suggesting some independence between sexual arousal and testosterone-mediated interest in sex. In other words, a lack of testosterone does not render a man "nonarousable" or impotent as is seen in most nonhuman males. Such men may rely more heavily on conditioned (erotic) stimuli than on an internally mediated (hormonal) state to trigger arousal. Furthermore, an important caveat should be noted. Because testosterone appears to contribute to feelings of sexual interest in men, one should not construe that an apparent lack of sexual interest in men can necessarily be traced to a lack of testosterone. Many psychological and relationship factors may explain a lack of sexual desire, including the perceived level of attractiveness of the partner, feelings of resentment and hostility toward the partner, attempts to exert control over the relationship, and difficulty of dealing with one's own or a partner's sexual dysfunction.

Whereas gonadal hormones appear to play a significant role in male sexual response, their role in human female sexual response remains unclear. In most female primates (apes, monkeys, humans), ovarian hormones influence, but do not control, the expression of sexual behavior. Furthermore, female primates may engage in sexual behavior even when gonadal hormones are minimal. In women, attempts to correlate desire, arousability, and arousal (measured through self-report and/or genital response measures) with different phases of the menstrual cycle, at points when different hormones dominate, have met with only partial success (see Davidson & Myers, 1988; Meuwissen & Over, 1992).

Interestingly, in women, sexual arousal may be associated with the presence of both estrogens (Cutler, Garcia, & McCoy, 1987; Grio, Cellura, Porpiglia, Geranio, & Piacentino, 1999) and androgens (Davis 1998, 2001; Sarrel, 1999). Recent thinking on the topic suggests that estrogens and androgens work together to enhance sexual arousal and response in the female (Wallen, 2001). Specifically, with respect to estrogen, a number of studies report higher libido in women during follicular (early in the cycle) and ovulatory (midcycle) phases of the menstrual cycle (Dennerstein et al., 1994; Wilcox et al., 2004) than during the luteal (late in the cycle) phase. With respect to androgens, which are secreted by both the ovaries and adrenal glands in women, deficiency at any age typically leads to complaints of loss of sexual function (Davis, 2001; Sarrel, 1999). Furthermore, in naturally and surgically menopausal women, administration of estrogen plus small amounts of testosterone provides greater improvement in psychological (e.g., lack of concentration, depression, and fatigue) and sexual symptoms (e.g., libido, sexual arousal, and ability to have an orgasm) than estrogen alone (Davis, 1998; Sherwin, Gelfand, & Brender, 1985). However, probably much more so than men, variability in sexual interest in women is likely to be contextual and partner-based, and as such, is less dependent on internally regulated biological endocrine systems.

While the specific mechanism through which gonadal hormones might facilitate sexual arousal in men and women is unknown, the effects are probably occurring at multiple levels. For example, these hormones may prime structures in the brain, thereby lowering the threshold to activation in the presence of sexually relevant stimuli. They may, however, also work on spinal and peripheral neural systems. For example, prepubescent males may experience genital stimulation as pleasant, but they seldom experience it as erotic. The rise of gonadal hormones during and after puberty may well be responsible for "eroticizing" certain types of sensory stimulation—perhaps by transforming ordinary somatic sensory stimulation (such as genital touching) into *autonomic* information. Autonomic activation is generally associated with emotional responding and is necessary for feelings of excitement and arousal (Motofei & Rowland, 2004, in press).

CENTRAL MECHANISMS OF SEXUAL MOTIVATION AND AROUSAL

Although models of human sexuality often distinguish among the desire, cognitive-emotional, arousal, and response aspects of sexuality, such distinctions become blurred at the level of the central nervous system and brain. For example, a physiological substrate in the brain for "desire" may be nonexistent. Desire might simply entail a state of high sensitivity (low threshold) in the pathways involved in arousal.

Even in relatively simple animal models of sexual behavior (e.g., rat), the interaction of a number of structures is essential for sexual response, as sensory, information-processing, motivational, and motor (movement) elements of sexual response are integrated to generate a "purposeful" action. Furthermore, the activity within these structures may themselves be under the influence of multiple internal and external modulators. For example, many of the structures known to be involved in the control of sexual arousal and behavior are also sensitive to the presence of circulating steroid (gonadal and adrenal) hormones (Pfaff & Schwartz-Giblin, 1988). Specifically, hormone-sensitive cells have been found in the medial preoptic area and parts of the hypothalamus (areas generally associated with biological motivation), extrahypothalamic limbic areas such as the hippocampus (areas generally associated with emotion, memory, and arousal), and in several midbrain structures (areas associated with reward) (see Figure 3.1).

In males of many species, several neural structures, particularly the medial preoptic area (MPOA) and other forebrain limbic areas, appear to play a central role in mediating sexual responses. This center may be responsible for translating sensory input into appropriate behavioral output (Baum, 1992; Pfaus et al., 2003; Sachs & Meisel, 1988). This structure does not operate in isolation but receives input about the organism's arousal state from the amygdala (part of the limbic system) and about the external environment (who, what, when, where, etc.) via cortical structures. Steroid hormones such as testosterone can modulate the activity of the MPOA, as can input from the other brain areas.

The preoptic area is also involved in the regulation of sexual behavior in the female, but its role is inhibitory—MPOA activation inhibits sexual receptivity. The primary brain structure responsible for activating sexual behavior in the female appears to be the ventromedial nucleus (VMN) of the hypothalamus. Removal of this area interferes with sexual response in the female and reduces the tendency of the female to approach the male (Clark, Pfeifle, & Edwards, 1981). It is not clear whether the VMN is involved in the motivational or consummatory (i.e., response-executing) components (or both) of sexual response. However, as with the MPOA in the male, the VMN may act to facilitate sexual response in the female by increasing the connection between sexual sensory stimuli and autonomic/behavioral output. This effect might be achieved by raising the aversion threshold to mounting by the male (thereby increasing receptiveness to the stimulation), or by activating the sympathetic nervous system in preparation for both precopulatory behaviors such as soliciting by the female and copulation itself (Pfaff & Schwartz-Giblin, 1988).

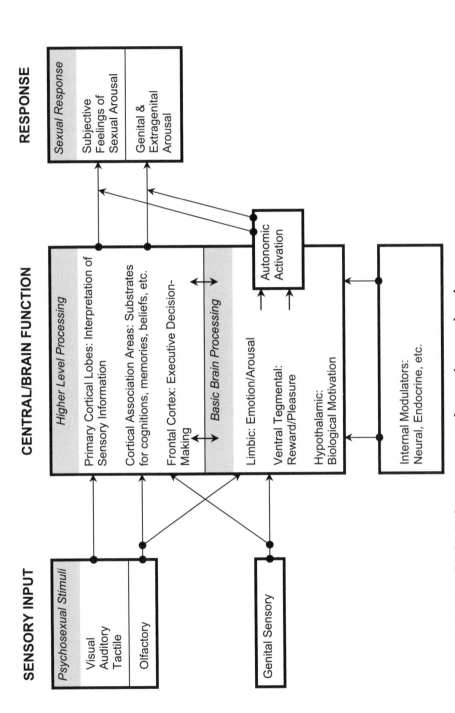

Figure 3.1. Psychobiological components of sexual arousal and response.

The extent to which the preceding findings apply to humans is only now being clarified through MRI and PET research, procedures that can detect changes in brain activity during states of sexual arousal. Interestingly, preliminary studies on humans suggest that some of the neural activation during sexual arousal may be shifted from lower (MPOA and VMN) to higher brain centers in men and women. This finding is not surprising in view of the fact that sexual response in humans depends more heavily upon contextual factors such as those arising from the relationship with the sexual partner, those related to social behavior, and those related to attitudes, beliefs, and moral codes. In men, changes have been noted in the ventral tegmental area, a midbrain-forebrain region involved in mediating pleasure and reward. Concomitant changes in the frontal, occipital, and temporal lobes have also been noted (Holstege et al., 2003; Stoléru et al., 1999). Generally, these brain regions are responsible for the processing of external (sensory) stimuli by giving meaning and interpretation to them and for evaluating, deciding, and executing specific appropriate motor/behavioral responses. Activity changes in hypothalamic and amygdaloid areas have also been noted in men, but not necessarily in the areas known for the involvement in sexual response in rodents. In women, many of these same structures appear to undergo change during arousal and orgasm (Karama et al., 2002). However, there appears to be less activation of hypo-thalamic and thalamic regions in women, perhaps offering an explanation for differences in sexual arousal typically seen across men and women when viewing erotica. The limitation of these MRI and PET studies is that although we have learned which specific brain areas are activated (or deactivated) during sexual arousal and orgasm in men and women, exactly how their activation relates to the subjective experience of arousal and orgasm is unclear (Levin, in press). Indeed, many of these same brain structures underlie other (i.e., non-sexual) cognitive and mental functions.

Nevertheless, several conclusions relevant to understanding human sexual behavior may be drawn from both animal and human studies.

1. Grouping human sexual response into discrete phases or components (e.g., sensory, motivational, affective, cognitive, etc.) is largely based upon introspective analyses. While such conceptualizations may prove useful for research and communication purposes, discrete neural analogs (in terms of structures or activities within the brain) for these constructs are unlikely to exist.

2. Although many similar brain regions appear to underlie sexual behavior across species, differences do emerge, at least when comparing rodents and cats with humans. Not surprisingly, in humans there appears to be a greater involvement of higher brain structures responsible for information processing and decision making, and less involvement of lower centers responsible for biologically motivated behaviors. Thus, substantial differences probably exist in the precise role that various neural structures play, as well as the way in which they interact with other structures.

3. Differences also occur across the sexes, both at the human and non-human level. With respect to these differences in humans, the findings imply that sexual arousal and response, although sharing common elements in many ways, may also be experienced quite differently by men and women.

PERIPHERAL AUTONOMIC AND SOMATIC (MOTOR) RESPONSES

One of the biological challenges of the mammalian organism with respect to sexual response is that of converting general sensory input into autonomic stimulation and response. These two neural systems—the somatic sensorimotor and the autonomic motor systems—are anatomically distinct and serve different purposes. The somatic sensorimotor system responds to information about the environment (visual, auditory, touch, etc.) and innervates striate muscles involved in making voluntary motor responses (movement of the arms, eyes, and so on) and executing overt behaviors. In contrast, the autonomic system is involved primarily in the control of internal, smooth muscle (involuntary) responses, ranging from heart muscle contractions, breathing, and digestion (to name a few) to erection and vaginal lubrication. But with respect to sexual arousal and response, both systems require activation, thereby necessitating both connection between and integration of these two systems. The way in which these two motor systems might function together to result in an integrated and coordinated sexual response is complex and not particularly well understood.

For now, let it suffice to say that during sexual arousal the autonomic nervous system (ANS) is activated via somatosensory stimulation to prepare and maintain the organism for sexual behavior. Activation of the autonomic system is responsible for mediating extragenital, smooth muscle changes—which are similar across the sexes—such as increased blood pressure, transient increases in heart rate, vasocongestion in the breast and pelvic regions, and, ultimately, an overall increase in muscle tension. Genital changes, though different, tend to follow parallel courses in men and women.

Mechanisms of Erection and Ejaculation

Both divisions of the autonomic nervous system—sympathetic and parasympathetic—are involved in arousal and activation of the genitals. Traditional functional classification of these systems (i.e., a homeostatic or regulatory role for the parasympathetic component and an emergency/arousal role for the sympathetic component) does not necessarily extend to activation of the genitals. Thus, the parasympathetic and sympathetic components of the ANS both appear to contribute to sexual excitement, penile erection, and ejaculation (for reviews, see Batra & Lue, 1990; Benson, 1988; Motofei & Rowland, in press). Stimulation of parasympathetic fibers of the pelvic nerve arising from the sacral area of the spinal cord can generate an erection. Recent studies, however, also suggest a possible role for the sympathetic nervous system in erection (Benson, 1988), since blockage of this system produces penile engorgement and erection as well (Rowland & Burnett, 2000; Siroky & Krane, 1983).

The ANS influences erectile tissue through changes in the dynamics of blood flow of the pudendal arteries (Rowland & Burnett, 2000). These arteries supply blood to the corpora cavernosa, the two lengthwise chambers on the back side of the penis, and the corpus spongiosum, the chamber that runs down the front side of the penis (i.e., if you are facing a man with a flaccid penis) and expands to form the glans penis. Erection is the result of increased arterial flow through vasodilation and shunting of the arterial blood away from immediate venal flow into the cavernous spaces of the penis. At first, this increase in arterial flow occurs without an increase in blood pressure, and therefore is probably the result of smooth muscle relaxation of the arterial walls. When full erection occurs, intracavernosal pressure is increased. Although restricted venal drainage from the increasingly erect penis presumably contributes to inducting or maintaining erection, its role has only recently received possible clarification (Batra & Lue, 1990). During erection, when intracavernosal pressure is high, small blood vessels are compressed against the relatively unyielding walls of the chambers, known as the tunica albuginea, and the resulting blockage may decrease venal outflow, increasing the effect of the inflow of blood in keeping the penis erect and firm.

Ejaculation is generally viewed as the efferent (motor) component of a reflex process resulting from sensory stimulation of the coronal region of the penis, although in rare instances it appears that the sensory component is not critical to this process (e.g., spontaneous ejaculation). At the genital level, ejaculation involves two steps, including (1) seminal emission and bladder neck closure, and (2) forced expulsion of fluid (Motofei & Rowland, in press), and requires involvement of the sympathetic, parasympathetic, and somatic motor systems. During the first stage—emission—semen is deposited into the urethral tract, an event associated with "ejaculatory inevitability" in men. At this time, the bladder neck also closes to prevent urine from mixing in the urethral tract and semen from flowing back toward the bladder. The deposition of semen in the urethral tract then triggers the spasmodic (clonic) contractions responsible for ejaculation—a complex process that involves involuntary contraction of muscles that are normally under voluntary control. Local sensory receptors transmit this information to the brain, which is then associated with the subjective experience of orgasm. Obviously, the trigger for the ejaculatory sequence is under the control of brain systems and is related to the man's level of sexual excitement and arousal (Motofei & Rowland, in press). However, since ejaculation involves a series of muscle contractions, local mechanisms at the level of the pelvic musculature have also been suggested (e.g., stretching of muscles to a point of vigorous contraction). Furthermore, there is evidence to suggest that the posterior pituitary hormone, oxytocin, may facilitate these contractions (Carmichael et al., 1987). Exactly what makes these rapid contractions so rewarding is simply unknown. However, other autonomic functions in the pelvic region such as urination and defecation appear to share similar, though less intense, properties. For example, smooth muscle stretching and tension buildup from withholding urine and/or feces is associated with pleasant sensations when release finally does occur.

Mechanisms of Vaginal Lubrication and Female Orgasm

Although a number of internal (vagina, uterus) and external (clitoris, labia) structures respond to sexual stimulation in the woman, the vagina and clitoris are most directly involved in sexual response (see Levin, 2002, in press, for reviews). As with men, sympathetic, parasympathetic, and somatic pathways innervate the genital region and mediate these responses. Sympathetic and parasympathetic nerves connect via the pelvic and pudendal nerves, and their stimulation can produce increased blood flow to the vagina and affect smooth muscle tone in the vagina. It has been suggested that parasympathetic input dominates during the earlier stages of arousal and the sympathetic component dominates during orgasm. Somatic pathways are responsible for controlling striate muscles (those under voluntary control) around the vaginal opening and in the pelvic and abdominal areas.

During sexual arousal, vaginal smooth muscle shows a gradual increase in tone. In addition, autonomic input stimulates blood flow to the vagina through vasodilation, leading to vaginal vasocongestion (increased retention and volume of blood). The lining of the vaginal wall as well as the labia and clitoris becomes engorged with blood. Specifically, as sexual arousal occurs, an increasing number of the capillaries open and the flow through them increases (Wylie et al., 2004), processes that stimulate vaginal lubrication. At the peak of sexual arousal all the capillaries are open and the flow is maximal (Levin, in press).

The gradual accumulation of blood in the vaginal wall in response to sexual stimulation provides the stimulus for vaginal lubrication, a process akin to sweating (called transudation) from the blood circulating through the vessels underlying the vaginal lining. As the woman approaches orgasm, the uterus elevates to produce a "tenting" effect in the inner third of the vagina, and the outer vagina forms the orgasmic platform, a state of maximal vasocongestion (Levin, 2002, in press; Masters & Johnson, 1966). As in the male, the trigger for orgasm itself is unknown, but probably results from a reflexive muscle response to accumulating afferent input. Without entering the debate about the anatomical locus of orgasm (clitoral versus vaginal), it is probably safest to say that several pelvic and genital structures (clitoris, uterus, cervix, etc.) contribute to the overall experience of orgasm in women. Clearly, the clitoris and, possibly, the periurethral glans (area below the clitoris surrounding the urethra) are homologous to the penis and are for most women the epicenter of orgasm. While there is no universally accepted homologue to ejaculation in the female, some women may produce an ejaculate-like fluid from the anterior wall of the vagina, an area sometimes referred to as the G-spot (Alzate & Hoch, 1986; Levin, in press).

In contrast to the male, there is ongoing debate regarding the function of orgasm in the woman, as it plays no critical physiological role in successful reproduction (i.e., in women, pregnancy occurs without orgasm, whereas in men ejaculation/orgasm is necessary for reproduction). Hypotheses regarding the presumed role of female orgasm abound, and include such functions as preparation of the uterus for impregnation, facilitated transport of sperm toward the uterus, or even dissipation of vasocongestion in the vaginal region. Regarding this last point, Levin (in press) argues that relaxation of vaginal tone from orgasm allows continued blood flow through capillaries as muscle tone reaches a maximum and ensures maintained vaginal lubrication during sexual intercourse. A second function of female orgasm may be that of facilitating vaginal tenting and allowing for elevation of the cervix, a crucial movement for facilitated sperm transport toward the uterus.

Given these sex differences in structure and function related to orgasm, as well as the brain structures involved, the mechanisms of orgasm may be sufficiently dissimilar in women and men so that the experience of orgasm is different as well. Specifically, female orgasm tends to be more variable in its description, longer in duration, more dependent on learning factors, less reliable in its occurrence, and less sensitive to refraction than male orgasm. In reference to this last point, various studies have estimated that anywhere from 15 percent to 42 percent of women experience multiple orgasms—one orgasm right after another (Darling, Davidson, & Jennings, 1991). In contrast, multiple orgasm in men is still viewed as "case study" material, although the traditional view of a prolonged male refractory period (a time just after ejaculation during which no amount of stimulation will result in excitation) has recently been challenged by research suggesting that a subpopulation of men may be capable of achieving multiple orgasms, although each may not be accompanied by ejaculation (Dunn & Trost, 1989).

PSYCHOLOGICAL FACTORS AFFECTING SEXUAL AROUSAL

The long-held distinction between "physiological" and "psychological" is a somewhat artificial one (Rowland & Cooper, 2005; Sachs, 2003), as this dichotomy suggests that these domains are independent of one another. In fact, all "psychological" processes (such as sensing, feeling, learning, thinking, intending, and acting, as well as the self-awareness of these processes) are in actuality personal or subjective experiences of a set of underlying neurophysiological events. Nevertheless, because many sensory, cognitive, and affective processes impacting sexual arousal cannot be easily reduced to a specific physiological substrate or process, and because these psychological constructs or ideas relate well to people's own experiences, it is sometimes more beneficial to discuss them as "psychological" processes.

The Nature of Erotic Stimulation

What makes certain kinds of sensory stimulation erotic and other kinds not, or why one stimulus may be arousing for one individual but not for another, is surprisingly difficult to answer. Several overall principles, however, help explain individual and group differences in the arousal value of specific stimuli. First, much of what is arousing is probably established through a process of conditioning—particular visual, tactile, olfactory, and auditory stimulation become associated with the reward of sexual pleasure. Several studies have shown that sexual arousal can be readily conditioned to nonsexual or neutral stimuli (such as boots). Second, some stimuli may be more readily associated with sexual arousal than others because they are higher in their "biological relevance." Thus, heterosexual men's and women's sexual arousal is much more easily conditioned to the sight of the abdomen of a person of the opposite sex than to a neutral object (Hoffmann, Janssen, & Turner, 2004). Third, the capacity to translate ordinary sensory information into sexually arousing information may require (or at least be facilitated by) the presence of gonadal hormones. As mentioned earlier, eroticization of stimuli appears to coincide largely with the onset of puberty and the production of hormones from the testes and ovaries. And fourth, context is ever relevant in determining whether any particular stimulus at any particular time will have erotic value. As an example, repetition of the same psychosexual stimuli can either facilitate or inhibit arousal; that is, both familiarity and novelty of sexual stimuli—polar ends of a continuum—have the potential to increase (or decrease) sexual arousal, depending on a variety of other factors.

One specific area that has received substantial attention on this topic is that of gender differences in patterns of arousal to various kinds of sexual stimuli. Despite some long-standing beliefs, men and women do not seem to respond differentially to romantic versus explicit visual (erotic pictures or films) sexual material. Rather, the sexes are similar along one important dimension—the more explicit the material, the greater the self-reported arousal and genital response (see Rosen & Beck, 1988, for a review). However, qualifying factors are important. First, the context in which the sexual stimulation occurs appears to affect men's and women's arousal differently. For example, group-sex situations are not as sexually arousing to women as they are to men (Steinman, Wincze, Sakheim, Barlow, & Mavissakaliam, 1981). "Women-friendly" films which emphasize foreplay, stroking, enjoyment, and desire on the part of both male and female characters are rated more sexually arousing by women, although genital response is not necessarily affected (Laan, Everaerd, van Bellen, &

Hanewald, 1994). Second, while autonomic responses such as heart rate and pulse can be compared across sexes, and do indeed show similar patterns during arousal (e.g., Heiman, 1977), there is no means of directly comparing magnitude of penile versus vaginal responses. Third, even though both men and women may exhibit physiological arousal, they may report different emotions and feelings associated with the sexual stimuli. Finally, in studies of this type, participants tend to engage in a self-selection process, particularly when the study is conducted in a laboratory setting where sexual response is actually monitored (as opposed to surveys or questionnaires). Women volunteers for such studies tend to be less sex-role stereotyped than non-volunteers, whereas men volunteers tend to be more sex-role stereotyped (Wolchik, Brever, & Jensen, 1985). Because sex-role stereotyping could explain these findings as readily as sex differences per se, one has to be cautious about drawing strong conclusions regarding the nature of sexually arousing stimuli for the two sexes.

Recent research has also investigated the role of other sensory systems on sexual arousal. Olfactory stimulation from a potential mate is essential to normal copulatory behavior in most mammalian species, including nonhuman primates, but its role in human sexual attraction and arousal appears to be more subtle and variable (see Vandenbergh, 1988). Among humans, the scent of one's partner may play an important role in sexual arousal and response. The ability of olfactory stimuli to augment arousal may be more than just a conditioned response; some argue that mammals (including humans) are biologically predisposed to recognize and respond to certain smells as sexual. For example, women may find musky smells, a typical "male" smell that is a byproduct of androgen, to be sexy. In many species, musk presumably plays an important role in reproduction by serving as a male identifier and attractant to females seeking a fertile mate. The argument has been made that in humans the effect of such smells may be subliminal, that is, below people's level of conscious awareness (Cutler et al., 1987).

In contrast with the subtle and variable effects olfactory stimuli have on arousal, tactile stimulation of the genitals is strongly associated with sexual arousal in both men and women. Yet, even this most basic type of stimulation is context dependent. In laboratory studies on men, penile tactile stimulation presented without visual erotic stimulation is only mildly arousing compared with the same stimulation given in conjunction with visual sexual stimulation (providing an appropriate sexual context) (Rowland & Slob, 1992). Furthermore, loss of sensitivity in the genital region—from aging or disease—is associated with impaired sexual response in men, although this probably exacerbates existing problems rather than actually causing them (Rowland & Perelman, in press). In women, the role of genital sensory stimulation in sexual arousal has received only passing attention in laboratory studies, probably because its role is so obvious and because of difficulties in applying controlled tactile stimulation to the vaginal and clitoral regions. One recent study (Slob,

Bax, Hop, Rowland, & van der Werff ten Bosch, 1996) investigating the effect of vibratory stimulation of the labial region found that when women viewed an erotic videotape, the vibratory stimulation enhanced self-reported sexual arousal, but did not augment genital response.

A Role for Sexual Fantasy

Sexual fantasy and thoughts play an important role in arousal for many men and women. Sexual fantasies and thoughts alone (i.e., without any physical genital stimulation) can produce moderately high levels of sexual excitement and genital response (Rowland & Heiman, 1991; Whipple, Ogden, & Komisaruk, 1992). In fact, the use of sexual thoughts and fantasy provides a means for achieving some voluntary control over a response system that is largely viewed as involuntary. For example, training designed to increase the vividness of erotic fantasies can enhance both genital response and subjective sexual arousal or excitement (Smith & Over, 1990) and has been used as part of the treatment for a number of sexual problems in both men and women. On rare occasions, fantasy alone (in the absence of genital stimulation) has been known to lead to orgasm.

The Role of Emotional Response in Sexual Arousal

Emotions are frequently associated with sexual response, and they undoubtedly contribute to feelings of passion and intimacy toward one's partner, particularly during states of sexual arousal. Both sexual and emotional arousal involve activation of the autonomic nervous system, and this underlying commonality has led some researchers to posit that sexual arousal, for all practical purposes, fits the criteria of a positive emotion (energizing, rewarding, etc.). So it is not surprising that researchers and clinicians assume that people's emotional states are strongly interconnected with their sexual response.

The role of emotion (sometimes called "affect") in sexual response has, until recently, been presumed to be straightforward. Barlow (1986), for example, proposed that emotional response is determined largely by the contextual cues in which the sexual activity takes place. A positive emotional state (e.g., enjoyment, excitement) increases attention to erotic cues from the partner and/or situation, which in turn leads to autonomic and genital arousal. In some instances, the sexual situation may evoke a negative emotional response (embarrassment, guilt, aversion, etc.) that then interferes with sexual arousal and enjoyment. This intuitively appealing model offers a reasonable framework for interpreting the way sexual arousal and emotions interact, but it also oversimplifies it.

In order to understand the complex way in which emotions and sexual arousal interact, it is first necessary to realize that emotions are comprised of multiple dimensions. These include a positivity-negativity dimension, a level of physiological arousal, and a cognitive recognition and labeling process (i.e., interpreting the situation as fear, anger, joy, or whatever, depending on the situation). Each of these dimensions has the potential to affect sexual arousal differently. For example, are positive emotions likely to affect sexual arousal differently than negative emotions? Is the intensity of the emotional state (and thus the level of physiological activation) important? Finally, is the particular emotion relevant—for example, might one negative emotion (such as embarrassment) have a different impact on sexual arousal than another negative emotion (such as sadness or distress)? Research to date suggests that each of these elements may affect sexual arousal in different ways. For example, even though positive emotions are generally associated with sexual arousal, a high level of positive *mood* (i.e., a positive state that is devoid of physiological arousal) does not necessarily facilitate sexual arousal (Laan, Everaerd, van Berlo, & Rijs, 1994; Mitchell, DiBartolo, Brown, & Barlow, 1998). Yet, increasing a person's general physiological arousal level (i.e., by getting them excited or upset but not in a sex-related way) may increase sexual arousal in both men and women, independent of whether the state is experienced as positive or negative (Beck, Barlow, Sakheim, & Abrahamson, 1987; Hoon, Wincze, & Hoon, 1977). And finally, specific emotional statements impact arousal differently—embarrassment and guilt are much more strongly associated with impaired sexual response than sadness or disgust (Rowland, Tai, & Slob, 2003).

A second important aspect regarding the interaction between emotions and sexual arousal is that emotion comes into play at several points and at several levels within the context of a sexual situation. Specifically, an individual's emotional state may be influenced by events or circumstances unrelated to the sexual situation, but these emotions may impinge upon the sexual situation. Or, the sexual situation itself may evoke a positive or negative emotional response. Or, the specific acts/events of sexual arousal and sexual behavior, because of their typically rewarding nature, may engender a strong emotional response. Thus, as is described in the next paragraphs, the role of emotion is likely to be quite different at distinct points in the process of sexual arousal or in distinct sexual situations.

Consider situations that evoke emotional feelings but that are not tied specifically to the sexual situation. Most studies indicate that any emotional stimulus, positive or negative (consider anxiety and anger as examples of the latter), that induces a general state of arousal has fairly strong potential for increasing sexual arousal. For example, the negative feelings experienced by a person upset over an incident in the workplace might well enhance sexual arousal (because the person's general level of arousal is increased). Yet, this relationship may hold only when those levels of arousal are mild to moderate. Extreme emotional arousal has strong potential to interfere with basic genital response (erection, vaginal lubrication). Specifically, the sympathetic nervous system activation associated with strong emotional arousal is generally incompatible with the initial phases of erectile response and vaginal lubrication, processes requiring strong parasympathetic activation.

On the other hand, emotions that are derived specifically from the sexual context may have more direct effects on sexual response. These effects depend on a complex interplay between the arousal strength of the stimulus, the specific emotional state that is elicited (anger, fear, frustration, excitement, enjoyment, etc.), and the degree to which the feeling is tied to sexual performance and self- or partner-evaluation within the sexual situation. As an example, positive feelings and expectations associated with an attractive and/or familiar sex partner might well facilitate sexual arousal. But negative feelings associated with worry and fear of evaluation by the partner (performance anxiety) may inhibit sexual arousal and response. If the fear and worry emanate from the sexual situation but are not evaluative in nature, then as indicated before, they may *not* inhibit sexual arousal. A couple may find having sex in forbidden places (e.g., the mile high club) highly arousing even though the situation induces a certain level of anxiety and fear. In contrast, the evaluative nature of sexual interactions, either from oneself or from one's partner, can often generate feelings of "sexual" anxiety (am I attractive? am I able to please my partner? am I responding okay? etc.) that interfere with sexual arousal and response. (Elliott & O'Donohue, 1997; Rowland & Heiman, 1991). Indeed, psychotherapy for men and women with sexual dysfunctions is often aimed at reducing sexual anxiety by reframing the sexual experience from one that involves fear, embarrassment, and worry about performance to one that emphasizes greater self-efficacy, confidence, and positive expectations.

Finally, emotional states during sexual arousal itself are consistently associated with high levels of positive emotion. That is, when the emotional state is measured as a part of the sexual response, positive emotion clearly dominates. And generally, the higher the sexual arousal, the greater is the positive emotional response. In fact, multivariate statistical procedures typically identify these two concepts as being part of the same dimension, at least in sexually functional men and women. Such findings imply that sexual arousal may itself represent a type of emotional state.

Those who view sexual arousal as a type of "emotional state" typically subscribe to "cognitive arousal theory," which holds that the experience of an emotion depends on both physiological arousal and a cognitive interpretation of that arousal, an interpretation that relies heavily on contextual cues and past experiences (Schachter & Singer, 1962). Sexual arousal nicely fits this general model (Everaerd, 1988). In a sexual context, appraisal of a situation as "sexual" elicits physiological arousal and primes a cognitive (thought) labeling process so that the experience is identified and stored in memory as one that is "sexual" (Janssen & Everaerd, 1993). The autonomic and sympathetic nervous system responses that follow (e.g., Meston & Gorzalka, 1996) may further augment the subjective experience of the emotion. Although there are few studies showing a common underlying basis for emotion and sexual arousal, one recent report (Everaerd & Kirst, 1989) used "prototypes" (clusters of attributes or qualities that people use to describe that emotion) of various emotional states and compared them against ones for sexual arousal. The prototype for sexual arousal overlapped considerably with the emotional prototypes for "joy," "warm feeling," and "merry." Given the above, it is not surprising that in sexually functional individuals, sexual arousal and positive affect appear to be strongly interwoven (Rowland et al., 2003).

Perhaps in summary, one can safely say that positive feelings both facilitate and result from sexual arousal and successful performance. At the same time, negative emotions (fear, embarrassment, worry, or anxiety), particularly when they emanate from issues of performance evaluation, are often associated with sexual impairment and may contribute to, maintain, or result from the dysfunction. Yet, negative emotions, because of their ability to increase general levels of arousal, may in some instances also facilitate sexual arousal.

The Role of Cognition in Sexual Arousal

The cognitive component of sexual arousal refers to the way in which information is processed and interpreted in a sexual situation. Unlike emotions, which can easily be categorized as either positive or negative, the thought processes that occur during sexual response can literally be infinite. Therefore, this aspect of sexual arousal has focused on particular strategies of information processing that might account for variability in sexual response, particularly comparing sexually functional men and women with those having a sexual problem (Cranston-Cuebas & Barlow, 1990; Janssen & Everaerd, 1993; Sbrocco & Barlow, 1996). Furthermore, because emotions include a cognitive component (e.g., recognizing, identifying, and labeling the situation as such), the suggestion has been that the characteristics that distinguish sexually functional from sexually dysfunctional men and women is actually the cognitive component of the negative emotion that is being experienced. In the broadest of terms, two interrelated cognitive strategies have emerged as significant differentiators of sexually functional and dysfunctional men and women: attentional focus and self-perceptions (the latter includes attributions and negative expectancies).

The role of *attention* has occupied a prominent position in the search for cognitive factors that affect sexual arousal. Since it is not possible for an individual to process all information from the environment, selectivity is required. Within a sexual situation, attention typically focuses on cues relevant to generating sexual arousal. Not surprisingly, tasks that distract the individual from erotic cues diminish sexual response (see Cranston-Cuebas & Barlow, 1990 for review). Tasks that focus the individual's attention on the endpoint of becoming sexually aroused, a situation analogous to performance demand (Heiman & Rowland, 1983), generally increase sexual arousal. However, this pattern of responding to attentional cues appears to be quite different for men and women with problems of sexual arousal (e.g., erectile dysfunction). They show inhibited response in situations where they feel increased demand to become sexually aroused (Abrahamson, Barlow, & Abrahamson, 1989; Beck, Barlow, & Sakheim, 1983). This increased demand results in a process called "spectatoring," whereby individuals detach themselves from the sexual experience as they monitor their own sexual responses. In doing so, their attention is drawn away from the erotic cues of the situation and partner toward distracting and "less productive (arousing)" stimuli. In fact, sexually functional men and women show less arousal when distracting tasks are introduced into a sexual situation, whereas dysfunctional men and women show no difference or even improved arousal under these conditions. Thus, as Sbrocco and Barlow (1996) note, performance demand, spectatoring, and fear of inadequacy are all forms of task-irrelevant activities that distract individuals from processing relevant stimuli from the sexual context (van Lankveld & van den Hout, 2004; van Lankveld, van den Hout, & Schouten, 2004).

Self-perceptions of physiological and emotional responses also constitute an important part of information processing during sexual arousal. Sexually functional individuals of both sexes tend to be reasonably accurate in estimating their level of genital response in comparison with dysfunctional individuals. Dysfunctional men and women tend to underestimate their genital arousal. Why such a difference? It might well be part of a strategy of setting low expectations (negative expectancies) so as to minimize the embarrassment of failure, or an underestimation simply resulting from low self-efficacy. Consistent with this notion, sexually dysfunctional people tend to attribute their failure to perform adequately to things about themselves ("internal attribution style" interpreted as "something's wrong with me"). In contrast, sexually functional men and women tend to attribute failure to perform adequately (when it does happen) to things outside of themselves ("external attribution style" interpreted as "something's wrong with the situation") (Nobre & Pinto Gouveia, 2000; Weisberg, Brown, Wincze, & Barlow, 2001). Along with this, dysfunctional men and women are less likely to attribute their successes in performance to themselves and more to circumstances or factors outside themselves. In other words, dysfunctional men and women exhibit a cognitive style in which they tend to take blame for their failures while not accepting credit for their successes.

There is no doubt that such cognitive sets become part of a vicious cycle, whereby failure induces negative expectancies, increasing focus on task-irrelevant cues, decreased arousal and performance, and eventual avoidance of sexual situations altogether. Such avoidance may have significant effects on the partner, who may interpret these behaviors as not wanting intimacy or contact, as being unattractive or undesirable, and so on. Fortunately, cognitive-behavioral therapeutic approaches to sexual problems have identified ways to break the negative feedback cycle and place the individual back on a track that regains a sense of self-efficacy regarding arousal and performance. In doing so, the positive association typically characteristic of sexual interaction and intimacy can be reestablished.

CONCLUDING THOUGHTS

Individuals vary considerably in the intensity and frequency of sexual arousal and behavior. These differences can be attributed to myriad physiological, psychological (cognitive-affective), and sociocultural factors. Specifically, physiological systems involved in sexual response can be altered by such conditions as disease, aging, pathophysiological agents, and pharmacological substances. For example, prolonged and heavy use of a pathophysiological agent such as nicotine, which diminishes vasomotor response, may have deleterious effects on erectile response in men; antidepressant drugs are known to inhibit ejaculation in men and produce anorgasmia in women. Some conditions may affect sexual response in one sex, while having minimal or no effect in the other. Diabetes, a condition known to produce peripheral neuropathy, often interferes with erectile ability in men but appears to have negligible effects on sexual arousal in women (Slob, Koster, Radder, & van der Werff ten Bosch, 1990). At the other end of the spectrum, some physiological agents may facilitate sexual arousal and response. Throughout the ages, reports abound on the use of putative aphrodisiacs (e.g., the bark of the yohimbine tree supposedly enhances arousal) (see Rowland & Tai, 2003, for a review).

The importance of psychological factors to functional sexual response cannot be overstated. Numerous factors, ranging from the erotic value of the stimuli, expectations of the situation, and self-efficacy on the one hand, to affective response, self-perceptions, and methods of cognitive processing on the other, have been shown to impact sexual arousal significantly, and may account for differential patterns of responding between sexually functional and dysfunctional individuals. Even when a sexual dysfunction has a strong somatic basis, psychological factors are implicated. Men and women who fail sexually, whether from somatic or psychogenic causes, are likely to react with worry and feelings of loss of control which affects future sexual responses.

Beyond physiological and psychological influences, relationship and sociocultural factors play important roles in sexual arousal. Among other things, the quality of the relationship between the sexual partners, the individual's personal priorities and values, and customs and expectations of one's culture play critical roles in defining any sexual situation, and therefore will impact sexual arousal and behavior.

REFERENCES

Abrahamson, D. J., Barlow, D. H., & Abrahamson, L. S. (1989). Differential effects of performance demand and distraction on sexually functional and dysfunctional males. *Journal of Abnormal Psychology, 98,* 241–247.

Alzate, H., & Hoch, Z. (1986). The G-spot and female ejaculation: A current appraisal. *Journal of Sex and Marital Therapy, 11,* 211–220.

American Psychiatric Association. (2000). *Diagnostic and statistical manual of mental disorders* (4th Ed., Text revision). Washington, DC: Author.

Bancroft, J. (1989). *Human sexuality and its problems.* Edinburgh: Churchill Livingston.

Barbach, L. G. (1974). *For yourself: A guide to female orgasmic response.* New York: Doubleday.

Barlow, D. H. (1986). Causes of sexual dysfunction: the role of anxiety and cognitive interference. *Journal of Consulting and Clinical Psychology, 54,* 140–148.

Basson, R. (2002). A model of women's sexual arousal. *Journal of Sex and Marital Therapy, 28,* 1–10.

Batra, A. K., & Lue, T. F. (1990). Physiology and pathology of penile erection. *Annual Review of Sex Research, 1,* 251–263.

Baum, M. J. (1992). Neuroendocrinology of sexual behavior in the male. In J. Becker, S. M. Breedlove, & D. Crews (Eds.), *Behavioral endocrinology* (pp. 97–130). Cambridge, MA: MIT Press.

Beck, J. G., Barlow, D. H., & Sakheim, D. K. (1983). The effects of attentional focus and partner arousal on sexual responding in functional and dysfunctional men. *Behavior Research and Therapy, 21,* 1–8.

Beck, J. G., Barlow, D. H., Sakheim, D. K., & Abrahamson, D. J. (1987). Shock threat and sexual arousal: The role of selective attention, thought content, and affective states. *Psychophysiology, 24,* 165–172.

Benson, G. S. (1988). Male sexual function: Erection, emission, and ejaculation. In E. Knobil & J. Neill (Eds.), *The physiology of reproduction* (pp. 1121–1139). New York: Raven Press.

Byrne, D., & Kelley, K. (Eds.) (1986). *Alternative approaches to the study of sexual behavior.* Hillsdale, NJ: Erlbaum.

Carmichael, M. S., Humbert, R., Dixen, J., Palmisano, G., Greenleaf, W., & Davidson, J. M. (1987). Oxytocin increase in human sexual response. *Journal of Clinical Endocrinology and Metabolism, 64,* 27–31.

Carter, C. S. (1992a). Hormonal influences on human sexual behavior. In J. Becker, S. M. Breedlove, & D. Crews (Eds.), *Behavioral endocrinology* (pp. 131–142). Cambridge, MA: MIT Press.

Carter, C. S. (1992b). Neuroendocrinology of sexual behavior in the female. In J. Becker, S. M. Breedlove, & D. Crews (Eds.), *Behavioral endocrinology* (pp. 71–95). Cambridge, MA: MIT Press.

Clark, A. S., Pfeifle, J. K., & Edwards, D. A. (1981). Ventromedial hypothalamic damage and sexual proceptivity in female rats. *Physiology & Behavior, 27,* 597–602.

Cranston-Cuebas, M., & Barlow, D. H. (1990). Cognitive and affective contributions to sexual functioning. *Annual Review of Sex Research 119*(1), 161.

Cutler, W. B., Garcia, C. R., & McCoy, N. (1987). Perimenopausal sexuality. *Archives of Sexual Behavior, 16*(3), 225–234.

Daly, M., & Wilson, M. (1978). *Sex, evolution and behavior.* North Scituate, MA: Duxbury Press.

Darling, C. A., Davidson, J. K., & Jennings, D. A. (1991). The female sexual response revisited: Understanding the multiorgasmic experience in women. *Archives of Sexual Behavior, 20*, 527–540.

Davidson, J. M., & Myers, L. (1988). Endocrine factors in sexual psychophysiology. In R. Rosen & G. Beck (Eds.), *Patterns of sexual arousal: Psychophysiological processes and clinical applications* (pp. 158–186). New York: Guilford.

Davis, S. R. (1998). The clinical use of androgens in female sexual disorders. *Journal of Sex and Marital Therapy, 24*(3), 153–163.

Davis, S. R. (2001). Testosterone deficiency in women. *Journal of Reproductive Medicine, 46*(3), 291–296.

Dennerstein, L., Gotts, G., Brown, J. B., Morse, C. A., Farley, T. M., & Pinol, A. (1994). The relationship between the menstrual cycle and female sexual interest in women with PMS complaints and volunteers. *Psychoneuroendocrinology, 19*(3), 293–304.

Dunn, M. E., & Trost, J. E. (1989). Male multiple orgasms: A descriptive study. *Archives of Sexual Behavior, 18*(5), 377–388.

Elliot, A. N., & O'Donohue, W. T. (1997). The effects of anxiety and distraction on sexual arousal in a nonclinical sample of heterosexual women. *Archives of Sexual Behavior, 26*(6), 607–624.

Everaerd, W. (1988). Commentary on sex research: Sex as an emotion. *Journal of Psychology and Human Sexuality, 2*, 3–15.

Everaerd, W., & Kirst, T. (1989). Sexuele opwinding: een emotie? [Sexual arousal: An emotion?]. Unpublished manuscript.

Fisher, W. A., Byrne, D., White, L. A., & Kelley, K. (1988). Erotophobia-erotophilia as a dimension of personality. *Journal of Sex Research, 25*, 123–151.

Geer, J. H., & Broussard, D. B. (1990). Scaling sexual behavior and arousal: Consistency and sex differences. *Journal of Personality and Social Psychology, 58*, 664–671.

Grio, R., Cellura, A., Porpiglia, M., Geranio, R., & Piacentino, R. (1999). Sexuality in menopause: Importance of adequate replacement therapy. *Minerva Gynecology, 51*(3), 59–62.

Heiman, J. R. (1977). A psychophysiological exploration of sexual arousal patterns in females and males. *Psychophysiology, 14*, 266–274.

Heiman, J. R., & Rowland, D. L. (1983). Affective and physiological response patterns: The effects of instructions on sexually functional and dysfunctional men. *Journal of Psychosomatic Research, 27*, 105–116.

Hoffmann, H., Janssen, E., & Turner, S. L. (2004). Classical conditioning of sexual arousal in women and men: Effects of varying awareness and biological relevance of the conditioned stimulus. *Archives of Sexual Behavior, 33*(1), 43–53.

Holstege, G., Georgiadis, J. R., Paans, A. M. J., Meiners, L. C., van der Graaf, F. H. C. E., & Reinders, A. A. T. S. (2003). Brain activation during human male ejaculation. *Journal of Neuroscience, 23*(27), 9185–9194.

Hoon, P. W., Wincze, J. P., & Hoon, E. (1977). A test of reciprocal inhibition: Are anxiety and sexual arousal in women mutually inhibitory? *Behavior Therapy, 8,* 694–702.

Janssen, E., & Bancroft, J. (in press). The dual-control model: The role of sexual inhibition and excitation in sexual arousal and behavior. In E. Janssen (Ed.), *The psychophysiology of sex.* Bloomington: Indiana University Press.

Janssen, E., & Everaerd, W. (1993). Male sexual arousal. *Annual Review of Sex Research 4,* 211–245.

Kaplan, H. S. (1974). *The new sex therapy.* New York: Brunner/Mazel.

Karama, S., Lecours, A. R., Leroux, J.-M., Bourgouin, P., Beaudoin, G., Joubert, S., et al. (2002). Areas of brain activation in males and females during viewing of erotic film excerpts. *Human Brain Mapping, 16,* 1–13.

Laan, E., Everaerd, W., van Bellen, G., & Hanewald, G. (1994). Women's sexual and emotional responses to male- and female-produced erotica. *Archives of Sexual Behavior, 23,* 153–170.

Laan, E., Evereard, W., van Berlo, R., & Rijs, L. (1994). Mood and sexual arousal in women. *Behavior Research and Therapy, 33,* 441–443.

Levin, R. J. (2002). The physiology of sexual arousal in the human female: A recreational and procreational synthesis. *Archives of Sexual Behavior, 31,* 405–411.

Levin, R. J. (in press). The role of sexual arousal in human reproductive mechanisms: A critical account. *Annual Review of Sex Research, 16.*

Masters, W. H., & Johnson, V. E. (1966). *Human sexual response.* Boston: Little, Brown.

Meston, C. M., & Gorzalka, B. B. (1996). Differential effects of sympathetic activation on sexual arousal in sexually dysfunctional and functional women. *Journal of Abnormal Psychology, 105*(4), 582–591.

Meuwissen, I., & Over, R. (1992). Sexual arousal across phases of the menstrual cycle. *Archives of Sexual Behavior, 21,* 101–120.

Mitchell, W. B., DiBartolo, P. M., Brown, T. A., & Barlow, D. H. (1998). Effects of positive and negative mood on sexual arousal in sexually functional males. *Archives of Sexual Behavior, 27*(2), 197–207.

Motofei, I. G., & Rowland, D. L. (2004). The physiological basis of human sexual arousal: Neuroendocrine sexual asymmetry. *International Journal of Andrology, 27,* 78–87.

Motofei, I. G., & Rowland, D. L. (in press). Neurophysiology of ejaculation: Developing perspectives. *BJU International.*

Nobre, P., & Pinto Gouveia, J. (2000). Erectile dysfunction: An empirical approach based on Beck's cognitive theory. *Sexual and Relationship Therapy, 15*(4), 351–366.

Pfaff, D. W., & Schwartz-Giblin, S. (1988). Cellular mechanisms of female reproductive behaviors. In E. Knobil & J. Neill (Eds.), *The physiology of reproduction* (pp. 1487–1568). New York: Raven Press.

Pfaus, J. G., Kippin, T. E., & Coria-Avila, G. (2003). What can animal models tell us about human sexual response? *Annual Review of Sex Research, 14*, 1–63.

Robinson, P. (1976). *The modernization of sex.* New York: Harper & Row.

Rosen, R. C., & Beck, J. G. (1988). *Patterns of sexual arousal: Psychophysiological processes and clinical applications.* New York: Guilford.

Rowland, D. L., & Burnett, A. (2000). Pharmacotherapy in the treatment of male sexual dysfunction. *Journal of Sex Research, 37*, 226–243.

Rowland, D. L., & Cooper, S. E. (2005). Behavioral and psychologic models in ejaculatory function research. *Current Sexual Health Reports, 2*, 29–34.

Rowland, D. L., & Heiman, J. (1991). Self-reported and genital arousal changes in sexually dysfunctional men following a sex therapy program. *Journal of Psychosomatic Research, 35*, 609–619.

Rowland, D. L., & Perelman, M. (in press). Inhibited or retarded ejaculation. In M. O'Leary (Ed.), *Handbook of premature ejaculation.* Abingdon, Oxon, UK: Taylor & Francis.

Rowland, D. L., & Slob, A. K. (1992). Vibrotactile stimulation enhances sexual arousal in sexually functional men: A study using concomitant measures of erection. *Archives of Sexual Behavior, 21*, 387–400.

Rowland, D. L., & Tai, W. (2003). A review of plant-derived and herbal remedies in the treatment of sexual dysfunction. *Journal of Sex and Marital Therapy, 29*(3), 185–205.

Rowland, D. L., Tai, W., & Slob, A. K. (2003). Preliminary exploration of emotional response in men with premature ejaculation: Effects of clomipramine treatment. *Archives of Sexual Behavior, 32*, 145–154.

Sachs, B. D. (2003). The false organic-psychogenic distinction and related problems in the classification of erectile dysfunction. *International Journal of Impotence Research, 15*, 72–78.

Sachs, B. D., & Meisel, R. L. (1988). The physiology of male sexual behavior. In E. Knobil & J. Neill (Eds.), *The physiology of reproduction* (pp. 1393–1486). New York: Raven Press.

Sarrel, P. M. (1999). Psychosexual effects of menopause: Role of androgens. *American Journal of Obstetric Gynecology, 180*, 319–324.

Sbrocco, T., & Barlow, D. H. (1996). Conceptualizing the cognitive component of sexual arousal: Implications for sexuality research and treatment. In P. M. Salkovskis (Ed.), *Frontiers of cognitive therapy* (pp. 419–449). New York: Guilford.

Schachter, S., & Singer, J. (1962). Cognitive, social, and physiological determinants of emotional state. *Psychological Reports, 69*, 379–399.

Schnarch, D. M. (1988). Talking to patients about sex—Part II. *Medical Aspects of Human Sexuality, 22,* 97–106.

Schnarch, D. M. (1991). *Constructing the sexual crucible: An integration of sexual and marital therapy.* New York: W.W. Norton.

Sherwin, B. B., Gelfand, M. M., & Brender, W. (1985). Androgen enhances motivation of females: A prospective crossover study of sex steroid administration in the surgical menopause. *Psychosomatic Medicine, 47,* 339–351.

Siroky, M. B. & Krane, R. J. (1983). Neurophysiology of erection. In R. Krane, & M. Siroky, & I. Goldstein (Eds.), *Male sexual dysfunction* (pp. 9–20). Boston: Little, Brown.

Slob, A. K., Bax, C. M., Hop, W. C. J., Rowland, D. L., & van der Werff ten Bosch, J. J. (1996). Sexual arousability and the menstrual cycle. *Psychoneuroendocrinology, 21,* 545–558.

Slob, A. K., Koster, J., Radder, J. K., & van der Werff ten Bosch, J. J. (1990). Sexuality and psychophysiological functioning in women with diabetes mellitus. *Journal of Sex and Marital Therapy, 16,* 59–68.

Smith, D., & Over, R. (1990). Enhancement of fantasy-induced sexual arousal in men through training in sexual imagery. *Archives of Sexual Behavior, 19,* 477–490.

Steinman, D. L., Wincze, J. P., Sakheim, D. K., Barlow, D. H., & Mavissakaliam, M. (1981). A comparison of male and female patterns of sexual arousal. *Archives of Sexual Behavior, 10,* 529–547.

Sternberg, R. J., & Barnes, M. (1988). *The psychology of love.* New Haven, CT: Yale University Press.

Stoléru, S., Grégoire, M. C., Gérard, D., Decety, J., Lafarge, E., Cinotti, L., et al. (1999). Neuroanatomical correlates of visually evoked sexual arousal in human males. *Archives of Sexual Behavior, 28*(1), 1–21.

Tiefer, L. (1991). Historical, scientific, clinical and feminist criticisms of "The Human Sexual Response Cycle" model. *Annual Review of Sex Research, 2,* 1–23.

Vandenbergh, J. G. (1988). Pheromones and mammalian reproduction. In E. Knobil & J. Neill (Eds.), *The physiology of reproduction* (Vol. 2, pp. 1679–1698). New York: Raven Press.

van Lankveld, J. J. D. M., & van den Hout, M. A. (2004). Increasing neutral distraction inhibits genital but not subjective sexual arousal of sexually functional and dysfunctional men. *Archives of Sexual Behavior, 33*(6), 549–558.

van Lankveld, J. J. D. M., van den Hout, M. A., & Schouten, E. G. W. (2004). The effects of self-focused attention, performance demand, and dispositional sexual self-consciousness on sexual arousal of sexually functional and dysfunctional men. *Behaviour Research and Therapy, 42,* 915–935.

Wallen, K. (2001). Sex and context: Hormones and primate sexual motivation. *Hormones and Behavior, 40,* 339–357.

Weisberg, R. B., Brown, T. A., Wincze, J. P., & Barlow, D. H. (2001). Causal attributions and male sexual arousal: The impact of attributions for a bogus erectile difficulty on sexual arousal, cognitions, and affect. *Journal of Abnormal Psychology, 110*, 324–334.

Whipple, B., Ogden, G., & Komisaruk, B. (1992). Physiological correlates of imagery-induced orgasm in women. *Archives of Sexual Behavior, 21*, 121–134.

Wilcox, A. J., Day Baird, D., Dunson, D. B., McConnaughey, D. R., Kesner, J. S., & Weinberg, C. R. (2004). On the frequency of intercourse around ovulation: Evidence for biological influences. *Human Reproduction, 19*(7), 1539–1543.

Wolchik, S. A., Brever, S. L., & Jensen, K. (1985). Volunteer bias in erotica research: Effect of intrusiveness of measure and sexual background. *Archives of Sexual Behavior, 14*, 93–107.

Wylie, K., Levin, R. J., & Goddard, A. (2004). Vasomotion and the vaginal response to sexual arousal assessed by photoplethysmography—a proposed new quantitative analysis. (11th World Congress of the International Society for Sexual and Impotence Research, October 17–21, Buenos Aires, Argentina). *Journal of Sexual Medicine, 1*(Suppl. 1), 92 (MP102).

4

An Evolutionary Perspective on Sexual and Intimate Relationships

David C. Geary ◆

After a hiatus of more than 100 years following Darwin's (1871) and other naturalists' early theories on human evolution, social and biological scientists are once again using our understanding of evolution to shed light on human behavior (Alexander, 1979; Betzig, 1986; Buss & Schmitt, 1993; Geary, 1998). The topics that have captured much of this recent attention are sexuality and sex differences in sexual preferences and behaviors. Fortunately, biologists have studied sexual and reproductive behavior and its evolution in hundreds of nonhuman species and now have a firm grasp of the how and why of these behaviors, including an understanding of when and why there is variation in their expression across social and ecological contexts (Amundsen, 2000; Andersson, 1994; Dunbar, 1995; Zahavi, 1975). In the first section, I provide a brief introduction to theory and research on sexual and other reproductive behaviors in nonhuman species. This introduction provides a new perspective for thinking about and coming to fully understand human sexuality, and associated sex differences. These topics are in fact quite broad and complex and so I focus on two features of human reproductive behaviors in the second section; specifically, the mate-choice preferences of women and men, and differences in these preferences. I conclude the section with a discussion of historical and cultural variation in mate-choice preferences and sexual behaviors. My goal here is to illustrate the power and utility of the evolutionary approach for conceptualizing human sexuality and sex differences in sexuality.

EVOLUTION AND SEXUAL BEHAVIOR

In addition to discovering the principles of natural selection, Darwin (1871) discovered the processes that operate within species and result in the evolution of sex differences. These processes are called *sexual selection*, and involve competition with members of the same sex over mates—*intrasexual competition*—and discriminating choice of mating partners—*intersexual choice*. In most species, these are largely restricted to male–male competition over access to females, and female choice of male mating partners (Andersson, 1994). I first describe why this pattern is so common, and why exceptions evolve. Because our interest is in mate choices, I then focus on the evolution of intersexual choice in nonhuman species.

Compete or Choose?

For most species, sexuality is about reproducing, and in order to reproduce one must compete for mates or chose the right mate. As I stated, males tend to compete and females, choose. But why this pattern of sex differences? About 100 years after Darwin's insights regarding sexual selection, scientists determined that sex differences in the tendency to compete or choose depend largely, but not exclusively, on the degree of each sex's investment in parenting (Trivers, 1972). The sex that provides more than his or her share of parental investment becomes, in effect, an important reproductive resource for members of the opposite sex. One important result is competition among members of the lower investing sex, typically males, over the parental investment of members of the higher investing sex, typically females. Members of the higher investing sex are thus in demand, and can be choosy when it comes to mates. In turn, any sex difference in the tendency to parent is related to a more fundamental sex difference in the potential rate with which males and females can produce offspring (Clutton-Brock & Vincent, 1991). This potential rate of reproduction interacts with social conditions, the operational sex ratio (OSR, which is discussed later) in particular, to create the mating dynamics that are observed in many species, including humans.

How Fast Can Males and Females Reproduce?

The basic issue is the biological limit on how many offspring males and females can "potentially" produce, in the best of all possible worlds, in their lifetime (Clutton-Brock & Vincent, 1991). For female mammals, this limit is determined by gestation time and length of postpartum suckling, whereas for males, the limit is determined by the number of females to which they gain sexual access. In any given breeding season, females will typically have one offspring, whereas males who successfully compete will have many offspring. Thus, the potential rate of reproduction is many times higher in male mammals than in female mammals; the same is true for most nonmammalian species.

One result of this sex difference in rate of reproduction is an evolved bias of mammalian females toward high levels of parental investment—which includes gestation and suckling—and mammalian males toward competition for mates and no parental investment. This is because males who successfully compete dominate the mating pool, and sire many more offspring through this competition than they would if they parented. Thus, the evolved behavioral biases for males are a preference for multiple mates, and more variability in reproductive outcomes than females. Some males sire many offspring, and many males sire no offspring, a dynamic that intensifies male-male competition.

Operational Sex Ratio

The OSR is the ratio of sexually active males to sexually active females in a given breeding population, and is closely related to the rate of reproduction (Emlen & Oring, 1977). An OSR of 1:1 occurs for populations with as many sexually mature females as males. However, any sex difference in the rate of reproduction will skew the OSR, because pregnant females typically leave the mating pool and may not return for many years. Female chimpanzees, for instance, will suckle their young for four to five years and are not sexually receptive during this time. The result is many more sexually receptive males than females in most populations, which, in turn, leads to intense male-male competition over access to a limited number of sexually receptive females. Male-male competition, in turn, creates the conditions under which female choosiness can evolve. For species in which females have a faster rate of reproduction, as when males incubate eggs, females compete and males choose (Amundsen, 2000).

In some situations, the sex with the higher potential rate of reproduction is better off by investing in parenting than in competing for mates, as is common in canines and about 15 percent of species of primates. For instance, in many species of the South American monkeys, shared territorial defense, concealed ovulation, female-on-female aggression, twinning, and perhaps other still unknown factors, functionally negate the sex difference in the potential rate of reproduction and result in a more balanced OSR, monogamy, and high levels of male parenting (Dunbar, 1995). Generally, male parenting occurs in species in which males are reproductively more successful when they parent than when they compete, although a mix of competing and parenting is evident in many species, including humans (Geary, 2000). In any case, when males parent, they become choosier and females compete for access to the best male parents.

Choosing a Mate

One of the advantages of investing more in parenting than in competing is that this investment becomes a valuable resource, one that members of the opposite sex will fight over (Andersson, 1994). The resulting demand for this investment creates the ability to choose mates. Because females invest more in parenting than males, female choice is much more common than male choice across bird, insect, fish, reptile, and mammal species. One result of female choice is the evolution of exaggerated male traits, such as the colorful plumage of the males of many species of birds. These exaggerated traits are often an indicator of the physical or genetic health of the male, or serve as an indicator of his ability (e.g., vigor in searching for food) to provide parental investment (Andersson, 1994; Zahavi, 1975).

The physical and genetic health of males is related, in part, to their immune system; specifically, the ability to resist infection by parasites, such as worms, viruses, and so forth in the local ecology (Folstad & Karter, 1992; Hamilton & Zuk, 1982). It appears that a healthy immune system is partly heritable, and thus the offspring of males with exaggerated traits survive in greater numbers than do the offspring of other males (Saino, Møller, & Bolzern, 1995). Thus, male ornaments are barometers that are strongly affected by the condition of the male, and female mate choice reflects the evolution of females' ability to read these barometers. Although the research is less extensive, there is evidence that similar mechanisms may operate in species in which males parent or females vary greatly in their reproductive success. In these species, males tend to be choosy when it comes to mates and females often have exaggerated traits (Amundsen, 2000; Andersson, 1994).

HUMAN MATE CHOICES

The same processes that govern sexual selection in nonhuman species help to explain sex differences and the dynamics of sexual and reproductive relationships in humans (Darwin, 1871; Geary, 1998). The literature in this area is in fact quite large, and thus I only focus on mate choices in the following sections; discussions of male-male and female-female competition can be found elsewhere (Campbell, 2002; Geary, 1998). Humans' mate choices are considerably more complicated than choices in most other species because many men invest heavily in their children. The reasons for the evolution of human fatherhood are beyond the scope of this chapter (Geary, 1998; 2005b), but once it evolved, it changed the dynamics of sexual selection. In addition to the standard mechanisms of male-male competition and female choice, men's parenting resulted in the evolution of female-female competition and male choice. Many of these features of sexual selection are of course related; for instance, women compete over traits that men prefer in a mate and vice versa (Buss, 1989). My focus in the first two subsections is on women's and men's mate-choice preferences, respectively. In the final subsection, I discuss how these preferences can be modified in response to cultural and social conditions.

Women's Mate-Choice Preferences

Intimate and often complicated relationships between women and men are a common theme in romance novels and other literatures that are more often read by women than by men (Whissell, 1996). Studies of themes that emerge across this genre suggest that the relationship dynamics and the traits of the central male character may reflect, at least in part, the evolved mate–choice preferences of women. The dynamics reflect the often conflicted interests and sexual tensions of the main characters, and the difficult time that women have in focusing the behavior of these men such that the men behave in ways that are consistent with the women's best interest. More often than not, the central male character is physically attractive, successful, and ultimately commits his time and resources, as in marriage, to the relationship with the central female character. In reality, these men are few and far between, if they exist at all, and thus a divide exists between women's preferred mates and their actual mate choices. The latter involve trade-offs between one trait, such as monetary success, against another trait, such as physical attractiveness (Gangestad & Simpson, 2000; Li, Bailey, Kenrick, & Linsenmeier, 2002). Here, I first describe research on the specifics of what women prefer in a mate, as well as the trade-offs they are willing to make when actually choosing a mate. I then describe the conditions under which some women seek short-term sexual relationships or multiple mating partners.

Long-Term Partners

Cultural success. One finding that has consistently emerged across Western and traditional societies is that women prefer long-term partners who are culturally successful, or are likely to become successful, all other things being equal (Buss, 1989; Irons, 1979; Sprecher, Sullivan, & Hatfield, 1994). The specifics of this success vary from one culture to the next, and can range from ownership of cows to ownership of stock portfolios. Across these contexts, culturally successful men are those who wield social influence and have control of the forms of resource that women can use for their own well-being and that of their children; money buys safe housing, health care, food, and social influence. The reason for this is clear: In all cultures that have been studied, the children of culturally successful men have lower mortality rates than the children of other men (Geary, 2000). Even in cultures where mortality rates are low, children of culturally successful men benefit in terms of psychological and physical health, longevity in adulthood, and opportunities (e.g., educational access) to become culturally successful themselves (Adler et al., 1994). These are exactly the conditions that would result in the evolution of women's preference for socially dominant and culturally successful marriage partners.

The salience of a prospective mate's cultural success is highlighted when women have to make trade-offs between a marriage partner's cultural success versus other important traits, such as his physical attractiveness. Li et al. (2002) studied these trade-offs by giving young women and men a marriage partner budget in which they could spend a fixed amount of "mate dollars" on their partner's traits; as spending on the trait increased, the partner's relative standing on the trait increased. Initial investments are made on necessities in a prospective mate, and any excess mate dollars are spent on luxuries. Across three studies, they found that women's initial investments were disproportionately in men's resources, such as their social level or yearly income, although women also invested in other traits (see below). As their budget increased and they had excess mate dollars, women invested proportionately more in other traits, such as kindness. In short, when women are forced to make trade-offs in a prospective marriage partner's traits, his cultural success is rated as a necessity and most other characteristics a luxury.

Personality and behavior. Women's preference for a culturally successful long-term partner is complicated by competition from other women and because these men are often self-serving and are better able to pursue their interest (see below) in multiple mating partners than are other men (Betzig, 1986, 1992; Pratto & Hegarty, 2000). A culturally successful partner who will not be focused on the relationship and any children from the relationship is not a good prospect for a long-term partner. The personal and behavioral characteristics of men are thus important considerations in women's mate choices. These characteristics provide information on the ability and the willingness of the man to make a long-term investment in the woman and her children (Buss, 1994). The bottom line is that women want culturally successful marriage partners, and they want some level of influence over the behavior of these men (Geary, 1998).

In addition to cultural success and social influence, women rate the kindness and intelligence of a prospective long-term partner very highly. In a multinational study, Buss (1989) found that women rated a prospective husband who was kind, understanding, and intelligent more highly than a prospective husband who was none of these, but had the potential to become culturally successful. In studies by Li et al. (2002), women rated a prospective marriage partner's kindness and/or intelligence as a necessity, along with his cultural success. As their budget increased, women added a few luxuries to this list, such as creativity, friendliness, and sense of romance. These studies indicate that women prefer culturally successful men and men who have the personal and social attributes that suggest they will invest these resources in a family.

However, the trade-offs women are willing to make, and the personal and behavioral attributes they prefer in a long-term mate, can vary from one context to another. As an example, many women prefer men with whom they can develop an intimate and emotionally satisfying relationship, although this appears to be more of a luxury than a necessity. In fact, the preference for this type of relationship is more common in middle-class and upper-middle-class Western culture than in many other cultures or, in fact, in the working-class of Western societies (Argyle, 1994; Hewlett, 1992). I am not saying that the development of an intimate relationship is not important or not preferred by women in non-Western cultures. Rather, in many non-Western contexts women are more focused on keeping their children alive than on developing intimacy with their husband.

Good looks and good genes. As I noted above, women will often make trade-offs between a partner's cultural success and his physical attractiveness. This does not mean that a partner's attractiveness is not important—it is—but, rather, it is more of a luxury than a necessity. Indeed, in romance novels and other literatures that appeal to many women, the central male character is almost always socially dominant, culturally successful, and handsome as well, and this makes biological sense (Whissell, 1996). Handsome husbands are more likely to sire children who are attractive and thus sought out as mating and marriage partners in adulthood, and these men and their children may be physically healthier than other men and their children, but these relations are complex and remain to be resolved (Geary, 2005b; Hume & Montgomerie, 2001; Weeden & Sabini, 2005). Whether or not handsome husbands are healthier, women prefer men who are somewhat taller than average, and have an athletic (but not too muscular) and symmetric body shape, and shoulders that are somewhat wider than their hips (Cunningham, 1986; Singh, 1995; Waynforth, 2001). Women rate symmetric facial features as attractive, as well as somewhat larger than average eyes, a large smile area, and prominent cheekbones and chin. When they can, women put these preferences into practice; for instance, physically smaller and less-robust men are less likely to be chosen as marriage partners than are taller and more-robust men (Nettle, 2002).

There is also evidence that women's mate and marriage choices are influenced by men's immune-system genes (Ober, Elias, Kostyu, & Hauck, 1992; Wedekind, Seebeck, Bettens, & Paepke, 1995). Women, of course, are not directly aware of these genetic differences: Immune-system genes are signaled through pheromones and women are sensitive to, and respond to, these scents, especially during the second week of their menstrual cycle, that is, when they are most fertile (Gangestad & Thornhill, 1998). And women show a preference for the scents of physically attractive men, even though they have never seen these men. This suggests that attractive and presumably healthy men have a variety of related physical and pheromonal traits that distinguish them from other men and that can influence women's choices of sexual partners. It is not simply the quality (i.e., presumed resistance to disease) of the man's immune-system genes; what matters is how these genes match up with those of the woman. In terms of disease resistance, the best outcome for offspring occurs when there is high variability in immune-system genes, and one way to achieve this is through having children with a partner with different immune-system genes. Women, in fact, find scents of men with dissimilar immune-system genes as more pleasant and sexy than the scents of men with similar immune-system genes, and conceive more easily with these men (Ober et al., 1992; Wedekind et al., 1995).

Some of the more intriguing research in this area has revealed that women's preference for physically attractive men varies across the menstrual cycle and with her physical attractiveness (Gangestad, Thornhill, & Garver, 2002; Little, Burt, Penton-Voak, & Perrett, 2001). Penton-Voak et al. (1999) demonstrated that women preferred men with masculine facial features (e.g., prominent chin) around the time of ovulation, and men with more feminine facial features at other times in their cycle; implications are discussed below, under "Short-term partners." Little et al. (2001) found that physically attractive women rated masculine looking men as more attractive long-term partners than did other women, presumably because attractive women are better able to keep these men focused on the primary relationship.

Short-Term Partners

Because women pay the cost of pregnancy, they are on average more sexually cautious than men, but do at times engage in short-term sexual relationships (Buss & Schmitt, 1993; Bellis & Baker, 1990; Essock-Vitale & McGuire, 1988; Gangestad & Thornhill, 1998; Oliver & Hyde, 1993; Symons, 1979). Sometimes women engage in these relationships when they perceive the potential for development of a longer-term relationship, suggesting that they sometimes use sexuality as a means to initiate a relationship with a potential marriage partner. At other times, women initiate a short-term sexual relationship outside of the context of a marriage or other long-term relationship, and in still other contexts women and their children may be better off when the women have multiple sexual partners (Bellis & Baker, 1990; Lancaster, 1989). I first provide a brief description of the dynamics of women's extra-pair relationships, and then describe the contexts in which most women benefit from multiple sexual relationships.

Extra-pair sex. It has been estimated that between 12 percent and 25 percent of women will engage in some type of affair during their lifetime (Banfield & McCabe, 2001; Bellis & Baker, 1990; Glass & Wright, 1992). The reasons for these affairs are many, but the most potentially volatile situation is one in which the woman's affair results in pregnancy by her extra-pair partner and cuckoldry of her husband; cuckoldry means that the husband has been deceived into raising the child of another man. The definitive study on how often this happens has not yet been conducted, but it is clear that it happens more frequently than many people wish to admit. The best estimate at this time is that as many as 10 percent of children may be the result of these relationships, although the rate varies widely across contexts and ranges from about 1 percent in Switzerland to more than 20 percent in many lower socioeconomic communities (Cerda-Flores, Barton, Marty-Gonzalez, Rivas, & Chakraborty, 1999; Sasse, Muller, Chakraborty, & Ott, 1994).

The dynamics of when women actually engage in an extra-pair sexual relationship appears to be influenced by hormone fluctuations (Gangestad & Thornhill, 1998; Gangestad, Thornhill, & Garver, 2002; Penton-Voak et al., 1999). Women show systematic changes in sexual fantasy and attractiveness to extra-pair men around the time of ovulation. Women are not only more likely to fantasize about, and sometimes engage in, an affair during this time, they are also more sensitive to and attracted by male pheromones (Gangestad et al., 2002). Gangestad and Thornhill (1998) found that the scent of facially symmetric men was rated as more attractive and sexy than was the scent of less symmetric men; but only during this fertile time frame. Penton-Voak et al. (1999) found that women rate masculine faces, those with a more prominent jaw, as especially attractive around the time of ovulation.

The emerging picture is one in which women may have an evolved sensitivity to cues to men's health (assuming attractiveness signals health) that peaks around the time women ovulate and are thus most likely to conceive. The pattern also suggests that, for some women, sexuality involves a mixed social and reproductive strategy (Gangestad & Simpson, 2000; Vigil, Geary, & Byrd-Craven, submitted). The mixed strategy may be most effective if these women are psychologically and socially attentive to the relationship with their primary partner and thus maintain his investment in her and her children, and only become attracted to extra-pair men at the time of ovulation. Many of these women never engage in an affair, and those who do seem to prefer an extra-pair partner with whom they have a level of emotional intimacy as contrasted with a stranger (Banfield & McCabe, 2001). In any case, when extra-pair relations do occur, they are typically initiated by the woman around the time of ovulation.

Serial monogamy and polyandry. For many women, marriage to a culturally successful and physically attractive man who is devoted to her and her children is not achievable. This is especially true in contexts where most men do not have the resources to support a family. To adjust to this circumstance, some women develop a successive series of relationships with a number of these men, or several men simultaneously, each of whom provides some investment during the course of the relationship. These women are practicing serial monogamy and sometimes polyandry, and in some circumstances are better off than are women monogamously married to men with low incomes. In recounting one such comparison of low-income women in the Dominican Republic, Lancaster (1989) noted that

> women who excluded males from the domestic unit and maintained multiple liaisons were more fecund, had healthier children with fewer pre- and post-natal mishaps, were able to raise more children over the age of five, had better nourished children (as measured by protein per

capita), and had better psychological adjustment (as measured by self-report and lower maternal blood pressure). (pp. 68–69)

Among the Ache and Barí, South American Indian societies, women will often engage in sexual relations with men who are not their social partners, especially after becoming pregnant (Beckerman et al., 1998; Hill & Hurtado, 1996). By tradition, these men are called secondary fathers and are socially obligated to provide food and other resources, as well as social protection, to the woman's child, although not all of them do so. The result seems to be a confused paternity such that both primary and secondary fathers invest in the child. The advantages of having a secondary father are substantial. The mortality rate of Ache children with one secondary father is about half that of children with no secondary father or two or more secondary fathers; with more than one secondary father paternity is too uncertain, and thus these men do not invest in the child. The benefit of a secondary father cannot be attributed to qualities of the mother, as 80 percent of Barí children with a secondary father survived to adulthood, as compared to 61 percent of their siblings without a secondary father (Beckerman et al., 1998).

Men's Mate-Choice Preferences

As anyone who has been involved in a heterosexual relationship knows, what women want and expect from a long-term, or even short-term, partner is not always what men want, although there are often many similarities. In the following sections, I describe men's preferences for long-term and short-term partners, respectively, and point out the most salient differences in relation to women's preferences.

Long-Term Partners

When men are looking for long-term partners, typically for marriage, they are in effect committing to invest a significant amount of their time and resources in the relationship with their partner and any resulting children. This is not to say that they are willing to invest as much as their partners would prefer for them to, as it is typically not the case. Still, from an evolutionary perspective, men are predicted to be, and are, more similar than different from women in terms of the traits they seek in a long-term partner (Kenrick, Groth, Trost, & Sadalla, 1993). In the following sections, I highlight a few of the key areas in which men and women differ in their mate preferences.

Cultural success. Outside of the strictures of Western culture, men are typically allowed to marry as many women as they can support, although only about 10–15 percent of men actually marry polygynously (Murdock, 1981); even in Western culture, the same end can be achieved with serial marriages (Forsberg & Tullberg, 1995). In these non–Western societies, men are more concerned with the traits described in the "Good looks and fertility" section than with their partners' cultural success (Gil-Burmann, Peláez, & Sánchez, 2002; Li et al., 2002; Sprecher et al., 1994). They do expect their wives to contribute to the family, as with foraging, but they are not typically concerned about their cultural success per se. In Western societies, monogamous marriages are socially imposed and thus marriage for culturally successful men—those who would have several wives in other societies—has a sexual and reproductive cost: Their sexual behavior is restricted, at least in terms of marriage vows, and sometimes legally, to a single relationship, and they typically have fewer children (Flinn & Low, 1986; Forsberg & Tullberg, 1995). As a result, culturally successful men in such cultures and those who strive for cultural success tend to be more choosy when it comes to marriage partners than other men, or successful men in polygynous cultures. For many of these men, the cultural success of their prospective wife is important, but is more of a luxury than a necessity, in contrast with women's expectations for the cultural success of their husbands.

Personality and behavior. When it comes to a marriage partner, men throughout the world prefer women who are intelligent and kind, although these traits are often a luxury and not a necessity (Buss, 1989; Li et al., 2002). One behavior that is a necessity for men, however, is their partner's sexual fidelity. Men's concern for their partner's sexual fidelity is an evolutionarily coupled feature of the earlier described cuckoldry risks, and the costs associated with investing in the child of another man. The social and psychological manifestation of this concern is sexual jealousy, which has a near universal influence on the dynamics of men's and women's relationships (Buss, 1994; Symons, 1979). It is not that women do not become sexually jealous, they do: it is a matter of degree and a matter of how men and women react to an actual or perceived infidelity. In one study, women reported their partner engaged in more monitoring of their behavior during the week the women were most likely to ovulate, the time frame when these same women reported an increase in sexual fantasy and interest in an extra-pair man (Gangestad et al., 2002). This and related studies are consistent with the view that men's sexual jealousy evolved at least in part as a response to women's ability to cuckold.

Good looks and fertility. Both women and men prefer attractive partners, but this preference is consistently found to be more important—a necessity and not a luxury—for men than for women (Buss, 1989; Li et al., 2002). Men's ratings of women's physical attractiveness are driven by several specific physical traits, including a waist-to-hip ratio (WHR) of 0.7; facial features that signal a combination of sexual maturity but relative youth; body and facial symmetry; and age (Cunningham, 1986; Kenrick et al., 1993; Kenrick & Keefe, 1992; Sprecher et al., 1994). A measure of leanness to obesity independent of height, that is, the body mass index (BMI), is also associated with rated attractiveness (Weeden & Sabini, 2005). Leaner women tend to be rated more attractive than heavier women, although, as noted later, the attractiveness of relatively thinner to relatively heavier women varies with availability of food and other resources (Anderson, Crawford, Nadeau, & Lindberg, 1992; Pettijohn & Jungeberg, 2004).

In any case, this combination of cues has been hypothesized to be indicators of women's health and fertility. To illustrate, women's fertility is low in the teen years, peaks at about age 25, and then gradually declines to near zero by age 45 (Menken, Trussell, & Larsen, 1986). Teenage mothers experience more complications during pregnancy than do women in their twenties, and these risks begin to increase in the thirties, and increase sharply after age 35. Given this, it is not surprising that men's preferences are sensitive to indications of a women's age (Kenrick & Keefe, 1992). Other aspects of men's preferences may or may not be indicators of health and fertility. In a review of this literature, Weeden and Sabini (2005) found that women with attractive faces, as rated by men, and a waist-to-hip ratio in the middle range tended to be in better health than their peers, but the strength of these relations was not large. Women with ratios greater than 0.85 are at risk for a number of physiological disorders and appear to have greater difficulty conceiving than do women with lower ratios. Other studies suggest that BMI might be a better predictor of health than WHR. Facial and body symmetry, in contrast, was not found to be consistently correlated with women's health. One possible exception is breast symmetry. Women with symmetric breasts are rated as attractive by men, and these women appear to be more fertile than other women (Møller, Soler, & Thornhill, 1995).

Short-Term Partners

Unlike women, men, like the males of most other species, often pursue short-term sexual relationships as an end initself. At least it seems to be so; but in fact, it can result in the currency of evolution—children. One important difference between these sexual relationships and those described in the "Long-term partners" section is men's investment in children; for short-term partners, men have no intention of investing in any resulting children, whereas for long-term partners they typically do. That men are interested in short-term sexual partners and differ in important respects from women on this dimension of sexuality is illustrated in the respective sections below on sexual attitudes and fantasy, and use of prostitutes.

Sexual attitudes and fantasy. Some of the largest sex differences in this area involve attitudes toward casual sex and the frequency of masturbation (Buss & Schmitt, 1993; Clark & Hatfield, 1989; Oliver & Hyde, 1993). About four out of five men were more enthusiastic about the prospect of casual sex than the average woman, and about six out of seven men report masturbating more frequently than the average woman; the latter suggests that men are more likely on average to be sexually frustrated than women. Men's attitudes toward casual sex are put into practice if the opportunity arises. In a set of studies in which undergraduates approached attractive but unfamiliar members of the opposite sex and asked them for a date, to go to their apartment, or to engage in casual sex, Clark and Hatfield (1989) found that one out of two of the men and one out of two of the women accepted the date. When asked to engage in casual sex, three out of four men agreed, but none of the women agreed.

There are also differences in the quantity and nature of the sexual fantasies of men and women (Geary, 1998). Young men are twice as likely as young women to report having sexual fantasies at least once a day, and four times as likely to report having fantasized about sex with more than 1,000 different people. Although there were no sex differences in feelings of guilt over sexual fantasies, men and women differed considerably in the content of their fantasies. Women are two and a half times as likely to report thinking about the personal and emotional characteristics of their partner, whereas men are nearly four times as likely to report focusing on the physical attractiveness of their partner. Moreover, women are twice as likely to report fantasizing about someone with whom they are currently romantically involved with or had been involved with, whereas men are three times as likely to fantasize about having sex with someone they are not involved with and have no intention of becoming involved with. The latter is of course consistent with a desire for short-term sexual relationships as an end in itself.

Prostitution. The demand for prostitutes is driven almost entirely by men (Bonnerup et al., 2000; Turner et al., 1998). It is difficult to estimate the number of men who have resorted to prostitution as a means to secure short-term sexual partners, because men are reluctant to admit to this behavior. In a survey of 1,729 adolescents and young men between the ages of 15 and 19 in the United States, 2.5 percent reported having had sex at least once with a prostitute (Turner et al., 1998). Given the age range in this sample, the percentage of men who resort to prostitution at some point in their lifetime must be considerably higher than 2.5 percent. Indeed, for a random sample of 852 Danish and Swedish adults between the ages of 23 and 87, one out of six men, but none of the women, reported having visited a prostitute at least once (Bonnerup et al., 2000).

Historical and Cross-Cultural Variation

Although there are sex differences in mate preferences and sexual behavior, it should be clear that there is not one reproductive strategy for women and another for men. In addition to common themes in women's and men's preferences, such as for an attractive partner, the strategies adopted by both sexes often vary across contexts, historical periods, and characteristics of the individual (Anderson et al., 1992; Flinn & Low, 1986; Gangestad & Simpson, 2000; Guttentag & Secord, 1983; MacDonald, 1995; McGraw, 2002; Pettijohn & Jungeberg, 2004). Individuals with traits that are desired by the opposite sex, such as culturally successful men or physically attractive women, are in higher demand than are their same-sex peers and therefore are able to exert more influence in their inter-sexual relationships. However, wider social and ecological factors also influence the sexual behavior and choices of marriage partners of these and other people, as I briefly overview in the following sections.

Operational Sex Ratio

Recall that the OSR is the term used by biologists to describe the ratio of reproductive-age males to reproductively available females in the local population, and imbalances in the ratio influence the reproductive strategies adopted by both sexes, including humans (Guttentag & Secord, 1983). In industrial societies, population growth or "baby booms" can skew the OSR such that there are too many women. The oversupply results from the preference of women for older marriage partners and of men for younger marriage partners (Kenrick & Keefe, 1992). With an expanding population, the younger generation of women will be selecting marriage partners from a smaller pool of older men. The resulting imbalance in the OSR can influence more general social patterns, including divorce rates, sexual mores, and the willingness of men to invest in their children, among others. As Guttentag and Secord (1983) noted, "Sex ratios by themselves do not bring about societal effects, but rather that they combine with a variety of other social, economic, and political conditions to produce the consequent effects on the roles of men and women and the relationships between them" (p. 137).

One of the more extreme of these social effects occurred in the United States from 1965 through the 1970s. During this time, there were more women than men looking for marriage partners in many parts of the country, which enabled men to better pursue their sexual preferences. In comparison to other historical periods, this epoch and others in which a similar skew occurred are characterized by liberal sexual mores (i.e., many short-term sexual partners for both sexes); high divorce rates; increases in the number of out-of-wedlock births and the number of families headed by single women; an increase in women's participation in the workforce; and a lower willingness of men to invest in fatherhood. During these periods, men are better able to express their preferences for a variety of sexual partners and relatively low levels of investment in children. A sharply different pattern emerges when there is an oversupply of men. During these epochs, women are better able to enforce their preferences than are men. As a result, these periods are characterized by an increase in the level of commitment of men to marriage, as indexed by declining divorce rates and a greater willingness of men to invest in their children.

Cultural Mores and Resource Availability

Wider social mores or values also influence the dynamics of sexual relationships, and one of the most important of these is the prohibition against polygynous marriages (MacDonald, 1995). In societies in which polygyny is not constrained by formal or informal rules, culturally successful men (about 10–15 percent of men) will typically marry several women. One crucial consequence is some men sire many children and many men sire no children. The result is an increase in male-on-male aggression and other changes in reproductive dynamics.

Western culture has a history of monogamous marriages, but polygynous sexual relationships by culturally successful men, that is, these men typically had a single wife with whom heirs were sired, as well as many mistresses (Betzig, 1986, 1992). In Western Europe, cultural prohibitions emerged slowly during the Middle Ages such that the ability of dominant men to engage in polygyny was gradually reduced (MacDonald, 1995). The result is a system of socially imposed monogamy, whereby nearly all men have the potential to develop sexual and reproductive relationships. One consequence is that culturally successful men become especially choosy when it comes to marriage partners, as they are constrained to invest their resources in a single woman and her children. The intensity of competition among women to marry these men is also predicted and appears to increase accordingly (Geary, 1998). These days, polygyny is achieved in Western culture through serial monogamy, which has an important reproductive consequence for men but not for women (Forsberg & Tullberg, 1995). This is because men, but not women, who engage in serial monogamy have more children than their peers who stay monogamously married.

The resources needed to raise a family and the availability of these resources in the local ecology also influence sexual behavior and reproductive patterns (Flinn & Low, 1986). When resources are scarce and it takes the efforts of both parents to keep children alive, the ability of a prospective long-term partner to secure resources becomes crucial in the mate-choice decisions of both sexes. In these societies, polygyny is rare, and monogamy and high levels of fathers' investment in children are the norm. A parallel pattern is found even in wealthy societies, at least for women. In the United States, women's criteria for marriage partners vary with the cost of living. In cities with a high cost of living, women placed a greater emphasis on the man's earning potential than did women living in other cities (McGraw, 2002). In Spain, women with economic resources appear to place less emphasis on men's socioeconomic status than do women with fewer resources (Gil-Burmann, Pelaez, & Sanchez, 2002).

More general, culture-wide standards of beauty also vary with ecological conditions. In an analysis of cross-cultural differences in the relative plumpness or thinness of women—waist-to-hip ratio stays steady with moderate changes in weight due to the pattern of fat distribution—as the preferred body type, Anderson et al. (1992) found that relative plumpness was preferred in nearly twice as many societies (44 percent) as relative thinness (19 percent). Plumpness tended to be favored in societies in which the food supply was unpredictable, but thinness was not necessarily the preferred standard in societies with excess food. In a related study, Pettijohn and Jungeberg (2004) found that economic and social well-being in the United States were related to the facial and body features of the *Playboy* playmate of the year. When times were difficult (e.g., increase in unemployment rate), the playmates tended to be taller, heavier, and had more mature (e.g., smaller eyes) facial features. Thinner playmates tended to be found with economic prosperity and higher levels of social well-being. These studies suggest that cultural and historical variation in the ideal for women's beauty varies, at least in part, with stability and availability of food and other resources.

CONCLUSION

Many people are uncomfortable with the proposal that human behavior in general and human sexuality in particular are the result of a long evolutionary history and are essentially about surviving and reproducing. But this discomfort does not make these proposals incorrect, and in fact an evolutionary perspective on human sexual behavior is the only theoretical lens that provides the full range of explanation and understanding of these phenomena. Darwin's (1871) insights on the processes of sexual selection and later discoveries regarding the importance of parenting and potential rates of reproduction for shaping the evolution and here-and-now expression of sexual behavior and sex differences in this behavior have provided compelling explanations of these behaviors in hundreds of species (Andersson, 1994; Clutton-Brock & Vincent, 1991; Trivers, 1972). It readily follows that these same mechanisms will yield many insights on human sexuality and human sex differences (Geary, 1998; Symons, 1979), and this is indeed the case, as I illustrated with women's and men's mate preferences and variation in these preferences across historical periods and different cultures. With this chapter, I have in fact only scratched the surface regarding the power of this approach and hope that it has piqued the readers' interest in reading more and thinking more about this topic.

REFERENCES

Adler, N. E., Boyce, T., Chesney, M. A., Cohen, S., Folkman, S., Kahn, R. L., & Syme, S. L. (1994). Socioeconomic status and health: The challenge of the gradient. *American Psychologist, 49*, 15–24.

Alexander, R. D. (1979). *Darwinism and human affairs.* Seattle, WA: University of Washington Press.

Amundsen, T. (2000). Why are female birds ornamented? *Trends in Ecology and Evolution, 15*, 149–155.

Anderson, J. L., Crawford, C. B., Nadeau, J., & Lindberg, T. (1992). Was the Duchess of Windsor right? A cross-cultural review of the socioecology of ideals of female body shape. *Ethology and Sociobiology, 13*, 197–227.

Andersson, M. (1994). *Sexual selection*. Princeton, NJ: Princeton University Press.

Argyle, M. (1994). *The psychology of social class*. New York: Routledge.

Banfield, S., & McCabe, M. P. (2001). Extra relationship involvement among women: Are they different from men? *Archives of Sexual Behavior, 30*, 119–142.

Beckerman, S., Lizarralde, R., Ballew, C., Schroeder, S., Fingelton, C., Garrison, A., & Smith, H. (1998). The Barí partible paternity project: Preliminary results. *Current Anthropology, 39*, 164–167.

Bellis, M. A., & Baker, R. R. (1990). Do females promote sperm competition? Data for humans. *Animal Behaviour, 40*, 997–999.

Betzig, L. (1986). *Despotism and differential reproduction: A Darwinian view of history*. New York: Aldine.

Betzig, L. (1992). Roman polygyny. *Ethology and Sociobiology, 13*, 309–349.

Bonnerup, J. A., Gramkow, A., Sorensen, P., Melbye, M., Adami, H.-O., Glimelius, B., & Frisch, M. (2000). Correlates of heterosexual behavior among 23–87 year olds in Denmark and Sweden, 1992–1998. *Archives of Sexual Behavior, 29*, 91–106.

Buss, D. M. (1989). Sex differences in human mate preferences: Evolutionary hypothesis tested in 37 cultures. *Behavioral and Brain Sciences, 12*, 1–49.

Buss, D. M. (1994). *The evolution of desire: Strategies of human mating*. New York: Basic Books.

Buss, D. M., & Schmitt, D. P. (1993). Sexual strategies theory: An evolutionary perspective on human mating. *Psychological Review, 100*, 204–232.

Campbell, A. (2002). *A mind of her own: The evolutionary psychology of women*. New York: Oxford University Press.

Cerda-Flores, R. M., Barton, S. A., Marty-Gonzalez, L. F., Rivas, F., & Chakraborty, R. (1999). Estimation of nonpaternity in the Mexican population of Nuevo Leon: A validation study with blood group markers. *American Journal of Physical Anthropology, 109*, 281–293.

Clark, R. D., & Hatfield, E. (1989). Gender differences in receptivity to sexual offers. *Journal of Psychology and Human Sexuality, 2*, 39–55.

Clutton-Brock, T. H., & Vincent, A. C. J. (1991, May 2). Sexual selection and the potential reproductive rates of males and females. *Nature, 351*, 58–60.

Cunningham, M. R. (1986). Measuring the physical in physical attractiveness: Quasi-experiments on the sociobiology of female beauty. *Journal of Personality and Social Psychology, 50*, 925–935.

Darwin, C. (1871). *The descent of man, and selection in relation to sex*. London: John Murray.

Dunbar, R. I. M. (1995). The mating system of callitrichid primates: I. Conditions for the coevolution of pair bonding and twinning. *Animal Behaviour, 50*, 1057–1070.

Emlen, S. T., & Oring, L. W. (1977, July 15). Ecology, sexual selection, and the evolution of mating systems. *Science, 197*, 215–223.

Essock-Vitale, S. M., & McGuire, M. T. (1988). What 70 million years hath wrought: Sexual histories and reproductive success of a random sample of

American women. In L. Betzig, M. Borgerhoff Mulder, & P. Turke (Eds.), *Human reproductive behaviour: A Darwinian perspective* (pp. 221–235). Cambridge, UK: Cambridge University Press.

Flinn, M. V., & Low, B. S. (1986). Resource distribution, social competition, and mating patterns in human societies. In D. I. Rubenstein & R. W. Wrangham (Eds.), *Ecological aspects of social evolution: Birds and mammals* (pp. 217–243). Princeton, NJ: Princeton University Press.

Folstad, I., & Karter, A. J. (1992). Parasites, bright males, and the immunocompetence handicap. *American Naturalist, 139*, 603–622.

Forsberg, A. J. L., & Tullberg, B. S. (1995). The relationship between cumulative number of cohabiting partners and number of children for men and women in modern Sweden. *Ethology and Sociobiology, 16*, 221–232.

Gangestad, S. W., & Simpson, J. A. (2000). The evolution of human mating: Trade-offs and strategic pluralism. *Behavioral and Brain Sciences, 23*, 573–644.

Gangestad, S. W., & Thornhill, R. (1998). Menstrual cycle variation in women's preferences for the scent of symmetrical men. *Proceedings of the Royal Society of London B, 265*, 927–933.

Gangestad, S. W., Thornhill, R., & Garver, C. E. (2002). Changes in women's sexual interests and their partner's mate retention tactics across the menstrual cycle: Evidence for shifting conflicts of interest. *Proceedings of the Royal Society of London B, 269*, 975–982.

Geary, D. C. (1998). *Male, female: The evolution of human sex differences*. Washington, DC: American Psychological Association.

Geary, D. C. (2000). Evolution and proximate expression of human paternal investment. *Psychological Bulletin, 126*, 55–77.

Geary, D. C. (2005a). Evolution of life history trade-offs in mate attractiveness and health: Comment on Weeden and Sabini (2005). *Psychological Bulletin, 131*, 654–657.

Geary, D. C. (2005b). Evolution of paternal investment. In D. M. Buss (Ed.), *The evolutionary psychology handbook* (pp. 483–505). Hoboken, NJ: John Wiley.

Gil-Burmann, C., Peláez, F., & Sánchez, S. (2002). Mate choice differences according to sex and age: An analysis of personal advertisements in Spanish newspapers. *Human Nature, 13*, 493–508.

Glass, S. P., & Wright, T. L. (1992). Justifications for extramarital relationships: The association between attitudes, behaviors, and gender. *Journal of Sex Research, 29*, 361–387.

Guttentag, M., & Secord, P. (1983). *Too many women?* Beverly Hills, CA: Sage.

Hamilton, W. D., & Zuk, M. (1982, October 22). Heritable true fitness and bright birds: A role for parasites? *Science, 218*, 384–387.

Hewlett, B. S. (1992). Husband-wife reciprocity and the father–infant relationship among Aka pygmies. In B. S. Hewlett (Ed.), *Father-child relations: Cultural and biosocial contexts* (pp. 153–176). New York: Aldine de Gruyter.

Hill, K., & Hurtado, A. M. (1996). *Ache life history: The ecology and demography of a foraging people*. New York: Aldine de Gruyter.

Hume, D. K., & Montgomerie, R. (2001). Facial attractiveness signals different aspects of "quality" in women and men. *Evolution and Human Behavior, 22,* 93–112.

Irons, W. (1979). Cultural and biological success. In N. A. Chagnon & W. Irons (Eds.), *Natural selection and social behavior* (pp. 257–272). North Scituate, MA: Duxbury Press.

Kenrick, D. T., Groth, G. E., Trost, M. R., & Sadalla, E. K. (1993). Integrating evolutionary and social exchange perspectives on relationships: Effects of gender, self-appraisal, and involvement level on mate selection criteria. *Journal of Personality and Social Psychology, 64,* 951–969.

Kenrick, D. T., & Keefe, R. C. (1992). Age preferences in mates reflect sex differences in human reproductive strategies. *Behavioral and Brain Sciences, 15,* 75–133.

Lancaster, J. B. (1989). Evolutionary and cross-cultural perspectives on single-parenthood. In R. W. Bell & N. J. Bell (Eds.), *Interfaces in psychology: Sociobiology and the social sciences* (pp. 63–72). Lubbock: Texas Tech University Press.

Li, N. P., Bailey, J. M., Kenrick, D. T., & Linsenmeier, J. A. W. (2002). The necessities and luxuries of mate preferences: Testing the tradeoffs. *Journal of Personality and Social Psychology, 82,* 947–955.

Little, A. C., Burt, D. M., Penton-Voak, I. S., & Perrett, D. I. (2001). Self-perceived attractiveness influences human female preferences for sexual dimorphism and symmetry in male faces. *Proceedings of the Royal Society of London B, 268,* 39–44.

MacDonald, K. (1995). The establishment and maintenance of socially imposed monogamy in Western Europe. *Politics and the Life Sciences, 14,* 3–46.

McGraw, K. J. (2002). Environmental predictors of geographic variation in human mate preferences. *Ethology, 108,* 303–317.

Menken, J., Trussell, J., & Larsen, U. (1986, September 26). Age and infertility. *Science, 233,* 1389–1394.

Møller, A. P., Soler, M., & Thornhill, R. (1995). Breast asymmetry, sexual selection, and human reproductive success. *Ethology and Sociobiology, 16,* 207–219.

Murdock, G. P. (1981). *Atlas of world cultures.* Pittsburgh, PA: University of Pittsburgh Press.

Nettle, D. (2002). Height and reproductive success in a cohort of British men. *Human Nature, 13,* 473–491.

Ober, C., Elias, S., Kostyu, D. D., & Hauck, W. W. (1992). Decreased fecundability in Hutterite couples sharing HLA-DR. *American Journal of Human Genetics, 50,* 6–14.

Oliver, M. B., & Hyde, J. S. (1993). Gender differences in sexuality: A meta-analysis. *Psychological Bulletin, 114,* 29–51.

Penton-Voak, I. S., Perrett, D. I., Castles, D. L., Kobayashi, T., Burt, D. M., Murray, L. K., & Minamisawa, R. (1999, June 24). Menstrual cycle alters face preference. *Nature, 399,* 741–742.

Pettijohn, T. F., & Jungeberg, B. J. (2004). *Playboy* playmate curves: Changes in facial and body feature preferences across social and economic conditions. *Personality and Social Psychology Bulletin, 30*, 1186–1197.

Pratto, F., & Hegarty, P. (2000). The political psychology of reproductive strategies. *Psychological Science, 11*, 57–62.

Saino, N., Møller, A. P., & Bolzern, A. M. (1995). Testosterone effects on the immune system and parasite infestations in the barn swallow (*Hirundo rustica*): An experimental test of the immunocompetence hypothesis. *Behavioral Ecology, 6*, 397–404.

Sasse, G., Muller, H., Chakraborty, R., & Ott, J. (1994). Estimating the frequency of nonpaternity in Switzerland. *Human Heredity, 44*, 337–343.

Singh, D. (1995). Female judgment of male attractiveness and desirability for relationships: Role of waist-to-hip ratio and financial status. *Journal of Personality and Social Psychology, 69*, 1089–1101.

Sprecher, S., Sullivan, Q., & Hatfield, E. (1994). Mate selection preferences: Gender differences examined in a national sample. *Journal of Personality and Social Psychology, 66*, 1074–1080.

Symons, D. (1979). *The evolution of human sexuality.* New York: Oxford University Press.

Trivers, R. L. (1972). Parental investment and sexual selection. In B. Campbell (Ed.), *Sexual selection and the descent of man 1871–1971* (pp. 136–179). Chicago: Aldine.

Turner, C. F., Ku, L., Rogers, S. M., Lindberg, L. D., Pleck, J. H., & Sonenstein, F. L. (1998, May 8). Adolescent sexual behavior, drug use, and violence: Increased reporting with computer survey technology. *Science, 280*, 867–873.

Vigil, J. M., Geary, D. C., & Byrd-Craven, J. *Trade-offs in low income women's preferences for long-term and short-term mates: Within-sex differences in reproductive strategy.*

Waynforth, D. (2001). Mate choice trade-offs and women's preference for physically attractive men. *Human Nature, 12*, 207–219.

Wedekind, C., Seebeck, T., Bettens, F., & Paepke, A. J. (1995). MHC-dependent mate preferences in humans. *Proceedings of the Royal Society of London B, 260*, 245–249.

Weeden, J., & Sabini, J. (2005). Physical attractiveness and health in Western societies: A review. *Psychological Bulletin, 131*, 635–653.

Whissell, C. (1996). Mate selection in popular women's fiction. *Human Nature, 7*, 427–447.

Zahavi, A. (1975). Mate selection—A selection for a handicap. *Journal of Theoretical Biology, 53*, 205–214.

5

Love

Pamela C. Regan ◆

Well, I can't speak for anyone else, but for me, the only way I'd have sex with someone was if we were deeply in love. If two people are in love, then sex seems like a natural way to express those feelings. (19-year-old woman interviewed by the author)

The decision to have sex is a personal choice that everyone should be free to make. Some people have sex just because they enjoy it, or because they have the chance to do it. That's fine; it's a personal decision. Other people, and I'm one of them, think that sex is best when it's done out of love, with someone you're involved with. (20-year-old man interviewed by the author)

As the quotations above illustrate, many people view love and sex as intimately connected. In fact, attitude surveys conducted around the United States reveal that the majority of adults and teenagers feel that sexual activity is most appropriate when it occurs between two people who are involved in a loving, committed relationship (Reiss, 1964; Sprecher, McKinney, Walsh, & Anderson, 1988). And being in love—and wanting to express those feelings of love to the partner—is one of the primary reasons couples engage in intercourse with one another (Jessor, Costa, Jessor, & Donovan, 1983; Leigh, 1989). Love also is related to many other significant interpersonal events in human life, including marriage and other forms of long-term pair-bonding, reproduction and child rearing, and intimacy and social support. Thus, it is hardly surprising that most people eagerly seek out love and believe that forming a successful love relationship is essential for their personal happiness (Berscheid & Regan, 2005). This chapter explores the topic of love. We begin by considering general theories of love and the measurement instruments that are associated with them. Next, we explore the two types of love that are most closely related to sexuality; namely, passionate love and companionate love. Specifically, we examine theories about the nature of passionate and companionate love, consider how scientists typically measure or assess feelings of love, and discuss research that illuminates the role that these two important varieties of love play in people's lives.

WHAT IS LOVE? GENERAL THEORIES ABOUT THE NATURE OF LOVE

Throughout history, scholars from a variety of disciplines have speculated about the nature of love. In their efforts to determine what is common to all types of love and what is unique to each particular variety, they have tended to follow two general approaches. Early theorists developed their classification systems from a consideration of existing literature and from previous philosophical, theological, and scientific discourse. Contemporary theorists have relied on empirically based methods (derived from the collection and analysis of data provided by research participants). Despite their different approaches, both early and contemporary theorists agree that love is a multifaceted phenomenon.

Early Taxonomies of Love

Early scholars interested in understanding the nature of love focused on identifying and cataloging different proposed varieties or types of love. One of the earliest known written treatises on love appeared in France during the late twelfth century. Written by Andreas Capellanus, *The Art of Courtly Love* considers the origins, manifestations, and effects of love, as well as how love can be acquired, increased, decreased, and terminated. Capellanus (ca. 1184/ 1960) argued that love consists of two basic varieties—pure love and common love. Pure love is durable (it "goes on increasing without end"), is based on affection, and is the kind of love "that anyone who is intent upon love ought to embrace with all his [or her] might." Common love is fragile and based upon sexual feelings and desires. According to Capellanus, this particular variety of love "gets its effect from every delight of the flesh and culminates in the final act of Venus" (p. 122).

Other early scholars also proposed that multiple varieties of love exist, each containing specific features and characteristics. For example, in the late 1800s,

William James (the founder of American psychology) differentiated between maternal love, which he argued was largely altruistic in nature, and another variety of love (to which he neglected to give a label) that was characterized by sexual appetite, emotional intensity, and exclusivity (i.e., directed toward one particular individual to the exclusion of all others) (1950). During the same period of time, the German physician Richard von Krafft-Ebing (1945) identified four distinct types of love. These were *true love*, a hardy mixture of altruism, affection, closeness, and sexuality; *sensual love*, a fleeting, fragile love based on sexual desire and romantic idealization of the loved one; *sentimental love*, about which Krafft-Ebing had little to say other than that it was self-indulgent and "nauseating"; and *platonic love*, which was grounded in compatibility and feelings of friendship.

Half a century later, psychotherapist Albert Ellis (1954) proposed an even greater number of possible love varieties, ranging from parental love and familial love, to conjugal love, romantic love, and sexual love, to self-love, religious love, love of animals, and love of humanity. Existential theorist Erich Fromm (1956) also believed that love existed in a number of different forms. According to his taxonomy, varieties of "real love" include brotherly love, motherly love, fatherly love, erotic love, self-love, and love of God. Each of these types of love contains four basic features—caring, respect, responsibility, and knowledge—along with its own unique features. For example, motherly love is distinguished by altruism and unconditional regard, whereas erotic love is short-lived and sexual.

Unlike his contemporaries Ellis and Fromm, religious writer and theorist C. S. Lewis proposed the existence of only four primary types of love, each based on earlier distinctions made by Greek philosophers. *Affection* (called *storge* [stor-gay] by the Greeks) is based on familiarity and repeated contact and resembles the strong attachment seen between parents and children. This type of love is found among friends, family members, acquaintances, lovers, and between people and their pets. Affectionate love has a "comfortable, quiet nature" and consists of feelings of warmth, interpersonal comfort, and satisfaction in being together (Lewis, 1988). The second variety of love depicted by Lewis is *friendship* (*philias*). Common interests, insights, or tastes, coupled with cooperation, mutual respect, and understanding, form the core of this love type. More than mere companionship, Lewis argued that friendship develops when "two people . . . discover that they are on the same secret road" and become kindred souls (p. 67). *Eros*, or "that state which we call 'being in love,' " is the third variety of love (p. 91). Unlike the other kinds of love that exist, Lewis proposed that erotic love contains a mixture of fluctuating emotions ("sweetness" and "terror"), as well as a strong sexual component, feelings of affection, idealization of the loved one, and a short life span. The final love type he identified is *charity*, a selfless, altruistic love that is based on tolerance, forbearance, and forgiveness.

Psychometric Approaches to Love

As we have discussed, all of the early theorists agreed that love is a multifaceted experience and that more than one variety of love exists, and they developed their love classification systems by relying heavily on existing theoretical discourse and literature. Contemporary social scientists, while recognizing the importance of this earlier, theory-based work, have adopted a psychometric approach to understanding the nature of love. This approach involves collecting information about the love experiences of people involved in actual ongoing relationships, and then using statistical methods (including cluster analysis and factor analysis) to identify common themes and dimensions underlying those experiences. The assumption made by researchers who adopt this approach is that identification of the common elements in people's actual love experiences provides an effective way of distinguishing among different love varieties. The love taxonomies proposed by psychologist Robert Sternberg and sociologist John Lee were both developed using this approach.

The Triangular Theory of Love

On the basis of factor analysis of the self-reported experiences of men and women in dating relationships, as well as a consideration of previous social psychological theory and research on love, Sternberg (1986; 1998) suggested that love could be understood in terms of three basic components—intimacy, passion, and decision/commitment. Each of these components can be envisioned as forming the vertices of a triangle (see Figure 5.1).

The *intimacy component* of love is primarily emotional in nature and involves feelings of warmth, closeness, connection, and bondedness in the love relationship. Signs of intimacy include wanting to promote the welfare of the loved one; experiencing happiness, mutual understanding, and intimate communication with the loved one; having high regard for the loved one; giving and receiving emotional support; being able to count on the loved one in times of need; sharing oneself and one's possessions with the loved one; and valuing the presence of the loved one in one's life (Sternberg & Grajek, 1984). The *passion component* is motivational in nature and consists of the drives that are involved in romantic and physical attraction, sexual consummation, and related phenomena. Although passion takes the form of sexuality in many love relationships, Sternberg suggested that other needs (including the need for affiliation, for dominance over others, and for self-esteem) can contribute to the experience of passion. The *decision/commitment component* of love is primarily cognitive in nature and represents both the short-term decision that one individual loves another and the long-term commitment to maintain that love.

According to Sternberg, these three basic love components differ with respect to a number of properties, including stability and conscious controllability. For example, the intimacy and decision/commitment components are

Intimacy

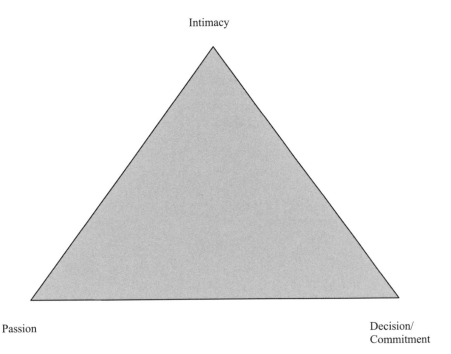

Passion

Decision/
Commitment

Figure 5.1. Sternberg's Triangular Theory of Love.

usually fairly stable in close relationships. Once we develop feelings of intimacy for someone and become committed to the relationship we have with that person, these features tend to endure over time. The passion component, however, tends to be less stable and predictable. In addition, although people possess a great deal of conscious control over the commitment that they make to a relationship, and even some degree of control over their feelings of intimacy, they usually have very little conscious control over the amount of passion that they experience for their partners.

The three basic components of love combine to produce eight different love types or varieties of love relationship, summarized in Table 5.1. *Nonlove* (no intimacy, passion, or decision/commitment) describes casual interactions that are characterized by the absence or very low amounts of all three love components. Most of our transient, everyday interactions or casual associations fall into this category. *Liking* (intimacy alone) relationships are essentially friendships. They contain warmth, intimacy, closeness, and the other positive emotions associated with intimacy, but lack passion and decision/commitment. *Infatuation* (passion alone) is an intense, "love at first sight" experience that is marked by extreme attraction and arousal in the absence of any real emotional intimacy and decision/commitment. In *empty love* (decision/commitment alone) relationships, the partners are committed to each other and the

Table 5.1. Sternberg's Taxonomy of Love Relationships

Kind of Love Relationship	Love Component		
	Intimacy	Passion	Decision/Commitment
Nonlove	Low	Low	Low
Liking	High	Low	Low
Infatuation	Low	High	Low
Empty love	Low	Low	High
Romantic love	High	High	Low
Companionate love	High	Low	High
Fatuous love	Low	High	High
Consummate love	High	High	High

Note: According to Sternberg, the three basic components of love—intimacy, passion, and decision/commitment—combine to produce eight different varieties of love.

relationship, but lack an intimate emotional connection and passionate attraction. Sternberg believed that this type of love characterized couples at the end of a long-term relationship (or at the beginning of an arranged marriage). *Romantic love* (intimacy + passion) consists of feelings of intimate closeness and connection coupled with strong physical attraction. *Companionate love* (intimacy + decision/commitment) relationships are essentially long-term, stable, and committed friendships that are characterized by high amounts of emotional intimacy, the decision to love the partner, and the commitment to remain in the relationship. This type of love is often seen between best friends or between partners in long-term romantic relationships in which sexual attraction has faded. Couples who experience *fatuous love* (passion + decision/commitment) base their commitment to each other on passion and desire rather than deep emotional intimacy. These "whirlwind" relationships are typically unstable and at risk for termination. Finally, *consummate love* (intimacy + passion + decision/commitment) results from the combination of high levels of all three components. According to Sternberg, this is the type of fulfilling, "complete" love that many individuals strive to attain, particularly in their romantic relationships.

Because the three basic components of love occur in varying degrees within a relationship, most love relationships will not fit cleanly into one particular category but will reflect some combination of categories.

The Colors (Styles) of Love

Using the metaphor of color, Lee (1973, 1977, 1988) developed a system in which the various types of love were classified as either primary or secondary. Like Sternberg, Lee not only drew on existing discourse but also employed psychometric techniques in his quest to understand the nature of love (including cluster analysis of love "symptoms" derived from literature, as well as factor analysis of data resulting from a card-sorting task in which men and women described their own personal love stories by sorting 1,500 cards containing brief descriptions of love-related events, behaviors, or emotions). The results of these analyses produced a taxonomy containing three primary and three secondary colors or styles of love.

The first of the three primary love styles is *eros*. Resembling passionate love, eros is an intense experience whose most typical symptom is an immediate and powerful emotional and physical attraction to the loved one. According to Lee, the erotic lover tends to be "turned on" by a particular physical type, is prone to fall instantly and completely in love with a stranger (in other words, experiences "love at first sight"), rapidly becomes preoccupied with pleasant thoughts about that individual, feels an intense need for daily contact with the beloved, and wishes the relationship to remain exclusive. Erotic love also has a strong sexual component. For example, the erotic lover experiences intense sexual attraction to the loved one, usually seeks some form of sexual involvement fairly early in the relationship, and enjoys expressing his or her affection through sexual contact. Lee (1988) described the typical erotic lover as being "eager to get to know the beloved quickly, intensely—and undressed" (p. 50).

The second primary color of love is *ludus*, a variety of love characterized by emotional control and a marked absence (and even active avoidance) of commitment. The typical ludic lover views love as a game that should be played with skill and cool detachment (and often with several partners at the same time). As the quintessential commitment-phobe, the ludic lover has no intention of including the current partner(s) in any future life plans or events and is bothered if a partner should show any sign of growing involvement, need, or attachment. In addition, people who adopt this love style tend to avoid seeing their partners too often, believe that lies and deception are justified, and expect their partners to maintain control of their emotions at all times. Like erotic love, ludus also has a physical or sexual component. However, unlike erotic lovers, ludic lovers tend to be attracted to a wide variety of physical types and they view sexual activity as an opportunity for pleasure rather than for intense emotional bonding.

Storge is the third primary love color. Described by Lee (1973) as "love without fever or folly" (p. 77), storge resembles the concept of "affection" described earlier by Lewis. This variety of love is stable and durable, and is based on a solid foundation of trust, respect, affection, and commitment. Indeed, the typical storgic lover views and treats the partner as a valued friend, does not experience the intense emotions or physical attraction to the partner associated with erotic love, prefers to talk about and engage in shared interests with the partner rather than to express direct feelings, is shy about sex, and tends to demonstrate his or her affection in nonsexual ways. To the storgic lover, love is an extension of friendship.

Like the primary colors, the primary love styles can be combined to form secondary colors or styles of love. The three secondary styles identified by Lee contain features of the primary styles, but they also possess their own unique characteristics. *Pragma* is a variety of love that combines elements of storge and ludus. Lee (1973) referred to this love style as "the love that goes shopping for a suitable mate" (p. 124). The pragmatic lover has a practical outlook to love and seeks a compatible lover. Essentially, he or she creates a shopping list of desirable attributes and selects a mate based on how well that individual meets these requirements (and, not surprisingly, the pragmatic lover will drop a partner who fails to "measure up" to expectation).

Mania is a secondary love style that reflects the combination of eros and ludus. However, manic lovers lack the self-confidence associated with eros and the emotional self-control associated with ludus. This obsessive, jealous love style is characterized by self-defeating emotions, desperate attempts to force affection from the loved one, and the inability to believe in or trust any affection the partner or loved one actually does display. The manic lover is desperate to fall in love and to be loved, begins immediately to imagine a future with the partner, wants to see the partner daily, tries to force the partner to show love and commitment, distrusts the partner's sincerity, and is extremely possessive. Lee (1973) felt that this was the most potentially destructive love style, calling it "irrational, extremely jealous, obsessive, and often unhappy" (p. 15).

The last secondary color of love is *agape*, which combines eros and storge. Agape is similar to Lewis's concept of "charity," and represents an altruistic, selfless love style that implies an obligation to love and care for others without any expectation of reciprocity or reward. This love style is universal in the sense that the typical agapic lover feels that everyone is worthy of love and that loving and caring for others is a duty of the mature person. With respect to personal love relationships, agapic lovers will put aside their own needs and interests and devote themselves to the partner, even stepping aside in favor of a rival who seems more likely to meet the partner's needs. Although Lee felt that many people respected and strived to attain the agapic ideal, he believed that the give-and-take that characterizes most romantic relationships precluded the occurrence of purely altruistic love.

Measuring Love Styles

The availability of a reliable measurement instrument is extremely important for the scientist (or anyone, for that matter) who is interested in understanding love and identifying the experiences and events with which love is associated. Not surprisingly, given its strong psychometric basis, Lee's classification system inspired the development of a multi-item scale that is designed to measure each of the proposed love styles (Hatkoff & Lasswell, 1977; Lasswell & Lasswell, 1976). This scale, originally created in the 1970s, was subsequently revised extensively by Clyde and Susan Hendrick and their colleagues (Hendrick & Hendrick, 1986, 1990; Hendrick, Hendrick, & Dicke, 1998; Hendrick, Hendrick, Foote, & Slapion-Foote, 1984). Called the Love Attitudes Scale, this instrument contains items that reflect the important components of the six love styles as originally conceptualized by Lee. Sample items include:

- My partner and I have the right physical "chemistry" between us. *Eros*
- I feel that my partner and I were meant for each other. *Eros*
- I believe that what my partner does not know about me would not hurt him/her. *Ludus*
- When my partner gets too dependent on me, I want to back off a little. *Ludus*
- Our friendship merged gradually into love over time. *Storge*
- Our love is really a deep friendship, not a mysterious, mystical emotion. *Storge*
- In choosing my partner, I believed it was best to love someone with a similar background. *Pragma*
- A main consideration in choosing my partner was how he/she would reflect on my family. *Pragma*
- When my partner does not pay attention to me, I feel sick all over. *Mania*
- I cannot relax if I suspect that my partner is with someone else. *Mania*
- I cannot be happy unless I place my partner's happiness before my own. *Agape*
- I would endure all things for the sake of my partner. *Agape*

The Love Attitudes Scale has been used in many empirical investigations. In general, the results of these studies reveal that love experiences vary as a function of individual difference and group variables. For example, many researchers find that women score higher on the love styles of storge and pragma than do men, whereas men tend to score higher on ludus (Hendrick & Hendrick, 1988, 1987, 1995; Rotenberg & Korol, 1995). There also are multicultural and cross-cultural differences in love style. Within the United States, Asian American adults often score lower on eros and higher on pragma and storge than Caucasian, Latino, and African American adults (Dion & Dion, 1993; Hendrick & Hendrick, 1986). Latino groups, on the other hand, often score higher on ludus than Caucasian groups (Contreras, Hendrick, & Hendrick, 1996). Cross-cultural comparisons reveal that Americans tend to endorse a more storgic and manic approach to love than do the French, who, in turn, tend to demonstrate higher levels of agape (Murstein, Merighi, & Vyse, 1991).

Interestingly, only a few researchers have examined the role of love styles in ongoing romantic relationships. In general, there is a tendency for individuals to pair with people who have a similar love style—erotic lovers fall passionately in love with other erotic lovers, agapic people pair with other equally selfless individuals, and so on (Davis & Latty-Mann, 1987; Morrow, Clark, & Brock, 1995). In addition, there is some evidence that love styles are associated with relationship outcomes. For example, research on dating couples conducted by Hendrick and her colleagues revealed that men and women who adopted an erotic style of loving tended to feel particularly satisfied with their romantic relationships (Hendrick, Hendrick, & Adler, 1988). In addition, the partners of women who scored high on eros (erotic or passionate love) or agape (selfless love) were highly satisfied, whereas the partners of women who scored high on ludus (game-playing love) were not very satisfied. More recently, Brenda Meeks, Susan Hendrick, and Clyde Hendrick (1998) examined the correlation between relationship satisfaction and various love styles in a sample of dating couples. Their results revealed that men and women who endorsed an erotic or storgic approach to love also tended to be highly satisfied with their relationships. Those who possessed a ludic love style, however, were less satisfied. Taken as a whole, these results suggest that game playing, lack of friendship, and lack of passion are not conducive to interpersonal happiness.

When considering this particular area of research, it is important to keep in mind that not everyone possesses one style of loving. Some people may have several love styles that characterize their approach to relationships. It is also possible for a person's love style to change over his or her lifetime or during the course of a given relationship. For example, the emotional intensity and passionate attraction associated with an erotic love style, or the jealous preoccupation associated with a manic love style, may occur more often during the beginning stages of a romance when the partners are uncertain about their feelings and the future of their relationship. Over time, however, these feelings may be replaced by more storgic or agapic feelings as the partners grow closer and their attachment stabilizes.

Both Sternberg and Lee developed their love classification systems by examining the self-reported experiences of adult men and women involved in romantic (dating, cohabiting, or marital) relationships. Similarly, the measurement instrument developed to reflect Lee's theory of love, the Love Attitudes Scale, also focuses on these kinds of relationships (for example, respondents are instructed to answer the items with respect to their current or previous romantic partner). Thus, the classification systems proposed by Sternberg and Lee probably are more appropriately considered taxonomies of adult romantic love rather than of general love varieties.

The Prototype Approach: Identifying Mental Models of Love

Like psychometric theorists, researchers who adopt the prototype approach also rely on empirical methods in their efforts to understand love. Unlike Sternberg, Lee, and other psychometric theorists, however, prototype researchers typically do not confine their investigations to romantic varieties of love. In addition, they focus more specifically on people's knowledge, beliefs, and attitudes—their mental representations—of the concept of love. Researchers who follow this approach seek to determine what people think when they are asked about love, how people cognitively differentiate love from related concepts (e.g., liking), how mental representations of love are formed over time, and how these conceptualizations or mental representations influence people's behavior within their ongoing interpersonal relationships.

The Hierarchy of Love

Eleanor Rosch (1973, 1975, 1978) was an early pioneer in the use of prototype analysis for understanding natural language concepts. According to Rosch, natural language concepts (for example, *love, dog,* or *apple*) have both a vertical and a horizontal dimension. The vertical dimension has to do with the hierarchical organization of concepts; that is, with relations among different levels of concepts. Concepts at one level may be included within or subsumed by those at another, higher level. For example, the set of concepts *fruit, apple,* and *Red Delicious* illustrates an abstract-to-concrete hierarchy with superordinate, basic, and subordinate levels, as does the set of concepts *mammal, dog,* and *Golden Retriever.*

Using the methods originally developed by Rosch, some social scientists have investigated the hierarchical structure of the concept of love. Psychologist Phillip Shaver and his colleagues found evidence that *love* is a basic-level concept contained within the superordinate category of *emotion* and subsuming a variety of subordinate concepts that reflect types or varieties of love (e.g., *passion, infatuation, liking*) (Shaver, Schwartz, Kirson, & O'Connor, 1987). In other words, most people consider passion, infatuation, and liking to be types of love, which, in turn, is viewed as a type of positive emotion.

The Prototype of Love

Concepts also vary along a horizontal dimension. This dimension concerns the differentiation of concepts at the same level of inclusiveness (e.g., the dimension on which such subordinate level concepts as *Red Delicious, Fuji,* and *Granny Smith* apples vary, or along which the concepts of *Golden Retriever, Collie,* and *Poodle* dogs vary). According to Rosch, many natural language concepts have an internal structure whereby individual members of that category are ordered in terms of the degree to which they resemble the prototypic member of the category. A *prototype* is the best, clearest example of the concept—the most applelike apple (e.g., Red Delicious) or the "doggiest" dog (e.g., Golden Retriever).

People use prototypes to help them decide whether a new item or experience belongs or "fits" within a particular concept. For example, in trying to decide whether or not she is in love with her partner, a woman might compare the feelings ("I'm happy when he's here and sad when he's not"), thoughts ("I think he's very attractive," "I wonder what our children would look like"), and behaviors ("I arrange my schedule so that we can spend time together," "We go everywhere together") that she has experienced during their relationship with her prototype—her mental model—of "being in love" ("People who are in love miss each other when they're apart, think about each other a lot, imagine a future life together, and spend a lot of time with each other"). If what she is experiencing matches her prototype, she will probably conclude that she is, in fact, in love with her partner.

The prototype approach has been used to explore the horizontal structure of a variety of relational concepts, including love. Beverley Fehr and James Russell (1991), for example, asked men and women to generate as many types of love as they could in a specified time and then asked another sample of individuals to rate these love varieties in terms of "prototypicality" or "goodness of example." Of the ninety-three subtypes of love that participants generated, *maternal love* was rated as the best or most prototypical example of love, followed by *parental love, friendship, sisterly love, romantic love, brotherly love,* and *familial love. Infatuation* and *puppy love* were considered two of the least prototypical examples of love.

Researchers also have identified the prototypic features (as opposed to types) of love. For example, Fehr (1988) asked one group of participants to list the characteristics of the concept love and a second group of participants to rate how central each feature was to the concept of love. Features that her participants believed were central or prototypical to love included the following:

- Trust
- Caring
- Honesty
- Respect
- Concern for the other's well-being
- Loyalty
- Commitment
- Acceptance

Features that were considered unimportant or peripheral to the concept of love included:

- Fear
- Uncertainty
- Dependency
- Seeing only the other's good qualities
- Euphoria

Researchers who use the prototype approach have provided a wealth of information about people's thoughts and beliefs about love, as well as the ways in which individuals differentiate love from related concepts like joy, anger, and liking. However, this approach has not yet been able to successfully identify how people actually form their conceptualizations of love, and how these mental representations guide and influence people's behavior in real-life relationships.

As can be seen from the foregoing discussion, scholars throughout history, and across disciplines, who have sought to understand love have not always come to the same conclusions. They disagree about the exact number of different kinds of love that exist. Capellanus and James, for example, contented themselves with a mere two varieties, whereas Krafft-Ebing and Lewis argued in favor of four distinct types, and Sternberg and Ellis each identified close to a dozen types. They also disagree about what to label the varieties of love that they believe to exist, and in many cases they have not been able to specify the unique causes, characteristics, and consequences of the various types of love.

These areas of disagreement notwithstanding, early and contemporary scholars have reached some consensus with respect to the topic of love. First, they all agree that the experience of love is intimately associated with the quality of individual human life and that, consequently, the study of love is a necessary and important scientific endeavor. Second, they agree that love exists in many different forms or varieties (a view that is supported by analyses of people's mental representations of love). Third, typologies of love and people's reports of their experiences in romantic relationships suggest that love (at least, adult romantic love) is composed at a minimum of two distinct varieties. The first type (generally called passionate or erotic love) is emotionally intense, fragile, and sexually charged, and the second type (known as companionate, friendship-based, or affectionate love) is durable, slow to develop, and infused with warmth and intimacy. These two varieties of love have received a great deal of attention from contemporary love researchers, in part because of their important association with personal and species survival—as noted by Lewis (1988), "Without Eros none of us would have been begotten and without Affection none of us would have been reared" (p. 58). We turn now to a consideration of these two kinds of love.

PASSIONATE LOVE

Out of all the many varieties of love that theorists and researchers have identified, *passionate love* has received the most sustained attention. This focus is justified by the fact that passionate love appears to be a universal human experience. Social scientists have found evidence for the existence of passionate love in virtually all known human societies (Jankowiak & Fischer, 1992; Sprecher et al., 1994). Additionally, many people place a high degree of value on this particular kind of love. For example, increasing numbers of men and women around the world are basing their selection of marital and other long-term romantic partners on passionate love (Goodwin, 1999). Cross-cultural surveys reveal that most people say that they will not marry unless they are in love with their partner (Levine, Sato, Hashimoto, & Verma, 1995; Simpson, Campbell, & Berscheid, 1986). And finally, passionate love appears to be a unique experience. As we will discuss below, this particular variety of love possesses several features that clearly differentiate it from other kinds of love.

What Is Passionate Love? Classic and Contemporary Theories

Early theorists suggested that passionate love consists of a number of unique features, including the following:

- swift and sudden onset
- fairly brief life span
- idealization of the loved one
- mental preoccupation with the loved one or the love relationship
- intense and often fluctuating emotions
- physiological arousal and its bodily sensations
- sexual desire or lust
- exclusivity (a focus on one specific individual)

For example, Krafft-Ebing (1945) posited that sensual love (his label for passionate love) consisted largely of the romantic idealization of the loved one's qualities coupled with intense sexual desire, and he stated that this particular variety of love was "never true or lasting" and died quickly. In the 1940s, noted love theorist and psychotherapist Theodor Reik (1944, 1945) expressed a similar view of passionate love, arguing that it was a mixture of three unique characteristics—sexual desire or the "sex urge," a short life span, and idealization of the loved one—combined with affection (which he believed was present in many types of love). A decade later, Ellis (1954) also concluded that the distinguishing features of passionate love were the unrealistically positive evaluation and "fictionalization" of the loved one, intense and changeable emotions and feelings, fragility, exclusivity, and sexual desire. He believed that sexual desire, in particular, was the most powerful force behind the development of passionate love, and that this type of love would inevitably perish once desire was sated—"sexual and marital consummation indubitably, in the vast majority of instances, maims, bloodies, and finally kills romanticism" (p. 116).

Like their predecessors, contemporary love theorists have continued to emphasize the intense, idealistic, emotional, sexual, and short-lived nature of passionate love. As we have discussed earlier, Lee (1973, 1977) viewed erotic (passionate) love as a combination of emotional intensity, sexual attraction, and mental preoccupation. Sternberg, too, considered emotional intimacy and passionate attraction to be important components of what he termed romantic love. He also was keenly aware of its fleeting and fragile nature. Drawing an analogy to substance addiction, Sternberg (1988) suggested that the rapid development of passion is inevitably followed by habituation, so that over time, the partner is no longer as physically and mentally "stimulating" as he or she once was.

Other theorists have reached similar conclusions. For example, psychologists Kenneth and Karen Dion (1973) suggested that passionate love is a mysterious and volatile experience characterized by such symptoms as daydreaming, sleep difficulties, impaired ability to concentrate, and fluctuating emotions. Similarly, in their analysis of the elements of passionate love relationships, Keith Davis and Michael Todd (1982) proposed that the exclusivity that characterizes this type of love can produce both intensely positive and negative emotional states (ranging from euphoria to jealousy, possessiveness, and dependency).

Among contemporary theorists, social psychologists Ellen Berscheid and Elaine Hatfield (formerly Walster) (1971, 1974) have devoted the most sustained attention to defining passionate love. In their original theoretical papers on the nature of passionate love, they proposed that this variety of love blossoms when a person is highly aroused physiologically and when situational cues (like the presence of another individual) indicate that "being in love" is the appropriate label for that arousal. These theorists suggested that emotions that are associated with strong physiological arousal (including fear, frustration, and excitement) can produce and enhance passionate attraction between two people. In addition, like Ellis, Lee, and Sternberg, Berscheid and Hatfield theorized that sexuality (in particular, sexual attraction or desire) is strongly linked with the experience of passionate love. More recent discourse provided by these authors and their colleagues continues to emphasize the transitory, emotional, and sexual nature of this kind of love (Berscheid, 1988; Berscheid & Regan, 2005; Hatfield & Rapson, 1993; Regan & Berscheid, 1999).

Dorothy Tennov (1979, 1998) characterized *limerence* (the state of being passionately in love) as a subjective experience that is marked by persistent, intrusive thoughts about the loved one, an acute longing for reciprocation of one's feelings, mood fluctuations, intense awareness of the loved one's actions, physical reactions, emotional peaks and valleys depending on the loved one's actions and perceived reciprocity, and idealization of the loved one's qualities. Exclusivity is one particularly important hallmark of limerence. Like many of the earlier theorists, Tennov (1998) suggested that there can be only one object of passionate love at a time, and that once someone is selected, "limerence cements the reaction and locks the emotional gates against competitors" (p. 86). She also believed that sexual attraction is a necessary component of limerence:

> Sexual attraction is not "enough," to be sure. Selection standards for
> limerence are, according to informants, not identical to those by which

"mere" sexual partners are evaluated, and sex is seldom the main focus of limerence. Either the potential for sexual mating is felt to be there, however, or the state described is not limerence. (1979, p. 25)

In sum, passionate love is believed by most theorists to be a short-lived state that is characterized by idealization of the loved one, preoccupation and obsessive thinking, and intense emotions. In addition, passionate love is presumed to be an exclusive rather than an inclusive or generalized experience. That is, unlike affectionate love, agapic love, familial love, and so on, which can be felt for many other people at the same time, passionate love is assumed to be directed at one and only one particular individual. Finally, most theorists propose that sexuality (most notably, sexual desire or attraction) is a distinguishing feature of passionate love.

The Measurement of Passionate Love

There are two common methods researchers use to measure passionate love, both involving self-report. The first includes single-item measures in which respondents are asked to report the quantity or the intensity of passionate love they experience for their partner using a rating scale. Examples of such items include:

Q. How much passionate love do you currently feel for your partner?

1	2	3	4	5	6	7	8	9
None at all								A great deal

Q. Rate the intensity of your feelings of passionate love for your current partner.

1	2	3	4	5	6	7	8	9
Not at all intense								Extremely intense

Q. How deeply are you in love with_____?

1	2	3	4	5	6	7	8	9
Not at all in love								Very much in love

Q. How strong are your feelings of passionate love for_____?

1	2	3	4	5	6	7	8	9
Extremely weak								Extremely strong

Single-item measures such as these are easy to administer and appear to be relatively valid (that is, they seem to provide a general assessment of the extent to which someone is experiencing feelings of passionate love). However, many researchers prefer to use larger, multi-item scales that have been developed specifically to measure the various elements of passionate love that theorists believe to be important. Although several different passionate love scales have been constructed over the years, the most commonly utilized and empirically sound measures are the erotic love subscale of the Love Attitudes Scale (discussed earlier in this chapter) and the Passionate Love Scale developed by Elaine Hatfield and Susan Sprecher (1986).

The Passionate Love Scale represents the most complete measure of passionate love currently available. Drawing on previous theory, existing measurement instruments, and in-depth personal interviews, Hatfield and Sprecher created a series of thirty items designed to assess the various components of the passionate love experience. For example:

- Sometimes my body trembles with excitement at the sight of____.
- Since I have been involved with___, my emotions have been on a roller coaster.
- Sometimes I cannot control my thoughts; they are obsessively on_____.
- For me,____is the perfect romantic partner.
- In the presence of____, I yearn to touch and be touched.

The items clearly reflect what theorists believe are the essential ingredients of passionate love: Intense physiological arousal, emotional turbulence and intensity, cognitive preoccupation, idealization of the loved one, and physical or sexual attraction.

Research on Passionate Love

Many of the suppositions that theorists have made about the nature of passionate love have received empirical support. For example, passionate love does appear to be more fragile and less durable than other kinds of love. Research conducted with married couples generally reveals that levels of passionate love decline over time (Hatfield, Traupmann, & Sprecher, 1984). Researchers who have surveyed dating couples find similar results. For example, with a sample of 197 dating couples, Susan Sprecher and Pamela Regan (1998) examined whether the number of months that each couple had been dating was related to the amount of passionate love they reportedly felt for each other. These researchers found evidence that passionate love was related to the age or duration of the relationship; specifically, the longer a couple had been together, the lower were their passionate love scores (although passionate love scores were high in all couples). It is important to keep in mind that these results do not imply that passionate love is completely lacking between partners involved in long-term relationships. Rather, these findings simply provide evidence that the intense feelings and sensations characteristic of the first stages of "falling in love" gradually stabilize over time.

Researchers also have found evidence in support of the notion that passionate love is a highly emotional state. Interestingly, whether a passionate lover's emotions and sentiments are positive or negative depends to some extent on whether his or her feelings are reciprocated by the loved one. *Requited* (reciprocated) love is an almost uniformly positive experience. In one study, men and women who were asked to identify the essential features of requited passionate love cited a panoply of positive emotions ranging in intensity from warmth and tenderness to joy, rapture, and giddiness (Regan, Kocan, & Whitlock, 1998). Similarly, couples who are in love with one another report experiencing many more positive than negative emotions (Sprecher & Regan, 1998). In fact, jealousy appears to be the only negative emotion that is consistently associated with the experience of requited passionate love; most partners report having felt jealous at some point during their relationship.

Unrequited passionate love has several of the same positive emotional features as requited passionate love, yet, at the same time, is a much more intensely negative experience. In one of the first studies to explore unrequited passionate love, Roy Baumeister, Sara Wotman, and Arlene Stillwell (1993) asked a group of people who had been in this situation to write autobiographical accounts of their experiences. Many (44 percent) would-be suitors reported that their unreciprocated passion caused them pain, suffering, and disappointment; jealousy and anger (which were usually directed at the loved one's chosen partner); and a sense of frustration. Similarly, 22 percent experienced worries and fears about rejection. In addition to these unpleasant experiences, however, the lovelorn suitors also reported many pleasant emotional outcomes; in fact, positive feelings far outweighed negative ones in the accounts they gave of their experience. For example, happiness, excitement, the blissful anticipation of seeing the beloved, sheer elation at the state of being in love, and other positive emotions were reported by the majority (98 percent) of would-be suitors. Over half (53 percent) also looked back upon their unrequited love with some degree of positive feeling. Thus, passionate love—whether it is requited or not—is clearly an emotional experience.

Passionate love is also a sexual experience. A number of studies demonstrate that both behavioral (e.g., intercourse and other sexual activities) and physiological (i.e., sexual excitement, sexual arousal) aspects of sexuality are associated with feelings of passionate love. For example, people who are more passionately in love report experiencing higher levels of sexual excitement when thinking about the partner, and engaging in more frequent sexual activities with that partner, than individuals who are less passionately in love (Aron & Henkemeyer, 1995; Hatfield & Sprecher, 1986; Sprecher & Regan, 1998). In addition, sexual activity is one of the primary ways in which couples express love to one another. Researchers Peter Marston, Michael Hecht, Melodee Manke, Susan McDaniel, and Heidi Reeder (1998) interviewed a sample of in-love couples about the ways in which they communicated their feelings of passion to each other. The most common method of expressing passionate attraction was through sexual activities, including "making love."

As the majority of love theorists have speculated, one particular aspect of sexuality—sexual desire or sexual attraction (i.e., lust)—appears to have the strongest association with passionate love. Many men and women certainly seem to think so. For example, Robert Ridge and Ellen Berscheid (1989) asked a sample of college-aged men and women whether they believed that there was a difference between the experience of "being in love" with someone and the experience of "loving" someone. Fully 87 percent emphatically claimed that there was indeed a difference between the two experiences. In addition, when asked to specify the nature of that difference, participants uniformly cited sexual attraction as descriptive of the passionate, "being in love" experience and not of the "loving" experience. Similar results have been reported by Regan et al. (1998). These researchers asked a sample of men and women to list in a free response format all of the features that they considered to be characteristic or prototypical of the state of "being in love." Out of 119 spontaneously generated features, *sexual desire* received the second highest frequency rating (66 percent; *trust* was first, cited by 80 percent). In other words, when thinking about passionate love, two-thirds of the participants automatically thought of sexual desire.

Person perception experiments provide additional support for these prototype results. Person perception experiments are commonly used in social psychological research and essentially involve manipulating people's perceptions of a relationship and then measuring the impact of that manipulation on their subsequent evaluations and beliefs. In one such experiment, Regan (1998) provided a sample of forty-eight undergraduate men and women with two self-report questionnaires ostensibly completed by "Rob" and "Nancy," a student couple enrolled at their university. The members of this couple reported that they were passionately in love with each other, that they loved each other, or that they liked each other. Participants then estimated the likelihood that the members of the couple experience sexual desire for each other and the amount of desire that they feel for each other. Analyses revealed that participants perceived partners who are passionately in love as more likely to experience sexual desire than partners who love each other or who like each other. Similarly, partners who are passionately in love were believed to experience a greater amount of sexual desire for each other than partners who love each other or who like each other. Sexual desire is viewed, at least by young men and women, as an important feature or component of passionate love relationships—and not of relationships characterized by feelings of loving (i.e., companionate love) or liking (i.e., friendship).

Not only do people believe that passionate love is characterized by sexual desire, but most men and women report experiencing sexual desire for the people with whom they are passionately in love. For example, Ellen Berscheid and Sarah

Meyers (1996) asked a large sample of undergraduate men and women to list the initials of all the people they currently loved, the initials of all those with whom they were currently in love, and the initials of all those toward whom they currently felt sexual attraction/desire. Their results indicated that 85 percent of the persons listed in the "in love" category also were listed in the "sexually desire" category, whereas only 2 percent of those listed in the "love" category (and not cross-listed in the "in love" category) were listed in the "sexually desire" category. Thus, the objects of respondents' feelings of passionate love (but not their feelings of love) also tended to be the objects of their desire.

Research with actual dating couples yields similar results. Regan (2000) found that the self-reported amount of sexual desire experienced by men and women for their dating partners was significantly positively correlated with the level of passionate love they felt for those individuals. Their feelings of desire were unrelated, however, to the amount of companionate love and liking they experienced for their partners. In other words, the more sexual desire a person reported feeling for his or her partner, the more strongly he or she reported being in love with (but not liking or loving) that individual. In sum, research reveals that passionate love is a sexualized experience that is strongly associated with feelings of sexual desire for the partner, tends to result in the occurrence of sexual activity, and appears to be linked with sexual arousal and excitement.

COMPANIONATE LOVE

In addition to passionate love, most early and contemporary love theorists include a type of love known today as *companionate love* in their classification schemes. Variously described as affectionate love, friendship love, true love, attachment, storge, and conjugal love, companionate love reflects "the affection and tenderness we feel for those with whom our lives are deeply entwined" (Hatfield & Rapson, 1993).

What Is Companionate Love? Theory and Research

The majority of love theorists conceive of companionate love as containing several basic characteristics, including a relatively slow onset, durability, interdependence, and feelings of affection, intimacy, and commitment. Krafft-Ebing (1945) called this type of love "true love" and stated that it "is rooted in the recognition of the moral and mental qualities of the beloved person, and is equally ready to share pleasures and sorrows and even to make sacrifices" (p. 12). This conceptualization resembles Lewis's definition of "affection" and Ellis's description of conjugal love, as well as the definitions provided by contemporary love theorists. For example, relationship scholar Sharon Brehm (1985) describes this variety of love as built upon a solid foundation of respect, admiration, and interpersonal trust and rewards. Sternberg (1988) similarly depicts companionate love as composed of feelings of emotional intimacy coupled with a firm commitment to the relationship and the partner. He suggests that companionate lovers possess mutual understanding, share themselves and their possessions with one another, give and receive emotional support, and demonstrate various other signs of intimate connection, affection, and mutuality.

Other contemporary theorists have speculated that, unlike passionate love, companionate love may grow stronger over time because it is grounded in intimacy processes (including caring, understanding, and attachment) that require time to develop fully (Hatfield & Rapson, 1993). Still others have proposed that romantic relationships may progress in a linear fashion from passionate love to companionate love. For example, love theorist Bernard Murstein (1988) wrote:

> With unimpeded access to each other and as a result of habituation, bit by bit generalized, overriding passion and longing evaporate and are replaced by liking or trust, although in good marriages, passion may return on specific occasions. . . . Out of the evolving network of shared experiences as a couple—children, family, married life—comes something less ephemeral and more permanent than romantic love.

Research on companionate love is less plentiful than that conducted on passionate love. Nonetheless, at least two general conclusions can be drawn. First, there is some evidence that companionate love is relatively impervious to the passage of time. Although the dating couples in Sprecher and Regan's (1998) study reported lower levels of passionate love over time, their companionate love scores did not change as a function of the length of their relationship. It made no difference how long a couple had been together—the partners continued to report feeling the same high level of affectionate, warm love for each other. Thus, time does not appear to have had any negative impact on companionate love.

Second, in accordance with theoretical supposition, companionate love is associated with uniformly positive emotional experiences—and these positive feelings and sentiments are much less extreme than those commonly produced by passionate love. Helmut Lamm and Ulrich Wiesmann (1997) asked university students to explain in writing how they could tell that they "loved" (as opposed to "liked" or were "in love with") another person. The most common indicator of companionate love generated by the participants was *positive mood* (listed by 53 percent). Distinctive indicators (elements that were listed significantly more frequently for companionate love [loving] than for passionate love [being in love] or friendship [liking]) included such positive emotional states as *trust* (41 percent), *tolerance* (21 percent), and *relaxedness or calmness* (12 percent). The participants in a study conducted by psychologist

Donna Castañeda (1993) provided almost identical answers when asked to indicate the qualities and characteristics they believed to be important in a companionate love relationship. Specifically, participants mentioned *trust, mutual respect, communication and sharing, honesty,* and *affection,* along with a number of other positive emotions and experiences.

Research with dating couples substantiates these survey results. Sprecher and Regan (1998) found that positive emotions (including joy, trust, liking, contentment, satisfaction, and respect) were positively associated with the amount of companionate love reported by a sample of romantically involved couples. In addition, not only did companionate lovers feel high degrees of emotional intimacy and warmth, but they also reported relatively more feelings of sexual intimacy than did passionate lovers. Specifically, the higher a couple's companionate love scores, the more the partners reported being able to communicate openly and honestly with each other about sexuality. Thus, feelings of intimacy—emotional and, perhaps, sexual—are a hallmark of the companionate love experience.

The Measurement of Companionate Love

Like passionate love, companionate love can be measured with single items that provide a general sense of how much a person loves his or her partner:

Q. How much caring, affectionate love do you feel for ___?

1	2	3	4	5	6	7	8	9
None at all								A great deal

Q. How deeply do you love ___?

1	2	3	4	5	6	7	8	9
Not at all								Very much

Companionate love can also be assessed with multi-item scales that are designed to reflect the features that theorists believe to be important elements of this particular variety of love. For example, the storge subscale on the Love Attitudes Scale (discussed earlier in this chapter) has been used as a measure of companionate love. Perhaps the most commonly utilized measure of companionate love, however, is the thirteen-item Love Scale created by psychologist Zick Rubin (1970). Sprecher and Regan (1998) subsequently modified this scale by adding an item that assesses interpersonal trust and removing several items that reflected a more passionate love experience. Sample items on the resulting Companionate Love Scale include:

- feel that I can confide in ___ about virtually everything.
- would forgive ___ for practically anything.
- care about ___.
- feel that I can trust ___ completely.

SUMMARY

In an effort to understand the nature of love, scholars from a variety of disciplines have proposed various typologies or classification schemes that specify types of love. Although there is disagreement about the number and the nature of the different love types, there are several points of rapprochement. Virtually all early and contemporary love theorists agree that love is intricately associated with the quality of human life, that different varieties of love exist, and that at a minimum, there are two commonly experienced types of adult romantic love—a passionate variety that is intense, emotional, fragile, and sexually charged, and a companionate variety that is durable, stable, and infused with warmth, intimacy, affection, and trust. These theoretical suppositions are largely supported by empirical research on people's implicit conceptions of love and self-reports of ongoing experiences in love relationships. Of course, it is important to recognize that other types of love also exist and are experienced by men and women over the course of their lifetimes, ranging from the vague liking felt for casual acquaintances to the intense devotion often experienced for family members, children, and beloved pets. An important task for future researchers is to determine the unique features and consequences of these other important varieties of love.

REFERENCES

Aron, A., & Henkemeyer, L. (1995). Marital satisfaction and passionate love. *Journal of Social and Personal Relationships, 12*, 139–146.

Baumeister, R. F., Wotman, S. R., & Stillwell, A. M. (1993). Unrequited love: On heartbreak, anger, guilt, scriptlessness, and humiliation. *Journal of Personality and Social Psychology, 64*, 377–394.

Berscheid, E. (1988). Some comments on love's anatomy: Or, whatever happened to old-fashioned lust? In R. J. Sternberg & M. L. Barnes (Eds.), *The psychology of love* (pp. 359–374). New Haven, CT: Yale University Press.

Berscheid, E., & Meyers, S. A. (1996). A social categorical approach to a question about love. *Personal Relationships, 3*, 19–43.

Berscheid, E., & Regan, P. (2005). *The psychology of interpersonal relationships.* Upper Saddle River, NJ: Pearson.

Berscheid, E., & Walster, E. (1974). A little bit about love. In T. L. Huston (Ed.), *Foundations of interpersonal attraction* (pp. 355–381). New York: Academic Press.

Brehm, S. S. (1985). *Intimate relationships.* New York: Random House.

Capellanus, A. (ca. 1184/1960). *The art of courtly love.* (J. J. Parry, Trans.). New York: Columbia University Press.

Castañeda, D. M. (1993). The meaning of romantic love among Mexican-Americans. *Journal of Social Behavior and Personality, 8,* 257–272.

Contreras, R., Hendrick, S. S., & Hendrick, C. (1996). Perspectives on marital love and satisfaction in Mexican American and Anglo couples. *Journal of Counseling and Development, 74,* 408–415.

Davis, K. E., & Latty-Mann, H. (1987). Love styles and relationship quality: A contribution to validation. *Journal of Social and Personal Relationships, 4,* 409–428.

Davis, K. E., & Todd, M. J. (1982). Friendship and love relationships. In K. E. Davis & T. O. Mitchell (Eds.), *Advances in descriptive psychology* (Vol. 2, pp. 79–122). Greenwich, CT: JAI Press.

Dion, K. L., & Dion, K. K. (1973). Correlates of romantic love. *Journal of Consulting and Clinical Psychology, 41,* 51–56.

Dion, K. L., & Dion, K. K. (1993). Gender and ethnocultural comparisons in styles of love. *Psychology of Women Quarterly, 17,* 463–473.

Ellis, A. (1954). *The American sexual tragedy.* New York: Twayne Publishers.

Fehr, B. (1988). Prototype analysis of the concepts of love and commitment. *Journal of Personality and Social Psychology, 55,* 557–579.

Fehr, B., & Russell, J. A. (1991). The concept of love viewed from a prototype perspective. *Journal of Personality and Social Psychology, 60,* 424–438.

Fromm, E. (1956). *The art of loving.* New York: Harper & Row.

Goodwin, R. (1999). *Personal relationships across cultures.* London: Routledge.

Hatfield, E., & Rapson, R. L. (1993). *Love, sex, and intimacy: Their psychology, biology, and history.* New York: HarperCollins.

Hatfield, E., & Sprecher, S. (1986). Measuring passionate love in intimate relationships. *Journal of Adolescence, 9,* 383–410.

Hatfield, E., Traupmann, J., & Sprecher, S. (1984). Older women's perceptions of their intimate relationships. *Journal of Social and Clinical Psychology, 2,* 108–124.

Hatkoff, T. S., & Lasswell, T. E. (1977). Male-female similarities and differences in conceptualizing love. In M. Cook & G. Wilson (Eds.), *Love and attraction: An international conference* (pp. 221–227). Oxford, UK: Pergamon Press.

Hendrick, C., & Hendrick, S. S. (1986). A theory and method of love. *Journal of Personality and Social Psychology, 50,* 392–402.

Hendrick, C., & Hendrick, S. S. (1988). Lovers wear rose colored glasses. *Journal of Social and Personal Relationships, 5,* 161–183.

Hendrick, C., & Hendrick, S. S. (1990). A relationship-specific version of the Love Attitudes Scale. *Journal of Social Behavior and Personality, 5,* 239–254.

Hendrick, C., Hendrick, S. S., & Dicke, A. (1998). The love attitudes scale: Short form. *Journal of Social and Personal Relationships, 15,* 147–159.

Hendrick, C., Hendrick, S. S., Foote, F. H., & Slapion-Foote, M. J. (1984). Do men and women love differently? *Journal of Social and Personal Relationships, 1,* 177–195.

Hendrick, S. S., & Hendrick, C. (1987). Love and sex attitudes and religious beliefs. *Journal of Social and Clinical Psychology, 5,* 391–398.

Hendrick, S. S., & Hendrick, C. (1995). Gender differences and similarities in sex and love. *Personal Relationships, 2,* 55–65.

Hendrick, S. S., Hendrick, C., & Adler, N. L. (1988). Romantic relationships: Love, satisfaction, and staying together. *Journal of Personality and Social Psychology, 54,* 980–988.

James, W. (1890/1950). *The principles of psychology* (Vol. 1). New York: Dover.

Jankowiak, W. R., & Fischer, E. F. (1992). A cross-cultural perspective on romantic love. *Ethology, 31,* 149–155.

Jessor, R., Costa, F., Jessor, L., & Donovan, J. E. (1983). Time of first intercourse: A prospective study. *Journal of Personality and Social Psychology, 44,* 608–626.

Krafft-Ebing, R. von (1886/1945). *Psychopathia sexualis* (12th ed.). New York: Pioneer Publications.

Lamm, H., & Wiesmann, U. (1997). Subjective attributes of attraction: How people characterize their liking, their love, and their being in love. *Personal Relationships, 4,* 271–284.

Lasswell, T. E., & Lasswell, M. E. (1976). I love you but I'm not in love with you. *Journal of Marriage and Family Counseling, 38,* 211–224.

Lee, J. A. (1973). *Colours of love: An exploration of the ways of loving.* Toronto: New Press.

Lee, J. A. (1977). A typology of styles of loving. *Personality and Social Psychology Bulletin, 3,* 173–182.

Lee, J. A. (1988). Love-styles. In R. J. Sternberg & M. L. Barnes (Eds.), *The psychology of love* (pp. 38–67). New Haven, CT: Yale University Press.

Leigh, B. C. (1989). Reasons for having and avoiding sex: Gender, sexual orientation, and relationship to sexual behavior. *Journal of Sex Research, 26,* 199–209.

Levine, R., Sato, S., Hashimoto, T., & Verma, J. (1995). Love and marriage in eleven cultures. *Journal of Cross-Cultural Psychology, 26,* 554–571.

Lewis, C. S. (1960/1988). *The four loves.* New York: Harcourt Brace.

Marston, P. J., Hecht, M. L., Manke, M. L., McDaniel, S., & Reeder, H. (1998). The subjective experience of intimacy, passion, and commitment in heterosexual love relationships. *Personal Relationships, 5,* 15–30.

Meeks, B. S., Hendrick, S. S., & Hendrick, C. (1998). Communication, love and relationship satisfaction. *Journal of Social and Personal Relationships, 15,* 755–773.

Morrow, G. D., Clark, E. M., & Brock, K. F. (1995). Individual and partner love styles: Implications for the quality of romantic involvements. *Journal of Social and Personal Relationships, 12,* 363–387.

Murstein, B. I. (1988). A taxonomy of love. In R. J. Sternberg & M. L. Barnes (Eds.), *The psychology of love* (pp. 13–37). New Haven, CT: Yale University Press.

Murstein, B. I., Merighi, J. R., & Vyse, S. A. (1991). Love styles in the United States and France: A cross-cultural comparison. *Journal of Social and Clinical Psychology, 10*, 37–46.

Regan, P. C. (1998). Of lust and love: Beliefs about the role of sexual desire in romantic relationships. *Personal Relationships, 5*, 139–157.

Regan, P. C. (2000). The role of sexual desire and sexual activity in dating relationships. *Social Behavior and Personality, 28*, 51–60.

Regan, P. C., & Berscheid, E. (1999). *Lust: What we know about human sexual desire.* Thousand Oaks, CA: Sage.

Regan, P. C., Kocan, E. R., & Whitlock, T. (1998). Ain't love grand! A prototype analysis of romantic love. *Journal of Social and Personal Relationships, 15*, 411–420.

Reik, T. (1944). *A psychologist looks at love.* New York: Farrar & Rinehart.

Reik, T. (1945). *Psychology of sex relations.* New York: Grove Press.

Reiss, I. L. (1964). The scaling of premarital sexual permissiveness. *Journal of Marriage and the Family, 26*, 188–198.

Ridge, R. D., & Berscheid, E. (1989, May). *On loving and being in love: A necessary distinction.* Paper presented at the annual convention of the Midwestern Psychological Association, Chicago, IL.

Rosch, E. (1973). On the internal structure of perceptual and semantic categories. In T. E. Moore (Ed.), *Cognitive development and the acquisition of language* (pp. 111–144). New York: Academic Press.

Rosch, E. (1975). Cognitive representations of semantic categories. *Journal of Experimental Psychology, 104*, 192–233.

Rosch, E. (1978). Principles of categorization. In E. Rosch & B. B. Lloyd (Eds.), *Cognition and categorization* (pp. 27–48). Hillsdale, NJ: Erlbaum.

Rotenberg, K. J., & Korol, S. (1995). The role of loneliness and gender in individuals' love styles. *Journal of Social Behavior and Personality, 10*, 537–546.

Rubin, Z. (1970). Measurement of romantic love. *Journal of Personality and Social Psychology, 16*, 265–273.

Shaver, P., Schwartz, J., Kirson, D., & O'Connor, C. (1987). Emotion knowledge: Further exploration of a prototype approach. *Journal of Personality and Social Psychology, 52*, 1061–1086.

Simpson, J. A., Campbell, B., & Berscheid, E. (1986). The association between romantic love and marriage: Kephart (1967) twice revisited. *Personality and Social Psychology Bulletin, 12*, 363–372.

Sprecher, S., Aron, A., Hatfield, E., Cortese, A., Potapova, E., & Levitskaya, A. (1994). Love: American style, Russian style, and Japanese style. *Personal Relationships, 1*, 349–369.

Sprecher, S., McKinney, K., Walsh, R., & Anderson, C. (1988). A revision of the Reiss premarital sexual permissiveness scale. *Journal of Marriage and the Family, 50*, 821–828.

Sprecher, S., & Regan, P. C. (1998). Passionate and companionate love in courting and young married couples. *Sociological Inquiry, 68*, 163–185.

Sternberg, R. J. (1986). A triangular theory of love. *Psychological Review, 93*, 119–135.

Sternberg, R. J. (1988). Triangulating love. In R. J. Sternberg & M. L. Barnes (Eds.), *The psychology of love* (pp. 119–138). New Haven, CT: Yale University Press.

Sternberg, R. J. (1998). *Cupid's arrow: The course of love through time.* Cambridge, UK: Cambridge University Press.

Sternberg, R. J., & Grajek, S. (1984). The nature of love. *Journal of Personality and Social Psychology, 47,* 312–329.

Tennov, D. (1979). *Love and limerence.* New York: Stein and Day.

Tennov, D. (1998). Love madness. In V. C. de Munck (Ed.), *Romantic love and sexual behavior: Perspectives from the social sciences* (pp. 77–88). Westport, CT: Praeger.

Walster, E., & Berscheid, E. (1971). Adrenaline makes the heart grow fonder. *Psychology Today, 5,* 47–62.

6

Sexual Desire Issues and Problems

Anthony F. Bogaert and Catherine Fawcett ◆

Have you ever met someone who just cannot get enough sex? Or someone who just is not interested in sex at all? Maybe you have noticed that your own sexual desire changes, sometimes clearly depending on your circumstances (e.g., just met a new and exciting partner) but sometimes for no apparent reason at all.

This variation in sexual desire (also called sex drive or libido) is what this chapter is about. We will review scientific knowledge related to sexual desire and interest—what might increase, or at least maintain, it and what might decrease it—along with addressing issues/problems related to sexual desire.

THE NATURE OF SEXUAL DESIRE (WHAT IS IT?)

For many people, sexual desire is the feeling of passion and lust (in everyday language, "horniness") that expresses itself within the context of heterosexual relationships. However, if we assume that this is the case for everyone, then we can have only a limited view of sexual desire issues and problems. For example, let us say you know a coworker—let us call him Fred—and you think you know him reasonably well, although you would not call him a good friend and you have never been over to his apartment. He does not talk much about himself, but you know that he lives alone and that he has never been married; he has never mentioned dating or ever having had a girlfriend. You also note that he never seems flirtatious with his female coworkers; and although you do not follow him around at work (hopefully!), you have never noticed him to have a "wandering eye" for any of the new and attractive women who happen to come to your place of employment. What are you to conclude? A classic case of a person with lifelong low sexual desire; perhaps you might even consider him to be an "asexual?" But wait. A reasonable alternative to this conclusion (at least if you are not blind to human diversity) is that he is gay and effectively hides his interest in, and sexual activity with, men from his coworkers. Another alternative is that he does have sexual desires for women, but he is very shy and withdrawn; thus, he may have an active fantasy and masturbation life but does not express this desire within the context of his public life; still another alternative is that he has some level of desire for women, but that this sexual desire is secondary to a strong preference for some illegal activity (e.g., voyeurism) or a nonhuman object (e.g., a fetish), and he again expresses these desires in a very private manner.

How can we incorporate all of these alternatives, along with, of course, the expression of the sexual desires that often occur in standard heterosexual relationships? Kaplan (1995) argues that sexual desire is "an interest in sexual activity, leading the individual to seek out sexual activity or to be pleasurably receptive to it." Note that in this definition there is no assumption about the gender of the partner(s); in fact, there is no assumption that a partner is even necessary (it could be fantasy or even masturbation). Our own definition of sexual desire is similar to Kaplan's, and includes one or more of the following aspects: (1) the interest in (or being pleasurably receptive to) stimulation of one's own genitals and sexual release (e.g., orgasm); (2) the interest in (or being pleasurably receptive to) genital/sexual contact with another; and (3) interest in (or being pleasurably receptive to) thinking about, seeing, approaching, and touching one's preferred sexual partners and/or objects (e.g., a partner's genitals). Note that in our definition, we specify what is "sexual" in sexual desire (i.e., genital stimulation/contact); in Kaplan's definition, it is implied. Keep these definitions in mind when you read the remainder of the chapter.

Aside from these definitions, it is also important to draw a distinction at this point between desire and another aspect of sexual functioning, arousal. Sexual arousal has to do with the physical changes that occur during sexual activity, such as an erection and vaginal lubrication. Often, desire for sex (e.g., feelings of "horniness") comes before and leads to physical stimulation and arousal. For example, let's say Sally has been feeling sexual desire ("horny") all day, and when she goes home, she masturbates, arousing herself (e.g., vaginal lubrication) until she has an orgasm. However, one's subjective desire for sex can also occur (or at least intensify) once physical stimulation and arousal has occurred. For example, Marcia has been feeling tired and not very sexy all day. When she goes home after work, her boyfriend, Ted, starts to massage her body, including her breasts and labia, she becomes physically aroused and her desire for sex intensifies; soon they begin to engage in passionate lovemaking. Recent research indicates that it is common for people, particularly women, to indicate that desire and arousal aspects of their sexuality overlap (Graham, Sanders, Mihausen, & McBride, 2004) and that—as the example with Marcia indicates—sexual desire sometimes occurs during or even after arousal. On the other hand, although very related and often reinforcing, it is important to note that one can feel desire without physical arousal, and one can feel arousal without desire. Furthermore, sexual desire disorders may not necessarily accompany sexual arousal problems (e.g., erectile problems) and vice versa. Sexual desire issues (and not arousal per se) will be the topic of this chapter.

WHAT AFFECTS SEXUAL DESIRE?

Before we review issues and problems of sexual desire, let us briefly review some of the factors that seem to affect it. One factor is hormones. One sex hormone in particular, testosterone, has been found to be important in stimulating sexual desire in both men and women. Testosterone, produced by the testes in men and the ovaries and adrenal glands in women, acts as a kind of fuel that helps stimulate the feelings of "horniness" that make us want to seek out and engage in sex. One of the reasons why children do not have an adultlike interest in sex is because the testes, ovaries, and adrenal glands are not mature and hence do not produce adult levels of hormones. For example, studies of adolescents (e.g., Udry, Billy, Morris, Groff, & Raj, 1985) show that those with high levels of testosterone, unlike those who are less mature and have low levels, show a high interest in sex, including masturbation experience and planning to have intercourse. Other studies show similar results for adults who are deprived of normal levels of testosterone. For example, studies of sex offenders who were physically castrated (i.e., had their testicles removed) and others who were chemically castrated (i.e., given a drug that inactivates the offenders' testosterone) showed that, although a few continued to be interested in sex, at least for a while, there was a dramatic decline in sexual interest within a few months (Heim, 1981). In addition, there is evidence that postmenopausal women, who have declining functioning of the ovaries (and thus lower levels of testosterone), sometimes have a lower sex desire, and these women's interest in sex can sometimes be increased by administering testosterone (Sherwin, 1991).

How does testosterone affect sexual desire? As mentioned, it likely acts as a kind of fuel to stimulate sexual feelings. It does so by acting on nerve cells (neurons) in the brain and body (typically the genitals) especially sensitive to testosterone. These cells are sensitive because they have special parts called receptors that are able to bind with or receive testosterone molecules. Cells with these receptors are particularly concentrated at the base of the brain. Specifically, areas at the base of the brain running from a section called the preoptic area back to a structure called the hypothalamus seem to be particularly important and sensitive to testosterone (Hull & Dominquez, 2003; Paredes & Baum, 1997). Note that there are several other areas, including the midbrain and hippocampus, which contain hormone receptor sites, but most of the relevant areas seem to be concentrated at the base of the brain (e.g., hypothalamus; see Chapter 2 in this volume).

A minimal level of testosterone is important to sexual interest, but it is important to keep in mind that sexual desire in humans is also a function of numerous psychosocial factors, including learning (memories), fantasies, and the quality of one's relationships. Thus, higher brain areas and the social context, not just testosterone and basic areas of the brain, are important.

One psychosocial factor that may be important in affecting desire is one's learning or conditioning history with regard to sex (see Ågmo, Turi, Ellingsen, & Kaspersen, 2004). Some people have had a history of sexually positive experiences, and this would likely maintain, or even increase, one's sexual interest. On the other hand, some people may have had primarily neutral or even negative experiences, which may serve to decrease sexual interest. What are these "positive" or "negative" (or "neutral") experiences? The most relevant positive experience is sexual pleasure, including orgasm. The neutral experiences would be a lack of pleasure (e.g., no orgasm), and the negative experiences would include boredom, fear, anxiety, and perhaps even pain. From a learning perspective, whether we have positive, neutral, or negative experiences during sex has consequences. Specifically, the more we have positive experiences (e.g., orgasm), the stronger the association or conditioning between these positive, rewarding experiences and the stimuli/context that brings it about. It should also increase the incentive or motivation to seek out those stimuli or contexts in which the reward takes place. So, let us say that Wendy has been masturbating (and having orgasms) since age 15. During college, she was sexually active with a number of boyfriends, and then later, with her husband, Mark. She typically has had orgasms with all of her partners including Mark. Now, at 45, she is still strongly interested in sex, and desires it regularly. From a learning perspective, this may be because she has learned to have positive associations/memories to sex throughout her adolescence and adulthood, and these positive associations/memories maintain her incentive to engage in it regularly.

Is there any research support for this perspective? There is, although most of it is indirect. First, orgasm frequency has been found to be an important factor in sexual behavior and motivation (Bentler & Peeler, 1979; Arafat & Cotton, 1974). For example, those activities in women that most consistently induce an orgasm (e.g., cunnilingus) are rated as the most satisfying (Hurlbert, Apt, & Rabehl, 1993). Second, because women are less likely than men to have an orgasm consistently, one might expect that more women than men should be diagnosed with low sexual desire. This is in fact the case (also see "Gender Differences in Sexual Desire," below). Third, animal models of sexual desire have demonstrated that in rats injected with naloxone, which prevents a positive affective state (reward), sexual behavior takes on aversive properties (Ågmo et al., 2004). Fourth, there is some evidence that people who have had sex early and more frequently in their lives (e.g., in adolescence and young adulthood) are the ones most likely to continue to engage in it later on in life (Laumann, Gagnon, Michael, & Michaels, 1994). Although alternative explanations may account for this (e.g., a person may have had a strong sex drive in the first place), one plausible explanation is that these people have built up a reward history with regard to sex and now the incentives and motivations for sex continue throughout their lives.

Sexual fantasies are another factor affecting sexual desire. Although they are difficult to define, sexual fantasies or daydreams are considered acts of the imagination; thoughts that are not simply orienting responses to external stimuli or immediately directed at solving a problem or working on a task (Leitenberg & Henning, 1995). They can be realistic or bizarre, elaborate or fleeting, and can result from memories or be entirely made up. Sexual fantasies can occur spontaneously or intentionally, and can be provoked by other thoughts, feelings, and sensory cues. They can take place during sexual activity, or outside of it, often during masturbation. In short, the term "sexual fantasy" refers to almost any mental imagery that is sexually arousing or erotic to the individual (Leitenberg & Henning).

Factor analysis has revealed that the majority of sexual fantasies fall into one of four basic categories:

1. conventional intimate heterosexual imagery with past, present, or imaginary lovers who are usually known to the person;
2. scenes suggesting sexual power and irresistibility (e.g., seduction scenes, multiple partners);
3. scenes involving varied or "forbidden" sexual imagery (e.g., different sex positions, questionable partners, etc); and
4. submission-dominance scenes in which some physical force or sadomasochistic imagery is involved or implied.

The first category is by far the most common. The content of sexual fantasies in gay men and lesbian women tends to be the same as in their heterosexual counterparts, except that homosexuals imagine same-sex partners rather than opposite-sex partners (Leitenberg & Henning, 1995).

Although some traditional approaches (e.g., classical psychoanalysis) have advocated negative views about sexual fantasies, it is now often considered a sign of pathology *not* to have sexual fantasies rather than to have them (Leitenberg & Henning, 1995). For instance, infrequent sexual fantasy is one of the defining criteria for hypoactive sexual desire disorder (HSDD), described in the *Diagnostic and Statistical Manual of Mental Disorders* (American Psychiatric Association, *DSM-IV*, 1995). In addition, a positive association has been found between sexual fantasy frequency and orgasmic frequency during intercourse, for both men and women (Arndt, Foehl, & Good, 1985; Epstein & Smith,

1957; Lentz & Zeiss, 1983). The experience of sexual fantasy is also positively associated with sexual arousability (Stock & Greer, 1982). Considering these findings, it is not surprising that individuals with sexual desire disorders are often encouraged by sex therapists to use sexual fantasies during masturbation, intercourse, and even nonsexual activities (Leitenberg & Henning, 1995). Research has also shown that frequency of sexual fantasy is either positively correlated with ratings of general satisfaction (particularly in women), or unrelated to sexual satisfaction. In addition, in contrast to the popular belief that sexual deprivation leads to more sexual thoughts, those with the most active sex lives seem to have the most sexual fantasies (Crepault, Abraham, Porton, & Couture, 1976). Thus, sexual fantasy is generally considered a normal and healthy part of one's sexuality.

Relationship factors are also likely important in sexual desire. For example, have you ever started a sexual relationship with someone and you just cannot get enough of them (at least, sexually speaking)? For some reason, those "horny" feelings just seem to stay with you, and all you want to do is stay in bed with them (the only interruption being room service). Of course, this intensity of sexual desire usually fades, despite the affection and love that may persist and begin to grow for a partner over time. Thus, on the other side of novelty is familiarity and boredom, and these may dampen one's sexual desires. Research supports this view: sexual activity typically decreases for couples over time. For example, data from a well-conducted American study indicates that married couples in their forties have intercourse, on average, about 1.3 times per week, whereas married couples in their twenties have intercourse, on average, 2.2 times per week (Laumann et al., 1994). Part of this decline may be an age factor (e.g., declining health), but a large part of it probably has to do with "habituation," the tendency to lose interest in one's partner with increasing familiarity. For example, this habituation explanation makes sense of recent findings suggesting that there is usually a sharp decline after the first year of a relationship and then a slow and fairly steady decline thereafter (Call, Sprecher, & Schwartz, 1995). This trend is probably best explained by habituation/boredom rather than age and declining health.

Aside from novelty factors in a relationship, there are other relationship issues that can increase or decrease desire. Physical attractiveness may be one of them. Those who perceive themselves and/or their partners to be physically attractive may have more interest in, and desire for, sex. The role of one's partner's attractiveness in increasing desire may be obvious because the more attractive the partner, the more desirable sex with that partner may be. However, the role of one's own (perceived) sexual attractiveness is also likely to be important, particularly for women (see Ackard, Kearney-Cooke, & Peterson, 2000). This is partly because women, relative to men, place a higher value on their ability to attract and turn on a partner with their own beauty/sexiness. Indeed, part of the "turn on" for a woman in sexual situations may be the knowledge that she is beautiful and sexy in her partner's eyes. Thus, if a woman perceives (rightly or wrongly) that she does not possess this ability, her desire to put herself into sexual situations may be low. If, however, she believes that her body is very sexy and beautiful to her partner(s), then her desire for sexual situations may be high. For example, Holly likes it when men look at her body appreciatively, and when she has sexual fantasies, she often begins them by imagining herself wearing underwear (e.g., a teddy and a lace bra) that she believes will turn on her partners. When interacting with her boyfriend, Luke, her desire is similar: she likes it when he tells her how beautiful and sexy she is, and her interest for sex is usually increased by wearing underwear that she knows will turn him on. In contrast, Maria has a very negative image of her own body and does not believe that men like looking at her. She also believes that her body is unattractive to her husband, Jack, and that there is little that she can do to increase her attractiveness in his eyes. Consequently, she does not desire sex and tends to avoid sexual thoughts and situations.

Another relationship issue is satisfaction and conflict. The more a relationship is mutually satisfying with a high degree of intimacy, the more the couple may have desire for sex. Conversely, frequent arguments, anger, and resentment may lead to a lack of sexual interest in one's partner. After all, it is hard to have desire for someone who you currently disdain! Also, such conflict and distress may work to diminish sexual desire indirectly by causing anxiety and/or depression in a partner, which has been shown to be negatively related to sexual desire (van Minnen & Kampman, 2000; Trudel, 1991).

GENDER DIFFERENCES IN SEXUAL DESIRE

In North American culture, there is a commonly held belief that men generally have more frequent and intense sexual desires, and therefore higher sex drives, than women. Indeed, research has indicated that a gender difference does exist, and it is reflected in a variety of measures, such as self-reported desired frequency of sex, desired variety of sexual acts and partners, frequency of fantasy, frequency of masturbation, number of partners, frequency of thinking about sex, and willingness to make sacrifices in other spheres to obtain sex. For instance, in a U.S. sample, more than half of the men reported thinking about sex every day, whereas only one fifth of the women reported thinking about sex that often (Laumann et al., 1994). Men have also been shown to have more intrusive, unwanted, and even personally unacceptable thoughts about sex than women (Byers, Purdon, & Clark, 1998).

Sexual fantasies are also a good indicator of sexual desire because they are explicitly sexual and require conscious attention but are not constrained by opportunities, social pressures, or other external factors (Baumeister, Catanese, & Vohs, 2001). Gender differences in sexual fantasy have been examined in many studies, which have generally concluded that men have more frequent and more varied fantasies than women. That is, men's fantasies occur more often than women's, include increased variety in partners than women's, and extend to a broader variety of sexual acts than women's (Baumeister et al., 2001). Such findings are consistent with a view that men have a higher sex drive than women. Other indicators of desire differences include preferences for number of sexual partners (see Baumeister et al., 2001, for a review) and masturbation frequency (Laumann et al., 1994), on which men score higher than women.

Gender differences in sexual desire are also highlighted by the study of sexual dysfunctions and their consequences. If the optimal strength of sex drive is intermediate, and women on average are toward the lower end of that range, then they should be more vulnerable than men to pathological or problematic patterns of very low (inadequate) sexual desire (Baumeister et al., 2001). In addition, cases in which one member of a partnership does not want to have sex should be more distressing to the partner who has a high sex drive (typically, men). Indeed, women have been found to suffer significantly more than men from low desire problems (e.g., HSDD). Female sexual reluctance has also been found to be a far more common source of disagreement than male reluctance (O'Sullivan & Byers, 1995). Some research has indicated that differences in sexual desire among females may be due to differential levels of free testosterone, which have, in some cases, been found to be significantly lower in people with low sex drive (Riley & Riley, 2000). Cultural/learning factors may also play a role in these gender differences in low desire. Regardless of the explanations, however, these findings are consistent with the view that women on average have less sexual desire than men to begin with, and so more women than men will fall into the spectrum of very low sex drive (Baumeister et al., 2001).

Of course, the gender difference in sex drive does not mean that women do not enjoy or desire sex. It also does not mean that men have a greater overall sexuality, as women may be just as capable of having and enjoying sex as men. In addition, the findings discussed here are based on averages. There are presumably many females who have greater sexual desire than their male partners, but the fact remains that, in general, men have, as indicated by a number of measures (e.g., sexual fantasies), higher sex drives than women. These differences can be partially explained by biological factors, such as differential levels of androgens (e.g., testosterone), which, as mentioned, have been implicated in determining sex drive. Cultural influences may also play a part in discouraging some aspects of female sexuality, although Baumeister et al. (2001) argue that gender differences exist even in spheres where culture has supported and encouraged female sexual desire, such as marital sex.

WHAT DESIRE LEVEL IS A PROBLEM?

Should little or no interest in sex be considered a health or psychological problem? Or should it be considered a harmless, even healthy, variation in human behavior? The answer depends on one's perspective and the social/

historical context. For example, most religions have strong prescriptions against liberal sexual practices, and some (e.g., Buddhism, Roman Catholicism) see complete abstinence as a virtue. In this view, sexual activity is sanctioned only within certain contexts (e.g., reproduction), and it is often considered a sin if this activity occurs outside of these contexts (e.g., for recreation). Thus, for many groups around the world the concept of a "disorder" for those having a low or nonexistent sexual desire would probably be perceived as nonsensical.

Until recently, influential Western institutions beyond religious ones would also not have deemed low sexual desire as a disorder, particularly in women. In fact, the situation was typically the opposite. For example, even until the 1950s, some segments of the medical community deemed low sexual activity to be healthy, and suggested that various maladies follow from high levels of nonreproductive sexual activity (e.g., masturbation). As Sigusch (1998) suggests, this started to change in the 1950s and 1960s when sexuality began to be viewed as separate from reproduction and thus could be performed for its own intrinsic values (e.g., physical pleasure, recreation).

In the wake of this decoupling of sex from reproduction, it is perhaps not surprising that low sexual desire emerged as a potential problem. Sexuality as a (healthy) recreational activity was becoming fully a part of the modern sensibility of many (although not all) Western people. However, it was not until 1980 that "inhibited sexual desire" appeared as a diagnostic category in the *Diagnostic and Statistical Manual of the Mental Disorders* (*DSM-III*, 1980). The name was changed in the next edition (*DSM-IV*, 1995) to "hypoactive sexual desire disorder (HSDD)." In 1989, the term "lack or loss of sexual desire" appeared in the *International Statistical Classification of Diseases and Related Health Problems* (*ICD-10*, World Health Organization, 1992).

The *DSM-IV* currently defines hypoactive sexual desire disorder (HSDD) as "persistently or recurrently deficient (or absent) sexual fantasies and desire for sexual activity. The judgement of deficiency or absence is made by the clinician." A diagnosis must also include that "the disturbance causes marked distress and interpersonal difficulty" (p. 510). Note that the *DSM* subdivides HSDD into certain subcategories, such as "generalized" versus "situational" and "lifelong" versus "acquired." The *DSM* also specifies related diagnoses. One is a "discrepancy of sexual desire" disorder. In this case there would have to be a significant difference in sexual desire between the two members of a couple. Another variation is sexual aversion disorder, where an aversion for genital contact occurs (e.g., extreme anxiety when a sexual encounter presents itself). Finally, a diagnosis of HSDD and related problems must exclude evidence of certain well-known medical conditions, such as depression or the use of certain drugs, known to lower sexual desire.

At the other end of the spectrum, excessive desire for sex or hyperactive sexual desire disorder is not a diagnosable condition from the perspective of the *DSM-IV*, although proposals have been made to include it in the *DSM-V* and *ICD-II* (Vroege, Gijs, & Hengeveld, 1998). One of the reasons that it is not a diagnosable disorder is because hyperactive sexual desire disorder often accompanies paraphilias (e.g., fetishes, exhibitionism). However, this is not always the case. Thus, one argument in favor of including hyperactive sexual desire disorder as a diagnosable problem is that it may be associated with nonparaphilic activities (e.g., masturbation or sexual activity with a partner) and may be a source of significant distress for the individual. Given that hyperactive sexual desire is not yet a diagnosable phenomenon, this chapter will primarily address issues of low sexual desire.

HOW PREVALENT ARE SEXUAL DESIRE DISORDERS?

It is impossible to know for certain how prevalent such disorders are because representative samples of people have not been assessed for such disorders by clinicians. However, there have been a number of large-scale, representative studies that have included questions about problems with sexual desire. One of the most surprising findings in the last twenty years in sex research has emerged from these studies: a very high number of people indicate they have problems with low sexual desire! For example, 33 percent of women and 15 percent of men reported low desire in the past year in a representative sample of U.S. residents (Laumann et al., 1994; Laumann, Paik, & Rosen, 1999). In a representative sample of Swedish residents, 34 percent of women and 16 percent of men reported low sexual desire as a problem (Fugl-Meyer & Sjögren-Fugl-Meyer, 1999). In a representative sample of Danish residents, 11.2 percent of women and 3.2 percent of men indicated that they had low sexual desire (Ventegodt, 1998). In a representative sample of a region in Spain, 37 percent of women and 25 percent of men complained of low sexual desire (Arnal, Llario, & Gil, 1995). Some of the differences among these studies might reflect real differences in sexual desire problems across societies, but it might also reflect methodological differences between the studies (e.g., how the questions were posed or the answers classified). Another issue is that these figures do not address some of the subtleties of the diagnosis mentioned earlier (e.g., "generalized" versus "situational" or whether the issue reflects a discrepancy of sexual desire within a couple).

Despite the issues and differences in these studies, it is clear that low sexual desire is a common complaint. The figures in these studies also correspond well to data in twenty-two older studies, published over a fifty-year period, and reviewed by Nathan (1986). Note that many of these older studies predated the diagnostic category of hypoactive sexual disorder. Finally, these figures reinforce the observation from clinicians that low sexual desire issues may be the most common sexual dysfunction, particularly among women (Letourneau & O'Donohue, 1993).

On the other end of the spectrum, we do not know how prevalent hyperactive sexual desire disorders are because there is no comparable data (e.g., probability samples) on complaints about too much desire.

CAUSES OF ATYPICALLY LOW SEXUAL DESIRE

If one's learning history with regard to sex is important in sexual desire, then one might expect low sexual desire is (partly) the result of an inconsistent or complete lack of sexual rewards, which may act to dampen sexual desire through "conditioning" or learning processes (for a review, see Ågmo et al., 2004). As mentioned, from a learning perspective, repeated exposure to stimuli with a reward will enhance the strength of the association between a reward and the stimuli/context that brings it about. It should also increase the incentive or motivation to seek out those stimuli or contexts in which the reward takes place. Similarly, a weak reward will lead to a weak or decreased association or connection between that reward and the stimuli or context in which the (weak) reward occurs. In fact, the stimuli or context may eventually become associated with punishing outcomes (e.g., boredom, irritation). If so, it should lead to a decrease in the incentive or motivation to seek out those stimuli because a reward is absent and a punishment may be present. So, let us say that Sally was relatively sexually active in college but she rarely had an orgasm (a big reward). Now, married to Bob, this pattern has been similar: she has rarely had an orgasm. Without that reward, the stimuli or context (including Bob), becomes uninteresting and unappealing. Thus, she may develop a low desire for sex and very little interest in physical/genital contact with Bob.

There is some research in people with HSDD that directly supports the role of sexual rewards (e.g., orgasm) in sexual desire. For example, Trudel, Aubin, and Matte (1995) showed that sexual behavior, and the pleasure associated with these behaviors, was less extensive in couples with a partner diagnosed with HSDD than in "normal" couples. There is also evidence that the reduced pleasure preceded the onset of the diagnosis in the people with HSDD (Trudel, Fortin, & Matte, 1997), suggesting a possible causal role for a lack of sexual rewards in the onset of HSDD. Thus, some people with HSDD may "learn" that sex is an undesirable activity because their sexual behavior history contains few enduring memories of rewards.

There is also some suggestion that HSDD may result from abnormally low levels of hormones (e.g., testosterone). We have already reviewed evidence that testosterone plays an important role in men and women's sexual desire, so it is a reasonable suggestion that some cases of HSDD result from a deficiency of testosterone.

In women, there is some support for the idea that low testosterone plays a role in this condition, although the evidence is mixed. A couple of early studies did not find a difference in testosterone levels between hypoactive women and appropriate controls (Schreiner-Engel, Schiari, White, & Ghizzani, 1989; Stuart, Hammond, & Pett, 1987). However, two more-recent studies did show a difference (Guay, 2001; Riley & Riley, 2000). One of the reasons for the difference is that at least one of the significant studies (Riley & Riley) used a sample with only lifelong HSDD, whereas the two earlier studies did not restrict their sample in this way. It is also of note that there is evidence that certain events (e.g., menopause) may relate to low testosterone, and this may be important in a small minority of cases of women with HSDD (Warnock, 2002). Thus, there is some evidence that low testosterone may affect this condition in women, particularly in the most extreme (i.e., lifelong) cases of HSDD.

There is also some evidence for the role of low testosterone in men with low sexual desire. First, in rare cases of men with very low sex drive, hypogonadism (reduced or absent secretion of hormones from the testes) is indicated; however, this condition would likely preclude a clinical diagnosis of HSDD because hypogonadism is an obvious medical condition. Second, one study found that men clinically diagnosed with HSDD had lower levels of testosterone than a control group of men (Schiavi, Schreiner-Engel, & White, 1988). Other studies have examined sexual desire and its relationship to testosterone in general samples of men. One study found a relationship between low sexual interest and lower testosterone concentration in a group of 51-year-old men (Nilsson, Moller, & Solstad, 1995). It should be kept in mind, however, that most studies examining men with a normal range of testosterone (3–12 ng/ml) do not find a strong relationship between testosterone and sexual behavior (Sherwin, 1988).

Very recent research has examined the role of brain functioning. Stoléru et al. (2003) found that the pattern of activation (or deactivation) of a number of areas of the brain differs between men with HSDD and controls when viewing sexual activity. One area of interest is the medial orbitofrontal cortex. This area is known to inhibit motivated behavior and was deactivated when normal men viewed sexual stimuli, but it remained activated in men with HSDD. In other words, this area of the brain probably allows one to become sexually disinhibited when deactivated (i.e., lose one's restraint and become active pursuers of sexual activity), and yet it remained (abnormally) activated in HSDD men. It is as if a person with HSDD is unable to let go of the normal restraints that need to be discarded when a (potentially) desirable sexual encounter is presented to him (or her). Not only does this suggest there may be an abnormality in brain function associated with the pursuit of sexual goals in men with HSDD, but it also suggests that the HSDD may be less a problem with low intrinsic motivation/desire and have more to do with the "inhibition" of (relatively normal) sexual desire. Interestingly, an early name for HSDD, inhibited sexual desire, may have been, then, a well-chosen description of the phenomenon. More research needs to be done in this area, particularly in women diagnosed with HSDD. Perhaps a very different pattern of response (e.g., low intrinsic desire versus inhibition) occurs in women relative to men.

Kaplan (1995) argues that intrapsychic conflict, originating in childhood, along with neurotic interactions with one's partner, is the cause of desire problems. Note, however, that this explanation is largely based on her clinical experience, and additional supporting evidence is lacking. She also argues that a partner can take on negative attributes over time because of the failure to have satisfying sexual interactions. Thus, although she does not refer to this process as conditioning, a negative learning history, with, for example, a lack of pleasure and orgasms, seem to be implied.

As mentioned, relationship quality likely influences sexual desire, so it is not surprising that poor relationship/marital adjustment has been implicated in low sexual desire (Trudel, Boulos, & Matte, 1993). Thus, one might expect low desire for sex if partners actively dislike one another. Also, anxiety may accompany relationship difficulties, and such anxiety issues have been implicated in sexual desire disorders (Bozman & Beck, 1991; van Minnen & Kampman, 2000). However, research does not fully support this explanation. One study found that individuals with HSDD were not more likely than controls to have marital discord (Schiaivi, Karstaedt, Schreiner-Engel, Mandeli, 1992). Also, it is not clear whether marital discord is the cause of low sexual desire, or whether low desire can cause marital discord. After all, low sexual desire of one partner may cause stress and conflict in a relationship, particularly if the other partner desires greater sexual activity.

TREATMENT

Can low sexual desire be treated? Some degree of success has been reported in the literature. Examples of treatment strategies, along with the efficacy of these treatments, are presented below.

Hawton, Catalan, and Fagg (1991) used an intervention to treat low desire problems in women based on Masters and Johnson's (1970) classic approach to sex therapy. Masters and Johnson's approach to sex therapy was couple-oriented (i.e., must have a partner or a surrogate) and used an intensive two-week program with different techniques and homework assignments. One such technique was sensate focus, a technique still widely used today by many different therapists for a variety of sexual dysfunctions. While in the nude, partners take turns giving and receiving pleasurable stimulation to nongenital (e.g., face, back, belly) areas of the body. Because touching the genitals is off limits (at least initially), the sensate focus approach is meant to decrease the anxiety that may accompany sexual performance issues. Hawton et al. (1991) reported a high level of success in treating low desire in women using Masters and Johnson's approach, but their report should be viewed cautiously because they did not include an adequate control group.

LoPiccolo and Friedman's (1988) four-step intervention uses a number of traditional therapies (e.g., sensate focus) along with recent cognitive/behavioral techniques in an attempt to increase sexual desire. A cognitive/behavioral approach combines learning techniques and interventions designed to change negative thinking. The first step is *experiential/sensory awareness* training. This step is used because it is assumed that anxiety underlies many cases of low sexual desire. Here, sensate focus, body awareness (e.g., mirror exercises, monitoring of one's emotional responses), and fantasy training are used. The second step is *insight*. Here, the client is helped to try to understand factors that are contributing to his or her low sexual desire. For example, in this step, the client may come to understand that they have anxiety about sexual issues. The third step is *cognitive restructuring*. Here, the client's thoughts (or cognitions) are analyzed, and if irrational thoughts occur that prevent sexual desire, they are changed to more helpful, rational thoughts (e.g., "Just because I engage in sex doesn't mean I am a bad person"; p. 134). The fourth step is *behavioral interventions*. Here, certain practical interventions are used. They may expand on some elements of step one, experiential/sensory awareness (e.g., sensate focus), or use other novel interventions. These might include assertiveness, communication, along with other social-skills training. These skills may be useful not just in their current relationship (if they have one), but also in future social situations, where a possibility of dating and sex occurs. Another intervention is drive induction or "priming the pump." This makes sex more salient to the client or makes him/her more "ready" for a sexual state. According to the authors, this is particularly important for someone with low sexual desire because they tend to avoid all sexual situations. These "priming" exercises include fantasy breaks (e.g., taking a five-minute break at work to have a sex fantasy), showing physical affection to their spouse at regular points in time, looking at books with sexual content and renting an erotic video/ DVD. LoPiccolo and Friedman's four-step intervention has been reported to be successful, but it is unclear whether an adequate control group of low sexual desire was included in their assessment of efficacy.

Recently, a number of drug treatments for low sexual desire disorders have been tried. Given that postmenopausal women can have reduced testosterone, it is not surprising that testosterone has been found to improve desire in some postmenopausal women. For example, research has shown that treatment with both testosterone and estrogens increased the sexual desire of postmenopausal women with low sexual desire (for a review, see Cameron & Braunstein, 2004). There is also a recent study suggesting that testosterone can increase sexual desire in premenopausal women with HSDD (van Anders, Chernick, Hampson, & Fisher, 2005). This study is suggestive, but it was not a double-blind study (i.e., both the experimenters and participants do not know what treatment is administered to the participant), nor did it include a placebo control condition. Thus, more research needs to be done in this area, including in men. However, if HSDD is more of an inhibition (versus an intrinsic desire) problem (Stoléru et al., 2003), then one might expect that testosterone, which may be more associated with intrinsic desire issues, may only be modestly effective. Indeed, although administering higher-than-typical levels of this hormone did increase desire in the HSDD participants, they did not exhibit lower than typical levels of testosterone prior to treatment.

There is recent research on a drug known as buproprion in the treatment of low desire in women with HSDD. This drug is not a hormone but a chemical that affects neurotransmitters in the brain (dopamine, noradrenaline) thought to be important in sexual functioning. Evidence exists that this drug does indeed increase sexual desire in a substantial minority of women with HSDD (Segraves et al., 2001); although it is important to keep in mind that the majority did not respond. Interestingly, there is also evidence that buproprion also increases sexual desire in people with depression and other conditions that may relate to low sexual desire (Modell, Katholi, Modell, & Depalma, 1997). Some other chemicals may have an indirect effect on sexual desire through increasing physical arousal, including Viagra-like drugs and polyphenolics (Kang, Park, Hwang, Kim, Lee, & Shin, 2003). Polyphenolics 'are chemicals derived from plants and have a high concentration in certain foods (e.g., red wine). They seem to have positive (anti-oxidant) effects on the cardiovascular system and increase blood flow in certain areas of the body including the pelvic region. The use of polyphenolics has just begun within the context of sexual problems, and much more research, including with control groups, is necessary.

Another treatment is the use of certain behaviors that increase the likelihood of orgasm (i.e., orgasm consistency treatment). Note that this treatment is the only one recognized by the American Psychological Association as being efficacious (Chambless et al., 1998). This therapy is meant to build up a history of rewarding experiences (i.e., orgasm) with sex and thus to increase the incentives and interest in it. Usually, this begins by directed (or guided) masturbation and then later, by a coital alignment technique. This latter technique makes it more likely that an orgasm will occur because it entails adjustment of the position of the partners so that thrusting leads to more direct clitoral stimulation. There have been some reports of success with this treatment, at least in women (Hurlbert, 1993; Hurlbert, Apt, Rabehl, 1993; Hurlbert, White, Powell, & Apt, 1993; LoPiccolo & Stock, 1986; Pierce, 2000). However, although these results seem promising, it is unclear whether proper control groups were included in these studies as well.

In summary, a number of different approaches have been used to treat low sexual desire, with some degree of success, although more research is needed (e.g., more controlled studies). It is also important to note that low sexual desire issues have been considered difficult sexual dysfunctions to treat, and they will probably remain a challenge for therapists. Furthermore, not all people with low desire necessarily want treatment (e.g., are not distressed about it). Some of these individuals with low or absent desire, particularly if it is a lifelong phenomenon, may in fact feel that they have a separate sexual identity, unique from the three traditional sexual orientations (heterosexuality, homosexuality, bisexuality) routinely discussed in the sexuality literature. This unique fourth identity is called "asexuality." Research on asexuality is just beginning (Bogaert, 2004). Thus, we clearly need more research on low desire issues, along with potentially related phenomena such as asexuality, in the future.

ACKNOWLEDGMENTS

This research was supported by Social Sciences and Humanities Research Council of Canada Grant 410–2003–0943 to Anthony F. Bogaert (tbogaert@brocku.ca; 905-688-5550, ext. 4085). The authors wish to thank Carolyn Hafer and Luanne Jamieson for their help at various stages of this research.

REFERENCES

Ackard, D. M., Kearney-Cooke, A., & Peterson, C. (2000). Effect of body image and self-image on women's sexual behaviors. *International Journal of Eating Disorders, 28,* 422–429.

Ågmo, A., Turi, A. L., Ellingsen, E., & Kaspersen, H. (2004). Preclinical models of sexual desire: Conceptual and behavioral analyses. *Pharmacology, Biochemistry, & Behavior, 78,* 379–404.

American Psychiatric Association. (1980). *Diagnostic and statistical manual of mental disorders* (3rd ed.). Washington, DC: Author.

American Psychiatric Association. (1987). *Diagnostic and statistical manual of mental disorders* (3rd ed., rev.). Washington, DC: Author.

American Psychiatric Association. (1995). *Diagnostic and statistical manual of mental disorders* (4th ed.). Washington, DC: Author.

Arafat, I., & Cotton, W. (1974). Masturbation practices of males and females. *Journal of Sex Research, 10,* 293–307.

Arnal, A., Llario, R., & Gil, M. D. (1995). Estudio epidemiológico sobre la pravalencia de disfunciones sexuales en la comunidad valenciana [Epidemiological studies on the prevalence of sexual dysfunctions in a community of Valencia]. *Psicothema, 7,* 95–104.

Arndt, W., Foehl, J., & Good, F. (1985). Specific sexual fantasy themes: A multidimensional study. *Journal of Personality and Social Psychology, 48,* 472–480.

Baumeister, R., Catanese, K., & Vohs, K. (2001). Is there a gender difference in strength of sex drive? Theoretical views, conceptual distinctions, and a review of relevant evidence. *Personality and Social Psychology Review, 5,* 242–273.

Bentler, P. M., & Peeler, W. H. (1979). Models of female orgasm. *Archives of Sexual Behavior, 8,* 405–423.

Bogaert, A. F. (2004). Asexuality: Its prevalence and associated factors in a national probability sample. *Journal of Sex Research, 41,* 279–287.

Bozman, A. W., & Beck, J. G. (1991). Covariation of sexual desire and sexual arousal: The effects of anger and arousal. *Archives of Sexual Behavior, 20,* 47–60.

Byers, E., Purdon, C., & Clark, D. (1998). Sexual intrusive thoughts of college students. *Journal of Sex Research, 35,* 359–369.

Call, V., Sprecher, S., & Schwartz, P. (1995). The incidence and frequency of marital sex in national sample. *Journal of Marriage and the Family, 57,* 639–652.

Cameron, D. R., & Braunstein, G. D. (2004). Androgen replacement therapy in women. *Fertility and Sterility, 82,* 273–289.

Chambless, D. L., Baker, M. J., Baucom, D. H., Beutler, L. E., Calhoun, K. S., Crits-Cristoph, P., et al. (1998). Update on empirically validated therapies, II. *The Clinical Psychologist, 51,* 3–16.

Crepault, C., Abraham, G., Porto, R., & Couture, M. (1976). Erotic imagery in women. In R. Gremme & C. C. Wheeler (Eds.), *Progress in sexology* (pp. 267–285). New York: Plenum.

Epstein, S., & Smith, R. (1957). Thematic apperception, Rorsharch content, and ratings of sexual attractiveness of women as measures of sex drive. *Journal of Consulting and Clinical Psychology, 21,* 473–478.

Fugl-Meyer, A. R., Sjögren-Fugl-Meyer, K. (1999). Sexual disabilities, problems, and satisfaction in 19–74 year old Swedes. *Scandinavian Journal of Sexology, 2,* 79–105.

Graham, C. A., Sanders, S. A., Mihausen, R. R., & McBride, K. R. (2004). Turning on and turning off: A focus group study of the factors that affect women's sexual arousal. *Archives of Sexual Behavior, 33,* 527–538.

Guay, A. T. (2001). Decreased testosterone in regularly menstruating women with decreased libido: A clinical observation. *Journal of Sex and Marital Therapy, 27,* 513–519.

Hawton, K., Catalan, J., & Fagg, J. (1991). Low sexual desire: Sex therapy results and prognostic factors. *Behavioral Research and Therapy, 29,* 217–224.

Heim, N. (1981). Sexual behavior in castrated offenders. *Archives of Sexual Behavior, 10,* 11–22.

Hull, E. M., & Dominquez, J. M. (2003). Sex behavior. In M. Gallagher & R. J. Nelson (Eds.), *Handbook of psychology: Biological psychology* (Vol. 3, pp. 321–353). New York: John Wiley.

Hurlbert, D. F. (1993). A comparative study using orgasm consistency training in the treatment of women reporting hypoactive sexual desire. *Journal of Sex and Marital Therapy, 19,* 41–55.

Hurlbert, D. F., Apt, C., & Rabehl, S. M. (1993). Key variables to understanding female sexual satisfaction—an examination of women in nondistressed marriages. *Journal of Sex and Marital Therapy, 19,* 41–55.

Hurlbert, D. F., White, L. C., Powell, R. D., & Apt, C. (1993). Orgasm consistency training in the treatment of women reporting hypoactive sexual desire disorder: An outcome comparison of women-only groups and couples-only groups. *Journal of Behavior Therapy and Experimental Psychiatry, 24,* 3–13.

Kang, K., Park, Y., Hwang, H. J., Kim, S. H., Lee, J. G., & Shin, H. C. (2003). Antioxidative properties of brown algae polyphenolics and their perspectives as chemopreventive agents against vascular risk factors. *Archives of Pharmaceutical Research, 26,* 286–293.

Kaplan, H. S. (1995). *The sexual desire disorders: Dysfunctional regulation of sexual motivation.* New York: Brunner/Mazel.

Laumann, E. O., Gagnon, J., Michael, R., & Michaels, S. (1994). *The social organization of sexuality: Sexual practices in the United States.* Chicago: University of Chicago Press.

Laumann, E. O., Paik, A., & Rosen, R. C. (1999). Sexual dysfunction in the United States: Prevalence and predictors. *Journal of the American Medical Association, 281,* 537–544.

Leitenberg, H., & Henning, K. (1995). Sexual fantasy. *Psychological Bulletin, 117,* 469–496.

Lentz, S., & Zeiss, A. (1983). Fantasy and sexual arousal in college women: An empirical investigation. *Imagination, Cognition, and Personality, 3,* 185–202.

LeTourneau, E., & O'Donohue, W. (1993). Sexual desire disorders. In W. O'Donohue & J. H. Geer (Eds.), *Handbook of sexual dysfunctions: Assessment and treatment* (pp. 53–81). Needham Heights, MA: Allyn & Bacon.

LoPiccolo, J., & Friedman, J. M. (1988). Broad-spectrum treatment of low sexual desire: Integration of cognitive, behavioral, and systematic therapy. In S. R. Leiblum & R. C. Rosen (Eds.), *Sexual desire disorders* (pp. 107–144). New York: Guilford.

LoPiccolo, J., & Stock, W. E. (1986). Treatment of sexual dysfunctions. *Journal of Consulting and Clinical Psychology, 54,* 158–167.

Masters, W. H., & Johnson, V. (1970). *Human sexual inadequacy.* Boston: Little, Brown.

Modell, J. G., Katholi, C. R., Modell, J. D., & Depalma, L. (1997). Comparative sexual side effects of SSRIs and bupropion. *Clinical Pharmacological Therapy, 61,* 476–487.

Nathan, S. G. (1986). The epidemiology of the DSM-III psychosexual dysfunctions. *Journal of Sex and Marital Therapy, 12,* 267–281.

Nilsson, P., Moller, L., & Solstad, K. (1995). Adverse effects of psychosocial stress on gonadal function and insulin levels in middle aged males. *Journal of Internal Medicine, 237,* 479–486.

O'Sullivan, L., & Byers, E. (1995). Gender differences in response to discrepancies in desired level of sexual intimacy. *Journal of Psychology and Human Sexuality, 8,* 49–67.

Paredes, R. G., & Baum, M. J. (1997). Role of the medial preoptic area/anterior hypothalamus in the control of masculine sexual behavior. *Annual Review of Sex Research, 8,* 68–101.

Pierce, A. P. (2000). The coital alignment technique (CAT): An overview of studies. *Journal of Sex and Marital Therapy, 26,* 257–268.

Riley, A., & Riley, E. (2000). Controlled studies of women presenting sexual drive disorder: I. Endocrine status. *Journal of Sex and Marital Therapy, 26,* 269–283.

Schiaivi, R. C., Karstaedt, A., Schreiner-Engel, P., & Mandeli, J. (1992). Psychometric characteristics of individuals with sexual dysfunctions and their partners. *Journal of Sex and Marital Therapy, 18,* 219–230.

Schiaivi, R. C., Schreiner-Engel, P., & White, D. (1988). Pituitary gonadal function during sleep in men with hypoactive sexual desire and in normal controls. *Psychosomatic Medicine, 50,* 304–318.

Schreiner-Engel, P., Schiari, P. C., White, D., & Ghizzani, A. (1989). Low sexual desire in women: The role of reproductive hormones. *Hormones and Behavior, 23,* 211–234.

Segraves, R. T., Croft, H., Kavoussi, R. J., Ascher, J. A., Batey, S. R., Foster, V. J., et al. (2001). Bupropion sustained release (SR) for the treatment of hypoactive sexual desire disorder (HSDD) in nondepressed women. *Journal of Sex and Marital Therapy, 27,* 303–313.

Sherwin, B. B. (1988). A comparative analysis of the role of androgen in human male and female sexual behavior: Behavioral specificity, critical thresholds, and sensitivity. *Psychobiology, 16,* 416–425.

Sherwin, B. B. (1991). The psychoendocrinology of aging and female sexuality. *Annual Review of Sex Research, 2,* 181–198.

Sigusch, V. (1998). The neosexual revolution. *Archives of Sexual Behavior, 27,* 339–351.

Stock, W., & Geer, J. (1982). A study of fantasy based sexual arousal in women. *Archives of Sexual Behavior, 11,* 33–47.

Stoléru, S., Redouté, J., Costes, N., Lavenne, F., Le Bars, D., Dechaud, H., et al. (2003). Brain processing of visual sexual stimuli in men with hypoactive sexual desire disorder. *Psychiatry Research: Neuroimaging, 124,* 67–86.

Stuart, F. M., Hammond, D. C., & Pett, M. A. (1987). Inhibited sexual desire disorder in women. *Archives of Sexual Behavior, 16,* 91–106.

Trudel, G. (1991). Review of psychological factors in low sexual desire. *Sex and Marital Therapy, 6,* 261–272.

Trudel, G., Aubin, S., & Matte, B. (1995). Sexual behaviors and pleasures in couples with hypoactive sexual desire. *Journal of Sex Education and Therapy, 21,* 210–216.

Trudel, G., Boulos, L., & Matte, B. (1993). Dyadic adjustment in couples with hypoactive sexual desire. *Journal of Sex Education and Therapy, 19,* 31–36.

Trudel, G., Fortin, C., & Matte, B. (1997). Sexual interaction and communication in couples with hypoactive sexual desire. *Scandinavian Journal of Behavior Therapy, 26,* 49–53.

Udry, J. R., Billy, J. O. G., Morris, N. M., Groff, T. R., & Raj, M. H. (1985). Serum androgenic hormones motivate sexual behavior in adolescent boys. *Fertility and Sterility, 43,* 90–94.

van Anders, S. M., Chernick, A. B., Hampson, E., & Fisher, W. A. (2005). Preliminary clinical experience with androgen administration for pre- and postmenopausal women with hypoactive sexual desire. *Journal of Sex and Marital Therapy, 31*, 173–187.

van Minnen, A., & Kampman, M. (2000). The interaction between anxiety and sexual functioning: A controlled study of sexual functioning in women with anxiety disorders. *Sex and Relationship Therapy, 15*, 47–57.

Ventegodt, S. (1998). Sex and quality of life in Denmark. *Archives of Sexual Behavior, 28*, 295–307.

Vroege, J. A., Gijs, L., & Hengeveld, M. W. (1998). Classification of sexual dysfunctions: Towards DSM-V and ICD-11. *Comprehensive Psychiatry, 39*, 333–337.

Warnock, J. K. (2002). Female hypoactive sexual desire disorder. *CNS Drugs, 16*, 745–753.

World Health Organization. (1992). *International statistical classifications of diseases and related health problems* (1989 revision). Geneva: Author.

7

Sexual Arousal Disorders

Greg A. R. Febbraro ◆

This chapter will provide an overview of the sexual arousal disorders: female sexual arousal disorder (FSAD) and male erectile disorder (MED). The diagnostic features of FSAD and MED as well as their potential causes will be discussed. In addition, current available treatments for FSAD and MED will be briefly reviewed. Issues for future consideration will also be raised.

ESSENTIAL DIAGNOSTIC FEATURES OF SEXUAL AROUSAL DISORDERS

Occasional disturbances in sexual functioning are frequent. In the fairly recent National Health and Social Life Survey (NHSLS) conducted by Edward Laumann and colleagues, a little over 3,000 men and women were asked whether they had experienced various symptoms of sexual dysfunction (e.g., lacked interest in sex, were unable to achieve orgasm, had trouble maintaining/achieving erection) in the past twelve months. The overall prevalence rate of occasional disturbance was 43 percent for women and 31 percent for men (Laumann, Paik, & Rosen, 1999). Because these symptoms are fairly prevalent, people should not assume they need treatment if they occasionally experience sexual arousal problems. Symptoms have to be persistent or recurrent and should interfere with functioning in order for someone to be diagnosed with a psychological disorder.

Both FSAD and MED are classified under the "sexual dysfunctions" category in the *Diagnostic and Statistical Manual*, fourth edition, text revision (*DSM-IV-TR*). The *DSM-IV-TR* published by the American Psychiatric Association is the primary classification system used by mental health professionals in North America. Sexual dysfunctions are persistent and recurrent problems in the appetitive, excitement, and orgasm phases of the human sexual cycle. Dysfunctions are either psychological or psychophysiological in nature. Sexual arousal disorders are sexual problems that occur during the excitement phase and that relate to difficulties with feelings of sexual pleasure or with the physiological changes associated with sexual excitement (APA, 2000; Sue, Sue, & Sue, 2003). The diagnostic and associated features of FSAD and MED will now be discussed.

Female Sexual Arousal Disorder (FSAD)

FSAD is characterized by a lack of response to sexual stimulation, including lack of lubrication (APA, 2000). FSAD used to be referred to as "frigidity," a derogatory term that implies that the woman is emotionally cold, distant, unsympathetic, and unfeeling (Millner, 2005). Therefore, the current term, FSAD, is an improvement. The *DSM-IV-TR* criteria for FSAD include the following: (1) persistent inability to attain or maintain sexual excitement (e.g., lubrication and swelling of the genitalia, erection of the nipples) adequate for completion of sexual activity; (2) the sexual problem causes marked distress or interpersonal problems; and (3) the symptoms are not due to another psychological disorder (except another sexual dysfunction) or to the direct physiological effects of a drug or a general medical condition. The disorder involves both psychological and physiological components. As with other sexual dysfunctions, the problem can be: (1) lifelong or acquired, (2) generalized or situational, and (3) due to psychological or combined factors. A woman with lifelong FSAD has always had difficulty with sexual arousal. A woman with acquired FSAD, on the other hand, developed sexual arousal problems after a period of normal sexual arousal. As the terms imply, generalized FSAD refers to sexual arousal problems occurring in a variety of situations and not specific to certain types of stimulation or partners. Situational FSAD refers to sexual arousal problems limited to certain types of stimulation, situations, or partners. For example, a woman becoming aroused while masturbating but not when engaging in sexual intercourse may indicate that the arousal difficulties are due to relationship problems and not to a medical condition. Psychological-based FSAD means that psychological factors, such as anxiety, sadness, or anger, for example, fully account for the development of the disorder whereas FSAD that is determined to be due to combined factors involves psychological and biological factors (e.g., diseases, injuries). FSAD may result in painful intercourse, sexual avoidance, and marital or relationship difficulties (APA, 2000). Sexual avoidance may be exhibited in a variety of ways. For example, someone with FSAD may engage in infrequent sexual activity or only certain types of sexual activity. The impact of sexual avoidance on relationships is discussed later in this chapter, when reviewing interpersonal causal factors for sexual arousal disorders.

Prevalence rates for FSAD have been highly variable. More recent research indicates that between 10 percent and 20 percent of women experience the disorder over the course of a lifetime. Difficulties with lubrication itself were reported among 19 percent of women in the NHSLS study (Laumann, Paik, & Rosen, 1999). There are a couple of potential reasons for the variability in the estimates of FSAD. First, FSAD often co-occurs with sexual desire disorders (e.g., hypoactive sexual desire disorder) and orgasmic disorders (e.g., female orgasmic disorder), making it difficult to differentiate from those disorders (APA, 2000; Laumann, Gagnon, Michael, & Michaels, 1994; LoPiccolo, 1997). Second, some women with FSAD may have little or no subjective sense of sexual arousal, making its diagnosis difficult.

Male Erectile Disorder (MED)

MED is characterized by the inability to have an erection or maintain one. MED has historically been referred to as "erectile dysfunction," "inhibited sexual excitement," and "impotence." *DSM-IV-TR* criteria for MED are as follows: (1) persistent inability to attain or maintain an erection adequate for completion of sexual activity; (2) the sexual problem causes marked distress or interpersonal problems; and (3) symptoms are not due to another Axis I disorder (except another sexual dysfunction) or the direct physiological effects of a drug or a general medical illness. Like FSAD, MED can be lifelong or acquired, generalized or situational in nature, and occur due to psychological and combined factors. In lifelong erectile disorder, also referred to as primary erectile disorder, males have never been able to experience an erection that is satisfactory for intercourse. It should be noted that lifelong erectile disorder is considered rare. In acquired erectile disorder, also referred to as secondary erectile disorder, males have difficulty achieving or maintaining an erection but have achieved or maintained erections for intercourse at other times. Generalized MED refers to erectile difficulties occurring in a variety of situations and not specific to certain types of stimulation or partners. Situational MED, on the other hand, refers to erectile limited to certain types of stimulation, situations, or partners. For example, a male may not have any difficulty achieving an erection while masturbating, but may have difficulty doing so when engaging in sexual intercourse. This may indicate that the erectile difficulties are due to relationship problems and not due to a medical condition or substance abuse. Psychological-based MED means that psychological factors, such as negative emotions (e.g., anxiety, sadness, anger), fully account for the development of the disorder whereas MED that is determined to be due to combined factors involves psychological and biological factors (e.g., diseases, injuries) (APA, 2000; Hyde & DeLamater, 2006). MED often co-occurs with other sexual disorders, particularly hypoactive sexual desire and premature ejaculation disorders. Furthermore, individuals with mood disorders, such as depression, and substance-related disorders, like alcoholism, often report problems with sexual arousal (APA, 2000).

In the past, MED has been attributed primarily to psychological factors. For example, in their pioneering work on human sexuality, William Masters and Virginia Johnson estimated that only 5 percent of erectile dysfunctions were due to physical conditions (Masters & Johnson, 1970). However, more recent studies indicate that from 30 percent to 70 percent of erectile dysfunctions are caused by some form of vascular insufficiency, diabetes, atherosclerosis, traumatic groin injury, or other physiological factors (Hooper, 1998; Segraves, Schoenberg, & Ivanoff, 1983).

According to the NHSLS study, approximately 10 percent of men have experienced an erection problem within the past twelve months (Laumann, Paik, & Rosen, 1999). This statistic varies by age with only 7 percent of 18- to 29-year-olds experiencing erection problems, but 18 percent of 50 to 59-year-olds and 39 percent of men who were 60 years and older experiencing such problems. Similar rates for erection problems have been found in Germany and France (Hyde & DeLamater, 2006). Problems with erection are one of the most embarrassing ones many men can imagine or experience. In addition, depression may result from repeated experiences of erection problems. Furthermore, erection problems can also be a cause of concern for the male's partner.

CAUSES OF SEXUAL AROUSAL DISORDERS

A variety of causes for sexual arousal disorders have been offered. Biological, psychological (immediate and prior learning), and interpersonal causes have been the main ones examined in the literature. Therefore, these primary causes will now be briefly reviewed for FSAD and MED.

Biological Causes

As previously mentioned, Masters and Johnson (1970) had speculated that the large majority of sexual disorders were psychological in nature. However, the potential role of biological factors is increasingly being recognized (Rosen & Leiblum, 1995). Biological factors that explain the development of sexual disorders such as FSAD and MED include organic factors (e.g., diseases, injuries) and drugs. With regard to MED, approximately 50 percent or more of cases may result from organic factors or a combination of organic and other factors such as psychological factors (Buvat et al., 1990; Richardson, 1993).

Heart and circulatory diseases are often associated with MED as erections themselves depend on the circulatory system (Jackson, 1999). Troubles in the vascular system can create erection problems as the "production" of an erection depends upon having a large amount of blood flowing into the penis by way of the arteries, with simultaneous constricting of the veins so that the blood cannot flow out as rapidly as it is coming in. Damage to these arteries or veins can result in MED (Hyde & DeLamater, 2006). In women, vascular disease associated with diabetes can lead to FSAD (Phillips, 2000).

MED is also associated with diseases like diabetes mellitus and kidney problems. Diabetes, for example, can cause circulation problems and peripheral nerve damage, both impacting the ability to produce erections. Some studies have found that 28 percent of men with diabetes have erectile disorders, making it one of the most common medical causes (de Tejada et al., 2005). Hypogonadism, a condition characterized by the underfunctioning of the testes resulting in low testosterone levels, is also associated with MED (Morales & Heaton, 2001). MED is also associated with hyperprolactinemia, a condition characterized by the excessive production of prolactin (Johri, Heaton, & Morales, 2001).

Any injury causing damage to the lower part of the spinal cord may cause MED, since that is where the erection reflex center is located. MED may also result from some types of prostate surgery, although this is not a common phenomenon (Hyde & DeLamater, 2006).

Prior pelvic trauma, such as injury sustained during childbirth, can result in FSAD. In addition, urogenital atrophy (shrinkage of genital and urinary tissues) in menopausal and postmenopausal women can lead to FSAD (Phillips, 2000; Goldstein, 2000).

Drugs can also cause arousal and erectile problems. Examples of such drugs decreasing sexual arousal and causing erection problems include certain anti-hypertensive medications, certain antidepressants, overuse of alcohol, and the use of illicit substances like heroin and marijuana. Furthermore, long-term use of nicotine can also cause erection problems (Hyde & DeLamater, 2006).

FSAD can also result from the intake of antihistamines and hypertensive medications. Furthermore, antidepressants, such as selective serotonin reuptake inhibitors (SSRIs) and tricyclics (TCAs), can result in FSAD (Millner, 2005).

Psychological Causes

Psychological causes of sexual disorders are often categorized into immediate causes and prior learning. Immediate causes refer to problems occurring during intimacy that inhibit the sexual response. Prior learning refers to any beliefs or responses that people have learned or experienced earlier in life, that now affect their sexual response. Therefore, anxiety/fear can result in a vicious cycle, impacting sexual responding.

Immediate Psychological Causes

Four primary factors have been identified as immediate psychological causes of sexual disorders. These include fear of performance, cognitive interference, communication failure, and failure to engage in effective, sexually stimulating behavior.

Fear or anxiety about performance is often related to fear of failure during intercourse. Masters and Johnson theorized that such fear could cause sexual disorders. Such anxiety can create a self-fulfilling prophecy in which fear of failure produces a failure, which produces more fear, which produces another failure, and so on (Hyde & DeLamater, 2006).

Cognitive interference, a second immediate cause, refers to thoughts that distract the person from focusing on the erotic experience. This is a problem mainly of attention and of whether the person is focusing his or her attention on erotic thoughts or on distracting thoughts. Examples of distracting thoughts would include "Will my technique be good enough to please her?" or "Will my body be attractive enough to arouse him?" One type of cognitive interference is "spectatoring," a term coined by Masters and Johnson (1970), for an individual acting as an observer or judge of his or her own sexual performance (Hyde & DeLamater, 2006). People who engage in spectatoring are often asking themselves "I wonder how I'm doing?" types of questions.

In a series of experiments, David Barlow demonstrated how anxiety and cognitive interference combine to produce sexual disorders such as MED (Barlow, 1986). For example, when a male with MED is in a sexual situation, there is a performance demand causing him to experience negative emotions like anxiety. He then experiences cognitive interference and focuses his attention on nonerotic thoughts. This serves to increase the arousal of his autonomic nervous system, the part of the nervous system responsible for anxiety responses (e.g., flight or fight response). Someone with MED experiences this as anxiety whereas someone without MED, or any sexual disorder, experiences it as sexual arousal. The anxiety for someone with MED creates further cognitive interference, eventually causing problematic sexual performance, such as a failure to achieve an erection. This failure leads to an avoidance of sexual situations or to a tendency to experience anxiety when in a sexual situation. Like most cycles, it is repetitive, unless the person is able to recognize what is occurring and takes steps to unlearn it.

Steps to unlearn the above process often involve the use of cognitive restructuring. Cognitive restructuring is a technique in which a therapist helps someone recognize negative cognitions (i.e., thoughts) that are interfering with their sexual activity, and replace them with more positive cognitions. There are several ways to do this. Once negative thoughts that interfere with sexual performance are identified, the therapist can teach the client to challenge their negative thoughts. One strategy for challenging negative thoughts involves educating the person about the sexual process. A second strategy is to assist him or her in determining whether there is any factual evidence for the person's negative thoughts. A therapist would ask the person to describe what evidence he/she has that a negative belief is valid. During this process, the therapist can help identify any errors in the patient's thinking and challenge him/her to identify evidence that would suggest an alternative to their current belief. Finally, individuals can learn to de-catastrophize negative outcomes (Back, Wincze, & Barlow, 2001). For example, if an attempt at sexual activity is unsuccessful, the therapist can help the person recognize that although it may be very disappointing, it is not the end of the world. This helps the person put the situation in perspective and, in turn, can help them to relax more, and subsequently increase their chance for sexual arousal and sexual enjoyment.

In female sexual dysfunction, similar findings have been obtained regarding cognitive factors (Laan, Everaerd, van Aanhold, & Rebel, 1993; Palace & Gorzalka, 1990, 1992). In these studies, however, women have been less prone to the distracting effects of anxiety or social performance demands (Rosen & Leiblum, 1995).

Failure to communicate, a third immediate cause of sexual dysfunction, is one of the most important immediate causes. Many people do not communicate their sexual desires to their partners thus creating problems with intimacy (Hyde & DeLamater, 2006). Couples' rating their ability to communicate effectively with one another has been found to be the single best predictor of treatment outcome for erectile disorder. Lack of assertiveness and not knowing how to communicate their needs to their partner is common in women with FSAD (Hyde & DeLamater, 2006; Rosen & Leiblum, 1995).

Finally, a fourth immediate cause of sexual disorders is a failure to engage in effective, sexually stimulating behavior. This can often be the result of ignorance on the part of one or both partners. For example, a couple may seek therapy because of unsatisfactory sexual intercourse. During the course of therapy, it may be discovered that the reason for the unsatisfactory intercourse is one or both individuals being unaware of the needs of the other person. Furthermore, they may not be aware of sexual physiology and thus not know how to best stimulate the other person. Therefore, increased communication during intercourse may be all that is needed (Hyde & DeLamater, 2006).

Prior Learning

Prior learning as a psychological cause of sexual disorders may be due to various things learned or experienced during childhood, adolescence, or even adulthood. In some cases of sexual disorders, the person's first sexual act was traumatic. Child sexual abuse is one of the most serious of the traumatic early experiences that lead to later sexual disorders such as FSAD. A history of sexual abuse is frequently reported by women seeking therapy for problems with sexual desire, arousal, or aversion (Leonard & Follette, 2002). Similar findings emerge for men with desire or arousal problems (Wyatt, Chin, & Asuan-O'Brien, 2002; McCarthy, 1990).

Cultural or societal factors may also contribute to the development of sexual problems. For example, growing up in a very strict religious family where sex is viewed as being dirty and sinful can play a factor in the development of sexual disorders. In addition, parents punishing children severely for sexual activity such as masturbation can also play a factor (Hyde & DeLamater, 2006; Rosen & Leiblum, 1995).

Other Psychological Factors

As previously mentioned, negative emotions can affect sexual arousal and play a role in sexual disorders such as FSAD and MED. Specifically, emotions such as anxiety, sadness, and anger can interfere with sexual responding (Araujo et al., 1998). In regard to anxiety, for example, research has demonstrated that when people with sexual problems become anxious, their level of autonomic arousal (i.e., heart rate) increases and they tend to focus more on the negative consequences of not being able to perform. As a result, they do not become sexually aroused. In addition, research has demonstrated that when negative mood states are induced by the use of a musical mood-induction technique, there is an association with lower levels of physiological arousal. In regard to anger, research has found that suppression and expression of anger were associated with higher rates of erectile dysfunction (Back, Wincze, & Barlow, 2001).

Behavioral or lifestyle factors also play a role. For example, as previously mentioned, smoking, alcohol consumption, and obesity are all associated with higher rates of sexual disorders and are all behavioral problems (Hyde & DeLamater, 2006). Therefore, such behavior or lifestyle issues can be modified.

Interpersonal Causes

Problems in a couple's relationship are another leading cause of sexual disorders. Anger or resentment toward one's partner does not create an optimal environment for sexual satisfaction. Furthermore, in relationships in which there is anger or resentment, sex can be used as a weapon by one or both partners to psychologically hurt the other (e.g., by refusing to engage in any sexual behavior or in a particular sexual behavior the other desires). In addition, struggle for power in a relationship may add to sexual problems (Hyde & DeLamater, 2006).

Problems with intimacy are often an issue in relationships, which results in sexual disorders. Intimacy involves becoming emotionally close to one another. This may or may not involve physical contact. Intimacy problems typically represent a combination of individual psychological factors and relationship problems. Some individuals in relationships may enjoy the sex in the relationship but fear becoming intimate with their partner. Intimacy often involves allowing oneself to be emotionally vulnerable, and this is often very frightening to some individuals. Individuals with intimacy problems may be very good in the early stages of relationships but then lose interest or look for reasons to end relationships once it appears that things are becoming more serious and further commitment is necessary. This type of pattern may be repeated in a number of relationships, thus making it an interpersonal issue. Some theorists have suggested that individuals with intimacy problems may have learned this pattern early in life, potentially as far back as childhood (Rosen & Leiblum, 1995).

TREATMENT OF SEXUAL AROUSAL DISORDERS

The four major categories of therapies often used in the treatment of sexual disorders, including sexual arousal disorders, are behavior therapy, cognitive-behavioral therapy, couples therapy, and biomedical therapies. In addition to the above treatments, the use of bibliotherapy-based treatments has been increasing. Bibliotherapy-based treatments have been predominantly behavioral and fairly recently cognitive-behavioral in nature. Therefore, their use along with behavior, cognitive-behavioral, couples, and biomedical therapies will be briefly reviewed in this section. It should be noted that multicomponent treatments are usually necessary for all sexual disorders as it is often very difficult to disentangle biological from psychological factors for a sexual disorder.

Behavior Therapy

The basic assumption of behavior therapy is that sexual problems are the result of prior learning and that they are maintained by ongoing reinforcements and punishment (immediate causes). Therefore, problematic behaviors can be unlearned and replaced by more adaptive ones (Hyde & DeLamater, 2006). This is consistent with the basic principles of behaviorism and learning theory, major influences in psychology.

A variety of different behavioral techniques have been used to treat sexual problems. Historically, one of the key behavior therapy techniques has been systematic desensitization. This behavioral technique involves first, teaching individuals an incompatible behavior to anxiety/fear, usually muscle relaxation. Individuals also construct a fear hierarchy consisting of a series of increasing fearful situations. Once the fear hierarchy has been constructed, and individuals have learned how to use muscle relaxation, they are then asked to imagine each step of the fear hierarchy. When feeling anxious, they are asked to use their relaxation skills. Individuals cannot progress to the next step of the fear hierarchy until they have significantly reduced their fear to the preceding step (Hyde & DeLamater, 2006).

Most behavior therapy programs are multidimensional in nature. They include education about sexual anatomy and functioning, use of anxiety reduction techniques (e.g., systematic desensitization), structured behavioral exercises, and communication training. Behavior therapy programs for erectile dysfunction have had fairly good success rates. However, most of them have had fairly high relapse rates as well. Therefore, most behavior therapy programs should include what are called "relapse prevention procedures," should problems reoccur (Hyde & DeLamater, 2006). Relapse prevention procedures assist the individual in coping with setbacks.

Cognitive-Behavioral Therapy

Many sex therapists currently use a combination of behavioral strategies and exercises and cognitive therapy. This is referred to as cognitive-behavioral therapy (CBT). A key component of the cognitive approach to sex therapy is cognitive restructuring (Hyde & DeLamater, 2006). In cognitive restructuring, the therapist basically assists the client in restructuring his or her thought patterns, helping them to become more positive and realistic about sexual expectations. Often, negative attitudes are challenged, and individuals examine realistic alternatives to negative attitudes. Cognitive restructuring was previously described when reviewing psychological causes of sexual arousal disorders.

As for women with FSAD, they may have beliefs/attitudes about sexual activity that are associated with shame or guilt. Several myths have been identified that can create difficulties with sexual arousal in women. These include: (1) women must not be sexual, (2) women's responses to sex should be similar to men's responses, and (3) there are correct and incorrect ways to become aroused. Furthermore, a woman's negative beliefs or feelings about the partner can create negative sexual experiences (Charlton & Brigel, 1997). In CBT, the above myths would be challenged and modified.

Bibliotherapy

Bibliotherapy involves the use of written and other (e.g., use of videos) materials in the treatment of psychological and physical problems. Bibliotherapy materials typically describe how particular treatment methods are to be implemented by the individual. It can function as a stand-alone treatment or as a complement to ongoing therapy or medical care (van Lankveld, 1998).

To date, the vast majority of bibliotherapy approaches for sexual dysfunction have targeted orgasmic disorders. In addition, bibliotherapy approaches have predominantly used behavior therapy techniques pioneered by Masters and Johnson, or variations of them. A recent statistical review of bibliotherapy interventions targeting sexual dysfunctions conducted by Jacques van Lankveld found bibliotherapy to be moderately effective at the end of treatment. However, there was a relatively small effect at follow-up (van Lankveld, 1998). van Lankveld noted that 87 percent of the studies reviewed dealt with orgasmic disorders, thus limiting the generalizability of the findings.

More recently, bibliotherapy approaches have begun to use cognitive-behavioral techniques in the treatment of sexual dysfunction. In 2001, Jacques van Lankveld, Walter Everaerd, and Yvonne Grotjohann published the only cognitive-behaviorally-based BT study to date. In a randomized clinical trial, couples were assigned to either the BT group or a waiting-list group. After the ten-week BT treatment, participants (N = 199 couples) reported fewer complaints of low frequency of sexual interaction and general improvement of sexual problems, and lower male posttreatment ratings of problem-associated distress. Unlike previous studies, the above study targeted a wider variety of sexual problems, including sexual arousal problems.

Couples Therapy

Due to the role that interpersonal factors may play in sexual disorders, couples therapy is often used as part of an overall treatment strategy when relevant. Couples therapy assumes that the relationship difficulties between two people can cause sexual problems. Therefore, couple/relationship issues need to be addressed in order for sexual problems to improve. Couples therapy has often been combined with cognitive-behavioral therapy in the treatment of MED. A multicomponent treatment for MED developed by Raymond Rosen et al. (1994) involves sexual and performance anxiety reduction; education and cognitive intervention; script assessment and modification; conflict resolution and relationship enhancement; and relapse prevention.

For women with FSAD, many experts recommend that couples therapy should explore the type and quality of intimacy within a relationship. This would include exploring the willingness of each partner to trust the other, the ability of each partner to share self with the other, and fears of negative evaluation by one or both partners (Gehring, 2003). This approach to couples therapy is consistent with research findings that marital discord is often associated with the four factors of criticism, stonewalling, nonverbal or verbal expression of contempt, and defensiveness (Gottman, 1994).

Biomedical Therapies

There are an increasing number of biomedical treatments available for individuals experiencing sexual arousal disorders. These include medication/drug and surgical treatments, which will now be briefly reviewed.

Medication/Drug Treatments

The best-known medication currently is Viagra (sildenafil) released in 1998 for the treatment of erectile disorder. Viagra is taken orally before engaging in sexual activity. Viagra does not directly produce an erection; however, when males are stimulated sexually after taking Viagra, the drug facilitates the physiological processes that produce erection. Viagra serves to relax the smooth muscles in the corpora cavernosa, allowing blood flow in and creating an erection. In studies comparing Viagra to a placebo (i.e., an inert pill resembling the actual drug), approximately 57 percent of men responded successfully to the drug compared to 21 percent in the placebo group. Side effects appear to be minimal and include headaches, flushing, and vision disturbances. Overall, Viagra appears to be safe (Hyde & DeLamater, 2006).

Another drug that has been developed for MED is Cialis (tadalafil). The drug was developed as an alternative to Viagra. Like Viagra, Cialis relaxes the smooth muscle surrounding the arteries to the penis, thus facilitating engorgement (Brock et al., 2002; Montorsi & Althof, 2004; Padma-Nathan et al., 2001). Unlike Viagra, which lasts for only a few hours, Cialis is effective for as long as twenty-four to thirty-six hours. Levitra (vardenafil), another new drug, works much like Viagra. However, it appears to be somewhat more potent (Hyde & DeLamater, 2006).

Both Viagra and Cialis are peripherally acting drugs, meaning that they act on sites in the penis. An alternative to a peripherally acting drug is a centrally acting one, meaning that it acts on regions of the brain involved in arousal. One such drug is Uprima (apomorphine SL). It acts by increasing levels of dopamine, a neurotransmitter in the brain, particularly in the hypothalamus. Neurotransmitters help different nerve cells located in the brain and other parts of the body to communicate with one another. Uprima acts in twenty minutes and does not produce a spontaneous erection. Like Viagra, it has to be paired with sexual stimulation. Uprima has been demonstrated to be effective in 55 percent of cases (Heaton, 2001).

Currently, drug treatments for FSAD are limited. Typically, physicians have recommended the use of commercial lubricants, vitamin E, and mineral oils as potential treatments for sexual arousal in women (Phillips, 2000). In addition, estrogen replacement has been suggested for premenopausal women.

An equivalent of Viagra for women has been examined for the treatment of FSAD. However, clinical trials have not been successful. One possible reason for the failure of Viagra in women is that Viagra works by increasing vasocongestion, and inadequate vasocongestion is not likely what causes arousal and orgasmic difficulties in most women (Millner, 2005).

Women's sexual problems most often involve orgasm difficulties and low sexual desire. Low sexual desire becomes more of an issue as women age and their ovaries decline in the production of testosterone. At present, treatment for women often involves the administration of testosterone or any other androgen. One drug currently being tested in clinical trials is Instrinsa, a testosterone patch designed for postmenopausal women experiencing low sexual desire (Millner, 2005; Hyde & DeLamater, 2006).

The results of a preliminary study examining three strength levels of Femprox cream, produced by NexMed were announced at the Annual Meeting of the American Urological Association (AUA) in May 2005 ("Female sexual arousal," 2005). Femprox is applied topically and incorporates alprostadil, a vasodilator. Femprox cream was tested in 400 Chinese women (pre- and postmenopausal women between the ages of twenty-one and sixty-five) diagnosed with FSAD. Participants were randomly assigned to either a Femprox group (groups differed by strength of Femprox) or a placebo group. Overall, participants in the Femprox group showed improvement in sexual arousal over the course of treatment, compared to the placebo group. The results of this preliminary study are promising for women with FSAD.

Surgical/Medical Device Treatments

A variety of surgical/medical device treatments are available for the sexual arousal disorders, particularly for MED. These include intracavernosal injections, suction devices, and surgical therapy.

Intracavernosal injection (ICI) is a treatment for MED that involves injecting a drug, for example, alprostadil, into the corpora cavernosa of the penis. The drugs used for ICI procedures are vasodilators. Vasodilators dilate the blood vessels in the penis so that much more blood can accumulate there, resulting in an erection (Hyde & DeLamater, 2006). In one study, the erections produced by the ICI procedure lasted an average of thirty-nine minutes (Levitt & Mulcahy, 1995). ICI is now primarily used in instances where men do not respond to Viagra or similar medications. ICI is also used in combination with cognitive-behavioral therapy in cases where the cause of MED is determined to be psychological and biological in nature. It should be noted that there are some drawbacks to ICI procedures. One drawback is that some men experience penile pain from the procedure. Second, some men who have normal erections may potentially abuse this treatment by using it to obtain "super erections" (Hyde & DeLamater).

Suction devices are also used in the treatment of MED. An external, plastic tube, with a rubber band around it, is placed over the lubricated penis. Suction applied to the tube produces an erection. The erection is maintained by the constricting action of the rubber band, once the external plastic tube has been removed. Suction devices have been used effectively with diabetic men. They are also used in combination with cognitive-behavioral couples therapy for cases of MED that are primarily psychological in nature.

In severe cases of erectile disorder, surgical therapy is possible. The surgery involves implanting a penile prosthesis (Hellstrom et al., 2003a, 2003b; Kabalin & Kuo, 1997). In this procedure, a sac or bladder of water is implanted in the lower abdomen, connected to two inflatable tubes running the course of the corpus spongiosum, with a pump in the scrotum. Therefore, once the procedure is completed, men can inflate the penis so that they have a full erection.

A penile prosthesis is typically implanted as a last resort after sex therapy and drug therapy have been unsuccessful. The surgery destroys some portions of the penis so that a natural erection will never again be possible. Approximately 25 percent of men who undergo this procedure are dissatisfied afterward. Some of the reasons for the dissatisfaction include the penis being smaller when erect after the surgery and the experience of different sensations during both arousal and ejaculation (Steege, Stout, & Carson, 1986).

Another surgical therapy technique involves the implantation of a semi-rigid, silicone-like rod into the penis (Melman & Tiefer, 1992; Shandera & Thompson, 1994). This technique has fewer complications and is less costly than a penile prosthesis (Rosen & Leiblum, 1995).

With regard to FSAD, and female sexual dysfunction in general, a medical device available is the EROS-Clitoral Therapy Device. The device is designed to increase blood flow to the clitoris, and provides a vacuum suction to the clitoris in one of three levels of intensity. Several studies have provided preliminary evidence for the physiological effectiveness of the EROS device in women with FSAD (Billups et al., 2001; Munarriz, Maitland, Garcia, & Goldstein, 2003; Wilson, Delk, & Billups, 2001).

ISSUES FOR FUTURE CONSIDERATION

The sexual arousal disorders, FSAD and MED, are complex and multiply determined in nature. As a result of their complexity, their treatment is often multifaceted. With the above in mind, several suggestions are offered for future consideration. First, more research is necessary to accurately determine the prevalence of the sexual arousal disorders, as their prevalence has historically been highly variable. Second, more education is needed in helping people with sexual arousal problems better understand and recognize such problems. There has often been a stigma attached to sexual arousal problems, as with sexual problems in general, and improved education in terms of their prevalence and characteristics would be helpful to individuals experiencing them as well as to society in general. Third, professionals (e.g., physicians, psychologists, counselors) potentially working with individuals experiencing sexual arousal problems need to also be knowledgeable about such disorders. Professionals being better able to identify sexual arousal problems in patients/clients with whom they work can in turn help their patients confront such a problem sooner. In addition, proper identification of sexual arousal problems would lead to prompt treatment or referral to another professional who can appropriately assess and treat such problems. Finally, more research is needed in regard to the treatment of sexual arousal disorders, particularly in complex presentations of such problems. More studies examining the effectiveness of particular components in overall treatment packages need to be conducted. Therapies for sexual arousal disorders, particularly biomedical approaches, have come a long way, but more needs to be done.

REFERENCES

American Psychiatric Association. (2000). *Diagnostic and statistical manual of mental disorders* (4th ed., text revision). Washington, DC: Author.

Araujo, A., et al. (1998). The relationship between depressive symptoms and male erectile dysfunction: Prospective results from the Massachusetts Male Aging Study. *American Journal of Epidemiology, 152*, 533–541.

Back, A. K., Wincze, J. P., & Barlow, D. H. (2001). Sexual dysfunction. In D. H. Barlow (Ed.), *Clinical handbook of psychological disorders* (3rd ed.). New York: Guilford.

Barlow, D. H. (1986). Causes of sexual dysfunction: The role of anxiety and cognitive interference. *Journal of Consulting and Clinical Psychology, 54*, 140–148.

Billups, K. L., Berman, L., Berman, J., Metz, M. E., Glennon, M. E., & Goldstein, L. (2001). A new nonpharmacological vacuum therapy for female sexual dysfunction. *Journal of Sex and Marital Therapy, 27*, 435–441.

Brock, G. B., McMahon, C. G., Chen, K. K., Costigan, T., Shen, W., Watkins, V., et al. (2002). Efficacy and safety of Tadalafil in men with erectile dysfunction: An integrated analysis of registration trials. *Journal of Urology, 168* (178 Suppl. S.), 1332–1336.

Buvat, J., Buvat-Herbaut, M., Lemaire, A., Marcolin, G., & Quittelier, E. (1990). Recent developments in the clinical assessment and diagnosis of erectile dysfunction. *Annual Review of Sex Research, 1*, 265–308.

Charlton, R. S., & Brigel, F. W. (1997). Treatment of arousal and orgasmic disorders. In R. S. Charlton (Ed.), *Treatment of sexual disorders* (pp. 237–280). San Francisco: Jossey-Bass.

Female sexual arousal disorder, positive Femprox study results. *Medical News Today.* Retrieved on May 25, 2005, from www.medicalnewstoday.com/medicalnews.php?newsid=24977

Gehring, D. (2003). Couple therapy for low sexual desire: A systematic approach. *Journal of Sex and Marital Therapy, 29*, 25–38.

Goldstein, I. (2000). Female sexual arousal disorder: New insights. *International Journal of Impotence Research, 12*(Suppl. 2), S152–S157.

Gottman, J. M. (1994). *What predicts divorce?* Hillsdale, NJ: Lawrence Erlbaum.

Heaton, J. P. W. (2001). Key issues from the clinical trials of apomorphine SL. *World Journal of Urology, 19*, 25–31.

Hellstrom, W. J., Gittelman, M., Karlin, G., Segerson, T., Thibonnier, M., Taylor, T., et al. (2003a). Sustained efficacy and tolerability of vardenafil, a highly potent selective phosphodiesterase type 5 inhibitor, in men with erectile dysfunction: Results of a randomized double-bind, 26-week placebo-controlled pivotal trial. *Urology, 61*(4 Suppl. 1), 8–14.

Hellstrom, W. J., Overstreet, J. W., Yu, A., Saikali, K., Shen, W., Beasley, Jr., M., et al. (2003b). Tadalafil has no detrimental effect on human spermatogenesis or reproductive hormones. *Journal of Urology, 170*, 887–891.

Hooper, J. (1998, August). Science in the sack: Beyond Viagra. *Health and Fitness*, pp. 108–113.

Hyde, J. S., & DeLamater, J. D. (2006). *Understanding human sexuality* (9th ed.). New York: McGraw Hill.

Jackson, G. (1999). Erectile dysfunction and cardiovascular disease. *International Journal of Clinical Practice, 53*, 363–368.

Johri, A., Heaton, J., & Morales, A. (2001). Severe erectile dysfunction is a marker for hyperprolactinemia. *International Journal of Impotence Research, 13*, 176–182.

Kabalin, J. N., & Kuo, J. C. (1997). Long-term follow-up of and patient satisfaction with the Dynaflex self-contained inflatable penile prosthesis. *Journal of Urology, 158*, 456–469.

Laan, E., Everaerd, W., van Aanhold, M., & Rebel, M. (1993). Performance demand and sexual arousal in women. *Behaviour Research and Therapy, 31*, 25–35.

Laumann, E. O., Gagnon, J. H., Michael, R. T., & Michaels, S. (1994). *The social organization of sexuality*. Chicago: University of Chicago Press.

Laumann, E. O., Paik, A., & Rosen, R. C. (1999). Sexual dysfunction in the United States: Prevalence and predictors. *Journal of the American Medical Association, 281*, 537–544.

Leonard, L. M., & Follette, V. M. (2002). Sex functioning in women reporting a history of child sexual abuse: Clinical and empirical considerations. *Annual Review of Sex Research, 13*, 346–388.

Levitt, E. E., & Mulcahy, J. J. (1995). The effect of intracavernosal injection of papaverine hydrochloride on orgasm latency. *Journal of Sex and Marital Therapy, 21*, 39–41.

LoPiccolo, J. (1997). Sex therapy: A postmodern model. In S. J. Lynn & J. P. Garske (Eds.), *Contemporary psychotherapies: Models and methods*. New York: Guilford.

Masters, W. H., & Johnson, V. E. (1970). *Human sexual inadequacy*. London: Churchill.

McCarthy, B. W. (1990). Treating sexual dysfunction associated with prior sexual trauma. *Journal of Sex and Marital Therapy, 16*, 142–146.

Melman, A., & Tiefer, L. (1992). Surgery for erectile disorders: Operative procedures and psychological issues. In R. C. Rosen & S. R. Leiblum (Eds.), *Erectile disorders* (pp. 255–282). New York: Guilford.

Millner, V. S. (2005). Female sexual arousal disorder and counseling deliberations. *Family Journal, 13*(1), 95–100.

Montorsi, F., & Althof, S. (2004). Partner responses to sildenafil citrate (Viagra) treatment of erectile dysfunction. *Urology, 63*, 762–767.

Morales, A., & Heaton, J. (2001). Hormonal erectile dysfunction: Evaluation and management. *Urologic Clinics of North America, 28*, 279.

Munarriz, R., Maitland, S., Garcia, S. P., Talakoub, L., & Goldstein, I. (2003). A prospective duplex Doppler ultrasonographic study in women with sexual arousal disorder to objectively assess genital engorgement induced by EROS therapy. *Journal of Sex and Marital Therapy, 29*(1), 85–94.

Padma-Nathan, H., et al. (2001). On-demand IC351 (Cialis) enhances erectile function in patients with erectile dysfunction. *International Journal of Impotence Research, 13*, 2–9.

Palace, E. M., & Gorzalka, B. B. (1990). The enhancing effects of anxiety on arousal in sexually dysfunctional and functional women. *Journal of Abnormal Psychology, 99*, 403–411.

Palace, E. M., & Gorzalka, B. B. (1992). Differential patterns of arousal in sexually functional and dysfunctional women: Physiological and subjective components of sexual response. *Archives of Sexual Behavior, 21*, 135–159.

Phillips, N. A. (2000). Female sexual dysfunction: Evaluation and treatment. *American Family Physician, 62*(1), 127–136.

Richardson, J. D. (1993). Male sexual dysfunction: Ejaculatory problems. *Australian Family Physician, 22*(8), 1367–1370.

Rosen, R. C., & Leiblum, S. R. (1995). Treatment of sexual disorders in the 1990s: An integrated approach. *Journal of Consulting and Clinical Psychology, 63*(6), 877–890.

Rosen, R. C., Leiblum, S. R., & Spector, I. P. (1994). Psychologically based treatment for male erectile disorder: A cognitive-interpersonal model. *Journal of Sex and Marital Therapy, 20*, 67–85.

Segraves, R. T., Schoenberg, H. W., & Ivanoff, J. (1983). Serum testosterone and prolactin levels in erectile dysfunction. *Journal of Sex and Marital Therapy, 9*, 19–26.

Shandera, K. C., & Thompson, I. M. (1994). Urologic protheses. *Emergency Medicine Clinics of North America, 12*, 729–748.

Steege, J. F., Stout, A. L., & Carson, C. C. (1986). Patient satisfaction in Scott and Small-Carrion penile implant recipients. *Archives of Sexual Behavior, 15*, 393–400.

Sue, D., Sue, D. W., & Sue, S. (2003). *Understanding abnormal behavior* (7th ed.). Boston: Houghton Mifflin Company.

de Tejada, I. S., Angulo, J., Cellek, S., González-Cadavid, N., Heaton, J., Pickard, R. et al. (2005). Pathophysiology of erectile dysfunction. *Journal of Sexual Medicine, 2* (1), 26–39.

Van Lankveld, J. J. D. M. (1998). Bibliotherapy in the treatment of sexual dysfunctions: A meta-analysis. *Journal of Consulting and Clinical Psychology, 66*(4), 702–708.

Van Lankveld, J. J. D. M., Everaerd, W., & Grotjohann, Y. (2001). Cognitive-Behavioral bibliotheca for sexual dysfunctions in heterosexual couples: A randomized waiting-list controlled clinical trial in the Netherlands. *Journal of Sex Research, 38*(1), 51–67.

Wilson, S. K., Delk, J. R., & Billups, K. L. (2001). Treating symptoms of female sexual arousal disorder with the Eros-Clitoral Therapy Device. *Journal of Gender Specific Medicine, 4*(2), 54–58.

Wyatt, G. E., Chin, D., & Asuan-O'Brien, A. (2002). Child sexual abuse: Associations with the sexual functioning of adolescents and adults. *Annual Review of Sex Research, 13*, 307–345.

8

Orgasmic Problems and Disorders

Vaughn S. Millner ◆

What could possibly go wrong with orgasm? Orgasm, considered by many to be one of the most basic physiological functions and one of life's greatest pleasures, is an activity that can result in ecstasy, a child, a warm glow, or, at the very least, a mild purr.

As a sex researcher, therapist, counselor, educator, and human sexuality course instructor, I have had the opportunity to observe and hear reports from clients, students, and colleagues about many misconceptions regarding the natural phenomenon of orgasm. Consider the following examples. During a gynecological exam, a physician asked his 22-year-old, recently married patient if she had orgasms. "I don't know," she replied. He quickly added, "Then you haven't." On another day, the physician asked his 19-year-old, college student patient if he had engaged in sex yet. His patient honestly responded that he had not yet "gotten involved." Instead, had the physician asked his male patient if he had experienced intercourse yet, he would have received a different answer. Some college students believe they have not had sex unless they have an orgasm; and some believe that if they had engaged in anal intercourse, but not vaginal intercourse, then they have not had sex (Randall & Byers, 2003). The bottom line is that there is much confusion in North America about accurate information about sex, and imbedded in this misinformation is uncertainty about orgasmic function.

In this chapter, I will describe orgasm as well as orgasmic problems and the more serious orgasmic disorders. I also will ask readers to consider the context of the sexual experience and recognize how aging does and does not play a part in orgasmic satisfaction. In addition, readers will be provided a sampling of treatment options for orgasmic problems.

WHAT IS ORGASM?

Orgasm is considered to be the culminating event in what is termed the "sexual response cycle." Several versions of the sexual response cycle exist. Sex research pioneers Masters and Johnson (1966) described the male's and female's sexual response cycle in four parts: (1) the excitement phase, (2) the plateau phase, (3) the orgasmic phase, and (4) the resolution phase (also includes the refractory phase for males). This chapter focuses on the orgasmic phase; but it should be remembered that other phases are both directly and indirectly linked to the orgasmic phase. The first stage, excitement, refers to the body's physiological response to psychological and/or physical sexual stimulation. If the individual maintains the excitement phase, the second, or plateau, phase is entered. Sexual tension increases if the individual continues to find the sexual stimuli exciting. The ultimate release of continuing tension results in orgasm, contraction of the sex organs. During the orgasmic phase, involuntary climax is reached, with sensations occurring for females primarily in the clitoris, vagina, and uterus. For men, orgasm includes sensations mainly in the penis, prostate, and seminal vesicles. The final stage, resolution, is the inevitable loss of tension. Added to this cycle for men is the refractory period, the time during which the penis once again achieves tumescence. The refractory period varies considerably among men; and its description has been contradicted by some researchers, who rejoin that some men have multiple orgasms (Dunn & Trost, 1989).

The ejaculation process (i.e., the emission and expulsion of the whitish seminal fluid in men during the orgasm phase) is described by Masters and Johnson (1966) to occur within two stages. The first stage includes the expulsion of seminal fluid into the prostatic urethra via contractions. In this stage, the sphincter of the urinary bladder closes, or remains closed to prevent leakage into the bladder, as well as to contain the urine in the bladder, thereby effectively eliminating the possibility of the mixture of the urine and seminal fluid. In the second stage, the seminal fluid progresses from the prostatic urethra to the urethral opening. Subsequently, ejaculatory contractions project seminal fluid. Once males have begun ejaculatory contractions, the seminal fluid projections cannot be stopped, at least not in younger males. Not all older males have a clear differentiation of the two stages, that is, there may be a projection of the seminal fluid without the first stage's clear caution of irreversibility. Perry and Whipple (1981) studied female ejaculators and asserted that the two-phase ejaculatory process is as appropriate for women as it is for men.

In contrast to the Masters and Johnson (1966) model developed for both men and women, Walsh and Wilson (1987) developed a normal sexual response cycle for men and suggested five interrelated occurrences during the sexual cycle: libido (desire), erection, ejaculation, orgasm, and detumescence. All of these are related, of course, to orgasmic function. Kandeel, Koussa, and Swerdloff (2001) describe the stages as follows: The first stage, desire, varies in intensity and is influenced by many factors, including pharmacological agents and erotica. Desire may also be influenced by elevated levels of testosterone in older men, but not in younger men. Erection, the second stage, is the result of multiple stimuli that impact neurological and vascular pathways that eventually produce tumescence in the penis rigid enough for penetration. Tumescence occurs as a result of increased blood flow to the penis. The third stage, ejaculation, is a reflex, and results from action taking place in the sympathetic nervous system. The next phase, orgasm, is influenced by both physical and psychological factors. Orgasm involves contraction of the sex organs as well as pressure release in the urethra, contractions of the pelvic floor muscles, ejaculation, and, ultimately, release of tension. Orgasms, however, do not always include ejaculation. Orgasm and ejaculation, although two interrelated events, are separate physiological functions. Orgasm may occur with or without emission or ejaculation, and conversely, ejaculation can occur with or without orgasm (Kandeel et al., 2001; Wylie & Ralph, 2005). Finally, during the detumescence stage, the penis relaxes to a flaccid condition. The blood is drained away from the penis until, over time, it returns to the pretumescent level.

Overall, it is to be noted that orgasms for both men and women can occur alone or with a partner of either sex. Therefore, they can occur through coitus, oral sex, masturbation, or other means. In addition, orgasmic feelings can occur within the genital and pelvic area or extend to other areas of the body (Mah & Binik, 2002).

SEXUAL HEALTH AND THE SEXUAL EXPERIENCE

Having recognized the process of the orgasmic phenomenon, let us stop to consider what constitutes a healthy sexual experience overall before we discuss the factors influencing the satisfactory orgasmic experience. Perhaps the best way to proceed is to identify a reasonable definition of sexual health. Of the various definitions of sexual health established over time (see Edwards & Coleman, 2004, for a review), the working definition offered by an international consulting group on sexual health and published by the World Health Organization (2005) is the most compelling and appropriate one for the reader to keep in mind as he or she reads this chapter.

> Sexual health is a state of physical, emotional, mental and social well-being in relation to sexuality; it is not merely the absence of disease, dysfunction or infirmity. Sexual health requires a positive and respectful approach to sexuality and sexual relationships, as well as the possibility of having pleasurable and safe sexual experiences, free of coercion,

discrimination and violence. For sexual health to be attained and maintained, the sexual rights of all persons must be respected, protected and fulfilled. (p. 1)

I invite the reader to consider this inclusive understanding of sexual health as a helpful way to frame understanding of orgasmic function. The healthy orgasmic experience is more than "sexual activity" and reflects a positive approach to sexuality. Orgasms are part of the total sensual, sexual experience and can be influenced by many factors including emotions such as anger, guilt, and sadness, as well as negative thoughts, being in uncomfortable or fearful situations, feeling tired, not feeling attracted to the sexual partner, or not feeling attractive.

To what can orgasms be attributed—the mind or the body? Orgasmic satisfaction is related to the interpersonal, subjective experience as much as, if not more so than, the total sensory experience (Mah & Binik, 2005). Of course, much of the body is involved in the orgasmic experience of the sexual response cycle. The body's orgasmic response to sexual stimulation involves both widespread vasocongestion (accumulation of blood producing swelling) and an overall increase in muscle tension (Masters & Johnson, 1966). However, claims that the brain may be the body's biggest sex organ are not unfounded. The brain, with a complex relationship to the spinal cord, drives sexual behavior (Coolen, Allard, Truitt, & McKenna, 2004; Holstege et al., 2003; see also Chapter 2 in this volume).

Cognitive shifts are recognized in Basson's (2002) development of a woman's sexual arousal model. Basson (2002) contends that when a woman experiences genital congestion due to sexual stimuli, she may interpret that in one of several ways. A woman may decide to enjoy the experience or may reinterpret sexual stimuli through her thoughts and negate its influence. This is a reasonable view. Arousal can persist throughout a woman's sexual experience or can dwindle at some point during the sexual response cycle, thereby determining whether a woman will attain a fulfilling orgasmic experience or perhaps no orgasm at all (Millner, 2005). For instance, a woman may be engaged in a steamy sexual liaison with her male partner on the way to orgasm when she suddenly wonders if her 6-year-old child is still asleep. What if he gets up for a drink of water? What if he hears them? The cognitive shift from self to other can effectively reduce the possibilities of her achieving orgasmic release. Her male partner, on the other hand, may be more likely to be genitally focused and less distracted. The path to attaining orgasm is not always a straight or sure one.

NORMAL SEXUAL DEVELOPMENT

Humans develop sexually over time. By adolescence, one's sexual response is determined by a complex mix of messages determined by biology, gender differences promoted by society, sexual messages provided by family and friends as well as personal experiences, and individual differences. Include emotions and hormonal influences in this mix and we have a multidetermined sexual experience.

Generally for young males, problems with orgasms are not associated with adolescence. Adolescent and young adult females, however, may have difficulties having orgasm because of factors such as time pressures, less knowledge about their bodies, and lack of intimacy in relationships. Middle-aged adults have the added burden of reduced hormone levels. Overall, as women age, they tend to have fewer sexual problems, with the exception of lubrication, whereas sexual problems for aging men are positively associated with erection problems and lack of desire for sex (Laumann, Paik, & Rosen, 1999).

During a male's development, he usually does not have to concern himself with whether he will be able to reach orgasm. As an adolescent, hormones are typically coursing through his system and he finds himself experiencing spontaneous erections often without any external stimulation. As men grow older, orgasmic difficulties increase (Araujo, Mohr, & McKinlay, 2004). More attention must be given to what constitutes desire and how it can be attained. All phases of the male sexual response cycle (Masters & Johnson, 1966) are impacted by aging. Worldwide, for men, the biggest problem is premature ejaculation, followed by erectile difficulties for men over 40 (Laumann et al., 2004; Wylie & Ralph, 2005). It takes longer to achieve a full erection, and direct genital stimulation is needed to maintain the erection. With age, men's orgasms feel less intense, detumescence is quicker and there is a longer refractory period. In addition, there is less ejaculation (Kandeel et al., 2001). Although these age-related sexual changes are consistent (Dunn, Croft, & Hackett, 1999; Laumann et al., 1999), hormonal involvement in such changes is not clear.

For women, age-related physical changes include vaginal dryness, loss of vaginal elasticity, clitoral shrinkage, and lessened lubrication (Kingsberg, 2002). These often are related to menopause (the cessation of menstruation) and the corresponding decline of hormones. Androgens, namely, male sex hormones such as testosterone, play a role in women's sexual functioning, but the extent of the impact remains unclear (Bachman et al., 2002; Berman, Berman, & Goldstein, 1999). Women approaching menopause have about half of the androgens they had in their thirties and forties (Braunstein, 2002). Reduced estrogen levels as well as lower testosterone levels are associated with increased complaints of decreased desire and pleasure.

A developmental milestone for many young and middle-aged adults is pregnancy. Much is written and discussed about care for the mother and baby during pregnancy. Not so commonly discussed is the impact of pregnancy on a woman's sexual functioning. As the pregnancy progresses, some women report less ability to reach orgasm and less frequent coitus (Bogren, 1991; Gökyildiz & Beji, 2005). Changes in sexual functioning are due in part to changes in how women view their changing bodies and to the extent that they feel attractive to their partner. The greatest fear is that of harming the baby during sexual activity (von Sydow, 1999).

Another age-related factor that affects sexual functioning via impact to the uterus, hormones, and nerve endings is a hysterectomy. All women experience hormone fluctuation or hormone decline after a hysterectomy. In addition, as a result of the trauma on the body, both physically and psychologically, women can experience difficulties achieving orgasm postsurgery, although this is not an inevitable outcome (Sholty et al., 1984). Indeed, many women express increased sexual satisfaction after a hysterectomy (Goetsch, 2005). What is often missing from study analysis is the evaluation of women's subjective sexual experience, which may be the component that makes the difference between an orgasm or lack thereof.

PROBLEMS VERSUS DISORDERS

Apart from normal age-related orgasmic problems, many people have other types of orgasmic problems at least some of the time at some point during their lifetimes. Some have chronic, long-lasting conditions of difficulty achieving orgasmic satisfaction and never attain an orgasm. This is when a situational problem can turn into what clinicians call a "disorder."

Some are concerned about these circumstances whereas others are not worried. For example, some men ejaculate earlier than others. For those men, or their partners, who are concerned about this tendency, this is a problem. Others may decide to adapt in some way so that even though the condition still exists, they can create a pleasurable sexual experience for both partners. One of the distinguishing features of what constitutes a disorder is one's identification that the condition is problematic and impacts functioning. In other words, a sexual problem does not automatically translate into a sexual disorder. Individual perception can be key to identification of a sexual problem as a sexual disorder.

Therapists and other clinicians identify sexual disorders in their clients and patients based on the definitions used in the *Diagnostic and Statistical Manual of Mental Disorders—Fourth edition text revision* (American Psychiatric Association, 2000). This book is the "clinician's bible" as it provides a standardized definition of people's serious or persistent mental problems. The *DSM-IV-TR* bases its classification of sexual disorders largely on the previously described Masters and Johnson (1966) model of sexual response. The *DSM-IV-TR* sexual response cycle consists of the separate phases of desire, excitement, orgasm, and resolution. Problems may occur at one or more of these stages simultaneously.

To qualify as a *DSM-IV-TR* disorder, a person must experience considerable personal or interpersonal distress. Clinicians must specify as to whether the condition is (a) lifelong or acquired, (b) generalized or related to a particular situation or person, and (c) due to psychological or other factors.

Context is essential in the consideration of sexual problems (Bancroft, 2002; Kaschak & Tiefer, 2001). Masters and Johnson (1966) were careful to identify the importance of context in the sexual experience. They asked readers to limit the generalizability of their findings and called for more research, particularly as the research related to subjective feelings associated with physiological sexual reactions. Some subsequent clinicians did not heed their advice and proceeded to minimize the subjective component and emphasize only the physiological element.

The importance of context is illustrated in the following example: Sonya and José have been married for twenty years. In their first ten years of marriage, they had an active sexual relationship and Sonya experienced orgasm easily. In their eleventh year of marriage, José became distracted from their relationship and immersed himself in his work. Sonya also distanced herself from the relationship, concentrating instead on their children. Sonya began to fantasize frequently about other men. She became irritated when José initiated lovemaking because she sensed that he was merely seeking self-gratification rather than intimately reaching out to her. Mentally, she began to shut down and withdraw from José. When engaged in sexual activity with José, her thoughts of resentment continued unabated, and her body quickly responded by producing less lubrication and tensed muscles. She quit experiencing orgasms with José eleven years ago, although she could easily self-masturbate orgasmically. Does a woman have a sexual disorder if she is unable to have an orgasm with her husband of twenty years (one context), but can experience an orgasm by masturbation (a different context) or with a lover (another different context)? Should the woman be labeled with a disorder when it is possible that her husband does not stimulate her either psychologically or physically?

With these considerations in mind, the *DSM-IV-TR* still offers clarity and definition to what could be ambiguous sexual problems and recognizes three disorders involving problems with orgasms. The first is Female Orgasmic Disorder, also called Inorgasmia or Anorgasmia. According to the *DSM-IV-TR*, this condition is a "persistent or recurrent delay in, or absence of, orgasm in a female following a normal sexual excitement phase" (p. 547). Anorgasmia is distinguished by type. It includes women who have lifelong orgasmic problems versus acquired problems and women who have situational orgasmic problems versus more generalized problems. The clinician, in consultation with the woman, determines whether her orgasmic activity is adequate for age, sexual experience, and the satisfactoriness of the focus, intensity, and duration of sexual stimulation she is given.

About 50 percent of women attain orgasm through intercourse (Merck Manual, n.d.). Of the women who attain orgasms, they do so only about 40–80 percent of the time (Davidson & Darling, 1989). As recently as the 1970s and 1980s, these women would have been called "frigid" if they did not consistently experience orgasm during coitus. Such societal pressure has resulted in women "faking orgasms" out of embarrassment or shame that they are not equivalent to men in their orgasmic performance (Butler, 1976). In contrast, many women today are seeking help from physicians or sex therapists for orgasmic problems.

Anorgasmia can result from multiple factors, including inadequate arousal time for the woman during foreplay, ignorance of the woman's anatomy, and premature ejaculation (*Merck Manual*, n.d.). Other contributing factors include sexual side effects from pharmaceutical drugs or a woman's inability to release her inhibitions. Some of the treatment options include sex education, Kegel exercises to improve the pubococcygeus muscle tone, and sensate focus exercises (see under Treatment Options).

The second orgasmic disorder recognized by the *DSM-IV-TR* is Male Orgasmic Disorder. Described as a "persistent or recurrent delay in, or absence of, orgasm following a normal sexual excitement phase during sexual activity" (American Psychiatric Association, 2000, p. 552), it occurs in about 2–8 percent of the general population (Rowland, Keeney, & Slob, 2004). With the most common form of this condition, a man can ejaculate with manual stimulation from a partner, but is unable to reach orgasm during intercourse. Others may require prolonged stimulation to achieve orgasm during intercourse. Some men can attain orgasm by masturbation, but others are either unwilling or cannot masturbate to orgasm. Some, but not all of these men, experience full erections and nighttime emissions (Perelman, 2001).

The preceding *DSM-IV-TR* description needs further clarification. Although the manual states that men can have orgasms without the emission of semen, this distinction is not evident in the description of the disorder. If the reader will recall, orgasm and ejaculation are interrelated, but separate, physiological processes (Waldinger & Schweitzer, 2005). Advances continue in the clarification of the complex physiological processes that occur before, during, and after orgasm (Jannini & Lenzi, 2005; Kandeel et al., 2001; Ralph & Wylie, 2005; Waldinger & Schweitzer, 2005).

Male orgasmic disorder can result due to early prohibitive messages from childhood, early traumatic events, or lack of attraction to a partner. Also, it can occur as a result from a biological predisposition (Perelman, 2001), diseases such as multiple sclerosis and diabetes (Penson et al., 2003) as well as pelvic-region surgery and certain medications (Kandeel et al., 2001; Raja, 1999; Rosenberg, 1999). Treatment for male orgasmic disorder has not yet been standardized, but when there is a psychological etiology, some treat the condition with the introduction of stronger sexual stimulation such as erotic videos and a vibrator (Geboes, Steeno, & DeMoor, 1975). Others have found that low sexual arousal can be a general characteristic for these men (Rowland et al., 2004). Therefore, one treatment option that may be explored in couples sex therapy involves anxiety-reducing techniques such as conflict resolution and trust building. Perelman (2001) found success using a combination of treatment strategies such as sex education, pharmaceutical options such as sildenafil citrate (marketed as Viagra), and cognitive-behavioral techniques. A comprehensive approach utilizing the physiological, psychological, relational, and sexual education factors is usually the most effective one (McCarthy & Fucito, 2005).

The last orgasmic disorder listed by the *DSM-IV-TR* is rapid or premature ejaculation, the most common ejaculatory problem, affecting approximately 29 percent of men (Laumann et al., 1999). The opposite of male orgasmic disorder, premature ejaculation is "the persistent or recurrent onset of orgasm and ejaculation with minimal sexual stimulation before, on, or shortly after penetration and before the person wishes it" (American Psychiatric Association, *DSM IV-TR*, 2000, p. 552). This condition involves powerlessness to control ejaculation for a "satisfactory" amount of time prior to penetration. "Satisfactory" time typically means that a man ejaculates within one minute after he has penetrated the vagina, or he ejaculates too early for his partner to be satisfied in at least one half of his attempts at intercourse with that partner (Master & Turek, 2001; Waldinger, 2003). It can be caused by both physiological and psychological factors. Biologically determined factors include nervous system diseases, prostatitis, urinary tract infections, and physical injuries such as spinal cord injuries. Psychological factors include negative psychological states such as depression and anxiety in addition to a lack of psychosexual skills, relationship stress, and interpersonal problems (Metz & Pryor, 2000). Comprehensive assessment and treatment should consider both potential physiological and psychological causes and be targeted for the individual. Some treatment options include cognitive-behavioral therapy, couples communication training, pharmaceutical drugs such as selective serotonin reuptake inhibitors (SSRIs), or microsurgery.

In addition to the disorders listed in the *DSM-IV-TR*, Ralph and Wylie (2005), urologists in the United Kingdom, identified other ejaculatory problems. The following is a brief overview:

1. *Anejaculation*. There is no ejaculation. This condition can result from either psychological or physical causes. Psychological origins are usually involved when men are anorgasmic. This could occur either in one particular situation or in various settings. For example, a man may be able to masturbate and ejaculate, but is unable to ejaculate with a partner. Physical causes include diseases such as diabetes and neurological problems. Treatment depends on the origin of the problem, and can include sex therapy and pharmaceutical drugs such as ephedrine and imipromine. Another option is electroejaculation wherein an electrical current stimulates ejaculation.

2. *Aspermia*. This is the inability to ejaculate semen even with erection and orgasm (Papadimas et al., 1999). Aspermia may be the result of several factors such as obstruction, illness, or biological imperfections.

3. *Retrograde ejaculation*. Referring to the absence of ejaculation as a result of semen moving backward through the bladder neck into the bladder, retrograde ejaculation can be congenital, or can occur from diabetes, spinal cord lesions, or neurological or physical damage to the bladder neck. Retrograde ejaculation is considered to be the ejaculatory problem described as part of

male orgasmic disorder (Waldinger & Schweitzer, 2005). A physician can diagnose this condition by finding sperm and fructose in urine after a man experiences orgasm.

4. *Hematospermia.* With this condition, there is blood in the semen, generally a result of infection in the urogenital tract, especially in younger men (Feldmeier, Leutscher, Poggensee, & Harms, 1999). Other conditions associated with hematospermia could include cysts, polyps, or cancer of the prostate (Papp, Kopa, Szabó, & Erdei, 2003). An examination by a physician is necessary to determine the cause and type of treatment.

5. *Odynorgasmia.* Referring to painful ejaculation, this condition is rare. It is sometimes associated with cancer (Donnellan, Breathnach, & Crown, 2000) or occasionally radical prostatectomy (Koeman, van Driel, Schultz, & Mensick, 1996). In addition, antidepressant medication has been associated with painful ejaculation (Michael, 2000). A physician determines the diagnosis and treatment.

6. *Low volume of ejaculate.* This, too, is an unusual occurrence, and it can be biological in origin or related to lesions caused by surgery.

Overall, when considering if one has a disorder or a problem, it is important first to recognize that calling problems "disorders" can be problematic in itself in treatment. Labeling a woman "inorgasmic" can convince the woman that inorgasmia is something she "is" rather than a solvable condition she "has." This is an important distinction. A disorder is a condition that one possesses. With the exception of the limitations of some medical conditions, it is generally not an irreversible problem and does not define the person.

Medical Factors and Orgasmic Problems

There are a plethora of medical factors that impact orgasms. Some of these are diseases, injuries, physiological problems, and pharmaceutical options.

One of the most common causes of male sexual dysfunction is vascular insufficiency (Kandeel et al., 2001; Melman & Gingell, 1999). If blood cannot reach the cavernous tissue in the penis, then full erection is not possible. Men who experience vascular diseases, hypertension, diabetes, heart disease, high cholesterol, or a stroke tend to have increased likelihood of erectile problems (Laumann et al., 2004). Other organic components known to cause erectile dysfunction include liver disease, renal failure, blockage of small vessels in the penis of older men, chronic obstructive pulmonary disease, cancer (Kandeel et al., 2001), and neurological disorders such as Parkinson's or Alzheimer's disease (Lue, 2000). Some of the psychological origins include performance anxiety, depression, and a difficult relationship (Lue, 2000).

Diseases can impact sexual functioning in a variety of ways depending on the type of disease and treatment. A disease that can have both direct and indirect impact on sexual functioning is cancer, the second leading cause of death in the United States (Anderson & Smith, 2005). Cancer survivors, in an ever-increasing population, are living longer, and those who have been cured of cancer often have residual long-lasting psychosocial and sexual needs that formed during cancer treatment (Reuben, 2004). For example, consider surgery for prostate cancer. Prostate cancer sometimes results in a radical prostatectomy, removal of the prostate. This can result in erectile dysfunction. In recent years, however, surgery has advanced to the extent that men often regain their ability to engage in sexual intercourse within two years (Walsh, Marschke, Ricker, & Burnett, 2000). Many men, nevertheless, maintain a sense of embarrassment or shame, which prevents them from seeking help. For those men who express concern and are open to assistance, relief is available in the form of medication, injections, or penile implants (Burnett, 2005). Recognition of sexual needs during and after cancer treatment is an essential quality of life issue.

Another medical factor sometimes leading to orgasmic problems is injury to the body. One of the most debilitating injuries as it relates to sexual activity is a spinal cord injury (Charlifue, Gerhart, Menter, Whiteneck, & Manley, 1992; Sipski, Rosen, Alexander, & Gomez-Marin, 2004). The sympathetic arousal mechanism impacted by spinal cord injuries has been shown to influence genital sensitivity (Sipski et al., 2004), and anxiety and negative body image are often added to the physiological impairment. Such injuries do not inevitably cause sexual dysfunction, however. For instance, reports indicate that about one-half of women with spinal cord injuries report the ability to achieve orgasm (Charlifue, Gerhart, Menter, Whiteneck, & Manley, 1992; Sipski & Alexander, 1993). In some cases, research shows that for women who have injuries at T6 and above, the ability to experience orgasm is not related to their injuries (Sipski, Alexander, & Rosen, 1995); whereas those with total disruption have a much more difficult experience. One expert in this area, Sipski (2002), states that women with various types of spinal cord injuries can experience the sensations associated with orgasm. Sipski urges women with injuries to become more sexually self-aware, masturbate, and use mechanical devices such as vibrators to help improve their sexual response.

Sexual functioning can also be hampered by substances such as alcohol. A study by Johnson, Phelps, and Cottler (2004) found an association between inhibited orgasm and marijuana and heavy alcohol use for both men and women. Heavy drinking in this study was defined as seven or more drinks every day for a period of two weeks or longer, or drinking heavily at least once a week for a period of two months or longer. Drinking also interferes with one's ability to make wise sexual choices. Some mistakenly make decisions to drink based on the intention that alcohol will reduce their inhibition and enhance their sexual satisfaction. Instead, excessive drinking minimizes selectivity of a partner and creates vulnerability to sexual aggression (Klassen & Wilsnack, 1986).

Another substance-related contribution to orgasmic problems is medication side effects. Medication serves multiple roles in its association with sexual functioning. Although in some cases, pharmaceutical options such as sildenafil can positively enhance orgasmic functioning, medication can also wreak havoc on sexuality. Adverse reactions can be related to medications that alter physical processes that mediate sexual function or impact hormone levels, which could diminish sexual functioning. An example of the contradictory roles an antidepressant medication can play is when a man experiences enhanced sexual interest but cannot express it because of the medication's effect on erectile functioning.

Antidepressant medication is particularly well known for its relationship to lowered sexual functioning (Ashton & Rosen, 1998; Kennedy, Eisfeld, Dickens, Bacchiochi, & Bagby, 2000). However, one group of researchers, Rowland, Myers, Culver, and Davidson (1997) found that the oral antidepressant drug called bupropion (commonly known as Wellbutrin) had no such deleterious effect. Rowland and colleagues found that bupropion was not associated with erectile problems in either healthy men or men with diabetes. In addition, both groups of men generally reported that their sexual satisfaction remained intact or slightly improved with the use of bupropion. The researchers concluded that bupropion should be considered as a treatment for depression in diabetic men and others. Zimmerman et al. (2005), in a separate work, encouraged physicians to consider bupropion as a first treatment option for men with depression because of the lack of sexual side effects. Unfortunately, these findings have not consistently been demonstrated with women (Michelson, Bancroft, Targum, Kim, & Tepner, 2000).

Other Contributing Factors to Orgasm Problems

The body should be viewed holistically, that is, the sexual functioning of a human works optimally if the physical, mental, emotional, social, and spiritual aspects are balanced. Sexual problems and dysfunctions can occur at any point in the sexual response cycle with the occurrence of psychological conditions that influence satisfactory sexual experiences. Unfortunately, common negative mood states such as depression and anxiety can quickly and effectively eradicate the potential to encounter satisfactory orgasms. Psychological problems may stand alone or be directly related to a medical condition. Consider social phobia, that is, a relentless fear of social situations. For men, social phobia has been found to be associated with impaired arousal, orgasm, and sexual satisfaction. Women with social phobia also have problems with arousal and general sexual activity as well (Bodinger et al., 2002).

In a study by Laumann et al. (1999), factors that contributed to how likely one might experience sexual pleasure were identified. Some of the factors from the study include:

1. *Education.* Higher education generally meant more pleasurable sex. In addition, for women, higher education level was associated with fewer problems with orgasm.

2. *Attitudes.* Women who expected little from their relationships were also those women who reported an inability to reach orgasm. For men, erectile problems resulted from being in an uncommitted relationship.

3. *Health.* Poor health for women was associated with sexual pain whereas poor health for men was related to an increased risk of all sexual dysfunctions.

4. *Lifestyle factors.* For both women and men, low feelings of emotional satisfaction were associated with more sexual dysfunction, but especially so for women. In addition, infrequent sexual activity resulted in both lubrication and erectile problems.

5. *Sexual trauma.* Both men and women who experienced sexual victimization reported long-term problems in their sexual functioning. This is consistent with others' findings (Dennerstein, Guthrie, & Alford, 2004), wherein women who had been abused were found to have fewer sexual activities than women who had not experienced abuse.

6. *Stress.* For both men and women, all phases of the sexual response cycle are negatively impacted by emotional and stress-related problems.

Finally, the well-known factors of mood, timing, and environment are also influential in how most people experience sex and sexuality (Wells, Lucas, & Meyer, 1980). A discussion of other psychological and medical factors is imbedded in the subsequent dialogue regarding gender and orgasm.

GENDER AND ORGASM

It is difficult to know the number of people who experience sexual problems because many do not feel comfortable discussing their intimate life experiences with researchers or even family physicians. We do know that women report more sexual problems than men. This could mean that women are more open about reporting sexual problems than men, or it may mean that they do have more problems with sex than men. In the most recent analysis of a large, well-controlled survey involving about 13,600 men and 13,800 women from twenty-nine countries, Laumann et al. (1999) found that 43 percent of the women experienced sexual dysfunction as compared to 31 percent of the men. One overall conclusion was that sexual dysfunction is widespread, with sexual problems decreasing as women age, but increasing for aging men. Men aged 50 to 59 years were more than three times as likely to report problems with erection than men aged 18 to 29 years. Nonmarried women were one-and-a-half times more likely to report having orgasm problems than married women. Similarly, nonmarried men also reported higher rates of sexual problems than married men.

Sexual differences naturally involve physiology. A woman's clitoris is the only human organ with the sole purpose to initiate or elevate sexual tension.

A male has no such body part as his penis also serves other purposes. The range of physical differences is actually quite complex, and there is considerable ongoing study about the multiple interrelated physiological systems that distinguish men and women's sexual behavior.

Mentally and socially, there also appear to be differences in the ways men and women experience orgasm. Perhaps this is because right from birth women are socialized differently from men. Society impinges nonpermissive sexual messages upon women more so than with men. This could be one reason why men masturbate more often than women—a fact that leads to more frequent orgasms than women (Oliver & Hyde, 1993).

In examining sexual differences between men and women, Peplau (2003) found four other primary distinctions that I believe have implications for the orgasmic experience. The first difference was sexual desire. Men demonstrated greater sexual desire more consistently than women. Second, men were not as likely to stress committed relationship as a necessary ingredient for sexual behavior as women. Third, men were found to be more sexually aggressive than women. Aggression may be related to sexual self-concept, coercion in sexual relationships, and the decision as to who initiates sex. Fourth, men's sexual behavior did not change as much as women's sexual behavior over time. This fourth condition leaves one to ponder how willingness to change or adapt over a lifetime might very well influence orgasmic outcomes.

When considering differences, there is variability of orgasmic experiences within one's own gender, as well as between males and females. In the 1980s, a group of researchers (Sholty et al., 1984) studied a small group of women to determine how they experienced orgasm. Although the women differed considerably in their preferred methods, several factors positively influenced their orgasmic satisfaction, such as an improved attitude toward experimenting with sex with a long-term partner, improved sexual self-awareness, less fear of pregnancy due to better birth control measures, increased interest in sex and orgasm, and decreased level of shame and inhibition. In this study, women over the age of 40 were more likely to experience orgasm in several anatomic sites.

TREATMENT OPTIONS

Most sexual problems can be resolved with medical or psychological treatment. Generally, a combination of the two is the best approach, and both require education. In addressing treatment, there are several considerations.

First, treatment for orgasm problems must be designed to address the origin of the difficulty. Orgasmic problems and dysfunctions can result from interruption to normal sexual development, aging, medical conditions, restrictive social conditioning, relationship problems, and psychological challenges.

Successful treatment must begin with assessment of the problem. Generally, a physician should be consulted to rule out a physiological problem or medical diagnosis. Physicians can also check for medication side effects that impact sexual functioning. Physicians should be chosen for their expertise as well as their ability to accept that a sexual problem could have psychological, social, or physical origins. Of course, if it is obvious that the problem is purely psychological in origin, then treatment would begin with a mental health professional with expertise in sex therapy. For example, for a man or woman who has been sexually abused as a child and has sexual issues related to the abuse, therapy may be the best place to begin.

Second, it is important to remember that change will be required, and people are sometimes resistant to change. To overcome a sexual problem, one must generally implement changes in one's behavior, thoughts, or relationship. This will require self-awareness, intention to change, actually doing something different, and assessing the effectiveness of that behavior change.

Third, sex therapy often proves to be a useful and effective solution for orgasm problems (D'Amicis, Goldberg, LoPiccolo, Friedman, & Davies, 1985; Pierce, 2000; see also chapter 9 in this volume), but it is important to realize that the interventions vary according to the clinician as well as to the problem. Some clinicians concentrate on behavioral techniques whereas others may focus on relational dynamics. Others, such as Bianchi-Demicheli and Zutter (2005) base their interventions on a holistic approach addressing the origin of the problem including biological, intrapsychic, relational, social factors, or a combination of all. Their holistic model offers interventions that attempt to bridge psychological and physical components of sexual problems.

In the following sections, I briefly list a few medical options followed by a short sampling of psychological and behavioral treatments. Medical treatment options include both mechanical devices (for the physical component of orgasm) and pharmaceutical choices (for physical and, sometimes, mental components of orgasm). Psychological interventions include a wide range of therapies, usually involving some type of communication training for partners. Behavioral interventions begin with sex education and debunking of inaccurate sexual myths. Clients are subsequently taught new techniques to assist them in becoming more self-aware and to help them learn how to better please themselves or their partners. Often, sex therapy is fashioned from a combination of medical, psychological, and behavioral options. Collaborative relationships among a client's health care providers would probably best serve the client's interests (Millner & Ullery, 2002).

Medical Interventions

Clitoral Therapy Device

A rather new medical treatment option for female sexual dysfunction, the clitoral therapy device (available from Eros Therapy, Urometrics, St. Paul, Minnesota) is a battery-powered vibratory device. It is designed to provide a light vacuum over the clitoris with the expectation that the clitoral erectile chambers and labia would fill with blood (Bhugra, 2003). Approved by the U.S. Food and Drug Administration (FDA) for treatment of sexual arousal disorder and orgasm disorders in otherwise healthy women, the device also has shown to have promising results for women with sexual disorders resulting from cervical cancer radiation treatment (Schroder et al., 2005).

Pharmaceutical Options

The most popular treatment for men with orgasmic problems is sildenafil (McCarthy & Fucito, 2005). Not an "orgasm" pill, sildenafil (brand name is Viagra) helps men sustain erections by relaxing smooth muscles, expanding the arteries, and swelling the penis when they receive psychological or physical sexual stimulation (Lue, 2000; Rosenberg, 1999). If sildenafil fails as a treatment option, it may bring other issues into consideration, such as lack of desire. Sildenafil appears safe for most men, but there is a health risk for some, especially if they smoke or have underlying cardiovascular disease (Lue, 2000), diabetes, high blood pressure, high cholesterol, or certain eye problems (U.S. Food and Drug Administration, 2005). Sildenafil has not been approved by the FDA for women, although clinical trials are under way.

For women, pharmaceutical options such as estrogen creams and testosterone in combination with estrogen can offer a treatment option for vaginal irritation or dryness that occur with age-related changes (Kingsberg, 2002; "Overview: A Woman's Guide to Hormone Therapy," 2003; Sarrel, 1990). Estrogen, often combined with progestogen, helps to decrease cancer risk for women who have not had a hysterectomy. The risks and benefits are still being studied, however. Taking the hormones is not a simple decision-making process, and women should weigh the risks and the benefits of hormone replacement therapy with their physician.

There is a caveat when looking at a medication solution for sexual problems. Both men and women may choose a drug or medical device as a quick remedy to orgasmic problems that perhaps evolved from other factors such as social conditioning that created anxiety about sexuality (Tiefer, 2002). Although these rapid fixes work up to a point, medical interventions are most successful when partners are psychologically strong and solid in their relationships (McCarthy & Fucito, 2005). Partners may experience a great deal of relief and more satisfactory sexual performance if they focused additionally on the interpersonal aspects of the sexual experience. For example, as men age, arousal becomes increasingly important. Medication alone will not return the men to their adolescent sexual prowess. Additionally, older couples can benefit from learning how to redefine normal sexual activity (Kingsberg, 2002). Medication facilitates the sexual response, but ignoring the rest of the human sexual experience can result in an orgasmic experience that may not be psychologically stimulating (Mah & Binik, 2005).

Psychological and Behavioral Interventions

Intimacy

"What's love got to do with it?" asks a popular song title. This time-honored question as it relates to sexual satisfaction is important. Many people, especially women, require their own emotional investment before relaxing themselves enough to experience orgasm. Love, shown to be an emotion as well as a neurochemical reflection within the human brain, can be an integral component to intimacy, passion, and subsequently orgasm. For many, there is a relationship between intimacy and sexual function (McCabe, 1997), particularly orgasmic satisfaction (Mah & Binik, 2005). It has been shown that those who experience orgasm with a partner are reported to experience greater physiological satisfaction, more intimacy, and deeper pelvic feelings (Newcomb & Bentler, 1983).

One of the fundamental principles in intimacy-based sex therapy is that having an orgasm is not a requirement, but rather a part of an overall satisfactory, intimate sexual experience (Ellison, 2001). An orgasm may or may not happen and the outcome is irrelevant. What is relevant is having a mutually enjoyable sensual and sexual experience with a partner. With intimacy-based sex therapy, partners learn to express their feelings and thoughts truthfully.

Cognitive Restructuring

Cognitive restructuring techniques are interventions that facilitate changing internal, automatic thoughts that interfere with one's sexual functioning. Cognitive-behavioral techniques have been effective in treating several sexual problems such as female orgasm disorders and premature ejaculation (McCabe, 2001). For example, difficulty in attaining an orgasm may result from what thoughts are going through one's mind while engaged in sexual activity. For example, what might be the orgasmic outcome of a woman who says to herself, "I wonder if he's noticed my stomach is as big as a house" or "All men are creeps. This one's probably no different" or "He's just using me." In a second example, what would be the satisfactory sexual outcome of a man who bases his sexuality on performance, but who is not able to consistently achieve an erection? Thoughts may enter his mind such as "I'm a failure." Feelings of guilt, shame, self-rebuke, and embarrassment are negative feelings that often correspond with negative thoughts about self or partner. If these thoughts are going through one's mind, then it seems reasonable that thoughts of exultation and feelings of ecstasy are far away. It is important, therefore, for those experiencing orgasmic problems to examine cognitions, both before and during the sexual experience, for any pessimistic messages that could interfere with achieving sexual satisfaction. If thoughts are interfering with sexual functioning, then visits to a therapist or counselor would be advisable, particularly one who is trained in cognitive-behavioral therapy.

Sensate Focus Exercises

One common behavioral intervention developed by Masters and Johnson (1970) is sensate focus. Designed to help couples focus on sensations rather than performance, the goal is to decrease performance anxiety by focusing on an achievable task rather than to "have an orgasm." Couples are instructed to begin with nongenital touching while dressed in comfortable clothing. They eventually move to genital pleasuring with no focus on intercourse. The last step is a graduated movement to intercourse.

Orgasm Consistency Training

Orgasm consistency training, a structured cognitive-behavioral approach used by some therapists to help women improve their orgasmic functioning during intercourse (Hurlbert & Apt, 1994), has shown to be effective in the improvement of women's sexual desire and overall sexual functioning (Hurlbert, 1993). Prescriptions include masturbation, sensate focus exercises and male self-control techniques. Also incorporated in the program is the Coital Alignment Technique (CAT), namely, a coitus alignment position that requires a slight alteration from the male dominant missionary position (Pierce, 2000).

Sex Education and Sexual Sensitivity

Some basic sex education can increase partners' pleasure and add to intimacy. For example, while studying orgasm in a group of 868 female nurses, Darling, Davidson, and Cox (1991) found partner-related techniques that proved to enhance orgasm for women in the study, such as manual stimulation of the clitoral area with sexual intercourse, manual and oral stimulation of the clitoral area and the vaginal area, and manual and oral stimulation of the clitoral area and nipples without sexual intercourse. It could also be helpful for a woman's partner to know that a well-intended focus on direct clitoral stimulation may be uncomfortable for her and result in her eventual withdrawal from the sexual response cycle. This information is subject to considerable individual variation. Knowledge of sexual techniques and anatomy, while important, may not be enough to create ideal circumstances for partner orgasmic satisfaction. The best approach is to communicate one's personal preferences.

Communication Training

Partners who communicate about what is most pleasing for each are most likely to receive the most pleasurable experience. Usually, sex therapy involves some form of communication training ranging from assertiveness training to conflict resolution (Cupach & Comstock, 1990; Delaehanty, 1983; Kelly, Strassberg, & Turner, 2004; McCabe, 1999). Communication is especially crucial to satisfactory sexual experiences for women. If women have difficulty in expressing to their partner what pleasures them, then the result may very well be an unsatisfactory experience. Certainly, the same may be said for men.

FOUR PRINCIPLES FOR HEALTHY ORGASM EXPERIENCES

Orgasm can be a pleasant addition to life. It is not a necessary component to being happy, however. Sexuality can be experienced without orgasm. Societal pressure to perform and be orgasmic can create stress and frustration for individuals and couples. Remember, the context of the sexual experience as well as the orgasm can contribute to one's quality of life experiences.

A satisfactory orgasmic experience is related to a positive, respectful view of sexuality and is associated with all aspects of one's being. This positive approach to sexuality is reflected in one's thoughts, feelings, and behavior (sexual and otherwise). The four principles underlying the discussion in this chapter are:

1. *Self-awareness*. Self-awareness provides one with the ability to accurately discern what is pleasant or not pleasant, and allows one to acknowledge any sexual difficulty that may be interfering with one's quality of life. It also provides impetus into recognizing whether one's relationships (sexual or lacking thereof) are satisfactory. Further, self-awareness can help one to recognize negative thought patterns and pessimistic emotions about self or one's partner.

2. *Self-respect*. Self-respect can aid in the ability to address negative thoughts and emotions about sex. Self-respect gives one permission to admit to a sexual problem without shame. For those with medical or mental problems impacting sexuality, self-respect paves the way to negotiations with one's partner about sexual needs as well as finding the ability to assert oneself enough to discuss these problems with a physician and/or mental health professional. Self-respect also allows one to pursue life conditions such as sexual satisfaction that enhance quality of life. Further, self-respect prevents one from being coerced into unwanted sexual activity. Self-respect can help individuals to eliminate self-blame or self-pity, and facilitate action for their own sexual well-being.

3. *Healthy body, mind, and spirit*. Paying attention to all aspects of one's optimal functioning in the interrelated areas of physical, mental, and spiritual health creates conditions for positive orgasmic experiences. For those who are physically unable to experience orgasm, a healthy outlook of the majority of these components can often provide avenues to alternative satisfactory sexual experiences.

4. *Sexual knowledge and communication techniques.* Obtaining information about the human body, how it works, what interferes with sexual functioning and what enhances orgasmic satisfaction are helpful ingredients to satisfactory orgasmic functioning. Knowledge about the body and familiarity with sexual techniques create conditions for optimal sexual experiences, especially when self-awareness and self-respect are in place. With regard to communication, partners' abilities to be honest about whether they are ready to engage in sex is essential to an overall satisfactory sexual experience. If one partner is not interested, but does not want to hurt the other partner's feelings, this can, over time, turn into a pattern of dishonest communication, resulting in resentment and withdrawal. It is important for partners to be honest with themselves and each other, express their needs, and discuss what they like and do not like during sexual activity.

In conclusion, I remind the reader that many sexual problems can be alleviated. A healthy view of self and enthusiastic commitment to change are effective ways to begin to create intimate, satisfying orgasms. As Ralph Waldo Emerson once said, "Make the most of yourself, for that is all there is of you."

REFERENCES

American Psychiatric Association (2000). *Diagnostic and statistical manual of mental disorders* (4th ed., text revision). Washington, DC: Author.

Anderson, R. N., & Smith, B. L. (2005). Deaths: Leading causes for 2002. *National Vital Statistics Report, 53*(17). Hyattsville, MD: National Center for Health Statistics.

Anderson, K. E., & Wagner, G. (1995). Physiology of penile erection. *Physiological Reviews, 75*(1), 191–236.

Araujo, A. B., Mohr, B. A., & McKinlay, J. B. (2004). Changes in sexual function in middle-aged and older men: Longitudinal data from the Massachusetts Male Aging Study. *American Geriatrics Society, 52,* 1502–1509.

Ashton, A. K., & Rosen, R. C. (1998). Accommodation to serotonin reuptake inhibitor-induced sexual dysfunction. *Journal of Sex and Marital Therapy, 24*(3), 191–192.

Bachman, G., Bancroft, J., Braunstein, G., Burger, H., Davis, S., Dennerstein, L., et al. (2002). Female androgen insufficiency: The Princeton consensus statement on definition, classification, and assessment. *Fertility and Sterility, 77,* 660–665.

Bancroft, J. (2002). The medicalization of female sexual dysfunction: The need for caution. *Archives of Sexual Behavior, 31,* 451–456.

Basson, R. (2002). Are our definitions of women's desire, arousal and sexual pain disorders too broad and our definition of orgasmic disorder too narrow? *Journal of Sex and Marital Therapy, 28,* 289–300.

Berman, J. R., Berman, L. A., & Goldstein, I. (1999). Female sexual dysfunction: Incidence, pathophysiology, evaluation and treatment options. *Urology, 54,* 385–391.

Bhugra, D. (2003). Literature update: A critical review. *Sexual and Relationship Therapy, 18*(1), 120–124.

Bhugra, D., & Crowe, M. (1995). Physical treatments of erectile disorders. *International Review of Psychiatry, 7,* 217–223.

Bianchi-Demicheli, F., & Zutter, A. (2005). Intensive short-term dynamic sex therapy: A proposal. *Journal of Sex and Marital Therapy, 31,* 57–72.

Bodinger, L., Hermesh, H., Aizenberg, D., Valevski, A., Marom, S., Shiloh, R., et al. (2002). Sexual function and behavior in social phobia. *Journal of Clinical Psychiatry, 63,* 874–879.

Bogren, L. Y. (1991). Changes in sexuality in women and men during pregnancy. *Archives of Sexual Behavior, 20,* 35–45.

Braunstein, G. D. (2002). Androgen insufficiency in women: Summary of critical issues. *Fertility and Sterility, 77*(Suppl. 2), 94–99.

Burnett, A. L. (2005). Erectile dysfunction following radical prostatectomy. *Journal of the American Medical Association, 293*(21), 2648–2653.

Butler, C. A. (1976). New data about female sexual response. *Journal of Sex and Marital Therapy, 2,* 40–46.

Charlifue, S. W., Gerhart, K. A., Menter, R. R., Whiteneck, G. G., & Manley, M. S. (1992). Sexual issues of women with spinal cord injuries. *Paraplegia, 30,* 192–199.

Coolen, L. M., Allard, J., Truitt, W. A., & McKenna, K. E. (2004). Central regulation of ejaculation. *Physiology & Behavior, 83*(2), 203–215.

Cupach, W. R., & Comstock, J. (1990). Satisfaction with sexual communication in marriage: Links to sexual satisfaction and dyadic adjustment. *Journal of Social and Personal Relationships, 7,* 179–186.

D'Amicis, L. A., Goldberg, D. C., LoPiccolo, J., Friedman, J., & Davies, L. (1985). Clinical follow-up of couples treated for sexual dysfunction. *Archives of Sexual Behavior, 14*(6), 467–489.

Darling, C. A., Davidson, J. K., Sr., & Cox, R. P. (1991). Female sexual response and the timing of partner orgasm. *Journal of Sex and Marital Therapy, 17,* 3–21.

Davidson, J. K., Sr., & Darling, C. A. (1989). Perceived differences in the female orgasmic response: New meanings for sexual satisfaction. *Family Practice Research Journal, 8,* 75–84.

Delaehanty, R. (1983). Changes in assertiveness and changes in orgasmic response occurring with sexual therapy for preorgasmic women. *Journal of Sex and Marital Therapy, 8,* 198–208.

Dennerstein, L., Guthrie, J. R., & Alford, S. (2004). Childhood abuse and its association with mid-aged women's sexual functioning. *Journal of Sex and Marital Therapy, 30,* 225–234.

Donnellan, P., Breathnach, O., & Crown, J. P. (2000). *Scandinavian Journal of Urology and Nephrology, 35,* 158.

Dunn, K. M., Croft, P. R., & Hackett, G. I. (1999). Association of sexual problems with social, psychological, and physical problems in men and women: A cross sectional population survey. *Journal of Epidemiological Community Health, 53,* 144–148.

Dunn, M. E., & Trost, J. E. (1989). Male multiple orgasms: A descriptive study. *Archives of Sexual Behavior, 18,* 377–387.

Edwards, W. M., & Coleman, E. (2004). Defining sexual health: A descriptive overview. *Archives of Sexual Behavior, 33*(3), 189–195.

Ellison, C. R. (2001). Intimacy-based sex therapy: Sexual choreography. In P. J. Kleinplatz (Ed.), *New directions in sex therapy* (pp. 163–184). Ann Arbor, MI: Taylor & Frances.

Feldmeier, H., Leutscher, P., Poggensee, G., & Harms, G. (1999). Male genital schistosomiasis and haemospermia [Editorial]. *Tropical Medicine and International Health, 4*(12), 791–793.

Geboes, K., Steeno, O., & DeMoor, P. (1975). Primary anejaculation: Diagnosis and therapy. *Fertility and Sterility, 26,* 1018–1020.

Goetsch, M. F. (2005, June). The effect of total hysterectomy on specific sexual sensations. *American Journal of Obstetrics and Gynecology, 192*(6), 1922–1927.

Gökyildiz, S., & Beji, N. K. (2005). The effects of pregnancy on sexual life. *Journal of Sex and Marital Therapy, 31,* 201–215.

Holstege, G., Georgiadis, J. R., Paans, A. M. J., Meiners, L. C., Ferdinand, H. C. E., van der Graff, et al. (2003). Brain activation during human male ejaculation. *Journal of Neuroscience, 23*(27), 9185–9193.

Hurlbert, D. F. (1993). A comparative study using orgasm consistency training in the treatment of women reporting hypoactive sexual desire. *Journal of Sex and Marital Therapy, 19*(1), 41–55.

Hurlbert, D., & Apt, C. (1994). Female sexual desire, response, and behavior. *Behavior Modification, 18,* 488–504.

Jannini, E. A., & Lenzi, A. (2005). Ejaculatory disorders: Epidemiology and current approaches to definition, classification and subtyping. *World Journal of Urology, 23*(2), 68–75.

Johnson, S. D., Phelps, D. L., & Cottler, L. B. (2004). The association of sexual dysfunction and substance use among a community epidemiological sample. *Archives of Sexual Behavior, 33*(1), 55–63.

Kandeel, F. R., Koussa, K. T., & Swerdloff, R. S. (2001). Male sexual function and its disorders: Physiology, pathophysiology, clinical investigation, and treatment. *Endocrine Reviews, 22*(3), 342–388.

Kaschak, E., & Tiefer, L. (Eds.). (2001). *A new view of women's sexual problems.* New York: Haworth Press.

Kelly, M. P., Strassberg, D. S., & Turner, C. M. (2004). Communication and associated relationship issues in female anorgasmia. *Journal of Sex and Marital Therapy, 30,* 263–276.

Kennedy, S. H., Eisfeld, B. S., Dickens, M. A., Bacchiochi, B. A., & Bagby, R. M. (2000). Antidepressant-induced sexual dysfunction during treatment with moclobemide, paroxetine, sertraline, and venlafaxine. *Journal of Clinical Psychiatry, 61,* 276–281.

Kingsberg, S. A. (2002). The impact of aging on sexual function in women and their partners. *Archives of Sexual Behavior, 31*(5), 431–437.

Klassen, A. D., & Wilsnack, S. C. (1986). Sexual experience and drinking among women in a U.S. national survey. *Archives of Sexual Behavior, 15*(5), 363–392.

Koeman, M., van Driel, M. F., Schultz, W. C., & Mensick, H. J. (1996). Orgasm after radical prostatectomy. *British Journal of Urology, 77,* 861–864.

Laumann, E. O., Paik, A., & Rosen, R. C. (1999). Sexual dysfunction in the United States: Prevalence and predictors. *Journal of the American Medical Association, 281,* 537–544.

Laumann, E. O., Nicolosi, A., Glasser, D. B., Paik, A., Gingell, C., Moreira, E., et al. (2004). Sexual problems among women and men aged 40–80 years: Prevalence and correlates identified in the Global Study of Sexual Attitudes and Behaviors. *International Journal of Impotence, 17,* 39–57.

Lue, T. F. (2000). Erectile dysfunction. *New Journal of Medicine, 342,* 1802–1813.

Mah, K., & Binik, Y. M. (2002). Do all orgasms feel alike? Evaluating a two-dimensional model of the orgasm experience across gender and sexual context. *Journal of Sex Research, 39*(2), 104–113.

Mah, K., & Binik, Y. M. (2005). Are orgasms in the mind or the body? Psychosocial versus physiological correlates of orgasmic pleasure and satisfaction. *Journal of Sex and Marital Therapy, 31,* 187–200.

Master, V. A., & Turek, R. J. (2001). Ejaculatory physiology and dysfunctions. *Urologic Clinics of North America, 28,* 363–375.

Masters, W. H., & Johnson, V. E. (1966). *Human sexual response.* Boston: Little, Brown.

Masters, W. H., & Johnson, V. E. (1970). *Human sexual inadequacy.* Boston: Little, Brown.

McCabe, M. P. (1997). Intimacy and quality of life among sexually dysfunctional men and women. *Journal of Sex and Marital Therapy, 23*(4), 276–290.

McCabe, M. P. (1999). The interrelationship between intimacy, sexual functioning, and sexuality among men and women in committed relationships. *Canadian Journal of Human Sexuality, 8,* 31–38.

McCabe, M. P. (2001). Evaluation of a cognitive behavior therapy program for people with sexual dysfunction. *Journal of Sex and Marital Therapy, 27,* 259–271.

McCarthy, B. W., & Fucito, L. M. (2005). Integrating medication, realistic expectations, and therapeutic interventions in the treatment of male sexual dysfunction. *Journal of Sex and Marital Therapy, 31,* 319–328.

Melman, A., & Gingell, J. C. (1999). The epidemiology and pathophysiology of erectile dysfunction. *Journal of Urology, 161,* 5–11.

The Merck Manual of Diagnosis and Therapy. (n.d.). Female orgasm disorder. In *Sexual dysfunction in women* (chap. 243). Retrieved July 30, 2005, from www.merck.com/mrkshared/mmanual/section18/chapter243/243c.jsp

Metz, M. C., & Pryor, J. L. (2000). Premature ejaculation: A psychophysiological approach for assessment and management. *Journal of Sex and Marital Therapy, 26,* 293–320.

Michael, A. (2000). Venlafaxine-induced painful ejaculation. *British Journal of Psychiatry, 177,* 282–283.

Michelson, M. D., Bancroft, J., Targum, S., Kim, Y., & Tepner, R. (2000). Female sexual dysfunction associated with antidepressant administration: A randomized, placebo-controlled study of pharmacologic intervention. *American Journal of Psychiatry, 157*(2), 239–243.

Millner, V. (2005). Female sexual arousal disorder and counseling deliberations. *Family Journal, 11*(10), 1–6.

Millner, V. S., & Ullery, E. K. (2002). A holistic treatment approach to male erectile disorder. *Family Journal, 10*(4), 443–447.

Newcomb, M. D., & Bentler, P. M. (1983). Dimensions of subjective female orgasmic responsiveness. *Journal of Personality and Social Psychology, 44,* 862–873.

Oliver, M. B., & Hyde, J. S. (1993). Gender differences in sexuality: A meta-analysis. *Psychological Bulletin, 114,* 29–51.

Overview: A woman's guide to hormone therapy. (2003, April). *National Women's Health Report, 26*(2), 5.

Papadimas, J., Ioannidis, S., Kiouras, S., Tarlatzis, B., Papanicolaou, A., Bondis, I., et al. (1999). Spontaneous pregnancy following therapeutic approach of an infertile man with aspermia/obstructive azoospermia. *Archives of Andrology, 42,* 105–108.

Papp, G. K., Kopa, Z., Szabó, F., & Erdei, E. (2003). Aetiology of haemospermia. *Andrologia, 35,* 317–320.

Penson, D. F., Latini, D. M., Lubeck, D. P., Wallace, K. L., Henning, J. M., & Lue, T. F. (2003). Do impotent men with diabetes have more severe erectile dysfunction and worse quality of life than the general population of impotent patients? *Diabetes Care, 26,* 1093–1099.

Peplau, L. A. (2003). Human sexuality: How do men and women differ? *Current Directions in Psychological Science, 12*(2), 37–40.

Perelman, M. A. (2001). Integrating sildenafil and sex therapy: Unconsummated marriage secondary to erectile dysfunction and retarded ejaculation. *Journal of Sex Education and Therapy, 26,* 13–21.

Perry, D. P., & Whipple, B. (1981). Pelvic muscle strength of female ejaculators: Evidence in support of a new theory of orgasm. *Journal of Sex Research, 17,* 22–39.

Pierce, A. P. (2000). The Coital Alignment Technique (CAT): An overview of studies. *Journal of Sex and Marital Therapy, 26,* 257–268.

Raja, M. (1999). Risperidone-induced absence of ejaculation. *International Clinical Psychopharmacology, 14*(5), 317–319.

Ralph, D. J., & Wylie, K. R. (2005). Ejaculatory disorders and sexual function. *British Journal of Urology International, 95,* 1181–1186.

Randall, H. E., & Byers, E. S. (2003). What is sex? Students' definitions of having sex, sexual partner, and unfaithful sexual partner. *Canadian Journal of Human Sexuality, 12*(2), 87–96.

Reuben, S. H. (2004). Living beyond cancer: Finding a new balance. *President's Cancer Panel 2003–2004 Annual Report.* Washington, DC: U.S. Department of Health and Human Services.

Rosenberg, K. P. (1999). Sildenafil. *Journal of Sex and Marital Therapy, 25*, 271–279.

Rowland, D. L., Keeney, C., & Slob, A. K. (2004). Sexual response in men with inhibited or retarded ejaculation. *International Journal of Impotence Research, 16*, 270–274.

Rowland, D. L., Myers, L., Culver, A., & Davidson, J. M. (1997). Bupropion and sexual function: A placebo-controlled prospective study on diabetic men with erectile dysfunction. *Journal of Clinical Psychopharmacology, 17*(5), 350–357.

Sarrel, P. M. (1990). Sexuality and menopause. *Obstetrics and Gynecology, 75,* (Suppl. 4), 26S–30S.

Schroder, M. A., Mell, L. K., Hurteau, J. A., Collins, Y. C., Rotmensch, J., Waggoner, S. E., et al. (2005). Clitoral therapy device for treatment of sexual dysfunction in irradiated cervical cancer patients. *International Journal of Radiation Oncology, 61*(4), 1078–1086.

Sholty, M. J., Ephross, P. H., Plaut, S. M., Fischman, S. H., Charnas, J. F., & Cody, C. A. (1984). Female orgasmic experience: A subjective study. *Archives of Sexual Behavior, 13*(2), 155–392.

Sipski, M. L. (2002). Central nervous system based neurogenic female sexual dysfunction: Current status and future trends. *Archives of Sexual Behavior, 31*(5), 421–424.

Sipski, M. L., & Alexander, C. J. (1993). Sexual activities, response and satisfaction in women pre- and post-spinal cord injury. *Archives of Physical Medicine and Rehabilitation, 74*, 1025–1029.

Sipski, M. L., Alexander, C. J., & Rosen, R. C. (1995). Orgasm in women with spinal cord injuries: A laboratory-based assessment. *Archives of Physical Medicine and Rehabilitation, 76*, 1097–1102.

Sipski, M. L., Rosen, R. C., Alexander, C. J., & Gomez-Marin, O. (2004). Sexual responsiveness in women with spinal cord injuries: Differential effects of anxiety-eliciting stimulation. *Archives of Sexual Behavior, 33*(3), 295–302.

Tiefer, L. (2002). Beyond the medical model of women's sexual problems: A campaign to resist the promotion of "female sexual dysfunction." *Sexual and Relationship Therapy, 17*(2), 127–135.

U.S. Food and Drug Administration (2005). *Patient information sheet: Sildenafil citrate.* Retrieved July 30, 2005, from www.fda.gov/cder/drug/InfoSheets/patient/sildenafilPIS.htm

von Sydow, K. (1999). Sexuality during pregnancy and after childbirth: A meta-content analysis of 59 studies. *Journal of Psychosomatic Research, 47*, 27–49.

Waldinger, M. D. (2003). Use of psychoactive agents in the treatment of sexual dysfunction. *CNS Drugs, 6*(3), 204–216.

Waldinger, M., & Schweitzer, D. (2005). Retarded ejaculation in men: An overview of psychological and neurobiological insights. *World Journal of Urology, 23*(2), 76–81.

Walsh, P. C., & Wilson, J. D. (1987). Impotence and infertility in men. In E. Braunwald, K. J. Isselbacher, R. S. Petersdorf, J. D. Wilson, J. B.

Martin, & A. S. Fauci (Eds.), *Harrison's principles of internal medicine* (11th ed., pp. 217–220). New York: McGraw-Hill.

Walsh, P. C., Marschke, P., Ricker, D., & Burnett, A. L. (2000). Patient-reported urinary continence and sexual function after anatomic radical prostatectomy. *Urology, 55,* 58–61.

Wells, C., Lucas, M. J., Meyer, J. K. (1980). Unrealistic expectations of orgasm. *Medical Aspects of Human Sexuality, 14*(4), 59–71.

World Health Organization (2005). *Gender and reproductive right.* Retrieved June 30, 2005, from www.who.int/reproductive-health/gender/sexual_health .html

Wylie, K. R., & Ralph. D. (2005). Premature ejaculation: The current literature. *Current Opinions in Urology, 15,* 393–398.

Zimmerman, M., Posternak, M. A., Attiullah, N., Friedman, M., Boland, R. J., Baymiller, S., et al. (2005). Why isn't bupropion the most frequently prescribed antidepressant? *Journal of Clinical Psychiatry, 66*(5), 603–610.

9

Sex Therapy: How Do Sex Therapists Think about and Deal with Sexual Problems?

Peggy J. Kleinplatz ◆

This chapter will give the reader an overview of the field of sex therapy. There will be a brief description of sex therapy and its beginnings. This will be followed by a discussion of the major factors that lead to sexual difficulties. How to tell whether a sexual difficulty counts as a "problem" and what kind of expert to consult will be considered next. Of course, individuals and couples deal with all sorts of sexual concerns that are not necessarily classified as "official" sexual dysfunctions. Sex therapists deal with these issues daily, and some of the more common ones will be enumerated here. Then, the major male and female sexual dysfunctions will be discussed, followed by the most common problem for couples, that is, differences in sexual desire. Recommended resources follow the conclusion.

WHAT IS SEX THERAPY?

Sexual problems arise in most people's lives sooner or later, and in the offices of psychotherapists, counselors, and physicians daily. There is no one right way to deal with sexual problems. There is much debate about how to even conceptualize sexual problems both among lay people and professionals. Most people who confront sexual difficulties try to solve them by themselves for as long as possible, with the help of books, articles, and, increasingly, through the use of information on the Internet. Eventually, they may seek out or be referred to a sex therapist. Sex therapists (or at least board-certified sex therapists) are clinicians already trained in general psychotherapy and, usually, couples therapy. Some also have a background in medicine. They are then trained to deal with sexual problems in heterosexual/gay/lesbian individuals, couples, and, occasionally, groups. Traditionally, sex therapy has focused primarily on the treatment of the "sexual dysfunctions," though some professionals in the field deal with the whole realm of sexual problems and concerns including, for example, those related to unconventional sexual desires and practices. Sometimes this broader field is referred to as "clinical sexology."

Among professionals in the field, "sex therapy" has historically assumed brand-name proportions. It is the "Kleenex" of psychotherapy. It is often thought of as the home of one basic approach, first introduced and elaborated by its founders, William Masters and Virginia Johnson (see below). Their work provided brief, intensive, behaviorally oriented treatment which was very effective in reversing the obstacles to "natural" sexual functioning, especially in the short term. Whether it is wise to help couples return to "normal" sexuality in a sex-negative society is a continuing dilemma for experts in the field (Irvine, 1990; Reiss, 1990; Schnarch, 1991; Tiefer, 1996). Although Masters and Johnson's groundbreaking model continues to provide the cornerstone of much of the clinical work provided by sex therapists today, social and economic factors influence our perspective of what is seen as a problem; furthermore, clinical approaches are now more varied, with medical and particularly the pharmacological interventions receiving a great deal of attention (Rosen & Leiblum, 1995). At least in theory, sex therapists bring a biopsychosocial approach to working with sexual problems in therapy. In practice, with the increasing push toward medicalization of sexuality (Giami, 2000; Leiblum & Rosen, 2000; Schover & Leiblum, 1994; Tiefer, 1996, 2000, 2001; Winton, 2000, 2001), the services provided may be related directly to the particular professional one happens to be referred to or chooses to seek out.

HISTORY OF SEX THERAPY—AN OVERVIEW

Up until the 1960s, sexual problems typically were treated via psychoanalytically oriented psychotherapy. The focus was on unconscious causes of sexual disorders and on dealing with deeper personality processes in order to uncover and treat these difficulties. Although this approach was commendable for its orientation toward working with the whole person rather than merely a set of symptoms, it was very time consuming and cost intensive and was not known to be particularly effective.

The treatment of sexual problems was revolutionized in 1970. Gynecologist William Masters and his partner, social scientist Virginia Johnson, had established a laboratory in St. Louis, Missouri, for the study of sexuality in 1955. After studying the psychophysiology of sexual response in the laboratory for eleven years, Masters and Johnson released their findings in 1966. They described the stages of sexual arousal and response they had observed as the Human Sexual Response Cycle: excitement, plateau, orgasm, and resolution (Masters & Johnson, 1966). This model became the basis for their designation—and later, the entire field's ideas—of what constitutes "normal" sexual functioning. Deviations from this model during the stages they had described were designated as sexual dysfunctions. For example, difficulties among men during the sexual excitement phase were referred to as "impotence" (and are more commonly known today as "erectile dysfunction"). In 1970, Masters and Johnson released their second book, *Human Sexual Inadequacy*, in which they described the sexual dysfunctions in men and women and the approach they had developed for treatment of them. This was the genesis of the field of sex therapy and this new book became its Bible.

The dysfunctions described by Masters and Johnson were later enshrined in the third edition of the *Diagnostic and Statistical Manual of Mental Disorders* (*DSM*) published by the American Psychiatric Association (1980). The desire disorders were described by pioneers Helen Singer Kaplan (1977, 1979) and Harold Lief (1977). These dysfunctions continue to comprise the bulk of the categories of sexual difficulties listed in the current edition of the *DSM* (APA, 2000). The remaining categories of the *DSM* are not listed as dysfunctions but as disorders. These are the paraphilias, that is, various forms of unconventional sexuality, including cross-dressing and sexual sadomasochism (known as SM or BDSM colloquially) and the gender identity problems. There is considerable controversy over whether these categories belong in the *DSM* or their World Health Organization counterpart, the *International Classification of Diseases* (ICD; see below).

Early treatment methods in sex therapy were notably successful, at least in the reversal of the symptoms of sexual dysfunctions (Kaplan, 1974; Masters & Johnson, 1970). In fact, they were so impressive that the field was able to ignore the difference between treatment of symptoms versus attention to the underlying problems, not to mention overlooking the individuals or couples who were suffering. Solving mechanical problems expediently was sex therapy's initial claim to fame, but this approach made it all too convenient to focus on the "easy" cases and be caught unawares when confronted with an avalanche of "harder" cases, some of which resulted from earlier "successes." That is, the fact that sex therapy was so effective at eliminating the target symptoms meant that the field did not have to spend a lot of time considering and debating whether the minimal goals aspired to were all that could or should be achieved. Practitioners were operating—and often still do—without a theory of human sexual experience to ground and orient clinical work (Kleinplatz, 2003; Wiederman, 1998). As such, sex therapy may be very effective at helping couples to ameliorate their dysfunctional sex lives while being conspicuously ill-equipped to attain intense erotic intimacy (Kleinplatz, 1996, 2001; Schnarch, 1991; Shaw, 2001). For example, helping a couple learn to overcome a problem with early ejaculation does not guarantee that their sexual relationship will improve.

WHAT CAUSES SEXUAL PROBLEMS AND OBSTACLES TO SEXUAL FULFILLMENT?

It is important to have a good sense of what the problem is, what causes it, and even what purpose(s) it may serve for the individual and couple in order to determine how to deal with it in therapy. The field of sex therapy has often been accused of having a cookbook mentality, as in for problem X add remedy Y; one way of demonstrating that sex therapists are, indeed, attuned to the subtleties of sexual problems is by paying very close attention to their origins and meanings for the individuals in question.

Sexual problems do not usually originate from one cause or type of factor alone; rather, they are more often multidetermined or multifactorial (Kaplan, 1974). Theoretically, obstacles to sexual fulfillment can be divided into the four broad categories of biomedical, intrapsychic, interpersonal, and socio-cultural/economic/political causes but there tends to be quite a bit of overlap in the actual origins of sexual difficulties in any given individual. For example, a young, married couple may complain of lack of sexual desire. When questioned as to when the problem began, they answer that six months prior, their son was born; it was a difficult childbirth that left her with pain during intercourse; her maternity leave has concluded and both parents now must work full time outside the home; they are so busy that they barely have time for their child, let alone each other; she continues to breast-feed and is therefore sleep deprived; she is frustrated that her husband cannot seem to pick up the slack around the house. Both come from homes where conflict was managed poorly and do not know how to resolve their problems with one another without feeling threatened emotionally. As such, it is not surprising that these many factors lead to lack of sexual desire. This case also illustrates how many individuals/couples who come to sex therapy have all manner of problems that are not necessarily "sexual" in nature. However, when these underlying problems are ignored or left unresolved, eventually, they are manifested in the bedroom. It is at that point that such a couple may seek sex therapy when what is really required is time, public policy allowing longer maternity leave, gynecological attention to her pain during intercourse, conflict resolution skills, the development of trust, and a more equitable division of labor around the house (Working Group for a New View of Women's Sexual Problems, 2001).

Although sexual problems generally cannot be broken down into one factor versus another, for purposes of this chapter only, the following section breaks these factors down artificially as if they were separate when, in fact, they are intertwined.

Intrapsychic Factors

Intrapsychic factors are those psychological elements within the individual that bear on his or her sexual expression. Many of these are related to early childhood experiences and the messages received in childhood about sexuality. For example, what was the nature of the parents' sexual relationship and how was it perceived within the family? Were the parents sexually open and expressive, affectionate and demonstrative, or more reserved? Did they seem loving to one another and to the children, or cool and distant? Were they happily married, miserable together, or divorced? What did the parents teach about sex? What did the children learn from what the parents said or, more commonly, from what was never spoken, about sexuality? How did the family deal with nudity, self-stimulation in childhood, privacy, questions about where babies come from, and about what to expect during puberty? The values learned about one's body, and in particular the genitalia, as well as about pleasure and sexuality, overall, have a tremendous impact on future sexual attitudes, comfort, or discomfort. Too many young people are still being told, albeit nonverbally, "Sex is dirty—save it for someone you love." No wonder sex therapists often have extensive waiting lists!

Clearly, childhood sexual abuse or incest can lead to feelings of shame, guilt, and fear around sexuality and generally diminished self-esteem (Herman, 1992; Maltz, 1998). Many survivors of sexual abuse do not feel entitled to consensual, mutually respectful, and loving sexual relations. Furthermore, they are often unable to imagine sex that is chosen freely and how that would look and feel, rather than sex occurring for someone else's sake—to fulfill another's needs. These are often contributing factors to the future development of sexual problems including low sexual desire, sexual aversion, and various sexual dysfunctions. Unfortunately, given that many people raised in "normal" homes contend with sex-negative environments, they too are subject to anxiety and discomfort regarding sexuality with similar consequences, even if their concerns are not as intense as among those who were sexually abused. In other words, the notion that all sexual abuse survivors will develop sexual problems is an overstatement; correspondingly, in a sex-negative culture, "normal" sexual development may breed sexual problems.

Another common contributor to sexual problems is the focus on sex as performance rather than as a source of mutual pleasure. To the extent that one is observing one's body while in bed, concerned about getting or keeping an erection, reaching orgasm, or, more likely, reaching orgasm "soon enough" or delaying orgasm "long enough," one is typically unable to connect fully and joyfully with one's partner(s). Masters and Johnson (1970) referred to this as "spectatoring" and indeed, it often feels as if one is off in the bleachers, watching and worrying from a distance, instead of being embodied within and present with one's partner(s). Thus, performance anxiety interferes with sexual satisfaction even if it does not always technically impede "functioning."

Interpersonal Factors

Interpersonal factors include all those elements that affect one's ability to be engaged in sexual relationships or for a couple to be mutually engaged. These factors include difficulties with trust, fears of rejection, power struggles, disappointment, the aftermath of affairs, and "goodness of fit" (i.e., the extent to which partners share compatible visions of sex, eroticism, pleasure, etc.). The most prominently reported interpersonal factor is communication difficulties. Typically, couples arrive in sex therapists' offices complaining of problems with "communicating about intimacy." Sometimes this phrase is a euphemism for fears of talking openly about sexual likes and dislikes, wishes, preferences, and fantasies. However, the difficulty is often with conflict resolution per se and its impact on the couple's willingness to risk emotional and sexual intimacy together. Couples who cannot imagine disagreements as leading to anything other than attacks, recriminations, hurt feelings, and implicit or explicit threats eventually learn to avoid conflict. In fact, such couples may announce early in therapy that they are one another's best friends and that they get along beautifully . . . except for this one glitch around "intimacy." In such cases, it is not "sex" per se that is the problem; rather, these couples discover in therapy that couples who cannot really afford to get angry with one another also cannot afford to feel much of anything, let alone to share passion.

Above and beyond these "communication difficulties" is the difficulty in literally talking about and defining sexual terms. Many people associate their Latinate sex vocabularies with physicians' offices, and perhaps biology classes, and thus claim such terms "sound clinical." In contrast, the slang terms for sexual parts and functions (in English) have derogatory connotations and make people uncomfortable, too. As such, people are often at a loss as to how to ask for what they want. The usual default, nonverbal communication, is an inadequate substitute for simple, clear requests. Furthermore, the seriousness of this seemingly trivial problem is exacerbated by the lack of consensus as to what constitutes "sex." The Clinton-Lewinsky scandal highlighted how different individuals disagree on the meanings of the same terms and even manipulate language to obscure understanding. As such, it is fairly common for sex therapists to ask couples about their sexual behaviors, only to be met with euphemisms such as "making love" or "down there." These terms often turn out to signify entirely different things to each partner. Partners who argue endlessly about wanting to "take more time making love" may unknowingly have mistaken his self-doubts surrounding rapid ejaculation with her desire to receive more oral stimulation or their concerns about how frequently sex occurs.

Sociocultural/Economic/Political Factors

Personal and sociocultural values have an enormous impact on sexuality. In North America, sexual values tend to be sex-negative and thus contribute to the development of sexual difficulties. In fact, growing up with our culture's "sex script" (i.e., social blueprints for sexual norms, values, beliefs, attitudes, practices, and their justifications) tends to instill sexual shame and guilt in many, if not most, people to some extent (Gagnon & Simon, 1973). It has been said that the major developmental task of adolescence is overcoming the shame-engendering messages internalized during childhood.

Another major contributor to sexual dissatisfaction is ignorance. In American society, it is currently forbidden to offer comprehensive sexuality education in government-funded schools. By federal law, schools are to provide abstinence-only sex education, which teaches the basics of reproductive biology. Sex is equated with heterosexual intercourse. Conspicuously absent is any discussion of contraception or safer sex as ways of preventing unwanted pregnancies or sexually transmitted infections (STIs). Information about gay and lesbian sexuality is likely missing, too. By contrast, in Western countries where there are fewer restrictions on sex education, rates of unwanted pregnancies and STIs are significantly lower than they are in the United States (Advocates for Youth, 1999). More insidious perhaps is the exclusion of pleasure from sex education. As such, young people in abstinence-only sex education programs learn via silence that the ultimate taboo is not sex—it is discussion of sexual pleasure, not to mention wanting, seeking, and asking for pleasure.

Religion can provide its followers with a sense of their own value as sexual beings, with the belief that their bodies are sacred and that their accompanying desires are a divine gift. Alternately, religion can lead people to believe that they are inherently sinful, that their bodies are shameful, and that their desires must be overcome. It all depends on the religion, the parents, teachers, or clergy who teach it, and the perspective emphasized by them. Each of the major religions has sex-positive and sex-negative traditions, but many young people never learn of the breadth of spiritual streams available within their own backgrounds. Although many adult clients in sex therapy state that they have rejected the religious traditions in which they were raised, the gut-level impact of messages about sinfulness often remain, despite persuasive protests to the contrary.

The manifestations of ignorance and shame are pervasive when looking at sexual difficulties: both men and women suffer from body image problems which contribute to discomfort with nudity and with being touched. The sense of being inadequate or perhaps even defective is ubiquitous. Talk of sex is everywhere in the media, yet the capacity to express one's sexual wishes and preferences is limited by the taboo around asking for sexual pleasure. Many sexual problems could be prevented, or at least dealt with simply and expediently, if couples only felt free to show and tell what they find arousing. For many couples, however, even saying, "a little to the left, please" or "slower, gentler," is difficult enough; sharing one's deepest fantasies seems unimaginable.

Biomedical Factors

Any factor that affects the human body can affect sexuality. Although physicians may not specifically inquire as to the impact of medical conditions on one's sex life, the impact is there and should not be underestimated or ignored (Maurice, 1999). It is very useful for people to see their physicians and ask to be examined for any medical problems that might affect sexuality (Moser, 1999), particularly when embarking on sex therapy. A wide variety of diseases or their treatments can affect sexual desire, arousal, and response directly or indirectly. Particular categories of relevance here include any illness or injury that affects the neurological, endocrine (i.e., hormonal), or cardiovascular systems. For example, cardiovascular disease can create difficulties with sexual response, including difficulties with blood flow to the genitals in men and women. Actually having a heart attack often terrifies individuals and their partners into refraining from sexual relations, fearing that strenuous activity might trigger a subsequent heart attack. Unfortunately, providing the information that might help couples resume sexual relations safely in the presence of heart disease is often overlooked during a crisis and forgotten during the rehabilitation phase. Many health professionals are uncomfortable bringing up the subject of sexuality with their patients. Furthermore, medications for high blood pressure often create or exacerbate sexual dysfunctions. The fact that many patients are not warned about these potential side effects makes people feel all the more isolated and defective.

Chronic illness of any kind, disability and, ongoing pain, whatever the source, each has an impact on sexuality. These effects can be very subtle and barely noticeable at first, as might be the case with lower back pain, or sudden and dramatic, as in a spinal cord injury. Consideration of these effects should be included in the course of medical treatment or rehabilitation. Two medical problems that have a direct bearing on sexuality are sexually transmitted infections (STIs) and infertility. Diagnosis of these conditions often makes people feel defective immediately. People with STIs may describe feeling contaminated and untouchable. Infertility typically forces people to question their adequacy as sexual beings and their conceptions of "normalcy," while its treatment interferes with their previous sexual patterns.

A wide variety of commonly used drugs affect sexual functioning. For example, most psychotropic drugs, that is, medications used for psychiatric purposes, tend to affect sexual functioning adversely. A popular category of antidepressant medications, the selective serotonin reuptake inhibitors (SSRIs), which includes such drugs as Prozac and Paxil, can diminish or prevent sexual arousal, orgasm, or even sexual desire itself. On the other hand, this very side effect has been used to assist men who have been diagnosed with rapid ejaculation to slow their responses. In general, sexual side effects tend to be underreported, both because of the methodology used by pharmaceutical companies in their recording of adverse effects in the process of clinical trials, and because many people are too embarrassed to volunteer information about sexual difficulties. They may not even make the connection between medication usage and sexual problems. Some commonly used drugs do not even "count" in patients' minds when giving a sexual/medical history. Over-the-counter drugs such as antihistamines and decongestants dry out mucous membranes in the nose and mouth; as such, they may well limit a woman's lubrication, though it typically does not even occur to her that her allergy pills are making sex uncomfortable. Similarly, women using hormonal contraception (that is, oral contraceptive pills, "the patch," or injections, as in Depo-Provera) may not be aware of their possibly adverse effects on sexual desire in some women and, unfortunately, are not typically warned of such possibilities in advance. Recreational drugs need to be considered as well. People often use alcohol to "loosen up" before sex. However, the same cautions that apply to drinking and driving are relevant for sex as well. Because alcohol depresses the central nervous system, it affects reflexes and judgment. Alcohol can impair the ability to make clear and consensual choices about sex, thereby contributing to unwanted sex or unsafe sex. Furthermore, excess alcohol will also impair the mechanisms involved in sexual excitement and orgasm. Long-term alcoholism inevitably creates sexual dysfunction.

HOW DO YOU KNOW IF IT'S "NORMAL" OR IF IT'S A PROBLEM?

If it is bothersome, it could be a problem for the person who feels bothered. As obvious as that may seem, there is a lack of consensus among sex therapists as to whether or not distress is necessary or sufficient to indicate a problem. Some sex therapists believe that even when one feels no distress, certain symptoms should automatically qualify for diagnosis of pathology (Althof, 2001). Althof argues that until symptoms of sexual problems (e.g., women's difficulties with orgasm) are regarded as "objective" indicators of pathology regardless of subjective distress or lack thereof, sexual disorders will not be given their due and taken seriously as obstacles to patients' quality of life. This argument is analogous to the reasoning that although high blood pressure generally causes no symptoms, it signifies pathology and requires treatment nonetheless. Althof would say that there is a parallel with sexual problems. Others argue that personal distress is the most important criterion in determining whether or not we are to conceptualize some difficulty as worthy of treatment (Nathan, 2003). If it does not bother the individual in question, how can anyone else determine that the "patient" has a dysfunction, disorder, or even a problem?

Furthermore, these issues become even murkier when considering "problems" that create no distress for the "identified patient" but do bother others. For example, low sexual desire is not necessarily deemed problematic yet qualifies for the diagnosis of hypoactive sexual desire disorder (HSDD) when it creates "interpersonal difficulty" (APA, *DSM IV-TR* 2000, p. 539). In other words, as it stands currently, if a couple comprises of two people neither of whom want sex more than once a year and they are happy together, neither one receives a diagnosis. If, however, one wants sex twice a week while the other wants sex twice a year, the latter partner is diagnosed with HSDD. Some (e.g., Kafka & Hennen, 1999) would like to see an individual who wants sex twice a day receive a diagnosis, too, even if it creates no distress for anyone. There is much debate about the inclusion of such a diagnosis in future editions of the *DSM* and whether such high levels of sexual desire, without personal distress, should be conceptualized as "Compulsive Sexual Behavior" (Coleman, 1995), a "Sexual Impulse Control Disorder" (Barth & Kinder, 1987), "Sexual Addiction" (Carnes, 1991), or "Paraphilia-Related Disorder" (Kafka & Hennen, 1999), among other prospective designations.

There is, if anything, more controversy about whether or not sexual minorities should be thought of as having mental health problems. Does it count as a problem if it does not bother the individual in question but does create distress for others? For example, if a woman gets sexual arousal and pleasure from wearing women's lingerie, she would never be seen as mentally ill, regardless of others' reactions to her. If a man gets sexual arousal and pleasure from wearing women's lingerie, his wife's discovery of his proclivity sometimes creates distress for her. This situation often leads to treatment for him, even if he never considered it problematic until his wife felt threatened. Some consider it unreasonable, unfair, and without clinical justification to diagnose and treat people who do not feel distressed about their sexuality, even if their sexual inclinations are unusual and even if others are distressed by such interests (Moser & Kleinplatz, 2002, in press; Reiersøl & Skeid, in press). For individuals and couples who are seeking therapy but concerned about being judged for their unusual sexual desires, it may be helpful to choose a therapist more attuned to issues pertinent to unconventional sex practices. A good starting place may be at www.bannon.com/~race/kap/.

In addition, there are some aspects of sexuality that were once seen as problematic and in need of treatment which are now regarded quite differently. The most conspicuous example is homosexuality. At one time, it was regarded as a disorder but was declassified in 1973 by the American Psychiatric Association. Even though being gay or lesbian may cause distress to individuals or their families, particularly during the early "coming out" phase, ethical mental health professionals no longer "treat" homosexuality per se. They may, however, help people to adjust to being, or to loving, someone who is gay. This example illustrates how changes in sexual values over time affect the beliefs and practices of therapists. Similarly, in the 1950s, when simultaneous orgasms during intercourse were considered a marital ideal, women who were unable to attain orgasm during intercourse were often treated as "frigid" (see below). Today, it is recognized that the vast majority of women require direct clitoral stimulation in order to have orgasms. Thus, even though the client may feel distress, most sex therapists will provide reassurance and help to normalize the concern, but will not "treat" the alleged "frigidity."

Other couples come into therapy not because they have any problem but because they want more joy, meaning, eroticism, and intimacy out of sex. They are dismayed, disillusioned, and disgruntled by the quality of their sex lives. Although it would be hard to classify these couples as having dysfunctions or disorders, something seems to be missing. Such individuals often speak in terms of lack of connection or the absence of passion, or they state that the "mystery is gone." The excitement of the honeymoon phase of any relationship cannot be recaptured and must evolve into something deeper and ultimately more fulfilling (McCarthy & McCarthy, 2003). Nonetheless, erotic intimacy can be heightened in sex therapy by helping the people involved to grow as individuals and partners (Kleinplatz, 1996, 2001; Schnarch, 1991). The work of sex therapy in such cases may entail helping make the relationship safe enough to enable the individuals involved to be emotionally naked and to take the risks involved in being vulnerable.

Furthermore, some therapists consider using whatever concerns clients bring into therapy as openings toward personal growth and integration, regardless of whether or not their problems qualify for diagnosis (Mahrer & Boulet, 2001).

WHEN TO CHOOSE A SEX THERAPIST

Most people with sexual concerns start out by consulting a psychotherapist, a couple/marital therapist, or their family physicians. These individuals are generally able to assess the situation and refer the individual or couple to a specialist in sex therapy when appropriate. Sex therapy may be limited to the treatment of "official" sexual dysfunctions alone or may be more diverse and encompass the whole range of problems related to sexuality. The sex therapist's practice is often replete with concerns not necessarily listed in the usual nomenclatures. These include the impact of sexual assault and abuse, affairs and jealousy, aging, drug and alcohol abuse, eating disorders (which often accompany or exacerbate sexual problems), the ubiquitous "stress," communication problems, unconventional sexuality, sexual orientation issues, "sex addiction," sexual "malaise," and concerns about pornography and use of the Internet. Increasingly, sex therapists are called upon to deal with the sexual consequences of various medical problems and their treatment, including infertility, STIs, and myriad forms of chronic illness and disability including arthritis, heart disease, diabetes, cancer, and patients in/after rehab from traumatic injury. Many people are on medications that affect sexuality. Sex therapists frequently consult with family physicians and with specialists ranging from gynecologists and urologists to psychiatrists, endocrinologists, oncologists, internists, neurologists, and so on. Some sex therapists also have specialized training to deal with the needs of the transgendered (i.e., individuals who feel a disjunction between their biological sex and their sense of being male/female).

The most common presenting problems are related to sexual desire. These problems encompass low sexual desire, very high sexuality (often referred to as "sexual addiction"), sexual/erotic desire discrepancies, and unusual sexual desires (typically classified as the "paraphilias").

SEXUAL PROBLEMS IN INDIVIDUALS AND COUPLES AND HOW TO DEAL WITH THEM

Sexual problems tend to be classified into male versus female sexual dysfunctions and treated accordingly. Unfortunately, that division makes it too easy to overlook the extent to which sexual problems exist in interpersonal context. For example, when Masters and Johnson (1970) first attempted to define "premature ejaculation," now referred to as rapid ejaculation, they spoke in terms of the man being able to maintain his erection during inter-course to the point where the woman was able to achieve orgasm at least 50 percent of the time. The definition faltered and required revision on sev-eral grounds: Many, if not most, women will never achieve orgasm via vaginal stimulation alone; clitoral stimulation is required for most women to have orgasms. As such, a man could thrust for hours and yet have been diagnosed as dysfunctional. Second, the definition presupposed that men's partners are necessarily women and that whoever those partners might be, the focus of their sex lives is sexual intercourse. Finally, the definition presupposed that the criterion for sexual function versus dysfunction was a matter of performance, rather than his or their sexual pleasure. As such, most definitions of rapid ejaculation today focus on the man being able to keep his erection for as long as he and his partner would like, rather than in terms of some predetermined number of minutes or thrusts.

Classifications of male and female sexual dysfunctions do not capture the complexities of who has the problem, what makes it seem problematic—and to whom—and the context in which it creates problems. Nonetheless, for purposes of this section, the artificial division of men and women's sexual problems will follow.

Men's Sexual Problems and How to Deal with Them

Erectile Dysfunction

Of all male sexual dysfunctions, the one that has received the greatest attention in recent years has been erectile dysfunction, largely because of the marketing of pharmacological treatments for this condition since the late 1990s. Many people will have greater familiarity with erectile dysfunction than with other sexual problems. It will serve as the prototype here for sexual dysfunctions and their treatment, and will be discussed at greater length to introduce the basic principles of sexual problems and sex therapy.

Erections are triggered when men receive sexual stimulation, whether in the form of sexual thoughts and feelings or direct tactile contact. When men are young, mental stimulation is often sufficient to elicit an erection; typically, as men age, more direct physical stimulation is required to produce an erection. Sexual stimulation leads to an increase in blood flow into the arteries of the penis (more specifically, into highly vascular tissue in the chambers of the penis, especially the corpora cavernosa) faster than the veins can drain the blood back away. In fact, the now expanding arteries compress the veins, making it difficult for the blood flow to return until either the erection subsides or the man reaches orgasm.

Many things can interfere with erections. The factors are so numerous, from nervousness with a new partner, fear of pregnancy, job stress, to cardiovascular disease that virtually all men will have difficulties getting or maintaining erections from time to time. This is normal and does not require treatment. On the contrary, the problem sometimes occurs as a direct result of men worrying about what is normal. Men often believe that their masculinity is tied directly to their abilities to get erections automatically, whenever even a prospective opportunity arises, and to keep them endlessly (Zilbergeld, 1999). As such, occasional difficulties with getting or keeping erections can itself create the performance anxiety, which then generates the self-fulfilling prophecy of erectile dysfunction. It is noteworthy that although many people think of erectile dysfunction strictly as a problem of getting erections, the more common difficulty is with maintaining a hard penis during sexual contact rather than simply getting the initial erection.

In cultures where sexuality is defined in terms of intercourse, the prospect of erectile dysfunction can be so anxiety provoking that men have tried all manner of "treatments" to "cure" themselves of such an "affliction" from herbal potions through surgery. In sex therapy, the tradition has been to help the man and his partner to focus on pleasure rather than upon performance. To the extent that sex therapists can help the couple to broaden their sexual repertoire, they may be able to lift the pressure off the poor penis (not to mention the man attached to it!). As such, Masters and Johnson (1970) created a series of homework exercises, beginning with "sensate focus," to help couples circumvent performance anxiety. These short-term, behaviorally oriented exercises formed the cornerstone of all their treatments for sexual dysfunctions and remain fundamental to most sex therapy treatment paradigms to this day. Sensate focus exercises encourage the couple to caress one another with no expectation of engaging in intercourse. Indeed, in the initial stages of sex therapy, couples are typically forbidden from all genital contact, not to mention engaging in coitus. The idea is to reclaim pleasure for its own sake and for the couple to rediscover how to communicate through touch rather than to have to "perform." In the second stage, the couple is permitted to engage in "nondemand genital pleasuring," that is, genital stimulation but without intercourse. There were variations in homework depending on the nature of sexual problems and depending on how a given couple might respond to the initial sensate focus exercises in the course of therapy. For example, in the case of erectile dysfunction, the man was encouraged to allow himself to become sexually aroused and erect through penile stimulation by his partner, but to allow his erection to subside repeatedly. Eventually, his comfort level with, and enjoyment from, sexual contact would supersede his performance anxiety and thus enable him to return to engaging in intercourse without concern.

Although Masters and Johnson's approach was quite successful at alleviating the symptom of erectile dysfunction, at least in the short term, their method has been eclipsed by more recent medical interventions. Interestingly, as medically based treatments have become increasingly available, so has the popularity of the belief that sexual problems are caused by underlying medical disorders. Some have argued that this shift from the notion that sexual problems are primarily psychosocial to the current emphasis on the biomedical has been brought about by the pharmaceutical industry, which profits, quite literally, from the latter way of thinking (Tiefer, 2000, 2001). Others would say that men are only too eager to believe that their problems are organic because it relieves them of having to confront themselves in therapy. In any case, the notion that problems are either medical or psychosocial does a disservice to men. As discussed above, sexual problems are generally caused by a combination of factors but inevitably, have an impact on the whole person, mind, and body alike. Furthermore, regardless of who is identified as the patient, sexual difficulties typically affect all parties in a relationship. Therefore, attempts to deal with sexual problems should ideally include the "whole" person and the couple.

During the 1980s, urologist Giles Brindley discovered that injecting the penis with papaverine, an enzyme from a papaya extract, would cause automatic, hard, long-lasting erections. This breakthrough allowed men to ensure strong erections without having to engage in conventional sex therapy. In fact, they could do so without informing their partners and, for that matter, in the absence of any stimulation. These injections into the side of the penis, more specifically, into the corpora cavernosa, would create erections within about twenty minutes, regardless of what the man was feeling or doing. Whether that is a good or bad outcome is a value judgment. Nonetheless, it at least allowed men dealing with erectile dysfunction a new treatment option. (These intracavernosal injections would later be filled most commonly with a combination of papaverine, phentolamine and prostaglandin E1.) However, many men were understandably queasy at the thought of having to stick a syringe into their penises every time they wanted to produce an erection.

This obstacle was overcome with the introduction of sildenafil citrate, better known as Viagra, in 1998 (Goldstein et al., 1998). Viagra is ingested orally and, like the intracavernosal injections, works by dilating the arteries of the penis to permit an erection. Unlike the injection method, Viagra requires sexual stimulation to work effectively. If the man is not in the mood, it will not work. There is also a relatively high placebo rate. The same holds true for the other drugs in this class, vardenafil (i.e., Levitra) and tadalafil (i.e., Cialis), all known as PDE5 inhibitors. These relatively safe drugs have grown enormously popular, enough so to encourage the pharmaceutical industry to invest heavily in the development of products for the treatment of other sexual problems. Unfortunately, while these drugs may be effective at treating the symptom of sexual dysfunction, they often leave the problems within the man untouched, not to mention circumventing the couple entirely. For example, these drugs may allow the couple to temporarily ignore his feelings of worthlessness as a man unless he performs to an arbitrary and unrealistic standard; thus, his unspoken problems of self-doubt and resentment remain. Perhaps for this reason, or perhaps for other reasons (including embarrassment), articles have appeared on the problem of "patient compliance" (Althof, 1998; Perelman, 2000; Wise, 1999).

It is noteworthy that Masters and Johnson treated only couples—never individuals alone—but that practical considerations have led most sex therapists today to see people individually. Certainly, the increasing use of medical interventions and the lack of reimbursement in many American insurance plans mean that couples therapy is unlikely to occur as often as desired (Stock & Moser, 2001). Many experts still believe that ideally the relationship should be the target of sex therapy and continue to provide therapy to heterosexual or same-sex couples. Furthermore, in some instances, what appear to be mechanical difficulties in functioning can only be identified correctly as appropriate bodily responses to unsatisfactory sex or relationship issues when both partners are present (Kleinplatz, 2004; Schnarch, 1991). For example, it is only when both are in the same room that one detects the simmering conflict between them—or even their outright dislike for one another—such that his "dysfunction" is more likely a solution than a problem. Perhaps rather than being problematic, the man's soft penis provides evidence of good judgment demonstrated via his body.

Rapid Ejaculation

Notwithstanding the greater public attention to erectile dysfunction, rapid ejaculation is probably the most common male sexual dysfunction (Polonsky, 2000). As stated above, there has been considerable controversy in defining rapid ejaculation. How do you know how soon is too soon? All sorts of definitions have been proffered over the years with attempts at scientific objectivity. Some have focused on the number of minutes prior to ejaculation and others on the number of thrusts. There are several problems with such definitions: First, people who are enjoying sex rarely employ a stopwatch (fortunately!), so it is hard to ascertain what is "normal" and what is not. Second, much as scientist-clinicians seek objective criteria, how long sex lasts is only a problem when it creates distress. Surely, we can imagine the movie scene of lovers working feverishly to meet surreptitiously, ripping each other's clothes off in an empty corridor and enjoying a "quickie" before they can even catch their breath. In such instances, the sex seems torrid—not problematic. Thus, more recent approaches have focused on the man or the couple's subjective experience. For example, Metz and McCarthy (2003) feel that the best professional description of this problem is that "*the man does not have voluntary, conscious control, or the ability to choose in most encounters when to ejaculate*" (p. 1; emphasis in the original).

Typically, by the time men seek sex therapy for rapid ejaculation, they have already tried numerous delaying tactics regardless of the cost they may be paying. Common examples of "home remedies" include numbing creams, doubling up on condoms, and trying to think about disgusting things to turn themselves off. To the extent that these strategies "work," they deprive the man of pleasure, deprive the partners from feeling present with one another, and reinforce the notion that sex equals performing during intercourse.

Fortunately, rapid ejaculation generally responds quite readily to sex therapy. Most therapists deal with rapid ejaculation using a combination of sensate focus exercises, other cognitive-behavioral exercises and bibliotherapy. The tone set in therapy and in the exercises/readings is particularly important in counteracting the mindset common among men concerned about rapid ejaculation. The client's beliefs are explored and myths challenged both during therapy sessions and in assigned readings (e.g., Metz & McCarthy, 2003; Zilbergeld, 1999). For example, many men feel pressured to "last" as long as possible in the assumption that extensive thrusting is what it takes to satisfy female partners. Such men often feel quite relieved when they learn that most women prefer external, clitoral stimulation when seeking orgasm. As such, "lasting longer" becomes a choice for prolonging lovemaking, when he or they desire it, rather than an obligation. Therapists may have couples use sensate focus exercises in order to demonstrate that pleasure may abound regardless of the duration of intercourse. Other exercises are typically assigned to help the man gain more of a sense of voluntary control over his ejaculation. Ideally, the emphasis is on increasing his tolerance for high levels of pleasure rather than reducing his sensitivity to partner stimulation (Zilbergeld, 1999). The man or couple is then usually instructed in the use of the "squeeze" or "stop-start" techniques. Both techniques are used when the man is feeling very aroused and close to orgasm. The squeeze technique involves having the man or his partner apply pressure with the thumb and forefinger to the front and back of his penis—never the sides—either just under the penile glans or at the base of the penis to delay ejaculation. The stop-start technique is exactly what the name conveys: when the man feels that any further stimulation will lead to orgasm, he or they stop their activities until his level of excitement subsides. Then, stimulation is resumed. These exercises are intended to help him learn how it feels to be highly aroused without "going over the edge."

More recently, pharmacological treatment for rapid ejaculation has been available. The introduction of a popular class of antidepressants during the 1980s, the SSRIs, led to a wide range of adverse effects on sexual desire and response. In fact, the effects of drugs such as Paxil on orgasmic response were so dramatic, diminishing or even preventing orgasm in many patients, that the drug was later prescribed for men concerned about rapid ejaculation (Assalian, 1994). The SSRIs succeeded in slowing down men's ejaculations and have been used as an adjunct to, or instead of, conventional sex therapy for treatment of rapid ejaculation (Waldinger, 2003).

Delayed Ejaculation

On the other end of the spectrum are men who are unable to reach orgasm with a partner. (Men who have never had an orgasm in their lives under any circumstances, including via masturbation, probably have underlying medical problems requiring evaluation.) This problem had been known as "ejaculatory incompetence" and then later as "retarded ejaculation," but both these pejorative terms have been replaced by the term "delayed ejaculation." Most people do not think of men capable of thrusting away endlessly during intercourse as having a problem. On the contrary, many would be envious of such a capacity. As such, it has been estimated that delayed ejaculation is the most underreported of male sexual problems just as correspondingly, rapid orgasm in women is probably the most underreported of women's sexual difficulties. Many people would just scratch their heads at hearing of such conditions and ask, "So what's the problem?" The assumption in our sex scripts is that no man can stay hard for too long and that no woman can reach orgasm too soon. However, Apfelbaum (2000) would respond that men who cannot ejaculate with a partner are the misunderstood "workhorses" of the sex world. Apfelbaum has argued that although such men have often been treated as if they were withholding during sex, on the contrary, they are giving too much. These are individuals who are trying so hard to please their partners that they continue to perform while subjectively feeling minimal arousal, numb, or even turned off. It seems that their desires are out of sync with their penises, which continue to remain erect despite lack of excitement (Apfelbaum). Why this should be the case is not clear. During the 1970s and 1980s, sex therapy techniques involved attempting to stimulate such individuals ever more aggressively to the point of orgasm. Apfelbaum suggests instead that sex therapists help them to acknowledge their feelings. In other words, whereas previous treatment models had suggested that these men just keep on moving, even if this meant ignoring their own reluctance (a strategy associated with the work of Kaplan [1974] and referred to as "bypassing"), Apfelbaum recommends "counterbypassing." Here, the men are encouraged to pay more attention to their reluctance and lack of desire for intercourse—not to override them—and to be true to themselves by acknowledging these feelings. It is only via authenticity that enduring change can come about (Apfelbaum).

Pain Associated with Sex in Men—Dyspareunia

Most of the literature on pain associated with sex, known as dyspareunia, concentrates on female pain during intercourse. Unfortunately, there is insufficient attention to men's pain during or following various sexual acts. It is hard even to estimate just how prevalent such pain may be. Pain may occur anywhere in men's external or internal sexual and reproductive organs, that is, not only in the penis but also in the epididymis, vas deferens, prostate, and other parts. It may begin in the course of sexual arousal, orgasm, or thereafter. It can be related to anything from skin sensitivities and allergies to sexually transmitted or other infections and injury. These problems are usually assessed and treated by a physician.

There are only two articles in the literature on pain during anal penetration, known as anodyspareunia (Damon & Rosser, 2005; Rosser, Short, Thurmes, & Coleman, 1998). Both these articles focus on pain among men who have sex with men. This is striking given that most anal penetration of men and women occurs in heterosexual couples. This silence says more about the taboo surrounding anal sex than its actual popularity. (The best-selling "adult video" in recent years has been "Bend Over Boyfriend" [Rednour, 1998], notwithstanding or perhaps because of this silence.)

Women's Sexual Problems and How to Deal with Them

Difficulties with Orgasm

Women's difficulties with arousal and orgasm have been the subject of much speculation and far too many myths. These tend to go in and out of fashion along with the politics surrounding female sexuality. During the Victorian era, the very notion that women were capable of orgasms was scorned and scandalous. Freud argued that although little girls would naturally focus on the clitoris as their primary erogenous zone, "mature" women would and should be capable of orgasms via intercourse. This idea predominated through most of the twentieth century. During the 1950s, "marriage manuals" stated that the ideal was for husband and wife to achieve "simultaneous orgasm" during intercourse. Women who had problems with arousal or orgasm in the context of intercourse-oriented sex were deemed "frigid." During the 1960s, Masters and Johnson distinguished between arousal and orgasm and pointed out that it was normative for women to have orgasms via clitoral stimulation, whether during self-stimulation, manual stimulation by a partner, oral sex, or "somehow" during sexual intercourse.

The latter remains the goal for many couples, notwithstanding our expanding knowledge of female genitalia and sexuality. The number and intensity of nerve endings in the clitoris far exceed those in the vagina, and even those found in the vagina are located primarily near the entrance. (Any woman who has ever used tampons can remember her surprise upon first reading the package instructions; these indicated that once the tampon is inserted correctly, the woman will be unable to feel it in the course of normal activities.) It can be difficult for women to get enough direct clitoral stimulation during intercourse to bring about orgasm. Indeed, for some women the trick is to arrange enough external pressure and friction to trigger orgasm (almost) despite intercourse! Although this information is increasingly widespread, given a society that defines "sex" as intercourse—nothing else quite counts as "going all the way"—the objective of "climaxing during sex" endures. Even the obvious solution, for the woman or her partner to stimulate her clitoris manually during intercourse, strikes many people as "cheating," at least initially. It is as though the "hands-free orgasm" remains the cultural gold standard.

The pressure on women to perform corresponds to the pressure on men discussed earlier. If this theme is becoming repetitive, that is because its impact is ubiquitous. To the extent that sex must be heterosexual and that the ultimate end of sex is penis in vagina, we are creating obstacles to, and "dysfunctions" in the way of, sexual pleasure. Furthermore, we thereby limit what we can hope to attain during sex. For example, in 1982, sexologists Ladas, Whipple, and Perry wrote a best-selling book about the "G-spot" (i.e., the Grafenberg spot), which described a sensitive area that could be accessed via stimulation of the anterior wall, (the roof or front wall) of the vagina. (This area is now referred to as the "female prostate" [Zaviacic, 1999].) Rather than being welcomed as a new possibility for further sexual exploration, this important contribution was misinterpreted in some quarters as setting a new imperative, or perhaps reasserting the notion that there is one right way to reach orgasm after all (Tavris, 1992).

For the sex therapist, that leaves the problem of figuring out what constitutes a problem and precisely what requires "treatment." Increasingly, sex therapists have come to believe that couples who insist upon the woman achieving orgasm via sexual intercourse are in need of psychoeducational counseling rather than "treatment" as such. That is, they may need to learn enough about women's bodies to readjust their expectations and to expand their criteria for valid orgasm pathways (e.g., manual or oral sex). Alternately, they may be encouraged to use their hands or sex toys to provide direct clitoral stimulation during intercourse (Dodson, 2002).

But what of the woman who has never had an orgasm by any means and wants to do so? This problem is sometimes called inhibited female orgasm or anorgasmia. Some would say that the term really should be "preorgasmic" rather than "anorgasmic" because all women are capable of orgasm, whether it has happened yet or not (Barbach, 2000). In Masters and Johnson's (1970) approach, the couple began, as always, with sensate focus exercises. For many women, the taboo against exploring their bodies was strong enough to have prevented them from ever really discovering what gave them pleasure. Sensate focus exercises gave them permission to enjoy touching and being touched for their own sake. This theme has been emphasized in other programs for women who have difficulty with orgasm, such as those of Barbach (2000) and Heiman and Lo-Piccolo (1988). These popular cognitive-behavioral treatment plans involve teaching women about the anatomy of their genitalia and the physiology of sexual response, generally through readings and exercises, and via discussion during therapy sessions. Women also review their sexual histories, current beliefs, and especially myths to uncover the obstacles to pleasure. Individual or relationship problems, which make it hard to feel desirable, to feel worthy of sexual attention, to trust a partner, or to let go, are discussed and dealt with as necessary.

Bodily awareness and self-stimulation are emphasized, as most women who have never had an orgasm with a partner will probably find it easiest to experience it alone at first. There are often fewer inhibitions when one is alone, and the focused concentration on oneself makes it easier to discover one's own sensitivities and triggers to orgasm. It also seems safer to take all the time one needs alone; this is a serious consideration for many women (and their partners) who worry, "It's taking too much time. . . . I'm afraid [he/she] will get bored and give up on me." The implication that the couple should be able to rush through sex betrays their beliefs about sex and often the underlying fear of wanting more pleasure than entitled. It also suggests that the couple's existing sexual activities may not be particularly erotic, at least for her. As such, she will be encouraged to explore her own wishes and fantasies, too, on her way to orgasm and beyond.

Once she has found out how to have orgasms alone, she will need to show and tell her partner what pleases her. Here, it is often literally a matter of teaching her partner about her desires and her body, and demonstrating what kinds of stimulation she finds exciting. To the extent that they are able to communicate effectively and get over the initial awkwardness, this approach usually allows her to begin having orgasms with a partner in relatively short-term therapy.

Female Sexual Arousal Problems

Traditionally, there has been little attention focused directly on women's sexual arousal difficulties, at least in part because of the confounding of arousal per se with orgasm. However, it is possible for a woman to feel aroused and to lubricate without reaching orgasm and, less commonly, for women to reach orgasm while lubricating and feeling minimal levels of sexual arousal. Also, lack of arousal has been subsumed under treatment for difficulties with orgasm or desire.

Another reason for the lack of clinical or research attention to women's arousal difficulties is the conventional North American sexual script that emphasizes functioning over subjective experience. To the extent that men's difficulties with arousal are evident in erectile dysfunction, intercourse is impeded and, therefore, male arousal difficulties command the spotlight. Women's sexual arousal difficulties are manifest in terms of lack of vaginal lubrication and absent, minimal, or diminished subjective feelings of excitement. Neither of these difficulties necessarily obstructs intercourse per se and, therefore, they have been ignored by researchers. There has been a great deal of research on factors that might reduce or increase the blood flow to male genitalia. We need more data on factors affecting the psychology and physiology of female sexual response.

Women who see their gynecologists for lack of lubrication are sometimes assessed for underlying physical, psychological, or interpersonal causes and offered appropriate treatment; however, it is not unusual for them simply to receive instructions on the use of lubricants or hormonal creams. This treatment enables them to engage in intercourse whether or not they feel aroused. Lubricants are an important adjunct in helping women to engage in pain-free intercourse when their own, natural lubrication has been diminished by disease, by various prescription (e.g., antihypertensives, diuretics) or over-the-counter medications (e.g., antihistamines, decongestants), or by aging. However, such measures, when applied whenever women are slow to lubricate, are treating a symptom rather than what may be the underlying cause of the problem. It may simply be that she is not lubricating because the sex or her partner is not arousing to her. In such cases, the "treatment" may actually mask the problem—or the fact that there is no problem: it is healthy and normal *not* to be aroused if the sex or the relationship are not to one's liking or are actually a turn-off. The reasons that she is not lubricating or subjectively aroused warrant attention.

Given the paucity of literature on female sexual arousal problems, little is discussed in the way of treatment outside the use of lubricants and hormone creams. There are some valuable exceptions, including the integrated mind-body-relationship program of Foley, Kope, and Sugrue (2002). Their self-help program involves assessment and bodily awareness exercises for the woman, with emphasis on the pelvic floor muscles, sensate focus exercises for the couple, the use of fantasy, and designing the ideal sexual encounter.

It is worth remembering that some of the so-called inevitable changes associated with aging and decreasing hormone levels may be subject to prevention. Masters and Johnson, among others, would say "use it or lose it." Women who remain sexually active, whether alone or with partners, are less likely to have problems with vaginal dryness or lack of lubrication than women who undergo prolonged periods of abstinence.

Vaginismus

Perhaps the ultimate obstacle to intercourse is vaginismus. Vaginismus has been described as an involuntary, reflexive spasm of the muscles of the outer third of the vagina and perineum, preventing vaginal penetration. It varies in severity from women who cannot tolerate vaginal penetration in any form to women who can insert tampons and perhaps a finger during sexual stimulation. Some can even weather a gynecological exam (albeit, with hesitation and discomfort) but still tighten up at the prospect of intercourse. Men who attempt penile penetration with women diagnosed with vaginismus report that as they try to get past the vaginal entrance, "It feels like I'm hitting a brick wall." If they endeavor to push further, it will hurt the woman as well as the man's penile glans.

It is common for women with vaginismus to have orgasms via self-stimulation as well as manual and oral stimulation with a partner. What, then, brings them to therapy? Sometimes they seek treatment because they or their partners would like to be able to engage in intercourse. Sometimes they are referred for treatment by physicians unable to perform a pelvic exam. In many cases, the partners have developed a broad enough sexual repertoire such that they are able to satisfy one another (Hawton & Catalan, 1990; Kaplan, 1987; Pridal & LoPiccolo, 1993; Valins, 1992) with no particular desire for intercourse. In these instances, there is no need for therapy unless and until the couple wants to conceive a baby. Indeed, therapists note that the timing of couples seeking sex therapy for treatment of vaginismus is often linked to increased pressure from in-laws for grandchildren. It is striking that there is not a single case of vaginismus in lesbian couples reported in the literature.

There is extensive speculation about the origins of vaginismus. Certainly, any time a person feels tension or fear, the body responds accordingly: the muscles contract. Women diagnosed with vaginismus tend to have considerable anxiety about intercourse. More specifically, many are afraid of pain during intercourse, which results in the muscles at the vaginal opening tightening, making intercourse very difficult, if not impossible. Some, still virgins, are afraid based on horror stories they have heard about pain and bleeding on the wedding night. Others have already attempted intercourse but the pain they have dreaded leads to a self-fulfilling prophecy; sure enough, attempting intercourse when terrified leads the body to shut down, the vaginal muscles to shut tightly, and then inevitably to pain. Sometimes, vaginismus results from a history of pain during intercourse, in which case it is important to evaluate the cause of this pain. Others are afraid because of a prior history of sexual abuse and assault. (There is debate about the prevalence of trauma history among women with this condition.) Almost inevitably, women diagnosed with vaginismus come from sex-negative backgrounds with little to no sex education. One cue mentioned in gynecological textbooks for diagnosing vaginismus is that the vaginal muscles are positioned just as the lips might be in saying "no." Perhaps her body is sending a message about her reservations, which should be taken seriously rather than just trying, literally, to push past it. It may be advisable to conceive of the vaginal spasm as a symptom, related to her underlying fear(s) and feelings about intercourse rather than a disorder per se. However, all the speculation about causes, meaning, or even the purpose of vaginismus is generally considered irrelevant (at least in the literature) for treatment.

To the extent that the goal in treating vaginismus is for women to gain control over their vaginal muscles, thereby enabling intercourse, most of the time this objective is attained regardless. In fact, of all the sexual dysfunctions in women, vaginismus was long considered the easiest to treat, with the highest success rate (i.e., virtually 100 percent in the short term [Kaplan, 1974; Masters & Johnson, 1970]). The major treatment method involves the use of graduated, plastic, vaginal dilators. Women are trained in the insertion and "containment" of the dilators, progressing in size from the narrowest to the widest over the course of the treatment program. Women are encouraged also to learn and practice relaxation techniques and Kegel (i.e., vaginal muscle) exercises. Biofeedback is increasingly employed as an adjunct to therapy. Eventually, women are to make the transition from plastic dilators to penises, preferably with the man encouraged to lie motionless on his back until the woman feels comfortably in control.

Notwithstanding the effectiveness of these "desensitization" techniques in eliminating the symptom of vaginismus, this treatment approach has been criticized as dehumanizing to the woman and her partner (Kleinplatz, 1998; Nicolson, 1993; Shaw, 1994; Ushher, 1993). It may "work," but the therapy process may "succeed" at overcoming a vaginal spasm by ignoring the rest of the person. Overriding her anxieties and fears in order to achieve mastery over her body may leave her feeling disconnected and alienated from her partner. It also ignores the possibility that she may simply not be willing to engage in sexual intercourse. Suggested alternatives help the woman to become centered and integrated enough to deal with her feelings openly and directly rather than through the symptom of the vaginal spasm (Kleinplatz, 1998; Shaw, 1994).

Pain Associated with Sex in Women—Dyspareunia

Whereas there is minimal attention to pain associated with sex in men, there is quite an extensive literature on dyspareunia in women. Pain during sex, and during sexual intercourse in particular, is fairly common. Continuing and persistent pain associated with sex is less so.

There are an enormous number of possible causes for genital pain. It is hard to determine the precise origin of the pain without a careful clinical assessment, including a pelvic examination. Sometimes women come to sex therapy seeking help with genital pain after already having seen their physicians for their annual examination and having been pronounced healthy. However, unless the physician has been told specifically to investigate her genital pain, it is very unlikely that it will be detected. The "clean bill of health" does not mean much if the physician did not ask the right questions. It is important and helpful for the woman to tell her physician in as much detail as possible what is bothering her. Correspondingly, the physician will not be able to learn much without asking specific questions about where exactly it hurts, during which sexual (or other) acts, what triggers it and makes it stop, how intense the pain is and what is the nature of the pain. Given that many women and their physicians are uncomfortable discussing these subjects with one another, the sex therapist often plays the role of detective and facilitator.

The questions suggested above help to track the source of the pain. For example, burning pain on the external genitalia during oral sex or manual stimulation would likely lead to rather different investigations and diagnoses than sharp pain at the vaginal opening at the beginning of intercourse versus an aching thud on deep penetration. Pain can be caused by anything from STIs to yeast infections, endometriosis, allergies, hormonal changes, and vaginismus to episiotomy scars that have healed poorly. (An episiotomy is the incision often made into a woman's perineum during childbirth to prevent tearing. It is more routine in the United States than anywhere else. Research and experience in other countries have demonstrated clearly that most women usually do not need an episiotomy and that the risks outweigh the benefits.) Much of the recent focus has been on the pain of vulvar vestibulitis (i.e., generalized, chronic pain of the external genitalia [see Bergeron et al., 2002]) and vulvadynia (i.e., chronic pain at the vaginal opening).

There is quite a bit of controversy as to whether or not dyspareunia should be classified as a sexual dysfunction or as a pain disorder (Binik, Meana, Berkley, & Khalifé, 1999; Binik, 2005). As Binik et al. asked in the title of one of their articles, "Is the pain sexual or is the sex painful?" They argue that the current classification of dyspareunia as a psychologically based disorder manifested as a physical "sexual" symptom is erroneous and conspicuous. All other pain disorders (e.g., back pain, headaches) are classified and treated together using the same rationale; it is only dyspareunia that seems to have been singled out as different, with the focus on the sex rather than the pain. Binik (2005) states that our understanding of women's genital pain and its treatment must be revised. It should be reconceptualized as a pain disorder that interferes with a woman's quality of life, including but not limited to her sexual expression.

The treatment of dyspareunia must, of course, be related to the underlying cause of the pain. The ideal goal is to cure the source of the pain. When that is not possible, and even when it is, considering that she is now suffering from chronic pain, treatment should be multifaceted. Experts trained in sex therapy, biofeedback, pain management techniques, and physiotherapy will be required to work together with gynecologists and other physicians to diagnose and treat women or couples whose lives have been limited by pain.

COUPLES' PROBLEMS: DIFFICULTIES WITH SEXUAL DESIRE AND INTIMACY

The most common problem bringing individuals, and couples in particular, into sex therapy is low desire (known more formally as hypoactive sexual desire disorder). Actually, it is sexual desire discrepancy between the partners that brings couples into therapy more so than low (or high) levels of desire in the abstract. How low is too low? For that matter, how much is too much? And who is to make that determination? If two people want to have sex with each other three times per year and both are happy at that rate, these questions are moot—this couple will not be seeking sex therapy. The same is likely true for couples who want to have sex together three times per day. The context in which the problem arises is when one person wants more sex in that relationship than the other. Whom should the therapist treat, if anyone? These questions are more than merely academic. They are important both clinically and ethically. It is commonplace for two people to arrive for therapy wherein each feels strongly that the other has the problem and requires help. If one says, "If I never had sex again, I wouldn't miss it," is it feasible or right for the partner or a therapist to try to change someone who does not seek to change? Correspondingly, if one claims that the other is "oversexed" but the partner feels self-contentment, what is the therapist to do? It is a truism in couples therapy that people never change for others—at least not in the long term—but only for themselves. As such, in cases of sexual desire discrepancy the couple assuredly has a problem, which may or may not be amenable to change, but whether or not the individuals in question require "treatment" is a complex matter.

In order to ascertain how to proceed, the sex therapist needs to understand and appreciate the meaning of the problem in context. Is the low desire lifelong or recent? In either event, when and how did it come to be perceived as problematic, and by whom? What precipitated the diminishing of desire? Is there low desire in all situations and in all relationships or only with the current partner? Is there desire for others? (In the course of such an assessment, many individuals who are sure that their partners are utterly lacking in desire are stunned to hear that their partners self-stimulate to orgasm three times per week. Here the problem is not lack of desire—it is a lack of desire for sex or for the partner in that relationship.) Is the quality of the sex satisfactory to each partner? Is the type of sex they engage in mutually fulfilling? Sometimes people make assumptions based on the frequency of sex without considering the quality of the sex or the sexual relationship. To put it another way, is it any wonder if people who have different visions of ideal sexual relations ultimately appear to have a sexual desire discrepancy? How is the rest of the relationship? Sometimes, the problems lie elsewhere but are manifest in the bedroom. Often, when one is complaining of the other's low sexual desire, the other is dissatisfied with the relationship.

Key phrases for therapists to note include "The passion is gone" and "I don't feel any connection." Such statements may indicate that although nothing is wrong with either of them, there may not be anything right going on, either. The couple may be technically proficient and there may be no mechanical failures. However, the sex may be lackluster enough that it is not really worth wanting (Kleinplatz, 1996; Schnarch, 1991). Many people are justifiably disillusioned by their sex lives. One or both may be having their required quota of orgasms yet disappointed at the absence of eroticism during sex. In such cases, the question is: "What would make it worth your while to get excited?" It is all too common for people to be perceived as having low sexual desire when, actually, they refuse to settle for mediocre sex and are geared toward ecstasy (Ogden, 1999). Sometimes, sex therapists can be most helpful by going beyond the purely "clinical" to deal with all the dimensions of desire including the emotional, intellectual, erotic, and even spiritual (Ogden, 1999, 2001).

Given the complexity of sexual desire complaints, therapies must be individualized to deal with the particular problems of each unique individual or couple. There are few standardized therapy methods. This is greatly disappointing to many of those who come to therapy expecting quick-fix solutions. The popular discourse in the media suggests that desire is just a matter of hormones. Although hormone levels are relevant, simply increasing them is rarely sufficient to solve desire problems. Sometimes, the cause of the desire problems is primarily biochemical, as when a person's desire drops dramatically after starting to use certain drugs (e.g., SSRIs, sedatives, alcohol, cocaine). Even in these relatively straightforward instances, depending on how long it has been since the individual last experienced desire, it may be awkward getting back into having sex and may often require some coaching during sex therapy. Bibliotherapy may offer useful suggestions and exercises for couples who are struggling with uncomplicated desire problems or may be used as an adjunct to sex therapy (e.g., McCarthy & McCarthy, 2003). Couples must do their own work between sessions, arranging time to be both intimate and sexual (Ellison, 2001).

Most of the time, sexual desire problems require high levels of honesty in therapy in order to tease out the interplay of contributing factors and to deal with each of them. These may be as diverse as history of incest, treatment for cancer, arguments about child-rearing practices, reluctance to engage in oral sex, and distrust following an affair. Thus, a one-size-fits-all solution to these problems, all appearing as "low sexual desire," is unlikely to help.

CONCLUSION

Sex therapy is still in its infancy. For a field not yet fifty years old, a great deal has been accomplished. The complexity of sexual difficulties and the many reasons, meanings, and purposes underlying them remain a challenge.

Sexual difficulties—and whether or not a "symptom" even constitutes a "problem"—will never be understood in isolation but only in the context of lived human experience. In some respects, sex therapy has much to offer individuals and couples seeking to overcome the symptoms of the major sexual problems. Although the field does offer some remarkably rapid treatment options, the depths and heights to which many people aspire will require broader visions and innovative approaches. There remains plenty of room to grow, particularly with regard to sexual desire issues, whether dealing with "low" desire, "high" desire, unconventional desires, or desire discrepancies. Beyond helping couples overcome barriers to sex, much remains to be discovered about how to help couples attain the farther reaches of erotic intimacy.

REFERENCES

Advocates for Youth (1999). *European approaches to adolescent sexual behavior and responsibility*. Washington, DC: Author.

Althof, S. E. (1998). New roles for mental health clinicians in the treatment of erectile dysfunction. *Journal of Sex Education and Therapy, 23*(3), 229–231.

Althof, S. E. (2001). My personal distress over the inclusion of personal distress. *Journal of Sex and Marital Therapy, 27*(2), 123–125.

American Psychiatric Association. (1980). *Diagnostic and statistical manual of mental disorders* (3rd ed.). Washington, DC: Author.

American Psychiatric Association. (2000). *Diagnostic and statistical manual of mental disorders* (4th ed., Text Rev.). Washington, DC: Author.

Apfelbaum, B. (2000). Retarded ejaculation: A much misunderstood syndrome. In S. R. Leiblum & R. C. Rosen (Eds.), *Principles and Practice of Sex Therapy* (3rd ed., pp. 205–241). New York: Guilford.

Assalian, P. (1994). Premature ejaculation: Is it really psychogenic? *Journal of Sex Education and Therapy, 20*(1), 1–4.

Barbach, L. (2000). *For yourself: The fulfillment of female sexuality*. New York: Signet Books.

Barth, R. J., & Kinder, B. N. (1987). The mislabeling of sexual impulsivity. *Journal of Sex and Marital Therapy, 13*, 15–23.

Bergeron, S., Brown, C., Lord, M.-J., Oala, M., Binik, Y. M., & Khalifé, S. (2002). Physical therapy for vulvar vestibulitis syndrome: A retrospective study. *Journal of Sex and Marital Therapy, 28*(3), 183–192.

Binik, Y. M. (2005). Should dyspareunia be retained as a sexual dysfunction in DSM-V? A painful classification decision. *Archives of Sexual Behavior, 34*(1), 11–22.

Binik, Y. M., Meana, M., Berkley, K., & Khalifé, S. (1999). The sexual pain disorders: Is the pain sexual or is the sex painful? *Annual Review of Sex Research, 10*, 210–235.

Carnes, P. (1991). *Don't call it love: Recovery from sexual addiction*. New York: Bantam.

Coleman, E. (1995). Treatment of compulsive sexual behavior. In R. C. Rosen & S. R. Leiblum (Eds.), *Case studies in sex therapy* (pp. 333–349). New York: Guilford.

Damon, W., & Rosser, B. R. S. (2005). Anodyspareunia in men who have sex with men: Prevalence, predictors, consequences and the development of DSM diagnostic criteria. *Journal of Sex and Marital Therapy, 31*(2), 129–141.

Dodson, B. (2002). *Orgasms for two*. New York: Harmony.

Ellison, C. R. (2001). Intimacy-based sex therapy: Sexual choreography. In P. J. Kleinplatz (Ed.), *New directions in sex therapy: Innovations and alternatives* (pp. 163–184). Philadelphia: Brunner-Routledge.

Foley, S., Kope, S. A., & Sugrue, D. (2002). *Sex matters for women*. New York: Guilford.

Gagnon, J. H., & Simon, W. (1973). *Sexual conduct: The social sources of human sexuality*. Chicago: Aldine.

Giami, A. (2000). Changing relations between medicine, psychology and sexuality: The case of male impotence. *Journal of Social Medicine, 37*, 263–272.

Goldstein, I., Lue, T., Padma-Nathan, H., Rosen, R., Steers, W., & Wicker, P. (1998). Oral sildenafil in the treatment of erectile dysfunction. *New England Journal of Medicine, 338*, 1397–1404.

Hawton, K., & Catalan, J. (1990). Sex therapy for vaginismus: Characteristics of couples and treatment outcome. *Journal of Sex and Marital Therapy, 5*(1), 39–48.

Heiman, J., & LoPiccolo, J. (1988). *Becoming orgasmic: A sexual and personal growth program for women*. New York: Prentice Hall.

Herman, J. L. (1992). *Trauma and recovery*. New York: Basic Books.Irvine, J. M. (1990). *Disorders of desire: Sex and gender in modern American sexology*. Philadelphia: Temple University Press.

Kafka, M. P., & Hennen, J. (1999). The paraphilia-related disorders: An empirical investigation of nonparaphilic hypersexuality disorders in outpatient males. *Journal of Sex and Marital Therapy, 25*(4), 305–320.

Kaplan, H. S. (1974). *The new sex therapy*. New York: Brunner/Mazel.

Kaplan, H. S. (1977). Hypoactive sexual desire. *Journal of Sex and Marital Therapy, 3*(1), 3–9.

Kaplan, H. S. (1979). *Disorders of sexual desire and other new concepts and techniques in sex therapy*. New York: Brunner/Mazel.

Kaplan, H. S. (1987). *The illustrated manual of sex therapy*. (2nd ed.). New York: Brunner/Mazel.

Kleinplatz, P. J. (1996). The erotic encounter. *Journal of Humanistic Psychology, 36*(3), 105–123.

Kleinplatz, P. J. (1998). Sex therapy for vaginismus: A review, critique and humanistic alternative. *Journal of Humanistic Psychology, 38*(2), 51–81.

Kleinplatz, P. J. (2001). A critique of the goals of sex therapy or the hazards of safer sex. In P. J. Kleinplatz (Ed.), *New directions in sex therapy: Innovations and alternatives* (pp. 109–131). Philadelphia: Brunner-Routledge.

Kleinplatz, P. J. (2003). What's new in sex therapy: From stagnation to frag-mentation. *Sex and Relationship Therapy,* *18*(1), 95–106.

Kleinplatz, P. J. (2004). Beyond sexual mechanics and hydraulics: Humanizing the discourse surrounding erectile dysfunction. *Journal of Humanistic Psychology,* *44*(2), 215–242.

Ladas, A. K., Whipple, B., & Perry, J. D. (1982). *The G spot and other recent discoveries about human sexuality.* New York: Holt, Rinehart, and Winston.

Leiblum, S. R., & Rosen, R. C. (2000). Introduction: Sex therapy in the age of Viagra. In S. R. Leiblum & R. C. Rosen (Eds.), *Principles and practice of sex therapy* (3rd ed., pp. 1–13). New York: Guilford.

Lief, H. I. (1977). Inhibited sexual desire. *Medical Aspects of Human Sexuality,* 7, 94–95.

Mahrer, A. R., & Boulet, D. (2001). How can Experiential Psychotherapy help transform the field of sex therapy? In P. J. Kleinplatz (Ed.), *New directions in sex therapy: Innovations and alternatives* (pp. 234–257). Philadelphia: Brunner-Routledge.

Maltz, W. (1998). *The sexual healing journey: A guide for survivors of sexual abuse.* New York: HarperCollins.

Masters, W. H., & Johnson, V. E. (1966). *Human sexual response.* Boston: Little, Brown.

Masters, W. H., & Johnson, V. E. (1970). *Human sexual inadequacy.* New York: Bantam Books.

Maurice, W. L. (1999). *Sexual medicine in primary care.* St. Louis, MO: Mosby.

McCarthy, B., & McCarthy, E. (2003). *Rekindling desire: A step-by-step program to help low-sex and no-sex marriages.* New York: Brunner-Routledge.

Metz, E. M., & McCarthy, B. W. (2003). *Coping with premature ejaculation: How to overcome P.E., please your partner & have great sex.* Oakland, CA: New Harbinger.

Moser, C. (1999). *Health care without shame: A handbook for the sexually diverse and their caregivers.* San Francisco: Greenery Press.

Moser, C., & Kleinplatz, P. J. (in press). DSM-IV-TR and the Paraphilias: An argument for removal. *Journal of Psychology and Human Sexuality.*

Moser, C., & Kleinplatz, P. J. (2002). Transvestic fetishism: Psychopathology or iatrogenic artifact? *New Jersey Psychologist, 52*(2) 16–17.

Nathan, S. (2003). When do we say a woman's sexuality is dysfunctional? In S. Levine, C. Reisen, & S. Althof (Eds.), *Handbook of clinical sexuality for mental health professionals* (pp. 95–110). New York: Brunner-Routledge.

Nicolson, P. (1993). Public values and private beliefs: Why do women refer themselves for sex therapy? In J. M. Ussher & C. D. Baker (Eds.), *Psychological perspectives on sexual problems: New directions in theory and practice* (pp. 56–76). New York: Routledge.

Ogden, G. (1999). *Women who love sex.* Boston: Womanspirit Press.

Ogden, G. (2001). Integrating sexuality and spirituality: A group therapy approach to women's sexual dilemmas. In P. J. Kleinplatz (Ed.), *New directions in sex therapy: Innovations and alternatives* (pp. 322–346). Philadelphia: Brunner-Routledge.

Perelman, M. A. (2000). Integrating Sildenafil: Its impact on sex therapy. *Sexual Dysfunction in Medicine, 1*(4), 98–104.

Polonsky, D. C. (2000). Premature ejaculation. In S. R. Leiblum & R. C. Rosen (Eds.), *Principles and practice of sex therapy* (3rd ed., pp. 305–332). New York: Guilford.

Pridal, C. G., & LoPiccolo, J. (1993). Brief treatment of vaginismus. In R. A. Wells & V. J. Gianetti (Eds.), *Casebook of the brief psychotherapies* (pp. 329–345). New York: Plenum Press.

Rednour, S. (Director). (1998). *Bend over boyfriend* [Film]. San Francisco: Fatale Video.

Reiersøl, O., & Skeid, S. (in press). The ICD diagnoses of fetishism and sado-masochism. *Journal of Homosexuality, 50*(3/4).

Reiss, I. L. (1990). *An end to shame: Shaping our next sexual revolution*. Buffalo, NY: Prometheus Books.

Rosen, R. C., & Leiblum, S. R. (1995). The changing focus of sex therapy. In R. C. Rosen & S. R. Leiblum (Eds.), *Case studies in sex therapy* (pp. 3–17). New York: Guilford.

Rosser, B. R. S., Short, B. J., Thurmes, P. J., & Coleman, E. (1998). Anodyspareunia, the unacknowledged sexual dysfunction: A validation study of painful receptive anal intercourse and its psychosexual concomitants in homosexual men. *Journal of Sex and Marital Therapy, 24*(4), 281–292.

Schnarch, D. (1991). *Constructing the sexual crucible: An integration of sexual and marital therapy*. New York: W. W. Norton.

Schover, L. R., & Leiblum, S. R. (1994). Commentary: The stagnation of sex therapy. *Journal of Psychology and Human Sexuality, 6*(3), 5–30.

Shaw, J. (1994). Treatment of primary vaginismus: A new perspective. *Journal of Sex and Marital Therapy, 20*(1), 46–55.

Shaw, J. (2001). Approaching sexual potential in relationship: A reward of age and maturity. In P. J. Kleinplatz (Ed.), *New directions in sex therapy: Innovations and alternatives* (pp. 185–209). Philadelphia: Brunner-Routledge.

Stock, W., & Moser, C. (2001). Feminist sex therapy in the age of Viagra. In P. J. Kleinplatz (Ed.), *New directions in sex therapy: Innovations and alternatives* (pp. 139–162). Philadelphia: Brunner-Routledge.

Tavris, C. (1992). *The mismeasure of woman*. New York: Touchstone.

Tiefer, L. (1996). The medicalization of sexuality: Conceptual, normative, and professional issues. *Annual Review of Sex Research, 7*, 252–282.

Tiefer, L. (2000). Sexology and the pharmaceutical industry: The threat of co-optation. *Journal of Sex Research, 37*(3), 273–283.

Tiefer, L. (2001). The selling of "female sexual dysfunction." *Journal of Sex and Marital Therapy, 27*(5), 625–628.

Valins, L. (1992). *When a woman's body says no to sex: Understanding and overcoming vaginismus*. New York: Viking.

Waldinger, M. D. (2003). Rapid ejaculation. In S. B. Levine, C. B. Risen, & S. Althof (Eds.), *Handbook of clinical sexuality for mental health professionals* (pp. 257–274). New York: Brunner-Routledge.

Wiederman, M. (1998). The state of theory in sex therapy. *Journal of Sex Research, 35*(1), 88–99.

Winton, M. A. (2000). The medicalization of male sexual dysfunctions: An analysis of sex therapy journals. *Journal of Sex Education and Therapy, 25*(4), 231–239.

Winton, M. A. (2001). Gender, sexual dysfunctions and the *Journal of Sex & Marital Therapy. Journal of Sex and Marital Therapy, 27*(4), 333–337.

Wise, T. N. (1999). Psychosocial effects of sildenafil therapy for erectile dysfunction. *Journal of Sex and Marital Therapy, 25*(2), 145–150.

Working Group for a New View of Women's Sexual Problems (2001). A new view of women's sexual problems. *Women & Therapy, 24*(1/2), 1–8.

Zaviacic, M. (1999). *The human female prostate*. Bratislava: Slovak Academic Press.

Zilbergeld, B. (1999). *The new male sexuality*. New York: Bantam Books.

RECOMMENDED READINGS

Barbach, L. (2000). *For yourself: The fulfillment of female sexuality*. New York: Signet Books.

Courtois, C. (1988). *Healing the incest wound*. New York: W. W. Norton.

Dodson, B. (2002). *Orgasms for two*. New York: Harmony.

Daniluk, J. C. (1998). *Women's sexuality across the life span: Challenging myths, creating meanings*. New York: Guilford.

Ducharme, S. H., & Gill, K. M. (1997). *Sexuality after spinal cord injury: Answers to your questions*. Baltimore: Paul H. Brookes.

Ellison, C. R. (2000). *Women's sexualities*. Oakland, CA: New Harbinger.

Feuerstein, G. (1992). *Sacred sexuality: Living the vision of the erotic spirit*. New York: Putnam.

Foley, S., Kope, S. A., & Sugrue, D. (2002). *Sex matters for women*. New York: Guilford.

Francouer, R., Cornog, M., & Perper, T. (Eds.). (2000). *Sex, love and marriage in the 21st century: The next sexual revolution*. Chicago: University of Chicago Press.

Gottman, J. M. (1999). *The marriage clinic: A scientifically-based marital therapy*. New York: W. W. Norton.

Helminiak, D. A. (1996). *The human core of spirituality: Mind as psyche and spirit*. New York: State University of New York Press.

Herman, J. L. (1992). *Trauma and recovery*. New York: Basic Books.

Kaplan, H. S. (1974). *The new sex therapy*. New York: Brunner/Mazel.

Kaschak, E., & Tiefer, L. (Eds.). (2001). *A new view of women's sexual problems*. New York: Haworth.

Kleinplatz, P. J. (Ed.). (2001). *New directions in sex therapy: Innovations and alternatives*. Philadelphia: Brunner-Routledge.

Krotoski, D. M., Nosek, M. A., Turk, M. A. (Eds.). (1996). *Women with physical disabilities: achieving and maintaining health and well-being.* Baltimore: Paul H. Brookes.

Leiblum, S. R., & Rosen, R. C. (2000). *Principles and practice of sex therapy.* (3rd Ed.) New York: Guilford.

Levant, R. F., & Brooks, G. R. (Eds.). (1997). *Single Men and sex: New psychological perspectives.* New York: Wiley.

Levine, S., Althof, S., & Reisen, C. (Eds.). (2003). *Handbook of clinical sexuality for mental health professionals.* New York: Brunner-Routledge.

Lusterman, D. (1998). *Infidelity: A survival guide.* Oakland, CA: New Harbinger.

Malone, T. P., & Malone, P. T. (1987). *The art of intimacy.* New York: Prentice Hall.

Masters, W. H., & Johnson, V. E. (1970). *Human sexual inadequacy.* Boston: Little, Brown.

Moser, C. (1999). *Health care without shame: A handbook for the sexually diverse and their caregivers.* San Francisco: Greenery Press.

Nelson, J. B., & Longfellow, S. P. (1994). *Sexuality and the sacred: Sources for theological reflection.* Louisville, KY: Westminster/John Knox Press.

Ogden, G. (1999). *Women who love sex.* Boston: Womanspirit Press.

Reiss, I. L. (1990). *An end to shame: Shaping our next sexual revolution.* Buffalo, NY: Prometheus Books.

Schiavi, R. C. (1999). *Aging and male sexuality.* New York: Cambridge University Press.

Schnarch, D. (1991). *Constructing the sexual crucible: An integration of sexual and marital therapy.* New York: W. W. Norton.

Schnarch, D. (1997). *Passionate marriage: Love, sex, and intimacy in emotionally committed relationships.* New York: Wiley.

Schover, L. R., & Jensen, S. B. (1998). *Sexuality and chronic illness: a comprehensive approach.* New York: Guilford.

Schover, L. R. (1997). *Sexuality and fertility after cancer.* New York: Wiley.

Schwartz, P. (1994). *Peer marriage: How love between equals really works.* New York: Free Press.

Sipski, M. L., & Alexander, C. J. (Eds.). (1997). *Sexual function in people with disability and chronic illness: A health professional's guide.* Gaithersburg, MD: Aspen.

Tiefer, L. (2004). *Sex is not a natural act and other essays.* Boulder: Westview Press.

Treadway, D. (2004). *Intimacy, change and other therapeutic mysteries.* New York: Guilford.

Wincze, J. P., & Carey, M. P. (2001). *Sexual dysfunction: A guide for assessment and treatment.* New York: Guilford.

Zilbergeld, B. (1999). *The new male sexuality.* New York: Bantam Books.

To Locate a Certified Sex Therapist

The Board of Examiners in Sex Therapy and Counseling of Ontario, www.BESTCO.info

American Association of Sex Educators, Counselors, and Therapists, www
.AASECT.org

Major Sexology Associations and Opportunities for Continuing Education

Sex Information and Education Council of Canada, www.sieccan.org/
The Society for the Scientific Study of Sexuality (SSSS), www.sexscience.org/
Society for Sex Therapy and Research, www.sstarnet.org
American Association of Sex Educators, Counselors, and Therapists, www
.AASECT.org

Distributors of Sex Toys and Educational— Sexually Explicit—Videos

Come As You Are (An especially useful resource for sex toys and aids for the
disabled as well as the able-bodied.), www.comeasyouare.com
Good Vibrations, www.goodvibes.com

10

Sexual Compulsivity:
Issues and Challenges

Michael Reece, Brian M. Dodge,
and Kimberly McBride

For the most part, the world seems to operate under the assumption that sexual decision making occurs as a result of some logical and rational process. However, these logical and rational foundations become questioned when individuals participate in sexual activities that appear to be inconsistent with others' perceptions of their professional or societal roles or their personal perceptions of themselves. Perhaps one of the most famous public cases to be considered in recent times was the notion, widely circulated in the popular press, that President Bill Clinton was a "sex addict" due to the inconsistency between his role in society and his apparent inability to control his sexual urges. Mostly this was related to his affair with a White House intern and the ensuing public debate and attempts to remove him from office. This controversy launched the notion of "sexual addiction" into the national spotlight, with numerous television shows, magazines, newspapers, and Internet sites discussing the concept of sex addiction and using the behavior of the president of the United States as an example for debate and discussion.

While public discussion over this particular episode has subsided, one remaining artifact is that individuals throughout society continue to attempt to understand the sexual behaviors of others and themselves that they perceive to be "out of control" or "compulsive." These sexual behaviors and their characteristics have been called by many different names, with the most common being nymphomania, hypersexuality, sexual compulsivity, sexual addiction, and sexual impulsivity. These terms are used interchangeably by some professionals who work in the sexuality field, and often one's choice of a term reflects his or her personal beliefs and professional training. These terms are also used in different ways, depending on whether one is describing a psychological characteristic of an individual (i.e., someone is a "sex addict" or a "sexually compulsive person") or describing a particular behavior (i.e., some believe that excessive use of the Internet for sexual purposes is an example of a "sexually compulsive behavior"). That different terms are used to describe the phenomenon of a person being sexually "out of control" or that a behavior is "sexually compulsive" is also the result of the fact that there remains a great deal of debate as to whether the phenomenon of sexual compulsivity truly exists, and if it does, how it is measured. For consistency throughout this chapter, we will use the label "sexual compulsivity" to refer to behaviors and their characteristics that some people perceive to be problematic.

A range of sexual behaviors have been considered to be indicative of sexual compulsivity, such as excessive masturbation, having high numbers of sexual partners, excessive use of the Internet for sexual purposes (sexual chatting online, viewing sexually explicit videos, etc.), and looking for sex or having sexual interactions in public spaces (often called "cruising" or "dogging"), among others. However, the problem with any of these behaviors, either alone or in combination, being indicative of sexual compulsivity is that there are no established criteria for distinguishing among behaviors that are a normal part of one's sexual repertoire and when these behaviors have become excessive. How much masturbation is too much masturbation? How many sexual partners are too many? How many hours can one spend chatting with others about sex on the Internet before it is considered problematic? The lack of a solid answer to any of these questions makes reaching consensus on the phenomenon of sexual compulsivity very challenging for both professionals and members of the general population.

HISTORY AND MEANING OF SEXUAL COMPULSIVITY

The notion of excessive sexual behavior as a disorder or condition has been in existence since ancient times. Early descriptions date back to Greek myths, included in stories of the sexual activities of the god Dionysius. Over the past twenty-five years, there has been an increasing interest in the notion of "out-of-control" sexual behavior among therapists and scientists. Today, there is no single, dominant view of what sexual compulsivity is, how it should be assessed, and how it should be treated. Given below is a brief review of some of the dominant models that currently influence research and treatment in this area.

The issue of sexual compulsivity was brought to the forefront of people's attention in 1983 when Patrick Carnes published his book *Out of the Shadows: Understanding Sexual Addiction*. Carnes believed that out-of-control sexual behaviors represented a form of addiction, much like alcoholism, and advocated a twelve-step approach to treatment, similar to that used by Alcoholics Anonymous. Carnes was also among the first mental health practitioners to develop screening tests in an attempt to tap into and measure sexual addiction and compulsivity among diverse groups of individuals (see also Society for the Advancement of Sexual Health, 2005).

Shortly after Carnes published his book, researcher Eli Coleman wrote articles challenging Carnes's addiction model (Coleman, 1990). Coleman, instead, used the term "compulsive sexual behavior" and believed that the disorder was a form of obsessive-compulsive disorder (OCD). Further, Coleman conceptualized two types of compulsive sexual behavior (CSB), paraphilic and nonparaphilic. Paraphilic CSB, according to Coleman, involves the unconventional sexual behaviors, such as fetishes or pedophilia. Nonparaphilic CSB involves conventional or normative sexual behaviors, such as masturbation or sex with consenting adult partners.

By the mid-1990s, a number of ideas about the underlying causes of sexual compulsivity had been generated. One of the major contributors to research during this time was Seth Kalichman. Kalichman and his colleagues used the term "sexual compulsivity" and believed that poor impulse control was the driving factor behind the behavior. Kalichman's primary concern was not with the behavior itself, but more with the extent to which one's sexual behaviors were increasing the risk for human immunodeficiency virus (HIV) and the acquired immune deficiency syndrome (AIDS) and other sexually transmitted infections (STIs). Kalichman and his colleagues published a scale that has been widely used in research related to sexual compulsivity (cited in Kalichman & Rompa, 1995; Kalichman et al., 1994). Table 10.1 lists the items included in this scale, known as the Sexual Compulsivity Scale, which is also referred to later in this chapter.

In 2004, John Bancroft and his colleague Zoran Vukadinovic published a highly critical paper examining the concepts of sex addiction, sexual compulsivity, and sexual impulsivity. Their paper challenged the existing conceptualizations of sexual compulsivity and proposed that they may be of little scientific value. Bancroft and Vukadinovic questioned whether out-of-control sexual behavior existed at the extreme end of the range of normal sexual behavior, or whether it was qualitatively different in ways that make it problematic. Further, they advocated withholding labels such as sex addiction and sexual compulsivity in favor of the term out-of-control sexual behavior until the field had a better understanding of the underlying causes whereby appropriate treatments could be identified for such behavior.

Clearly, there is a great deal of interest and debate among scientists and practitioners when it comes to the notion of sexual compulsivity. While there has been a great deal of research in this area, to date, there is no consensus as to what the underlying causes are or what constitutes the most appropriate treatment. In fact, some people believe that sexual compulsivity does not exist at all. Because there is a lack of agreement, more research is needed to clarify

Table 10.1. Sexual Compulsivity Scale

Scale Items

My sexual appetite has gotten in the way of my relationships.
My sexual thoughts and behaviors are causing problems in my life.
My desires to have sex have disrupted my daily life.
I sometimes fail to meet my commitments and responsibilities because of my
    sexual behaviors.
I sometimes get so horny I could lose control.
I find myself thinking about sex while at work.
I feel that my sexual thoughts and feelings are stronger than I am.
I have to struggle to control my sexual thoughts and behavior.
I think about sex more than I would like to.
It has been difficult for me to find sex partners who desire having sex as much as I
    want to.

Key: Item responses range from 1 (Not at all like me) to 4 (Very much like me).

Source: Kalichman & Rompa, 1995.

these issues. In the meantime, it is important that we acknowledge what is unknown and proceed with caution.

A range of screening and assessment tools for sexual compulsivity are available to the general public, many of them from the Web site of the Society for the Advancement of Sexual Health (SASH), a leading professional association in the United States, addressing this issue (www.ncsac.org). Usually, such assessments tend to take one of the following three forms: assessments for men who identify as gay, assessments for men who identify as heterosexual, and assessments for women. No assessment tools have been developed for persons who identify as bisexual (those who have sex with both men and women or do not identify as exclusively heterosexual or gay). This may be due to existing biases that underlie previous research on sexual compulsivity, namely: (1) that sexual compulsivity is primarily a "male" problem (particularly for "gay men," who somehow face separate and distinct issues from "heterosexual men"), (2) that sexual compulsivity in women is not related to sexual orientation, and (3) that sexuality is dichotomous (not recognizing that many individuals who deal with compulsivity-related issues may not be confined to the polarized societal identity labels of "heterosexual" and "gay").

Rather than focus on whether sexual compulsivity is a psychological characteristic, a pathological condition, or simply a characteristic of one's sexual behaviors, SASH has offered a list of outcomes that could suggest that a person or their behaviors are sexually compulsive. An outcomes-based understanding of sexual compulsivity would suggest that individuals and their behaviors could be considered sexually compulsive if they find that their sexual behaviors (including those that they do alone, such as masturbation, and those that they do with other people, such as having intercourse) are leading to problems in various areas of their lives. For example, a person spending a great deal of time viewing sexually explicit materials on the Internet may not necessarily be indicative of sexual compulsivity, but if that behavior results in the individual's inability to relate to a romantic or relational partner or if it creates financial challenges, then it might indicate that their Internet-based sexual activities have become problematic. Table 10.2 provides a list of the impacts that could be indicative of sexually compulsive behavior.

Regardless of the lack of consensus on the meaning of sexual compulsivity, and on how to assess it and treat it, researchers have devoted a significant amount of energy into studying it and trying to understand how it is related to sexual health issues. In the following section of this chapter, we will present three examples of this work from our own research.[1] Three specific lines of research are presented, including work that has focused on sexual compulsivity and its associations with continued high-risk sexual behaviors among those

Table 10.2. Anticipated Impact of Sexually Compulsive (addictive) Behavior

Impact	Description
Social	Addicts become lost in sexual preoccupation, which results in emotional distance from loved ones. Loss of friendship and family relationships may result.
Emotional	Anxiety or extreme stress are common in sex addicts who live with constant fear of discovery. Shame and guilt increase, as the addict's lifestyle is often inconsistent with the personal values, beliefs, and spirituality. Boredom, pronounced fatigue, despair are inevitable as addiction progresses. The ultimate consequence may be suicide.
Physical	Some of the diseases which may occur due to sexual addiction are genital injury, cervical cancer, HIV/AIDS, herpes, genital warts, and other sexually transmitted diseases. Sex addicts may place themselves in situations of potential harm, resulting in serious physical wounding or even death.
Legal	Many types of sexual addiction result in violation of the law, such as sexual harassment, obscene phone calls, exhibitionism, voyeurism, prostitution, rape, incest and child molestation, and other illegal activities. Loss of professional status and professional licensure may result from sexual addiction.
Financial/ Occupational	Indebtedness may arise directly from the cost of prostitutes, cybersex, phone sex and multiple affairs. Indirectly, indebtedness can occur from legal fees, the cost of divorce or separation, decreased productivity, or job loss.
Spiritual	Loneliness, resentment, self-pity, and self-blame.

Source: NCSAC, 2005.

living with HIV, work exploring the extent to which sexual compulsivity is an issue among young adults, and research that looked into sexual compulsivity among individuals who seek sexual interactions in public places, known as cruising (which is perhaps one of the issues that is often cited as being a clear example of out-of-control sexual behavior).

SEXUAL COMPULSIVITY AND THE HIV/AIDS EPIDEMIC

The AIDS epidemic, and the continuing incidence of infections with the virus that causes it, HIV, provide a solid backdrop for considering the issue of sexual compulsivity. Given the devastating impact of this epidemic on society, sexuality and health professionals remain focused on the need to reduce the spread of this devastating infection and to promote the well-being of those already infected.

Recently, researchers in this area have focused much of their work on understanding the factors associated with the likelihood that an individual living with HIV will transmit the virus to another individual or expose themselves to other infections that can further compromise their health (Kalichman & Fisher, 1998). Numerous studies have documented that a significant proportion of individuals living with HIV will continue to participate in behaviors that present the potential for such outcomes (Heckman, Kelly, & Somlai, 1998; Kalichman, Kelly, & Rompa, 1997; Kalichman, Roffman, Picciano, & Bolan, 1997; Kalichman & Rompa, 2001; Marks, Burris, & Peterman, 1999; Reece, 2003; Reece, Plate, & Daughtry, 2001).

Researchers have been interested in the extent to which sexual compulsivity might have a role to play in the continuing high-risk sexual behaviors of individuals who know that they are infected with HIV. Studies have consistently documented an association between sexual compulsivity and one's participation in high-risk sexual behaviors following an HIV diagnosis (Benotsch, Kalichman, & Kelly, 1999; Gold & Heffner, 1998; Kalichman, Greenberg, & Abel, 1997; Kalichman & Rompa, 2001; Quadland & Shattls, 1987).

We have recently been examining the extent to which sexual compulsivity is associated with continued participation in unprotected sexual intercourse among individuals living with HIV (Reece et al., 2001; Reece, 2003). Several protracted findings have emerged. Among men living with HIV who identify as gay or bisexual, we find that those who report having been either the insertive or receptive partner in unprotected intercourse during the sixty days preceding the study also are those who have higher scores on a measure of sexual compulsivity. We find similar patterns among men who identify as heterosexual; those men with higher levels of sexual compulsivity also are the ones who were more likely to report being the insertive partner in unprotected sexual intercourse.

In a separate work, we also found some other trends that suggest we need to understand more about sexual compulsivity as we continue to respond to the challenges of the HIV/AIDS epidemic. Gay and bisexual men who scored highly on a measure of sexual compulsivity and who reported that they had been participating in unprotected intercourse indicated that they were most likely to participate in these behaviors with individuals they met in anonymous settings (sex clubs, bathhouses, etc.) and with men whose HIV status was unknown (Reese & Dodge, 2003, 2004).

These studies are highly consistent with the work of other researchers in the field of HIV/AIDS and, while certainly not conclusive, indicate a continuing need for us to understand whether knowledge of a phenomenon like sexual compulsivity may help public health professionals better target their efforts to reduce the incidence of HIV infections. It may be that those who are struggling to control their sexual behaviors are among those most appropriate for specialized interventions if we were able to more appropriately assess them and deliver programs to them in a way that does not further stigmatize them or label their sexual behaviors as pathological. (See HIV Case Scenario.)

HIV Case Scenario

Individual: Alfred, 31 years old, single bisexual man recently diagnosed with HIV

Issues: Presents for care at mental health clinic with concerns that his sexual behaviors are "out of control." His major concern is that he finds himself spending the vast majority of his evenings spending hours looking for men in Internet chat rooms who are interested in "no strings sex" because he does not want a relationship with another man and does not want to go to gay bars to meet them. Alfred tells his therapist that when he meets these men he "can't bring himself to tell them that he is living with HIV" and reports that "they almost never ask about it." He believes that he has probably transmitted HIV to some of his sexual partners given that he is strictly the insertive partner in sexual intercourse and almost never uses a condom. He is convinced that he is a "sex addict" and just does not know how to bring his sexual behaviors under control.

Considerations: Which aspects of Alfred's behaviors are "out of control?" Is it that he spends hours on the Internet seeking sex or that he is not telling his partners that he is living with HIV and has likely transmitted HIV to some? Is this truly an example of sexual compulsivity or is his Internet-based behavior related to his discomfort with his sexual interest in both men and women and that he does not know how to meet men other than on the Internet? Does he lack the skills to introduce condoms into his sexual interactions?

Linkages to Research: Alfred is obviously struggling to control his constant need to seek sexual partners on the Internet and this is something that he is wanting to better control. His Internet-based behavior seems compulsive on the surface, and his lack of HIV disclosure to his partners and his high rates of unprotected insertive intercourse is consistent with our research among men who score highly on measures of sexual compulsivity. It is certain that the potential for him to have transmitted HIV to other men is a problem that needs to be addressed immediately. However, rather than assume his claim that he is a "sex addict" is correct, his therapist may want to work with him to increase his knowledge of the non–bar-oriented venues for meeting men in his city, teach him skills for using condoms and ask him to make a commitment to use condoms in all sexual interactions, regardless of the extent to which his partners ask about HIV. While some aspects of his behaviors may be compulsive, Alfred is an example of those who are labeled (or who self-labeled) sexually compulsive, but perhaps his concerns over the inability to control his behavior can be resolved with strategic methods introduced by his therapist that increase his comfort with his bisexuality and his ability to use condoms consistently in all interactions.

SEXUAL COMPULSIVITY AND YOUNG ADULTS

A growing body of literature suggests that an association exists between sexual compulsivity and participation in sexual behaviors that are high risk in terms of HIV and other STIs. In most of these studies, sexual compulsivity has been measured using the Sexual Compulsivity Scale (SCS) mentioned earlier (Kalichman & Rompa, 1995). Across the studies mentioned previously, the SCS has demonstrated reliability and construct validity in several samples of individuals who can be classified as "high risk" for HIV, including men who have sex with men (MSM), substance abusers, and inner city, low-income men and women. The studies also demonstrated that compulsivity was significantly related to sexual risk behaviors in these samples. However, the relevance of sexual compulsivity among more general populations, such as college students, has rarely been explored.

To fill this gap in the literature, we designed and conducted a study, along with other colleagues, to assess sexual compulsivity among heterosexual college students (Dodge, Reece, Cole, & Sandfort, 2004). In this study, we examined whether sexual compulsivity was related to higher frequencies of sexual behaviors and higher numbers of sexual partners, and explored associations between sexual compulsivity and select demographic variables (gender, age, and race/ethnicity). Lastly, we ascertained whether sexual compulsivity was predictive of sexual behaviors considered risky in terms of HIV/STI in this population.

As in studies of "high-risk" individuals and those living with HIV, sexual compulsivity appeared to be a relevant construct for describing elevated levels of sexual practices with multiple partners in our sample of 899 heterosexual college students. We found higher levels of sexual compulsivity among individuals who reported higher frequencies of partner sex, solo sex, and public sex activities. Additionally, participants who reported involvement in non-monogamous sexual situations (i.e., multiple sexual partners) were more likely to have higher sexual compulsivity scores than those who reported involvement in monogamous sexual relationships and those who were not currently sexually active. Also consistent with other studies, men and younger participants were found to have higher compulsivity scores than women and older participants. Lastly, in relation to HIV/STI risk, men and women who had higher sexual compulsivity scores were more likely to report higher frequencies of unprotected oral, vaginal, and anal sex in the preceding three months.

That stated, in more practical terms, it is still not understood how sexual compulsivity functions in relation to sexual risk after the concept has been identified and measured. Considering this, we concluded that future studies are needed to determine the practical significance of sexual compulsivity in heterosexual college students and various other populations. (See Young Adult Case Scenario.)

Young Adult Case Scenario

Individual: Jason, 20 years old, single heterosexual college student

Issues: Presents for care at a university counseling center with concerns that his sexual behaviors are "out of control." His primary concern is that he spends a great deal of his time masturbating when he feels that he should be studying. He is also concerned because he has "hooked up" with a "large number" of young women at parties and did not use condoms on any of the occasions. Jason tells his therapist that he is worried that he is a "sex addict" and feels "guilty" about "leading girls on just to get sex." He believes that if he continues this pattern of behavior he will fail his courses and possibly get someone pregnant.

Considerations: Which aspects of Jason's behaviors are problematic? Is it that he spends time masturbating when he feels that he should be studying or is it that he does not use condom when he is "hooking up"? Is it his feeling of guilt? Is this an example of sexual compulsivity or is this an example of normal sexual behavior given Jason's age and the social norms of the college environment?

Linkages to Research: Jason is clearly uncomfortable with his sexual behaviors. However, research has yet to establish what sexual compulsivity truly looks like among young adults. Late adolescence and early adulthood are often a time of sexual exploration. Research conducted with college students has shown that having multiple sexual partners is not uncommon. Further, among young men, masturbation frequencies have been found to be higher than among older men or women. On the surface, it is difficult to assess whether or not Jason's behaviors truly are "out of control" or if they are relatively "normal." Certainly, his lack of condom use is an issue in terms of both pregnancy and HIV/STI transmission. If his masturbation is causing him to miss classes or perform poorly on homework assignments, then it may be indicative of sexual compulsivity. In this case, the therapist would need to assess to what extent Jason's behaviors are impacting his life. Often times young adults need education about what is normal sexual behavior and what is excessive. The therapist would definitely need to provide education about HIV and STI transmission and encourage condom use. The therapist should also determine how many women Jason has "hooked up" with and explore his feelings of guilt related to these encounters. Until a proper assessment is performed, it would be premature to make any assumptions about Jason's behavior.

SEXUAL COMPULSIVITY AND MEN WHO CRUISE FOR SEX WITH OTHER MEN

One sexual behavior that has received considerable attention in the literature, particularly as a potential threat to sexual health, is "cruising." Cruising, in a sexual context, has been defined and explored by a variety of researchers over the years. Cruising can be described as "referring to the ritual of seeking and interacting with potential sexual partners, usually those who were previously unknown to the participant" (Reece & Dodge, 2003). Among the general population, sexual compulsivity is often cited as one reason that an individual would seek sex with another person in public places.

Given that studies on sexual cruising and sexual compulsivity have generally existed as separate entities, they present a unique challenge to health and social service providers. There are studies that have documented associations between sexual compulsivity and high-risk behaviors, and there are some studies that have documented associations between the public nature of a venue and the likelihood that behavior in those venues will be high-risk. Further, there are a limited number of studies that have suggested associations among all three factors: sexual compulsivity, public venues, and high-risk behaviors. Based on this literature, it may be easy to understand why some have accepted the notion that sexual compulsivity is an important factor in the high-risk behaviors in cruising environments. However, this assumption may be inappropriate due to the lack of research specifically investigating cruising and sexual compulsivity.

To explore these issues, we conducted a primarily qualitative study to determine whether men who cruise for sex on college campuses have characteristics consistent with contemporary conceptualizations of sexual compulsivity (Reece & Dodge, 2004). We assessed the extent to which cruisers have elevated scores on a measure of sexual compulsivity, whether those scores have associations with their sexual behaviors, the health-related implications of those behaviors, whether men who cruise experience negative consequences commonly associated with sexually compulsive behaviors, and the potential for such negative consequences.

During in-depth interviews, men were asked to describe whether they had heard of sexual compulsivity, whether they had considered themselves to be sexually compulsive, or whether they ever thought of their cruising behaviors as being "out of control." All of the cruisers acknowledged that they had heard of the notion of an individual being "sexually compulsive." If participants had made the determination that their behaviors were compulsive, they typically reacted in two ways, by either (1) ending their cruising behaviors on their own, temporarily or permanently, or (2) seeking professional counseling or some type of social support or therapy group. Additionally, we conceptualized sexual compulsivity as having two primary components: (1) the drive to participate in behaviors in a compulsive manner, and (2) the existence of or potential for negative consequences to self or others. Participants reported a broad range of negative events that were associated with their cruising activities including social, emotional, physical, legal, financial/occupational, and spiritual.

This study provided insights into an issue that has been relatively unexplored in the literature. The findings suggest the need for additional consideration, debate, and research in order to better understand relationships between sexual compulsivity and cruising. Given the extent to which sexual compulsivity is openly discussed in the media, whether accurately or inaccurately, mental health and public health providers will continue to become engaged in interactions with clients and program participants, who are likely to introduce concerns related to sexual compulsivity. It is also likely, particularly among clients and program participants who are bisexual and gay men, that some of their sexual interactions will occur through cruising in public spaces, regardless of whether they are discussed openly. Therefore, it is important that we continue this dialogue and be open to exploring the nature and meanings of sexual interactions among men, in addition to the associations between their sexual behaviors and indicators of sexual compulsivity, in order to develop programs and interventions that are appropriate and effective. The Cruising

Case Scenario provides an example of some of the issues presented by participants in this study and the complexities associated with their behaviors and their perceptions of the impact of these behaviors on their lives.

Cruising Case Scenario

Individual: Bill, 35 years old, married self-identified bisexual man

Issues: Took part in research study on cruising for sex on a college campus. While he does not openly identify as "sexually compulsive," he often wonders if he is spending too much of his time seeking out anonymous sex.

> *I have definitely wondered whether or not I am a sex addict. Sometimes I get an uncontrollable urge to go out and seek out sex . . . the trigger happens when there is this conscious switch—this psychological switch and it feels like everything just drops down, blood . . . I don't know what physically . . . like it's a dropping sensation and an adrenaline rush . . . usually I'll end up breaking out into a cold sweat . . . for me the trigger is the opportunity.*

At times, he has spent hours upon end in the local parks and recreation areas waiting for sexual partners. This has often interfered with his ability to conduct his job (as a local government employee) effectively. It has also limited the time he spends at home with his family.

> *The cruising was almost second nature for a while. Sometimes I'd go just to be in the milieu. I'd go into the cruising areas and just sit for hours. I'd go daily. Three times a day sometimes.*

Bill has reported experiencing consistent and troubling rejection while cruising due to his weight and appearance. He has internalized these experiences to the point of almost becoming numb.

> *I've been turned down a lot . . . you learn quickly how to be rejected. You don't ask. You don't turn back. I know why they're doing it, because they are not physically attracted to me. I'm fat and . . . just not one of those suave guys. I learned not to question it.*

Last, Bill also worries about the social repercussions of his cruising behaviors, specifically needing to juggle his "multiple lives" in a small community. In addition, he recognizes that his behaviors are potentially "complicated" given that they are kept relatively secret in his everyday life.

> *I'm like a duck. I look good floating on the water but underneath it I'm paddling like hell just to stay afloat. . . . I have two different sex lives. With my wife, it's fine. . . . we don't have a wild sex life or anything because we*

are totally committed to our kids, and our nights are pretty full taking care of them. My other sex life . . . my cruising sex life is very intense. And those guys, I meet them all in public sex environments. I feel so "complicated" sometimes.

Considerations: Is Michael experiencing sexual compulsivity in his life or is he merely enjoying the "sexual freedom" that many individuals report as a reason for engaging in sex with multiple partners? At what point can the line be drawn? How are Michael's body image issues related to his cruising behaviors? Do his self-esteem issues act to reinforce, or hinder, the cruising? What are the implications of Michael's behaviors in terms of his job and home life, in terms of health, legal repercussions, etc.?

Linkages to Research: Although he does not explicitly identify "sexual compulsivity" as a problem in his life, Michael has presented concerns in terms of his sexual behaviors being out of control and causing problems in his life, particularly in terms of mental and social health. He has described problems in several key areas of the SASH (see Table 10.2) framework for understanding sexual compulsivity. Bill may benefit from consulting with a health care provider who is trained to diagnose and treat compulsive sexual behavior, if he is deemed to be dealing with such issues.

While these three areas of research indicate support for the notion that sexual compulsivity exists in some form among a diverse range of individuals and that it is associated with certain sexual behaviors, there is a need for much more research in these areas before any solid conclusions can be drawn. Additionally, there is a need to continue identifying ways of responding to sexual compulsivity among those who appear to be struggling with it by making available effective forms of treatment.

TREATMENT ISSUES

One of the most obvious challenges to providing treatment for clients presenting with sexual compulsivity is the lack of a clear set of diagnostic and treatment criteria. Without a clear set of criteria to serve as a guide, diagnosis and treatment can become an arbitrary endeavor. The *Diagnostic and Statistical Manual of Mental Disorders, Fourth Edition* (American Psychiatric Association, 1994) contains three general categories under which a diagnosis can be made: Paraphilia (either specific or not otherwise specified [NOS]); Impulse Control Disorder NOS; or Sexual Disorder NOS.

For mental health practitioners who may have little or no specialized training in the treatment of sexuality related issues, this ambiguity is problematic. Selecting the most effective treatment for a given disorder presumes a clear understanding of the underlying causes and knowledge of the appropriate treatment strategies. When there is no clear definition of the problem, and a number of competing approaches to treatment, the burden of deciding what sexual compulsivity is, and whether a given client suffers from it, rests on the mental health practitioner. While there is a great deal of debate among experts about issues related to the diagnosis and treatment of sexual compulsivity, a few approaches to treatment have been both widely used and empirically investigated. These are summarized briefly in the section that follows.

Twelve-Step Groups

The earliest approach to treatment, and one that is still common today, was adapted from the twelve-step model of Alcoholics Anonymous. The underlying premise of this approach is that sexual compulsivity represents a form of addiction much like alcoholism, drug addiction, or compulsive gambling. In this treatment paradigm, individuals are believed to be powerless over the amount or kind of sexual activity in which they engage (Carnes, 1989; Myers, 1995). One of the key components in this approach is the belief that the sexually addicted individual is overwhelmed by shame. In order for sex addicts to recover, they must progress through the twelve steps by admitting they have a problem, relinquishing control to God, admitting the nature of their wrongs, making amends when possible, and sharing the message with other addicts (Sex and Love Addicts Anonymous, 1985).

The twelve-step approach relies on groups of self-identified addicts coming together to share their stories and support one another through the recovery process. Typically, the groups do not include a trained facilitator or therapist. Instead, the groups are facilitated solely by members who encourage one another to abstain from problematic sexual behaviors and carry the message to other sex addicts. The only requirement for membership in such groups is the desire to stop acting out a pattern of sex addiction.

Cognitive-Behavioral Therapy

Cognitive-behavioral therapies refer to a set of techniques that are based on the assumption that behavior can be altered by changing cognitive processes (thoughts, beliefs, attitudes, assumptions). In this approach, maladaptive cognitive processes are assumed to be the underlying cause of maladaptive behaviors, and these negative thoughts are believed to be modifiable, both directly and indirectly, through therapeutic techniques (Montesinos, 2003).

Within the cognitive-behavioral approach, there are two different groups of strategies that are assumed to influence behavioral change. The first group of strategies is referred to as cognitive restructuring. Cognitive restructuring focuses specifically on changing maladaptive thought processes (internal dialogue or self-talk) in a clear and direct manner. The second group of strategies is called cognitive-behavioral coping skills. These strategies assume that there is a deficit of adaptive cognitions that maintain the problematic behavior. The goal of this strategy is to help the client acquire the skills that they lack.

Cognitive-behavioral approaches have been widely applied by mental health practitioners treating a variety of mental health issues. For example, cognitive-behavioral treatments have been used for treating anxiety, depression, phobias, eating disorders, and addictions.

Cognitive-behavioral approaches to treating sexual compulsivity include components of both cognitive restructuring and skills training. A therapist will usually guide a client through the cognitive restructuring process where they learn to modify distorted thoughts by identifying maladaptive thoughts as they occur and replacing them with more appropriate thoughts. The skills–training component of therapy may include social skills training and risk recognition (Myers, 1995). Usually techniques addressing relapse prevention are considered a key component to this type of treatment. Relapse prevention strategies focus on learning to identify risky situations and learning skills to cope with urges to relapse by focusing on individual, behavioral, and environmental factors that may precipitate a relapse.

Pharmacotherapy

The appropriateness of using psychotropic medications in the treatment of sexual compulsivity is still controversial in the scientific community. Certain scientists and therapists believe that medications called selective serotonin reuptake inhibitors (SSRIs, such as Prozac and Paxil), which are commonly used to treat depression, are highly effective for treating sexual compulsivity (Kafka, 1991; Ragan & Martin, 2000). Their argument is that these medications both decrease sexual urges and alleviate the depression that results from feeling out of control. Opponents to this approach argue that a common side effect of antidepressant medication is a diminished libido, therefore these medications may be temporarily masking the issues rather than treating it. So, unless an individual wants to commit to a lifetime of daily use, antidepressants should only be used in combination with other treatment approaches.

Antianxiety medications are another type of psychotropic drugs that have been used to treat sexual compulsivity. These medications are thought to reduce anxieties that either drive compulsive behaviors or result from them. Again, critics argue that these treatments may be useful in reducing the negative thoughts and feelings associated with sexual compulsivity but should not be used as a primary means of treatment.

Psychodynamic Psychotherapy

Psychodynamic therapy evolved from Sigmund Freud's psychoanalytic theory, which assumes that sexual and aggressive impulses are the primary determinants of behavior. The psychodynamic approach focuses on an individual's personality dynamics and seeks to draw out repressed feelings from childhood by discovering the kind of defense mechanism a client is using. The psychodynamic approach assumes that defense mechanisms help an individual guard against painful emotional experiences. Identifying the mechanisms that are being used allows the therapist to understand the client's internal motivations, ultimately directing the client's personality toward a more productive or functional state.

Psychodynamic therapeutic approaches to treating sexual compulsivity focus on uncovering childhood repressed feelings that may be driving the problematic sexual behaviors (Myers, 1995). This process often focuses on the idea the client has suffered parental deprivation early in life, most often maternal deprivation, and is filled with rage. The lack of parental love or closeness, combined with feelings of anger, is thought to be the root of the current problems. The relationship between the client and therapist, often called the therapeutic relationship, theoretically serves to repair the early deprivation and allows the client to develop appropriate behaviors. Change is also achieved by teaching the client to provide maternal nurturing for himself/herself.

Obviously, there are a wide variety of treatment methods being used by professionals to assist individuals who feel that their sexual behaviors have become compulsive. Individuals seeking assistance should take the time to explore the available options and choose one based on their particular situation, the experience of the provider, and after careful consideration of the philosophies and principles that underlie the specific treatment program. Table 10.3 provides an overview of some of the most popular and diverse treatment and information resources available on the Internet.

While there have been a variety of treatment approaches discussed in professional literature, few studies have systematically assessed treatment outcomes, particularly in large samples. Further, there has been virtually no effort to study the outcomes of treatment longitudinally by following individuals over time and assessing their changes in behavior after a range of different interventions. Therefore, we do not know if any of the available treatments are successful in altering problematic behaviors, especially over the long term. A limited number of case studies and small sample investigations have provided evidence for the use of pharmacotherapy, cognitive-behavioral therapy, psychodynamic treatment, and the twelve-step approach. However, these studies have been conducted among small groups of patients and have reported inconsistent findings, making the evidence that they provide weak at best. In order to establish the efficacy of the current approaches to treatment, or develop new approaches that may yield better results, further scientific investigation is needed.

Table 10.3. Selected Sexual Compulsivity Resources on the Internet

Organization	Web Address
Twelve-Step Program	
Sex Addicts Anonymous—SAA	www.sexaa.org
Sexual Compulsives Anonymous—SCA	www.sca-recovery.org
Sex and Love Addicts Anonymous—SLAA	www.slaafws.org
Sexaholics Anonymous—SA	www.sa.org
Sexual Recovery Anonymous—SRA	sexualrecovery.org
For Family and Friends	
Recovering Couples Anonymous (for couples when one member of the couple goes to another twelve-step group)	www.recovering-couples.org
Codependents of Sex Addicts (related to SAA)	www.cosa-recovery.org
S-Anon (related to SA)	www.sanon.org
Professional Association	
Society for the Advancement of Sexual Health	www.ncsac.org

SUMMARY

Clearly, there is a great deal of professional and public interest in the notion of sexual compulsivity. While much attention has been given to probable consequences of such behavior, particularly in terms of HIV/STI risk, little is actually known about the underlying causes or the actual outcomes of such behavior. As often is the case with any type of science, answering questions related to sexual compulsivity is an arduous process. Unfortunately, the pace at which research is being conducted is not keeping up with the demand of those who want or need answers. HIV and STDs continue to be transmitted, and a growing number of individuals are self-identifying, or are being identified by others, as "sex addicts." Further complicating the matter, a growing number of mental health practitioners are seeing clients with issues related to out-of-control sexual behavior without knowing if these treatments actually work. There are currently a number of efforts underway to answer these pressing questions; however, until the results are in, we cannot make assumptions about the behaviors or the individuals who present with them. It is highly likely that for some individuals certain sexual behaviors are, indeed, problematic. For others, applying the sexually compulsive label may be inappropriate and damaging. Until we know what sexual compulsivity really is and how it is manifested behaviorally, we need to acknowledge what we do not know and avoid unwarranted speculation and moral judgments.

NOTE

1. The studies were conducted by Reese, Dodge, and colleagues.

REFERENCES

American Psychiatric Association. (1994). *Diagnostic and statistical manual of mental disorders* (4th ed.). Washington, DC: Author.

Benotsch, E. G., Kalichman, S. C., & Kelly, J. A. (1999). Sexual compulsivity and substance use in HIV-seropositive men who have sex with men: Prevalence and predictors of high-risk behaviors. *Addictive Behaviors, 24*(6), 857–868.

Carnes, P. (1983). *Out of the shadows: Understanding sexual addiction.* Minneapolis, MN: Compcare.

Carnes, P. (1989). *Contrary to love: Helping the sex addict.* Center City, MN: Hazeldon.

Coleman, E. (1990). The obsessive-compulsive model for describing compulsive sexual behavior. *American Journal of Preventive Psychiatry and Neurology, 2*(3), 9–14.

Dodge, B., Reece, M., Cole, S., & Sandfort, T. G. M. (2004). Sexual compulsivity among heterosexual college students. *Journal of Sex Research, 41*(4), 343–350.

Gold, S. N., & Heffner, C. L. (1998). Sexual addiction: Many conceptions, minimal data. *Clinical Psychology Review, 18*, 367–381.

Heckman, T. G., Kelly, J. A., & Somlai, A. M. (1998). Predictors of continued high-risk sexual behavior in a community sample of persons living with HIV/AIDS. *AIDS and Behavior, 2*(2), 127–135.

Kafka, M. P. (1991). Successful antidepressant treatment of nonparaphilic sexual addictions and paraphilias in men. *Journal of Clinical Psychiatry, 52*(2), 60–65.

Kalichman, S. C., & Fisher, J. D. (1998). Introduction to the special issue on risk behavior practices of men and women living with HIV-AIDS. *AIDS and Behavior, 2*(2), 87–88.

Kalichman, S. C., Greenberg, J., & Abel, G. G. (1997). HIV-seropositive men who engage in high-risk sexual behavior: Psychological characteristics and implications for prevention. *AIDS Care, 9*(9), 441–450.

Kalichman, S. C., Johnson, J. R., Adair, V., Rompa, D., Multhauf, K., & Kelly, J. A. (1994). Sexual sensation seeking: Scale development and predicting AIDS-risk behavior among homosexually active men. *Journal of Personality Assessment, 62*, 385–397.

Kalichman, S. C., Kelly, J. A., & Rompa, D. (1997). Continued high-risk sex among HIV seropositive gay and bisexual men seeking HIV prevention services. *Health Psychology, 16*(4), 369–373.

Kalichman, S. C., Roffman, R. A., Picciano, J. F., & Bolan, M. (1997). Sexual relationships, sexual behavior, and HIV infection: HIV-seropositive gay and bisexual men seeking prevention services. *Professional Psychology: Research and Practice, 28*(3), 355–360.

Kalichman, S. C., & Rompa, D. (2001). The sexual compulsivity scale: Further development and use with HIV-positive persons. *Journal of Personality Assessment, 76*(3), 379–395.

Kalichman, S. C., & Rompa, D. (1995). Sexual sensation seeking and compulsivity scales: Reliability, validity, and predicting HIV risk behavior. *Journal of Personality Assessment, 65*, 586–601.

Marks, G., Burris, S., & Peterman, T. A. (1999). Reducing sexual transmission of HIV from those who know they are infected: The need for personal and collective responsibility. *AIDS, 13*(3), 297–306.

Montesinos, L. (2003). Behavioral analysis, therapy, and counseling. In J. Donnelly (Ed.), *Health counseling: Application and theory* (pp. 55–71). Belmont, CA: Thomson-Wadsworth.

Myers, W. A. (1995). Addictive sexual behavior. *American Journal of Psychotherapy, 49*, 473–483.

Quadland, M. C., & Shattls, W. D. (1987). AIDS, sexuality, and sexual control. *Journal of Homosexuality, 14*(1/2), 277–298.

Ragan, P. W., & Martin, P. R. (2000). The psychobiology of sex addiction. *Sex Addiction and Compulsivity, 7*, 161–175.

Reece, M. (2003). Sexual compulsivity and HIV serostatus disclosure among men who have sex with men. *Sexual Addiction and Compulsivity, 10*, 1–11.

Reece, M., Plate, P., & Daughtry, M. (2001). HIV prevention and sexual compulsivity: The need for an integrated strategy of public health and mental health. *Sexual Addiction and Compulsivity, 8*, 157–167.

Reece, M., & Dodge, B. (2003). Exploring the physical, mental and social well-being of gay and bisexual men who cruise for sex on a college campus. *Journal of Homosexuality, 46*(1/2), 111–126.

Reece, M., & Dodge, B. (2004). Exploring indicators of sexual compulsivity among men who cruise for sex on campus. *Sexual Addiction and Compulsivity, 11*, 87–113.

Sex and Love Addicts Anonymous. (1985). *Twelve steps and twelve traditions*. Retrieved October 1, 2005, from www.slaafws.org/12and12.html.

Society for the Advancement of Sexual Health. (2005). *Sexual addiction*. Retrieved October 3, 2005, from www.ncsac.org/addicts/papers_sexual_addiction.aspx

11

Chronic Disease, Disability, and Sexuality

Betty J. Fisher, Kelly E. Graham, and Jennifer Duffecy

The brain, it has been said, is the most important sex organ—the implication being that thoughts and feelings about sex may provide sufficient motivation to overcome some physical limitations and allow for a sexually satisfying experience despite physical disability or other obstacles. And the truth of this statement becomes quite clear when considering the sexual functioning of individuals living with spinal cord injuries, individuals recovering from heart attacks or strokes, and individuals living with other chronic health conditions that impede physical activity or functioning and interfere with the performance of sexual activities—especially in the manner presented by filmmakers and advertisers in mainstream media. In fact, many individuals living with disabilities (and especially disabilities associated with physical limitations) are seen as asexual. But sexuality is central to our being, regardless of physical appearance or health status (Kroll & Klein, 1995).

Sexuality, while fundamental, is a delicate area of life, and often the first area to suffer a major disruption in the face of stress or illness. For individuals in relationships with difficulties prior to the onset of illness or disability, these difficulties are likely to be magnified when health issues arise (Kievman, 1989; McGonigle, 1999; McInnes, 2003; Wallerstein & Blakeslee, 1996). This is especially true when such conditions result from accidents or when the disability comes about in an otherwise unexpected manner.

There can be considerable variation in the manner and degree to which an illness or disability affects sexuality. Conditions may be congenital or present from birth (e.g., cerebral palsy), acquired (e.g., spinal cord injuries or acute illness), or developed slowly over time (e.g., osteoarthritis or heart disease). Some conditions may have signs that are easily seen by even casual observers (e.g., paraplegia or paralysis) while others may not carry any outwardly visible signs (e.g., chronic pain or diabetes—the "invisible disabilities"). Many health problems significantly limit physical mobility due to functional impairments (e.g., muscular or nerve disorders) while others limit the functioning of specific body systems (e.g., cardiovascular or pulmonary disease). And finally, some conditions may directly affect sexual functioning (e.g., vascular or neurological disease resulting in erectile dysfunction) while others may have only indirect effects (e.g., chronic low back pain). Regardless of the distinctions that can be made and the various methods for categorizing chronic illness and disability, the impact on sexuality and sexual functioning can be significant, and, in nearly all cases, involves multiple factors.

Sexuality, likewise, involves multiple factors, and vital to any discussion of sexuality and disability is the reminder that sexuality is not just about activities culminating in sexual intercourse—it is about intimacy. Communication, trust, confidence, and pleasurable touching are all critical components of sexuality. Psychologist Jackson Rainer, who provides therapy to individuals with arthritis and other chronic health conditions, suggests redefining sexuality as "an energy that is healing, warming, and operates more outside of the genitals than in one specific place on the body" (Arthritis Foundation, 2004). When viewed in those terms, sex becomes less daunting—and becomes more about possibilities.

In the face of illness or disability, individuals and relationships may be redefined. And while the adverse effects on a relationship are the most obvious, some suggest that dramatic changes brought about by illness or disability disrupt the routine and create an opportunity for a new beginning—a chance to rediscover one's body and what feels good, or a chance to rebuild a relationship and improve sexual relations with a partner (Carlson, 1996; Kroll & Klein, 1995; Maurer & Strausberg, 1989; Wallerstein & Blakeslee, 1996).

In order to emerge from a health crisis with a "new, improved" sexual relationship, couples must overcome numerous obstacles. In addition to any direct disease/disability effects on sexuality, there are often undesirable side effects from interventions or medications used to treat the condition. The individual's psychological response to having a given disease or disability and the partner's response to changing roles are also key factors in determining the level of disruption to a couple's sexual life. While the focus of this chapter is a discussion of how various chronic diseases and disabilities impact sexuality, an underlying goal is to inform readers of the benefits that result when individuals with chronic health problems or disabilities can find ways to express sexuality and experience sexually satisfying activities.

The disabilities and chronic conditions included in this chapter are far from exhaustive but are believed to be representative of a wide range of conditions that can adversely affect sexual functioning. While there is necessarily some overlap in descriptions of conditions and treatment impact on sexuality, as well as the psychological impact on individuals with disabilities and their partners, we have attempted to minimize redundancy by beginning with an overview of some general concerns and factors that are shared by many chronic health problems and discussing the distinctive aspects in greater detail under the sections addressing specific disabilities, illnesses, or conditions.

CONCERNS COMMON TO VARIOUS DISABILITIES

For each of the disabilities and limitations discussed in this chapter, the challenge is twofold: not only is a person confronted with exploring and identifying changes in physical capacity and sexual response, but this may also occur in the context of psychological adjustment to a newly acquired or diagnosed disability. The role of both physical and psychological factors must be considered because both of these domains are essential to healthy sexual expression (Merritt, 2004). And because sexuality is affected by multiple factors, any difficulties that are present may require various forms of intervention. Therefore, assistance from a physician, psychologist, occupational or physical therapist, or personal attendant (or other health care provider) may be necessary to address issues adequately. If the assistance of a health care specialist is necessary, there is one caveat: the healthcare professional must have expertise in treating the disability and must be open and comfortable with frank discussions about sexuality.

Being comfortable with oneself and a partner is required when exploring or rediscovering sexual functioning and sexuality. Whether this exploration is through masturbation by oneself, or through mutual pleasuring, feeling comfortable with the process is key—if it does not feel safe, do not do it. For partners and individuals with disabilities alike, it is important to remember that communication about the experience is paramount. In order to break down stereotypes that the only "real" sex is genital intercourse, open and honest communication must play a central role. Individuals with disabilities must feel free to investigate what is arousing and pleasurable, and determine what physical capacity is available to meet these needs sexually, or how sex toys, a partner, or an attendant may be able to help meet these needs and desires. Limitations may force individuals to become creative in thinking about ways to give and receive pleasure. Being flexible in thinking about sex and having fun with it is essential. After all, "sex" is a broadly defined act, and encompasses anything and everything an individual and her/his partner(s) find satisfying.

While sexuality encompasses a broad range of activities that do not always involve genital contact, such activity may be part of intimate encounters. Disabilities, whether acquired or developmental, do not prevent sexually transmitted infections, nor do they always impact fertility (Hammond & Burns, 2000). Therefore, if sex involves intercourse or other contact with genitals, all individuals are encouraged to follow "safe sex" practices (i.e., use condoms to prevent transmission of sexually transmitted diseases and birth control methods to prevent unwanted pregnancies).

Communication and Intimacy

Many people with disabilities find the most difficult barrier to achieving a gratifying sex life is allowing oneself to feel sexy or to be sexual (Kaufman, Silverberg, & Odette, 2003). The capacity to be sexual with another person requires a degree of intimacy and trust that takes time to develop. Individuals with disabilities can feel sidelined in the dating scene by others' preconceived notions about disabilities and misconceptions about the physical or cognitive status of those with disabilities. Body-image issues and low self-esteem can hamper efforts at partnership and achieving sexual satisfaction with another person (Kaufman et al., 2003). Communication barriers can also hinder attempts to explore and process thoughts about sexuality, and addressing these can promote sexual satisfaction for individuals and partners.

Overcoming communication barriers in order to talk openly about sexual wants, needs, and fantasies greatly enhances the experience (Kaufman et al., 2003). When an individual can express these thoughts and feelings, this will serve to individualize and heighten the intimacy experience for those involved. And factors that can enhance intimacy are likely to enhance the sexual experience as well.

Sensation Changes

Changes in sensation occur with many different disabilities. To be sure, sensation is an important part of sexual arousal and response. After an injury or diagnosis, it is important to discover how different areas of the body are functioning with regard to sensation (Merritt, 2004). Sensation can be reduced or heightened, or hypersensitivity may even result. Changes in sensation can be explored alone or with a partner. While changes in genital sensation are the focus of most discussions, the whole body should be explored for erogenous zones and areas of sexual response. Individuals can be pleasantly surprised at the sexual responsiveness when an earlobe or inner arm is properly stimulated. Doing a "body mapping" exercise as described in Kaufman et al. (2003) can provide a wealth of information concerning sensate pleasure. For some partners, this may seem too "clinical," and can rob the spontaneity of exploring each other sexually. Clearly, each couple must decide on the best process for this or similar exercises. However, some partners begin such an exercise with "good intentions" and never complete the task because they become distracted by the pleasure they are giving and receiving along the way (Kaufman et al., 2003).

In addition to seeking pleasure through sensation, safety and skin integrity must be a focus as well. With loss in sensation comes the need to protect these areas with pressure management, appropriate repositioning, and a watchful eye toward possible areas of skin breakdown (Hammond & Burns, 2000).

Impaired Mobility

For individuals facing mobility challenges, exploring these with a partner or an attendant can be very helpful in promoting a quality sex life. As with reduced sensation, those with mobility limitations are at risk for skin breakdown and other injuries if care is not taken with positioning. Exploration of different sexual positions will enable partners to determine how to maximize pleasure and comfort. Additionally, employing pillows, furniture (and cushions), and sex toys can enhance the sexual experience for both partners. Other couples may choose to use specially designed foam positioning pieces, or slings to enable different positions (Hammond & Burns, 2000; Kaufman et al., 2003).

Spasticity

One challenge facing individuals with a variety of disabilities is spasticity (exaggerated, deep tendon reflexes and muscle cramps that are involuntary, and often, painful contractions of the muscles). Because sexual arousal can bring on spasms, it is important for people to understand how and when spasms occur, and take steps to prevent or minimize the effects of spasticity. Bathing in warm water is one technique for reducing spasticity, and the bath can be incorporated into the sex play (Kaufman et al., 2003). Taking medication for spasticity prior to engaging in sexual activity can also help reduce the disruptive effects of spasticity on the sexual experience. As an individual becomes more comfortable and accepting of spasticity experiences, it can be utilized to the their advantage to enhance the sexual experience. Some people report that tongue spasticity is wonderful for nipple stimulation, and others suggest that a hand tremor can be a convenient tool for genital or body stimulation. Learning to channel physical reactions into sex play can provide unusual but highly enjoyable enticement, which further enhances the sexual experience (Kaufman et al., 2003).

Psychological Effects

Persons who suffer a traumatic injury or who are diagnosed with a disabling condition can experience a variety of reactions, which can vary widely in nature and severity. Not all individuals become clinically depressed or anxious following such a life-altering event, and the person, treatment team, and support persons should not "expect" psychopathology to arise in the wake of an injury or diagnosis. However, adjustment to the disability and the resulting life changes can take time. For some, sexual activity can take a back seat to other life tasks during this process. Therefore, information regarding sex should be provided and processed at various points during the treatment and rehabilitation process, so that this important issue is not overlooked (Merritt, 2004).

NEUROLOGICAL/NEUROVASCULAR CONDITIONS

In the following section, sexuality issues associated with neurological and neurovascular disabilities will be addressed. Sections covering traumatic brain injury (TBI), spinal cord injury (SCI), and cerebrovascular accident ("stroke" or CVA) will provide more specialized information. Slightly less detailed sections will address issues specific to multiple sclerosis (MS), epilepsy, and cerebral palsy (CP). While this is clearly not an exhaustive review of sexuality and neurological conditions, it is hoped that the following sections will provide a jumping-off point for persons with disabilities and their partners to begin exploring sexuality in a healthy and fulfilling manner. At the end of the chapter, resources to promote further exploration and support are provided.

Traumatic Brain Injury

Physiological Impact

Physical changes following TBI are variable, depending on the nature of the injury. Very often, spinal cord injuries (SCI) occur concomitantly with the TBI (Merritt, 2004). Hemiplegia or hemiparesis (weakness or paralysis of one side of body) may also occur in varying degrees of severity and sensation may be impaired as well. Additionally, spasticity can be an issue depending on the nature of the injury. Cognitive deficits can often accompany a TBI, and like physical changes, these deficits can vary according to the location and severity of the injury to the brain. Issues that impact sexual functioning directly may be problems with social or interpersonal relationships, problems with accurately perceiving and expressing emotions, and limited insight into these concerns (Rosenthal & Ricker, 2000).

Psychological Impact

Given the complex nature of traumatic brain injury (TBI), those who suffer such injury and those who care for them can face a variety of issues postinjury. In particular, an individual with TBI may experience cognitive dysfunction, physical limitations, and personality changes, which can be distressing for both the individual and those in the individual's social support network. At times, personality changes can be more disturbing than any physical or cognitive difficulties, simply because friends and family may experience the person quite differently than before the injury. Anger, irritability, and disinhibition (leading to socially inappropriate behavior) may or may not be recognized by the individual but can be upsetting for support persons (Merritt, 2004). This can lead to divorce and isolation for many individuals with TBI. Psychotherapy, particularly family and couples therapy, along with education about how to cope with the effects of TBI, can improve the quality of relationships between the individual and her/his support persons. Additionally, support groups can offer both assistance in coping with these changes as well as social outlets and information dissemination. Resources will be provided at the end of the chapter for more information about these issues.

Spinal Cord Injury

Physiological Impact

Spinal cord injury (SCI) affects men and women in different ways. However, both genders will likely be concerned with mobility, sensation, and performance. As with other injuries, in SCI the level (cervical through sacral) and completeness of the injury (as measured by the ASIA scale) to the cord will have varying effects on physiological response. Men may experience changes in their ability to achieve or maintain an erection, whereas women may have reduced lubrication and ability to tighten vaginal muscles (Merritt, 2004). Both will experience varying levels of muscle control and sensation below the level of the injury, depending on the nature of the SCI.

For individuals with SCI, one negative side effect that can crop up during sexual activity is autonomic dysreflexia. Signs and symptoms include pounding headache, flushed skin, high blood pressure, slow pulse, and blurry or spotty vision. Prompt medical treatment is a must, as the person is at high risk for stroke, convulsions, or other medical complications if this is left untreated (Hammond & Burns, 2000).

For women, there are often no physiological changes after injury that prevent them from engaging in sexual activity (Jackson & Lindsey, 1998; Kaufman et al., 2003). Some women experience a diminished ability to produce vaginal lubrication owing to an interruption in the nerve signals from the brain to the genital area (Merritt, 2004). This is remedied by using a water-based lubricant; readily available at pharmacies or drugstores. Additional varieties of lubricants may be found online or at specialty sex shops. With the loss of muscle control that follows, some women may not be able to tighten vaginal muscles, resulting in reduced friction during intercourse. In order to improve friction, some women contract their urinary muscles to increase vaginal tightness. Different sexual positions may improve this as well (Kaufman et al., 2003).

The ability to achieve orgasm after SCI is another prominent concern for women. One study indicated that 54 percent of women were able to achieve orgasm after sexual activity, and another 30 percent reported extragenital pleasure. Some women report achieving orgasm after breast and upper body stimulation.

For men, the ability to achieve and maintain an erection is a primary concern. Men have two types of erections, psychogenic and reflex. In a psychogenic erection, sexual thoughts or feelings prompt signals from the brain to the penis that exit at the T–10 to L2 levels, resulting in an erection. Reflex erections, on the other hand, result from direct physical contact to the penis or stimulation of other erogenous zones such as the neck or nipples. A reflex erection is involuntary and can occur without sexual thoughts. The nerves that control impulses which stimulate a reflex erection are located in the sacral area (S2–S4) of the spinal cord. If the S2–S4 pathway is not damaged, men can generally have a reflex erection with proper stimulation (Merritt, 2004).

There are a variety of treatment options available to men who are unable to achieve an erection sufficient for sexual activity. Medications such as Viagra and Cialis are available with a prescription from a physician. Another option is penile injection therapy, in which medications are injected into the shaft of the penis, producing an erection for one to two hours following administration (Lindsey & Klebine, 2000; Merritt, 2004). Medicated Urethral System Erection or MUSE is another treatment option that involves placing a small, medicated pellet into the urethra. Once absorbed into the surrounding tissue, an erection can result (Lindsey & Klebine, 2000). Vacuum pumps enable the production of erections through mechanical means. Erections are maintained by placing a constriction ring (also termed "cock ring") around the base of the penis to prevent the blood from draining out prior to completion of sexual activity (Merritt, 2004). Use of the ring also prevents urinary leakage that can often occur during sex. Permanent penile prostheses are also available, but often are a last resort given the risk of infection or injury to the penis due to low levels of sensation (Lindsey & Klebine, 2000).

For both men and women, SCI can impact fertility levels. Following SCI, women may experience a disruption in their menstrual cycle, but as the body adjusts to the injury, normal cycles often resume with no effects on fertility (Jackson & Lindsey, 1998). Therefore, birth control should be employed accordingly, under the supervision of a physician. For women who wish to conceive, pregnancy can present some challenges physically and psychologically, making close prenatal monitoring essential. For men, ejaculation can be disrupted in upwards of 90 percent of men with SCI (Lindsey & Klebine, 2000). Retrograde ejaculation (where the semen travels up the urethra and is deposited in the bladder) can also occur. Sperm count does not change; however, the motility of sperm cells may decrease significantly. Treatment options such as penile vibratory stimulation and rectal probe electroejaculation are available to assist in the conception process (Kaufman et al., 2003; Lindsey & Klebine, 2000). Both of these treatment options are performed under the supervision of a physician.

Psychological Impact

Psychological adjustment to disability following a spinal cord injury is complex and can present significant challenges for individuals and their families. It can, of course, greatly affect sexual activities as well. After surviving the trauma of a serious injury, individuals often ask themselves and others if they are different, aside from the obvious changes in mobility. Basic personality features, styles of relating to others, or level of intelligence are unlikely to change. However, persons with SCI and their support persons may feel a variety of emotions including shock, sadness, and anger in response to the injury. This is very common following a traumatic event and part of the grieving process and part of psychological adjustment to the effects of the injury. While this is a natural part of recovering from an injury, professional assistance may be necessary if the emotional response becomes unmanageable and impedes progress in rehabilitation or life in general.

There are many ways to navigate the emotional recovery process, which can be as individualized as the rehabilitation process itself. Individuals with SCI and their partners/family members may begin examining their feelings and attitudes toward one another in addition to their feelings toward others with disabilities. Working on communication skills can promote healthy discussion between those with SCI and family members and can prepare a person with SCI to negotiate social situations following the injury. Issues such as maintaining friendships, dating, and engaging in sexual relationships are frequent concerns in promoting quality of life. Improving coping strategies, assertiveness training, and social skills during the adjustment phase can assist individuals with SCI and families in "getting back to life." When individuals with SCI and their significant others are given adequate support in regaining psychological intimacy, discussions concerning physical intimacy and experimentation with sexual expression are likely to follow. As alluded to in the previous section, psychological factors may play a more important role than the physiological factors in all aspects of sexual functioning following SCI (Kaufman et al., 2003; Merritt, 2004).

Multiple Sclerosis

Physiological Impact

Sexual dysfunction is commonly reported in MS. The areas of neurological involvement and the type of MS typically coincide with the type of sexual problems experienced by people living with MS. At times, sexual dysfunction itself may be the initial symptom prior to diagnosis. Men frequently experience erectile dysfunction (either an erection insufficient for intercourse, or an adequate erection for an insufficient duration), difficulties with sensation (either diminished or hypersensitivity), slowed ejaculation, diminished orgasm, and reduced libido/sex drive (Leonard, 2005). Women commonly experience reduced sensation, decreased vaginal lubrication, difficulty reaching orgasm, and reduced sex drive. Both genders can also have difficulty with spasticity in lower extremities (Leonard, 2005).

Psychological Impact

As with other disabilities, those who live with MS often experience persistent fatigue or low energy that can curtail sexual activity and diminish sexual drive (Devins & Schnek, 2000). Although incontinence does not typically interfere with sexual activity, the potential for it or the presence of catheters can be a source of anxiety or shame, which can detract from the sexual experience (Leonard, 2005). Depression, a common emotional correlate of MS, can also reduce libido and make it more difficult to become aroused.

Open communication, understanding and being flexible about sexual experiences can promote enjoyment for those involved. Varying the timing of sex play, positioning, and having a good understanding of sensation and mobility issues can enhance sexual encounters considerably (Merritt, 2004). Additionally, emptying bowel and bladder prior to engaging in sex and using adequate lubrication can engender additional comfort and pleasure (Leonard, 2005).

Epilepsy

Physiological Impact

As with MS, sexual problems associated with epilepsy are multifaceted, and can involve different areas of the brain, hormone levels, physical and psychological difficulties, along with sexual dysfunction associated with medications taken to control seizures (Morrell, 1997). Both genders may encounter low levels of sexual desire, and difficulties with arousal. Women report experiencing pain during intercourse (dyspareunia) and painful vaginal spasms during intercourse (vaginismus) (Epilepsy Foundation, 2005). Both of these issues are generally unrelated to diminished sexual desire or arousal, but can often lead to avoidance of sexual intercourse due to intense discomfort. Men with epilepsy can experience erectile problems, most often with achieving or sustaining erections. Ejaculation can be slowed as well. Individuals living with epilepsy can experience sexual arousal and sensations, physical exertion, and faster breathing similar to a preseizure aura (Morrell, 1997). Because the physiological symptoms of sexual arousal and climax are similar to preseizure auras, sexual activity can be an especially distressing phenomenon and can have profound effects on psychological and sexual functioning (Epilepsy and Sexuality, 2005).

Treatment Impact

Individuals living with epilepsy often take a variety of medications to control their seizure activity. Common side effects of these medications may interfere with both sexual desire and the ability to become aroused. Sedation is the most common side effect of antiepileptic medications and can be so severe as to interfere with sex play (Morrell, 1997). Because medications often affect individuals somewhat differently, a frank discussion with a health care provider can assist in finding a medication regimen that is effective in controlling seizure activity with fewer sexual side effects. For women experiencing pain during intercourse, there are gynecological treatments available to assist with this (Epilepsy and Sexuality, 2005).

Cerebral Palsy

Impact

For those coping with the effects of cerebral palsy (CP), addressing issues of sexual functioning can take many paths. To be sure, CP itself does not typically bring about any changes in arousal or erectile function (Disability and Illness, 2004). However, issues such as social stigma, communication, spasticity, pain, and positioning can affect sexual activity significantly. Research indicates that when compared to a sample of unmarried, able-bodied men, single men with CP demonstrated less facility with sexual information, experience, libido, and satisfaction, and experienced more psychological symptoms. Unmarried women with CP, conversely, demonstrated less satisfaction with body image as compared to single, able-bodied women (Cho, Park, Park, & Na, 2004). This highlights the idea that social stigma and psychological factors can significantly hamper efforts aimed at achieving satisfying sexual experiences (Disability and Illness, 2004). Partners may express concerns about spasticity and limited range of motion as new positions are explored. And as with other disabilities that limit mobility, this requires some patience, creativity, and openness to trying new positions, but this may lead to greater satisfaction and excitement with partners (Disability and Illness, 2004). Experimentation should be undertaken with consideration of the safety and comfort needs of those involved.

Cerebrovascular Accident

Physiological Impact

Much like TBI and SCI, stroke can affect a person's sexual functioning in a variety of ways. Physical difficulties caused by stroke include weakness, paralysis, diminished sensation, and pain (Westcott, 2002). Reduced sensation and pain are symptoms associated with other conditions, and the reader is referred to the later sections of this chapter for more detailed discussion regarding those symptoms.

Weakness and paralysis following a stroke may make coping with the physical changes a special challenge: activities of daily living such as bathing, dressing, grooming, and household chores take longer and are more energy consuming than before the stroke. Therefore, fatigue can interfere with intimacy (Westcott, 2002). Since sex does not always have to occur just prior to retiring for the evening, a couple should explore alternate times to engage in sexual activity, most notably, times when energy is higher (Merritt, 2004). Making time for sex when energy levels are higher can result in more satisfying sex (and potentially a cheerier attitude when tackling those other, less exciting activities of daily living). Trying different positions that compensate for limited mobility or low energy can also be of help. A "spooning" position with both partners lying on their sides (whatever side is more comfortable) and facing the same direction can allow for penetration, stroking of erogenous zones, and cuddling. Both partners lying on their sides facing one another can provide a similar result (Kaufman et al., 2003).

Treatment Impact

Some medications for high blood pressure are known to produce side effects that may have a negative effect on sexual desire and functioning (Caplan & Moelter, 2000). Sexual arousal and ability to achieve orgasm can also be affected by these medications. Discussing these side effects with a physician may allow him/her to prescribe different medications that may produce fewer side effects and promote effective blood pressure control. Individuals should not, under any circumstance, alter a dosage or stop taking these medications without discussing it with a health care provider first, as this may pose serious health risks.

Psychological Impact

One of the most common fears following a stroke is having another one, and many individuals fear engaging in sexual activities because of concern about increasing blood pressure to a level that might cause another stroke (Westcott, 2002). Because many underlying illnesses (such as diabetes) can increase a person's risk for stroke, it is important for individuals to have frank discussions with their physicians prior to resuming sexual activity. If fears of sexual activity causing a stroke cannot be put to rest by such a discussion, a referral for psychotherapy can assist with exploring underlying fears and issues that may be complicating the resumption of sexual activity.

Many individuals report other emotional changes following stroke, including depression, diminished self-esteem, and body image issues (Merritt,

2004; Caplan & Moelter, 2000). Sexual problems and emotional difficulties often coincide, especially following the traumatic experience of stroke. Emotional problems such as depression can result from the enormous adjustment process of recovery and coping with changes in physical and cognitive ability. However, some emotional issues can also be linked to damage in specific areas of the brain following the stroke. People may notice mood swings, inappropriate sadness or tearfulness, anger, depression, or anxiety, among other things. These changes should be discussed with a physician and a psychologist or neuropsychologist in order to receive the proper treatment to avoid prolonging or furthering the issues.

Lastly, communication difficulties can also hamper efforts to engage in fulfilling sexual activity. Frustration and anger are common reactions to problems with verbal expression or comprehension of what others are saying. Receptive and expressive aphasia are frequently associated with stroke and can present problems for those with a stroke and support persons alike. Patience is required for both the individual and partners or support persons. Individuals who experience communication difficulties often report that frustration and anger can further impede successful communication efforts and diminish affectionate or sexual feelings along the way. If communication issues are identified as a problem, a physician, speech therapist (preferably one specializing in assistive technology devices that can produce words or phrases), or psychologist may be able to assist in evaluating and treating this problem.

CARDIOVASCULAR DISEASE

Cardiovascular disease (CVD, or coronary heart disease; CHD) is the number one cause of death in men and women in the United States (National Heart, Lung and Blood Institute, n.d.). While the previous section on CVA, which included some of the factors affecting sexual activity following a stroke, is applicable here as well, CVD and sexuality requires further discussion. Approximately 25 percent of people with CVD report a discontinuation of sexual activity after a heart attack, and another 50 percent report a decrease in sexual activity. The percentages are smaller, but similar, for patients with cardiac chest pain, also called angina pectoris (Taylor, 1999). While this decline in sexual activity occurs primarily due to psychological factors, other factors include the effects of the disease on blood vessels and other body systems important to sexual functioning, the effects of medication on physical functioning, and the psychological effects on the individual's sexual partner.

Physiological Impact

Sexual dysfunction in men is frequently associated with cardiovascular disease because any condition that inhibits blood flow to the genital region can lead to erectile dysfunction (ED) in men and, some believe, to similar arousal problems in women (Buvat & Lemaire, 2001). While other common causes of the disruption of blood flow, including atherosclerosis (hardening of the arteries) and hypertension (high blood pressure), are frequently present before an individual suffers from a heart attack they may not be detected until afterward. Despite the well-known connection between cardiovascular disease and sexual dysfunction, many individuals are nervous about bringing up these concerns with physicians. Additionally, because some changes in sexual functioning are expected to occur as one ages, it is common for an individual to fail to mention such changes to her/his physician because these changes are mistakenly attributed solely to the aging process. And while some decline in sexual activity is normal as we age, current medical technology allows people to remain safely sexually active well into their eighties and nineties (Thorson, 2003). The first step to resuming sexual activity after a cardiac event is for the patient to discuss any worries with her/his physician or with another qualified health care provider. Physicians, too, may be hesitant to raise the topic of sexual functioning for fear of offending a patient or because of the physician's perceived lack of expertise, lack of time, or discomfort in discussing the topic (Haboubi & Lincoln, 2003; Stead, Brown, Fallowfield, & Selby, 2003; Sundquist & Yee, 2003).

After a cardiac event, many patients report being much more aware of heart activity (such as how fast it is beating) and other physical symptoms (such as rate of or difficulty breathing). Such a common response to a life-threatening event, such as a heart attack, can also change the focus of, and interfere with, engaging in sexual activity. Because of fears of recurrence of CHD symptoms, changes in the body during sex are to be expected and should not cause worry. However, the energy and effort required for sexual intercourse is the equivalent of mild to moderate physical activity and requires about the same amount of effort required to climb up two flights of stairs, meaning that for most people recovering from a heart attack, sexual activity is safe (Douglas & Wilkes, 1975; Hellerstein & Friedman, 1970; Stein, 1977).

More specifically, as one becomes sexually aroused, the body goes through many changes. The skin may become flushed, blood pressure rises, and heart beat increases to 90–130 beats per minute during orgasm. Increases in blood pressure and heart rate are considered safe even for those who have recently experienced a myocardial infarction.

Additional reassurance regarding the safety of sex is provided by guidelines developed to help determine the safety of sexual activity for individual cardiac patients. The Princeton Consensus Panel, a group of experts on sex and cardiac patients, determined that patients can be put into one of three risk categories: low, intermediate, or high. The majority of patients are in the low risk category, which includes patients with controlled hypertension (high blood pressure); mild, stable angina (chest pain); successful cardiac bypass surgery or stent placement; a history of an uncomplicated heart attack; mild heart valve disease; and no symptoms and less than three cardiac risk factors (Debusk et al., 2000). For individuals in this category, resuming sexual activity is generally safe within three to six weeks after a cardiac event.

Individuals in the other risk groups or those with lingering concerns should discuss the safety of resuming sexual activity with his/her physician. For such individuals a graded exercise tolerance test, or cardiac stress test, might be recommended. During a stress test, the patient is hooked up to monitors that measure heart and body functions. The patient is asked to walk on a treadmill or ride a stationary cycle at different speeds and levels of difficulty while the body's response is monitored. The physician can then determine how much physical activity the heart can safely handle and will be able to inform the patient whether sexual activity is safe.

As long as the physician has determined that it is safe, engaging in regular physical activity can be extremely helpful in returning to normal sexual routines. All individuals recovering from heart attack are encouraged to participate in exercise to strengthen the heart muscle, but physical activity has additional benefits as well. It can increase coordination and muscle tone as well as improve self-assurance, self-worth, and "staying power." Exercise not only leaves one in better health but also allows for better sexual performance.

Despite the popular belief that many people have heart attacks during sexual activity, it is simply not true. While having sex in an unfamiliar place or with a new partner can cause additional stress on the heart, even these kinds of activities do not lead to heart attacks very frequently. For healthy people with no previous history of cardiac disease, the chance of having a heart attack during sex is one to two in a million. For individuals with a previous heart attack, the risk increases to ten or twenty in a million (Kloner, 2000).

To further lower the risks of suffering a heart attack and increase the enjoyment of sexual activity, people are advised to be well rested before sex. This might mean having sex in the morning or soon after a nap. Food and drink (especially alcohol) should be avoided for one to three hours before having sex, as digestion diverts blood flow from the heart to the stomach. Very hot or cold showers or sitting in a sauna or whirlpool should also be avoided, as this can cause an additional increase in blood pressure.

Treatment Impact

Cardiovascular disease is frequently managed with a variety of medications. Most of the common classes of drugs used in the treatment of cardiovascular disease will not affect sexual functioning. These include ACE inhibitors (used to treat high blood pressure), calcium channel blockers (used to treat angina and high blood pressure), and statins (used to treat high cholesterol).

However, beta-blockers such as Toprol XL, Lopressor, and Tenormin (atenolol and metoprolol), which are used to treat high blood pressure, have been frequently associated with decreased sexual ability and erectile dysfunction. Beta-blockers can also be used to relieve angina (chest pain) and can help prevent additional heart attacks.

Despite the commonly made assumptions, a recent review of published articles and medical texts revealed that there are no scientific studies supporting the belief that the use of beta-blockers is highly associated with sexual dysfunction (Lama, 2002). This review failed to find any connection between erectile dysfunction or decreased libido and the use of beta-blockers. However, there has been difficulty separating out the effects of hypertension on sexual functioning from the contribution of age combined with the use of multiple medications. While there have been a number of well-reported, isolated cases linking beta-blockers and sexual dysfunction, reexamining the existing data suggests that the link is not strong.

While medications used to treat heart disease are of primary concern, medications used to treat other conditions may also raise special concerns for cardiac patients. Viagra (sildenafil) and other drugs of the same class including Levitra (vardenafil) and Cialis (tadalafil) have revolutionized the treatment of erectile dysfunction or ED. Along with that, it has also increased the awareness of risks of sexual activity in patients being treated for cardiovascular disease. According to current research, the only contraindication to Viagra use is the use of organic nitrates (such as nitroglycerin or isosorbide dinitrate, sold under the trade names of Isordil, Nitrogard, Nitrostat, Sorbitrate). Viagra causes a mild decrease in blood pressure, and when combined with nitrates, it can lead to a major decrease in blood pressure. How safe it is for people with recent (within six months) heart attack, unstable angina, stroke, or life threatening arrhythmias to use ED medication has not been adequately studied. It has been found that caution should be used by patients with unstable cardiac conditions when taking Viagra (Kloner, 2000). However, in patients with heart disease, placebo-controlled drug trials did not show an increase in heart attacks or serious cardiac events with the use of Viagra.

Psychological Impact

Any life-threatening event (such as a heart attack or stroke) can have an adverse psychological impact on an individual and on the individual's loved ones, making it difficult for life to return to normal. Patients often report a fear of death and anxiety about any activity that puts stress on the heart. Feelings of sadness following a cardiac event are also common and may be associated with changes in eating and sleeping habits. Some individuals may experience irritability and withdraw from those around them. Changes like those may be a sign of depression and should not be ignored. While about 85 percent of cases of depression following a heart attack resolve in about three months (American Heart Association, 1990), even moderate levels of depression can interfere with recovery from a heart attack (Carney, Freedland,

Rich, & Jaffe, 1995; Frasure-Smith, Lesperance, & Talajic, 1996). Depression can affect sexual desire, resulting in greatly reduced interest in sexual activity. Because there are so many effective treatments available for depression, it is important that health care providers be consulted when symptoms of depression persist.

Partners of individuals who have had a cardiac event also may experience depression or other psychological symptoms. Partners may become afraid or anxious (especially regarding sexual activities) and the negative impact of these fears on individuals recovering from heart attacks has been well documented (Ben-Sira & Eliezer, 1990; Levin, 1987; Thompson & Meddis, 1990). Often, partners have difficulties expressing their concerns directly, instead doing so by being patronizing and over-protective. Therefore, it is important for couples to make a special effort to communicate openly with each other about any fears or concerns in order to manage the new challenges following such an event.

When it comes to resuming sexual activity, couples can start out by just enjoying the sensations of being together. Cuddling and caressing are good ways to enjoy each other's bodies and affection without the performance-driven demands of sexual intercourse. Lowering one's expectations of a sexual encounter can help ease the stress as well. While orgasms are often seen as the goal of sex, feelings of tenderness and sensuality should also be appreciated. Physical affection can serve not only as a path back to sexual intercourse but also as a reward in its own right.

Once sexual intercourse has been resumed, one should be aware that research has suggested that no one sexual position is better than any other for cardiac patients, but there are a few guidelines to keep in mind (Taylor, 1999). In sexual positions where one partner is on top, this partner typically reaches a higher heart rate and engages in more strenuous physical exertion. Therefore, it may be better, particularly when first returning to sexual intercourse, for the person with cardiac disease to be on the bottom during sex.

Moreover, care should be taken when engaging in any positions that require the individual who has had a heart attack to put pressure on her/his arms for an extended amount of time, particularly for individuals who have had open-heart surgery, as this puts more stress on the incision. Some suggestions for less strenuous positions include both partners lying on their sides or sitting face to face in a chair. Oral sex is also an excellent way for couples to enjoy each other. Couples are encouraged to consult a physician prior to engaging in anal sex because it can lead to irregular heart rhythms (Cambre, 1990). When returning to sexual activity, the most important thing for couples to remember is to go slowly and not to do anything that makes either partner anxious. Still, some early research suggested that resuming sexual activity sooner, rather than later, after a heart attack could result in a faster recovery (Scalzi & Dracup, 1978), and a subsequent study showed similar benefits, with recovery being quicker when spousal fear is alleviated and sexual activities resumed (Beach et al., 1992).

DIABETES

Many individuals with cardiovascular disease also have other chronic health problems such as Type II diabetes mellitus, an endocrine disorder that results in poorly regulated blood glucose (sugar) levels due to reduced production of insulin (a hormone that helps turn sugar into stored energy) and insulin resistance (body's decreased sensitivity to insulin). Type II diabetes mellitus is frequently associated with ED in men (Wandell & Brorsson, 2000). Obesity is also commonly associated with Type II diabetes and makes it more likely that those who develop diabetes will also have heart disease and hypertension (high blood pressure). The previous sections have described the impact of cardiovascular and neurovascular conditions on sexuality and these apply to individuals who have Type II diabetes in addition to heart disease. And while cardiovascular disease may account for much of the sexual dysfunction observed in diabetes, there are several other ways in which Type II diabetes can impact sexual functioning.

Physiological Impact

In addition to the cardiovascular effects on sexual functioning, some research also suggests that obesity may negatively affect sexual functioning through hormonal changes that decrease sexual desire (Stahl, 2001; Trischitta, 2003). Individuals with poorly regulated Type II diabetes often report symptoms of fatigue, blurred vision, headache, and irritability—all symptoms that may interfere with an individual's desire for sexual activity. While those symptoms tend to be transient and associated with extremes in glucose levels, the complications that develop over years of poorly controlled blood glucose levels can be enduring and debilitating.

The complications of Type II diabetes affect multiple systems that directly and indirectly affect sexual functioning. These complications may include neuropathies (nerve damage) that reduce sensitivity to touch, especially in the feet and hands; retinopathy (damage to the blood vessels in the eye) that can lead to blindness; and nephropathy (kidney disease) that may lead to kidney failure and the need for hemodialysis (pumping blood through a machine that cleans the blood). Neuropathies and nephropathy have been associated, both directly and indirectly, with sexual dysfunction.

Nephropathy or kidney disease may progress to the point that the kidneys can no longer effectively clean the waste products out of the blood. When this happens, the individual may undergo hemodialysis. This generally requires visits to a dialysis center three times a week for three to five hours each visit. Studies of both men and women undergoing dialysis show that sexual dysfunction is common and related to changes in hormonal, nerve, and blood vessel conditions as well as psychological response to kidney disease and treatments (Gipson, Katz, & Stehman-Breen, 1999; Peng et al., 2005; Rosas et al., 2003).

Neuropathies may be associated with numbness, tingling, and decreased sensation but can also cause sharp, shooting and burning pains that can be quite distressing and disruptive. Decreased sensation due to nerve damage is thought to contribute to sexual problems in women with diabetes (Muniyappa, Norton, Dunn, & Banerji, 2005). Because neuropathies cause problems with feelings (especially in the feet), individuals may develop sores or have injuries without knowing it. If the individual does not get treatment soon enough, the damage may spread and become so severe that the foot or leg may have to be amputated (removed). Having a foot or leg amputated may create some difficulty with mobility, but a bigger concern is the psychological impact of losing a body part. Body image and confidence may be severely damaged so the individual believes she/he is less attractive as a result of amputation (Bodenheimer, Kerrigan, Garber, & Monga, 2000; Ide, 2004).

Treatment Impact

As discussed in the section on the treatment impact of cardiovascular disease, the beta-adrenergic blocking agents used to treat hypertension may be associated with ED. And because many individuals with Type II diabetes have high blood pressure and hyperlipidemia (too much fat in the blood), the information on medications from the section on treatment impact of cardiovascular disease also applies to those who have diabetes and cardiovascular disease.

In addition to medications taken to treat hypertension and elevated cholesterol, individuals with Type II diabetes may take oral medications (pills) to lower blood glucose or they may inject insulin. Medications to treat diabetes help lower blood glucose in different ways. Medications such as Glucotrol, Glucotrol XL, Mycronase, and Glynase help to reduce blood sugar levels by causing the pancreas to produce more insulin. Because there is more insulin present with these medications, it is possible for individuals to experience a low blood sugar reaction. A low blood sugar reaction can make one behave as if intoxicated (drunk) and can lead to death if not treated immediately.

Some diabetes medications lower blood glucose by making the body more sensitive to insulin and by reducing the amount of glucose produced in the body, while others slow the breakdown of starches into sugar. Some diabetes medications may cause serious liver damage. Other less serious, but sometimes intolerable side effects of these medications include: nausea, diarrhea, and other gastrointestinal distress. While these symptoms are generally not life threatening, they can be quite distressing and therefore interfere with sexual activity, particularly if they occur frequently.

Psychological Impact

As with other life-threatening conditions, a diagnosis of diabetes can lead to heightened anxiety and fear in both the individual with diabetes and his/her partner. In addition to any anxieties about the serious side effects of medicines, many individuals with diabetes report a depressed mood and extreme fatigue resulting from the rather burdensome regimen involved in diabetes care. In fact, some suggest that individuals with diabetes are twice as likely to develop depressive symptoms as those without the disease (Ciechanowski, Katon, Russo, & Hirsch, 2003; Lustman et al., 2000).

Depression, as stated previously, is associated with a significant decline in sexual desire. Other symptoms of depression include: decreased energy, appetite extremes, and difficulty with concentration and attention, all of which impact diabetes management. So in the context of depression, diabetes care declines and may lead to a cycle of worsening depression and increasing physical symptoms. Psychological interventions and/or antidepressants should be sought if symptoms persist beyond several weeks, bearing in mind that the SSRI (serotonin selective reuptake inhibitors) antidepressants are linked with disruption of sexual functioning at all stages of sexual response: desire, arousal, and climax (Stahl, 2001). Discussing any sexual side effects of the medication with a qualified health care provider is critical as there are medications available that may not interfere with sexual functioning.

When a partner's anxieties about an individual's health status persist despite reassurances by health care providers, marital or individual therapy may be indicated. Various kinds of professionals are available to address these concerns including psychologists, social workers, nurses, and counselors. A referral from a trusted health care provider is the first step to resolving any psychological factors disrupting sexual activity.

AUTOIMMUNE DISORDERS

While diabetes is most frequently thought of as an endocrine disorder, Type I diabetes is also classified as an autoimmune disorder because the individual's immune system has destroyed the cells in the pancreas responsible for producing insulin. Individuals with Type I diabetes share similar symptoms (e.g., fatigue, frequent urination, irritability) and complications (e.g., neuropathies, cardiovascular disease) as those with Type II diabetes. Many of the other more common autoimmune diseases also may be classified under the other categories, and they also may occur with, be accompanied by, or increase the risk for conditions from the other categories discussed in this chapter. Because the primary presenting symptoms of these conditions overlap considerably with those discussed in the other sections of this chapter, the reader is referred to the neurological, cardiovascular, endocrine, and chronic pain sections for information regarding the disease and treatment impact on sexual functioning. Some of the more common disorders include: (1) systemic lupus erythematosus (SLE), which can affect a wide range of body tissues (e.g., joints, skin, kidneys, heart, lungs, and blood vessels); (2) scleroderma ("hard skin"), which results in thickening and tightness of the skin of the fingers or toes but can affect other organs; and (3) rheumatoid arthritis (RA) in which the synovium or lining of joints becomes inflamed.

CHRONIC PAIN DISORDERS

Many of the disabilities and conditions discussed to this point have pain as a prominent symptom, and the pains described are caused by multiple factors. While cancer pain and pain associated with terminal illness are not addressed in any detail in this chapter, it is worth noting that these are considered acute pain because they are due to tissue damage. This tissue damage is secondary either to the disease itself or to the treatments provided (Swanson, 1999). Much of the information provided here can apply to cancer and other acute pains. But as with any health concern, a frank discussion with a physician or other qualified health care provider is suggested.

Chronic pain is defined as any pain that is present for longer than six months—beyond when all tissue healing should be completed. In many cases, physicians may not find evidence of tissue damage that could account for continuing pain. Chronic pain conditions are estimated to be one of the most common medical complaints and can result from a wide range of injuries or disease processes (Swanson, 1999).

Chronic low back pain (CLB) is one of the most common pain complaints and may be caused by muscle spasms, overexertion, or muscle strain. Herniated discs (the rupture of the fluid sac between the vertebrae in the spine) may cause pressure on nerves exiting the spinal cord and branching off to other areas of the body. CLB may also be caused by arthritis or degenerative joint disease. As discussed in the section on diabetes, neuropathic pain occurs when there is damage to nerves—and this can occur as a result of conditions such as alcoholism or MS (see section on neurological conditions).

Rheumatoid arthritis (RA) and osteoarthritis (OA) are two of more than 100 forms of arthritis—a set of conditions that cause painful inflammation of the joints and can result in restricted movement (American Pain Society, 2002). Fibromyalgia (FM) is a disorder in which "whole body" pain is the prominent symptom, but fatigue (feeling tired and having low energy) and intestinal distress are also common. There are, of course, many other types of chronic pain, including headache, facial pain, neck pain, abdominal, genital, and pelvic pain. But chronic pain conditions, regardless of location and type, can be equally debilitating.

Physiological Impact

Individuals living with pain often report decreased sexual activity with some estimates as high as 46 percent (Maigne & Chatellier, 2001). While the main reasons for decreased sexual activity in chronic pain are psychological in nature, sexuality can be affected by changes in sensation and mobility with some chronic pain conditions. As stated in the introductory section, chronic illness or neurological damage may cause reduced or heightened sensitivity to touch. Allodynia is a condition in which even a light touch is perceived as painful and may interfere with even the most basic physical forms of intimacy. Other, less severe pain sensations can also interfere with an individual's desire for physical contact. When these conditions are present, it is important for couples to experiment with, and gently explore, the individual's body in order to determine what types of stimulation on what areas of the body can be experienced as pleasure.

Reduced mobility is also a factor for individuals living with chronic pain—and especially those who have arthritis or muscle spasms. Experimenting with various positions and learning which activities are likely to trigger a spasm will increase the likelihood of satisfying sexual encounters. Taking pain and anti-spasmodic medications before any planned activities can help, as can a warm shower or bath timed appropriately. Individuals with RA often have decreased range of motion due to stiffness in the joints. One study found that women with high levels of stiffness in the morning reported more concerns about sexual functioning (Gutweniger, Kopp, Mur, & Gunther, 1999).

Fatigue is a common symptom of conditions such as Fibromyalgia and can interfere with sexual activities. In fact, many individuals living with chronic pain report fatigue and experience severe sleep disturbance, which can contribute to low energy and interfere with any desire for sex. Timing sexual encounters for periods when fatigue is less likely to interfere and employing positions that require less energy may promote satisfying sexual encounters.

Treatment Impact

Many of the medications used to treat chronic pain conditions can interfere with sexual functioning at all stages. Antiepileptics or anticonvulsant medications (e.g., gabapentin, carbamazepine, or lamotrigine) are often used to treat neuropathic or nerve pains. As described earlier, a common side effect of these medications is extreme sedation.

Sedation is also associated with the use of opioid analgesics, muscle relaxants, and benzodiazepines—especially at the initial stages of treatment. Tricyclic antidepressants (e.g., amitriptyline and nortriptyline) are often used in the treatment of neuropathies as well. These medications are well known for their sedating side effect; however, dry mouth, dizziness, and feeling as if one has a "hangover" (especially upon first awakening) are frequently reported and distressing side effects of amitriptyline and the other tricyclics. These side effects can interfere with one's ability to feel attractive and may reduce desire to engage in sexual activity. Having a frank discussion of these concerns with a physician or other members of the pain treatment team can lead to the appropriate medication changes.

Psychological Impact

Chronic pain conditions often lead to dramatic changes in lifestyle, and adapting to life with pain can be a lengthy process. Many chronic pain treatment centers have multidisciplinary teams comprised of physicians, nurses, behavioral health psychologists, occupational and physical therapists, and social workers because of the many factors that contribute to the chronic pain experience and the impact chronic pain has on various areas of life.

Individuals living with chronic pain frequently develop psychological symptoms as a result, and these can interfere with sexual activities in varying degrees. Some individuals may experience mild anxieties and fears about increased pain associated with sex while others develop major depressive disorders resulting in decreased libido. Furthermore, depression has been linked to increased pain severity—a vicious cycle that produces greater emotional distress followed by increasing pain severity (Swanson, 1999). If depression is implicated in the decreased desire for sex in a person with chronic pain, the first step to resolving this problem is discussing these concerns with a qualified health care professional. There are many effective treatments for depression, and treating depression may, as stated previously, result in decreased pain as well as improved mood.

SUMMARY

Many of the disabilities and chronic health conditions covered in this chapter directly impact sexual functioning because of damage to nerves or blood vessels, decreased hormone production, and chronic pain. The treatments for each of these conditions may also interfere with the satisfying expression of sexuality. Furthermore, there are often psychological factors such as depression or anxiety that individuals with chronic health problems experience. These psychological factors may also affect an individual's partner.

Despite the multiple factors that can adversely affect sexuality and intimacy, there remain a wide variety of means for achieving satisfying physical intimacy and enjoying the pleasures of sexual activity whether by oneself or with a partner. Sexuality is, as repeated throughout this chapter, an important aspect of life and critical to the quality of life and overall health and well-being of individuals living with disabilities and recovering from health crises.

REFERENCES

American Heart Association. (1990). *Sex and heart disease.* Dallas: Author.

American Pain Society. (2002). Guidelines for the management of pain in osteoarthritis, rheumatoid arthritis, and juvenile chronic arthritis. Glenview, IL: Author.

Arthritis Foundation. (2004). Guide to intimacy with arthritis. Retrieved June 30, 2005, from www.arthritis.org/resources/relationships/intimacy/hurts_hold_hands.asp.

Beach, E. K., Maloney, B. H., Plocica, A. R., Sherry, S. E., Weaver, M., Luthringerm, L., et al. (1992). The spouse: A factor in recovery after acute myocardial infarction. *Heart and Lung, 21*, 30–38.

Ben-Sira, Z., & Eliezer, R. (1990). The structure of readjustment after heart attack. *Social Science and Medicine, 30*, 523–536.

Bodenheimer, C., Kerrigan, A. J., Garber, S. L., & Monga, T. N. (2000). *Disability and Rehabilitation, 22*, 409–415.

Buvat, J., & Lemaire, A. (2001). Sexuality of the diabetic woman. *Diabetes & Metabolism, 4* (Suppl. 2), 67–75.

Cambre, S. (1990). *The sensuous heart: Guidelines for sex after a heart attack or surgery.* Atlanta: Pritchett and Hull.

Caplan, B., & Moelter, S. (2000). Stroke. In R. Frank & T. Elliot (Eds.), *Handbook of rehabilitation psychology* (pp. 75–108). Washington, DC: American Psychological Association.

Carlson, L. (1996). In sickness and in health: Sex, love, and chronic illness. New York: Dell.

Carney, R. M., Freedland, K. E., Rich, M. W., & Jaffe, A. S. (1995). Depression as a risk factor for cardiac events in established coronary heart disease: A review of possible mechanisms. *Advances in Cardiology, 31*, 237–241.

Cho, S., Park, E., Park, C., & Na, S. (2004). Characteristics of psychosexual functioning in adults with cerebral palsy. *Clinical Rehabilitation, 18*, 423–429.

Ciechanowski, P. S., Katon, W. J., Russo, J. E., & Hirsch, I. B. (2003). The relationship of depressive symptoms to symptom reporting, self-care and glucose control in diabetes. *General Hospital Psychiatry, 25*, 246–252.

Debusk, R., Drory, Y., Goldstein, I., Jackson, G., Kaul, S., Kimmel, S., et al. (2000). Management of sexual dysfunction in patients with cardiovascular disease: Recommendations from the Princeton Consensus Panel. *American Journal of Cardiology, 86*, 175–181.

Devins, G., & Shnek, Z. (2000). Multiple Sclerosis. In R. Frank & T. Elliot (Eds.), *Handbook of rehabilitation psychology* (pp. 163–184). Washington, DC: American Psychological Association.

Disability and illness: Cerebral palsy. (2004). Possible effects of cerebral palsy or CP on a person's sexuality. Retrieved June 15, 2005, from www.sexualhealth.com/article.php?Action=read&article_id=338&channel=3&topic=16

Douglas, J. E., & Wilkes, T. D. (1975). Reconditioning cardiac patients. *American Family Physician, 11*, 123–129.

Epilepsy Foundation. (2005). *Epilepsy and Sexuality.* Retrieved June 15, 2005, from www.epilepsyfoundation.org/answerplace/Life/adults/women/Professional/sexuality.cfm

Frasure-Smith, N., Lesperance, F., & Talajic, M. (1996). The impact of negative emotions on prognosis following myocardial infarction: Is it more than depression? *Health Psychology, 14*, 388–398.

Gipson, D., Katz, L. A., Stehman-Breen, C. (1999). Principles of dialysis: Special issues in women. *Seminars in Nephrology, 19,* 140–147.

Gutweniger, S., Kopp, M., Mur, E., & Gunther, V. (1999). Body image of women with rheumatoid arthritis. *Clinical and Experimental Rheumatology, 7,* 413–417.

Haboubi, N. H., & Lincoln, N. (2003). Views of health professionals on discussing sexual issues with patients. *Disability and Rehabilitation, 2,* 291–296.

Hammond, M. C., & Burns, S. C. (2000). (Eds.). *Yes you can! A guide to self-care for persons with spinal cord injury* (3rd ed.). Washington, DC: Paralyzed Veterans of America.

Hellerstein, H. K., & Friedman, E. H. (1970). Sexual activity and the post-coronary patient. *Archives of Internal Medicine, 125,* 987–999.

Ide, M. (2004). Sexuality in persons with limb amputation: A meaningful discussion of re-integration. *Disability Rehabilitation, 26,* 939–943.

Jackson, A., & Lindsey, L. (1998). *Pregnancy and women with SCI* [Brochure]. Birmingham: University of Alabama at Birmingham.

Kaufman, M., Silverberg, C., & Odette, F. (2003). *The ultimate guide to sex and disability: For all of us who live with disabilities, chronic pain, and illness.* San Francisco: Cleis Press.

Kievman, B. (with Blackmun, S.). (1989). *For better or worse: A couple's guide to dealing with chronic illness.* Chicago: Contemporary Books.

Kloner, R. (2000). Sex and the patient with cardiovascular risk factors: Focus on sildenafil. *American Journal of Medicine, 109*(9A), 13S–21S.

Kroll, K., & Klein, E. L. (1995). Enabling romance: A guide to love, sex and relationships for the disabled. Bethesda, MD: Woodbine House.

Lama, P. J. (2002). Systemic adverse effects of beta-adrenergic blockers: An evidence-based assessment. *American Journal of Ophthalmology, 134,* 749–760.

Leonard, M. (2005). *MS and sexual functioning.* MS Ireland, MS News. Retrieved June 19, 2005, from www.ms-society.ie/msnews/issue55/a10sexual.html

Levin, R. F. (1987). *Heart-mates: A survival guide for the cardiac spouse.* Englewood Cliffs, NJ: Prentice Hall.

Lindsey, L., & Klebine, P. (2000). *Sexual function in men with SCI* [Brochure]. Birmingham: University of Alabama at Birmingham.

Lustman, P. J., Anderson, R. J., Freedland, K. E., de Groot, M., Carney, R. M., & Clouse, R. E. (2000). Depression and poor glycemic control: A meta-analytic review of the literature. *Diabetes Care, 23,* 934–942.

Maigne, J. Y., & Chatellier, G. (2001). Assessment of sexual activity in patients with back pain compared with patients with neck pain. *Clinical Orthopedics, 385,* 82–87.

Maurer, J. R., & Strausberg, P. D. (1989). *Building a new dream: A family guide to coping with chronic illness and disability.* Reading, MA: Addison-Wesley.

McGonigle, C. (1999). *Surviving your spouse's chronic illness: A compassionate guide.* New York: Henry Holt.

McInnes, R. A. (2003). Chronic illness and sexuality. *Medical Journal of Australia, 179,* 263–266.

Merritt, L. (2004). Sexuality and Disability. In *e-Medicine*. Retrieved June 16, 2005, from www.emedicine.com/pmr/topic178.htm

Morrell, M. (1997). Sexuality in epilepsy. In J. Engel & T. Pedley (Eds.), *Epilepsy*. Philadelphia: Lippincott-Raven.

Muniyappa, R., Norton, M., Dunn, M. E., & Banerji, M. A. (2005). Diabetes and female sexual dysfunction: Moving beyond "benign neglect." *Current Diabetes Reports, 5*, 230–236.

National Heart, Lung and Blood Institute. (N.d.) *The heart truth: A national awareness campaign for women about heart disease*. Retrieved July 21, 2005, from www.nhlbi.nih.gov/health/hearttruth/whatis/index.htm

Peng, Y. S., Chiang, C. K., Kao, T. W., Hung, K. Y., Lu, C. S., Chiang, S. S., et al. (2005). Sexual dysfunction in female hemodialysis patients: A multicenter study. *Kidney International, 68*, 760–765.

Rosenthal, M., & Ricker, J. (2000). Traumatic brain injury. In R. Frank & T. Elliot (Eds.), *Handbook of rehabilitation psychology* (pp. 49–74). Washington, DC: American Psychological Association.

Rosas, S. E., Joffe, M., Franklin, E., Strom, B. L., Kotzker, W., Brensinger, C., et al. (2003). Associated decrease in quality of life and erectile dysfunction in hemodialysis patients. *Kidney International, 64*, 232–238.

Scalzi, C. C., & Dracup, K. (1978). Sexual counseling of coronary patients. *Heart and Lung, 7*, 840–845.

Stahl, S. M. (2001). The psychopharmacology of sex, part 2: Effects of drugs and disease on the 3 phases of human sexual response. *Journal of Clinical Psychiatry, 62*, 147–148.

Stead, M. L., Brown, J. M., Fallowfield, L., & Selby, P. (2003). Lack of communication between healthcare professionals and women with ovarian cancer about sexual issues. *British Journal of Cancer, 10*, 666–671.

Stein, R.A. (1977). The effect of exercise training on heart rate during coitus in the post myocardial infarction patient. *Circulation, 55*, 738–740.

Sundquist, K., & Yee, L. (2003). Sexuality and body image after cancer. *Australian Family Physician, 32*(1–2), 19–23.

Swanson, D. W. (1999). *Mayo Clinic on chronic pain*. New York: Kensington.

Taylor, H. A. (1999). Sexual activity and the cardiovascular patient: Guidelines. *American Journal of Cardiology, 84*(5B), 6N–10N.

Thompson, D. R., & Meddis, R. (1990). Wives' responses to counseling early after myocardial infarction. *Journal of Psychosomatic Research, 34*, 249–258.

Thorson, A. (2003). Sexual activity and the cardiac patient. *American Journal of Geriatric Cardiology, 12*(1), 38–40.

Trischitta, V. (2003). Relationship between obesity-related metabolic abnormalities and sexual function. *Journal of Endocrinological Investigations, 26*(3 Suppl.), 62–4.

Wallerstein, J., & Blakeslee, S. (1996). *The good marriage: How and why love lasts*. New York: Warner Books.

Wandell, P. E., & Brorsson, B. (2000). Assessing sexual functioning in patients with chronic disorders by using a generic health-related quality of life questionnaire. *Quality of Life Research, 9*, 1081–1092.

Westcott, P. (2002). *Sex after stroke* [Brochure]. London: Stroke Association.

ADDITIONAL RESOURCES FOR INFORMATION ON SEX AND DISABILITY

Video

Alexander, C. J., & Sipski, M. L. (Coproducers). (1993). *Sexuality reborn: Sexuality following spinal cord injury* [Videotape]. West Orange, NJ: Kessler Institute for Rehabilitation.

Books

Griffith, E., & Lemberg, S. (1993). *Sexuality and the person with traumatic brain injury: A guide for families.* Philadelphia: F. A. Davis.

Kroll, K., & Klein, E. (1992). *Enabling romance: A guide to love, sex and relationships for people with disabilities and the people who care about them.* Horsham, PA: No Limits Communications.

Web Sites

www.americanheart.org/presenter.jhtml?identifier=1200000
American Heart Association Web site that answers questions about heart disease and provides information about community supports, activities, and treatments.

www.arthritis.org/default.asp
A Web site about arthritis, community supports, healthcare providers, medications, and treatments.

www.nlm.nih.gov/medlineplus/healthtopics.html
A Web site designed to provide answers about health problems, medications, and organizations that offer support and services to individuals with specific health concerns.

www.sexualhealth.com
A Web site with a wealth of information about sexuality, education, counseling, therapy, medical attention, and other resources for persons with disabilities and their partners.

www.spinalcord.uab.edu/show.asp?durki=24434
A Web site by the University of Alabama at Birmingham. In addition to copious information about sexuality following spinal cord injury, there is abundant information about a variety of issues related to spinal cord injury.

www.newmobility.com
A Web site and magazine for persons with disabilities that addresses a variety of issues concerning living with disabilities.

Index

About the Editors
and Contributors

M. MICHELE BURNETTE holds a doctorate in clinical psychology and a master's of public health in epidemiology. Dr. Burnette was formerly a psychology professor at Western Michigan University, during which time she taught courses in human sexuality and conducted research on sexual function and health. She has also taught at the community college level and at the University of Pittsburgh. She is currently in private practice in Columbia, South Carolina, where she specializes in therapy for sexual problems. She has coauthored two textbooks with Richard D. McAnulty, *Human Sexuality: Making Healthy Decisions* (2004) and *Fundamentals in Human Sexuality: Making Healthy Decisions* (2003). She is also coeditor of this set.

RICHARD D. McANULTY is an associate professor of psychology at the University of North Carolina at Charlotte. He earned his Ph.D. in clinical psychology from the University of Georgia under the late Henry E. Adams. His research interests broadly encompass human sexuality and its problems. His books include *The Psychology of Sexual Orientation, Behavior, and Identity: A Handbook*, edited with Louis Diamant (Greenwood Press, 1994), and *Human Sexuality: Making Healthy Decisions* (2004) with Michele Burnette. He has served on the board of several journals, including the *Journal of Sex Research*.

ANTHONY F. BOGAERT, Ph.D., is professor of community health sciences and psychology at Brock University in St. Catharine's, Ontario. He has published extensively on various aspects of human sexuality. He is on the editorial board of *Archives of Sexual Behavior*. He is a recipient of Brock University's Chancellor's Chair for Research Excellence.

GEORGE J. DEMAKIS is an associate professor of psychology at the University of North Carolina at Charlotte. He has published widely on meta-analysis, as well as various areas of neuropsychology including Parkinson's disease, traumatic brain injury, multiple sclerosis, and malingering. He is on the editorial board of *The Clinical Neuropsychologist* and maintains an active practice in neuropsychological assessment and consultation in Charlotte, North Carolina.

BRIAN M. DODGE, Ph.D., is an assistant professor of public health programs in the College of Public Health and Health Professions at the University of Florida. His research has focused on various social and behavioral aspects of sexual health and HIV/AIDS. During his doctoral training at Indiana University and the Kinsey Institute for Research in Sex, Gender, and Reproduction, he worked as a research assistant in the Rural Center for AIDS/STD Prevention and in the Sexual Health Research Working Group. Dr. Dodge recently completed his postdoctoral training in the NIMH-funded Behavioral Sciences Research in HIV Infection Fellowship in the HIV Center for Clinical and Behavioral Studies at the Columbia University Department of Psychiatry and the New York State Psychiatric Institute. His ongoing research projects include HIV risk and prevention among at-risk men who have sex with both men and women, health and well-being among bisexual individuals, and sexual compulsivity among diverse populations.

JENNIFER DUFFECY, M.S., is a doctoral student in clinical psychology at the Illinois Institute of Technology/Institute of Psychology and a behavioral health psychology student at John Stroger Hospital of Cook County, Chicago. She has been selected as a predoctoral clinical psychology intern for the 2005–2006 academic year at Rush University Medical School in Chicago. Ms. Duffecy has served as research coordinator for the Cardiac Couples project (NIH-funded research at Rush University) since 2004 and expects to continue working with couples in which one partner is suffering from a chronic health condition. She is also interested in treatment adherence in various chronic illnesses.

CATHERINE FAWCETT is a graduate student in psychology at Brock University in St. Catharine's, Ontario. She recently received a graduate scholarship from the Social Sciences and Humanities Research Council of Canada (SSHRC).

GREG A. R. FEBBRARO is assistant professor of psychology at Drake University in Des Moines, Iowa. He holds a doctorate in clinical psychology and has published on the topics of self-administered interventions for anxiety disorders, phobias, self-regulatory processes, and the relationship between suicidality and problem solving. He has served as an ad hoc reviewer for several journals including the *Journal of Clinical Psychology* and the *Journal of Traumatic Studies*. Dr. Febbraro is a member of the American Psychological Association, the Association for Advancement of Behavioral and Cognitive Therapies, and the Iowa Psychological Association. His clinical interests include working with anxious, depressed, and traumatized populations.

BETTY J. FISHER, Ph.D. is a clinical psychologist at John Stroger Hospital of Cook County (formerly Cook County Hospital) in Chicago, where she serves as a behavioral health consultant. Dr. Fisher completed her master's degree in psychology at Ball State University and her doctorate in clinical psychology at Western Michigan University in 1996. She also completed a two-year postdoctoral fellowship in Behavioral Medicine at Johns Hopkins University School of Medicine. In addition to her interests in sexual functioning of individuals with chronic health conditions, Dr. Fisher has clinical and research interests in treatment adherence in chronic illness, lifestyle modification, coping, and social support.

DAVID C. GEARY is a professor in the Department of Psychological Sciences at the University of Missouri, Columbia. He has published more than 125 articles and chapters across a wide range of topics, including cognitive and developmental psychology, education, evolutionary biology, and medicine. His three books, *Children's Mathematical Development* (1994), *Male, Female: The Evolution of Human Sex Differences* (1998), and *The Origin of Mind: Evolution of Brain, Cognition, and General Intelligence*, were published by the American Psychological Association. Among his many distinctions is the Chancellor's Award for Outstanding Research and Creative Activity in the Social and Behavioral Sciences (1996).

KELLY E. GRAHAM, Psy.D., is a postdoctoral fellow at Missouri Rehabilitation Center. She received her doctorate in clinical psychology in 2004 from the Illinois School of Professional Psychology in Chicago. Dr. Graham completed her master's degree in rehabilitation counseling from Wright State University in 1996. Her research interests include neurocognitive and psychosocial sequelae of diabetes mellitus, adherence to treatment regimen in chronic illness, and decision-making capacity. Dr. Graham is currently involved in a research project in the Endocrinology Department at John Stroger Hospital of Cook County (Chicago), investigating factors associated with adherence to diabetic regimen.

PEGGY J. KLEINPLATZ, Ph.D., is a clinical psychologist, AASECT certified sex therapist, sex therapy supervisor, and sex educator. She teaches in the

Faculty of Medicine and in the School of Psychology, University of Ottawa, Canada. Kleinplatz has been teaching human sexuality since 1983 and was awarded the Prix d'Excellence by the University of Ottawa in 2000. She also teaches sex therapy at the affiliated Saint Paul University's Institute of Pastoral Studies. Her work focuses on eroticism and transformation. Kleinplatz is the editor of *New Directions in Sex Therapy: Innovations and Alternatives* (2001) and the forthcoming *Sadomasochism: Powerful Pleasures* (with Dr. Charles Moser, 2006).

KIMBERLY McBRIDE is a doctoral candidate in the Department of Applied Health Science at Indiana University and a predoctoral fellow at the Kinsey Institute for Research in Sex, Gender, and Reproduction. She earned her master's degree in counseling psychology from Humboldt State University in Arcata, California, in 2000. Her clinical work includes psychotherapy practicum experiences at Humboldt State University Counseling and Psychological Services, the Davis House Clinic, and the Kinsey Institute. Kim's primary research is focused on the relationship between mental health and sexuality, with particular interest in sexual risk-taking behaviors.

VAUGHN S. MILLNER, assistant professor of counselor education at the University of South Alabama, teaches graduate level counseling and educational psychology courses. As a licensed professional counselor, she also maintains a clinical practice. Her research and clinical interests include human sexuality, human relations training, and altruism. She is the editor of the Sex Therapy Section of the *Family Journal*, and her work has been published in both international and national peer-reviewed journals. She coauthored a book about human relations training and has provided human relations training both nationally and internationally.

MICHAEL REECE is the William L. Yarber Professor in Sexual Health in the Department of Applied Health Science at Indiana University, where he directs the Sexual Health Research Working Group. Dr. Reece's research interests are related to a range of sexual health topics and the mental health consequences of HIV infection. In 2005, Dr. Reece was awarded the Society Research Award from the Society for the Advancement of Sexual Health for his research on sexual addiction and other sexual health topics.

PAMELA C. REGAN is professor of psychology and director of the Social Relations Laboratory at California State University, Los Angeles. She has written extensively on love, passion, sexuality, and mate selection, and is the author of *The Mating Game: A Primer on Love, Sex, and Marriage* (2003), *The Psychology of Interpersonal Relationships* (2005, with E. Berscheid), and *Lust: What We Know about Human Sexual Desire* (1999, with E. Berscheid). Professor

Regan has served on the editorial board of *Personality and Social Psychology Bulletin*, *Personal Relationships*, the *Journal of Social and Personal Relationships*, and the *Journal of Psychology and Human Sexuality*.

DAVID L. ROWLAND received a Ph.D. from the University of Chicago in biopsychology in 1977, and has held fellowships at SUNY-Stony Brook, Stanford University, and Erasmus Medical Center in the Netherlands. His research focuses on understanding sexual problems in men and women, with publication of over 100 research articles and chapters. Currently, he serves as editor of the *Annual Review of Sex Research 2005–2009* and serves on the editorial boards of a number of journals in sexology and medicine. He currently holds the position of professor of psychology and dean of graduate studies at Valparaiso University and is senior associate in the Department of Population and Family Health Sciences in the Bloomberg School of Public Health at Johns Hopkins University.